THOUGHT CRIME

ASIA PACIFIC Asia-Pacific Culture, Politics, and Society
Editors: Rey Chow, Michael Dutton, H. D. Harootunian, and Rosalind C. Morris

A Study of the Weatherhead East Asian Institute, Columbia University

THOUGHT CRIME

MAX M. WARD

Ideology and State Power in Interwar Japan

Duke University Press   Durham and London   2019

© 2019 DUKE UNIVERSITY PRESS. *All rights reserved*
Printed in the United States of America on acid-free paper ∞
Designed by Courtney Baker
Typeset in Arno pro by Westchester Publishing Services

Library of Congress Cataloging-in-Publication Data
Names: Ward, Max M., [date] author.
Title: Thought crime : ideology and state power in interwar
Japan / Max M. Ward.
Description: Durham : Duke University Press, 2019. | Series: Asia
Pacific | Includes bibliographical references and index.
Identifiers: LCCN 2018031281 (print) | LCCN 2018038062 (ebook)
ISBN 9781478002741 (ebook)
ISBN 9781478001317 (hardcover : alk. paper)
ISBN 9781478001652 (pbk. : alk. paper)
Subjects: LCSH: Lese majesty—Law and legislation—Japan—
History—20th century. | Political crimes and offenses—Japan—
History—20th century. | Japan—Politics and government—
1926–1945. | Japan—Politics and government—1912–1945. |
Japan—History—1912–1945.
Classification: LCC KNX4438 (ebook) | LCC KNX4438 .W37 2019 (print)
LC record available at https://lccn.loc.gov/2018031281

Cover art: Newspaper clippings from the *Yomiuri Shimbun*, 1925-1938.
Courtesy of the *Yomiuri Shimbun*.

Dedicated to the punks, in the streets
and the ivory towers

CONTENTS

In *Thought Crime*, I analyze the transformations of an interwar Japanese antiradical law called the Peace Preservation Law (Chianijihō), from its initial
passage to suppress communism and anticolonial nationalism in 1925, to its
expansion in the 1930s into an elaborate system to "ideologically convert"
(*tenkō*) and rehabilitate thousands of political criminals throughout the Japanese Empire, to how the law's rehabilitation policies provided a model for
mobilizing the populations of the Japanese Empire for total war in the 1940s.
I am particularly interested in how the law provides a well-documented example of how a modern state deployed a combination of repression and rehabilitation when policing political threats (real or imagined), as well as how
such efforts reveal the underlying ideology particular to the prewar Japanese
imperial state. My interest in the Peace Preservation Law is therefore two-
fold. First, I want to intervene in the defining historical debates over the nature of the prewar imperial state and the consolidation of fascism in Japan
during the interwar period. Second, I utilize the particular history of the
Peace Preservation Law in order to consider the various modes of power that
states, not just the interwar Japanese state, use to police political threats, thus
reproducing and redefining their respective national polities in the process.

This latter aspect of my project became particularly clear to me as I was
finishing this book while on sabbatical in Tokyo in 2015–2016. I would often
take breaks from reading arcane interwar Japanese Justice Ministry reports
by catching up on the latest international news. One particular news story
caught my attention: the arrest of young Somali American men in Minneapolis, Minnesota, for allegedly trying to join ISIL in Syria.[1] Within the context
of the United States' perpetual state of exception called the war on terror, I
was not necessarily surprised by these arrests.[2] However, what was especially
intriguing was how the Minneapolis case was being framed by a discourse
of the radicalization of ideologies from abroad, and how the district court
in Minneapolis was considering ways to assess the defendants' degree of

radicalization.[3] These aspects resonated with what I was reading in Japanese documents from the 1920s and 1930s, when justice officials described domestic radical politics as the result of dangerous "foreign ideas" (*gairai shisō*) "infiltrating" (*sennyū*) the Japanese Empire and infecting it from within. These foreign ideas, it was said, turned imperial Japanese subjects into internal agents of a foreign enemy (here, the Soviet Union). Explained in this way, communism, anticolonial nationalism, and other ideologies were defined as "thought crime" (*shisō hanzai*), and by the 1930s, the Japanese state had established an extensive security apparatus to identify, assess, and ultimately rehabilitate thousands of so-called thought criminals (*shisō hannin*).

Today, this logic of external ideas producing internal enemies can be found in the discourse of homegrown terrorism, wherein foreign jihadist ideology ostensibly radicalizes citizens or recent immigrants in Europe and the United States so that they carry out the objectives of foreign enemies. Of course, the sociohistorical contexts and politico-ideological content of these two cases are extremely different. However, I was struck by the discursive similarities in how the two states defined their respective threats as, essentially, external ideas that were/are infecting their respective national polities, and how such a notion allowed the two states to generate fear and mobilize their populations. In particular, I became interested in the way such a definition authorized both states to diffuse their policing powers into communities, bringing together police, courts, prison officials, families, religious institutions, educators, and employers to assist with reforming those believed to have been led astray by dangerous foreign ideas. Indeed, at the time of this writing, many Japanese legal scholars are expressing strong criticism of the legal reinterpretations being carried out by the cabinet of prime minister Abe Shinzō in the name of the war on terror and national defense, pointing to similarities with prewar legal developments, and the Peace Preservation Law in particular. [4]

In both cases, state officials envisioned systems that, with collaboration from the local community, would monitor, assess, and rehabilitate those believed to be harboring dangerous ideas. In Japan, this system was actualized in a network of so-called Thought Criminal Protection and Supervision Centers (Shisōhan hogo kansatsu sho) in 1936. Although much more cursory and experimental than the prewar Japanese example, the Minneapolis District Court created a Terrorism Disengagement and Deradicalization Program in March 2016.[5] The first step in this new program was to assess the degree of a defendant's radicalization upon arrest so as to determine a sentence appropriate to the level of danger the defendant ostensibly posed. For example, a

Minneapolis district judge, Michael Davis, hired Daniel Koehler of the German Institute on Radicalization and Deradicalization Studies (GIRDS) to evaluate the degree of radicalization of four out of the nine defendants before they were sentenced.[6] The Minneapolis *Star Tribune* summarized Koehler's charge as to "identify the factors that drove the radicalization of the defendants, identify their risk of reoffending and specify strategies to steer them away from radical ideologies."[7] As we will see in *Thought Crime*, Koehler's charge echoes interwar Japanese Justice Ministry materials that instructed court procurators (*kenji*) to assess the danger posed by so-called thought criminals before their formal indictment or sentencing. Similar to Koehler, Japanese procurators produced official reports (*jōshinsho*) on each thought criminal, assessing the degree of a defendant's commitment to communist internationalism or anticolonial nationalism, and their potential to be rehabilitated through a multistage program of ideological conversion (*tenkō*). In both cases, ideas became the target of inquiry. For example, Koehler explained that his evaluations would assess "if these thoughts and ideas [i.e., jihad] actually determined this behavior and . . . led them to the point where they did something illegal."[8] The Minneapolis defendants had already been found guilty of conspiring to join ISIL. Thus Koehler's task was to interrogate the ideas motivating the defendants' actions in order to assess their reformability for sentencing.[9] Ultimately, Minnesota chief US probation officer Kevin Lowry summarized the objective of this program in this way, using rhetoric that could have come from the interwar Japanese example: "If a radicalized defendant or offender is not properly treated, they will continue to infect our communities . . . and they'll look to harm the community and martyr themselves if [they're not treated] with a balance between rehabilitation and public safety."[10] Here the radicalized defendants in Minneapolis embodied the danger of dangerous ideas spreading in their communities, and thus we can imagine that authorities would extend their balance between "rehabilitation and public safety" beyond pretrial interventions into postparole reform programs and preemptive monitoring to locate others who might be susceptible to becoming, in Lowry's terminology, "infected" by such ideas.

The Japanese interwar state similarly policed suspects by identifying the ideas that determined a communist's motives for joining the illegal Japanese Communist Party (JCP). In prewar Japan, conventional violence such as riot or lèse-majesté were already criminalized under the Civil Code or earlier antiradical laws such as the 1900 Public Peace Police Law (Chian keisatsu hō), which set strict parameters for political expression, publication, assembly, and activities. The 1925 Peace Preservation Law, in contrast, defined a criminal infringement as forming or joining an organization with the objective to "alter the national polity" (*kokutai o henkaku*) or "reject the private property system" (*shiyūzaisan seido o hinin*). In both the Japanese and US examples, the criminal act was primarily attempting to join an organization, and the burden for procurators and judges was to determine a defendant's commitment to the ideas that motivated him or her to allegedly join or support such groups. As one prominent justice official explained in regard to the Japanese Peace Preservation Law: "The peculiarity of this law is that it makes acts based on certain practical thoughts the object of punishment. The thoughts in thought crimes are not . . . theoretical, abstract thoughts, but practical, concrete thoughts."[11] Furthermore, in both cases, these pre-sentencing ideological assessments would decide if defendants received a prison sentence or were paroled into programs where they could be, in today's parlance, deradicalized.

Koehler told reporters that his risk assessments would anticipate what to do with the Minneapolis defendants "when they get out [of prison]" after serving their sentences.[12] This latter concern also dominated the discussions at Japanese Justice Ministry conferences in the mid-1930s, as Japanese officials worried that many incarcerated communists would soon complete prison sentences they were given in the late 1920s or early 1930s. These concerns over ideological recidivism (*saihan*) led Japanese officials in 1936 to establish the system of Thought Criminal Protection and Supervision Centers mentioned earlier, which coordinated between prisons, prosecutors, community leaders, employers, family members, and others to assist thought criminals to secure their ideological conversions while they transitioned back to society. Indeed, early in the Minneapolis investigations, the district court considered probation programs to deal with apprehended terror suspects who showed potential for reform.[13] In one case, a young man was temporarily released to a halfway house before his trial started.[14] There he received support from a nonprofit community organization which, as the *Star Tribune* reported, connected him with "a team of religious scholars, teachers and other mentors" in order to assess his potential for deradicalization and resocialization.[15]

In the end, however, District Judge Davis did not expand upon this rehabilitation experiment. Rather, citing the difficulty of balancing a defendant's rehabilitation with public safety, Davis ultimately emphasized public safety.[16] He sentenced the nine suspects to a range of jail terms—the harshest being thirty-five years in jail, with two others receiving thirty-year prison sentences. Only the young man temporarily released to a halfway house mentioned above was granted time served for turning state's witness, and given twenty years of supervised release.[17]

Many people involved in counterterrorism in the United States were watching the Minneapolis case closely.[18] The Department of Homeland Security under the Obama administration had created a counterterrorism program two years earlier in 2014 called the Countering Violent Extremism (CVE) program, with pilot programs targeting primarily Muslim and immigrant communities in Boston, Minneapolis, and Los Angeles.[19] The CVE program was designed to collaborate with community groups, families, and schools to identify individuals at risk for becoming terrorists, and would provide community and religious services to counter the appeal of radical ideologies. Almost immediately, the CVE program was critiqued for stigmatizing Muslim communities, as well as for attempting to turn educators and religious leaders into informants for the state.[20] Similar criticisms were directed at the Minneapolis Terrorism Disengagement and Deradicalization Program.[21] Despite these criticisms, the Minneapolis program was the first of its kind to so closely assess the beliefs of defendants and to consider methods for deradicalization. Officials were thus watching the Minneapolis case for aspects that could be incorporated into the national CVE program.

Following Donald Trump's election in November 2016 and his promise to take a hard line with suspected terrorists, it is doubtful that these kinds of soft approaches to preventing terrorism will be expanded in the US.[22] Indeed, in July 2017 the Department of Homeland Security informed various community organizations working to rehabilitate radicals—both alleged jihadists and white supremacists—that they would no longer receive funding from the department.[23] However, before we celebrate the Obama administration's approach as a lighter, more community-oriented way to counter radicalization, we should recognize that, in addition to the community criticisms of the CVE program mentioned earlier, the Obama administration escalated targeted drone strikes in Yemen and elsewhere, often killing civilians and radicalized American jihadists without the due process guaranteed under the Fourteenth Amendment of the US Constitution.[24] Furthermore, the Obama administration failed to fulfill a campaign promise to close the Guantánamo Bay detention camp, one of the most notorious examples of the US's deployment of extrajudicial repression in its war on terror. Indeed, the Trump administration has broken with convention and is, at the time of this writing, trying individuals in civilian court who have allegedly committed or planning acts of terror, rather than designating them enemy combatants and sending them to Guantánamo Bay.[25] In many cases, the Trump administration is enacting policies that go explicitly against his earlier campaign rhetoric of getting tough with terrorists. Ultimately, we should recognize that the discourse of radicalization legitimated, and continues to legitimate, both repression and rehabilitation, even as the balance between these two shifts between administrations and their rhetoric on how to adequately deal with so-called homegrown terrorists.

To be clear, the question that I pursue in *Thought Crime* is not whether repression or rehabilitation is the more effective approach to combat domestic radicals. Rather, I am interested in how, at particular historical conjunctures, states define political threats as essentially ideological and foreign in nature, and how such definitions provide the conditions for states to experiment with different combinations of repression and rehabilitation. Ultimately, I am interested in what kinds of policing methods such a definition informs, and how communities are brought within campaigns to ostensibly eradicate ideological influences. Furthermore, I believe such experiments reveal more about the underlying ideologies informing the varying modes of power that a state deploys than they do about the purported threats they are meant to combat, whether we are discussing the prewar Japanese imperial state's interwar thought crime policy or the United States' war on terror.[26]

Thus, as I was completing this book in Tokyo in 2015–2016, I found myself conducting a kind of parallax analysis, simultaneously reading historical documents related to the prewar Japanese thought crime system and contemporary news reports on the United States' CVE experiments with deradicalization. I hope that *Thought Crime*, in addition to contributing to the historical literature on interwar Japan, can also provide a historical vantage point from which we can consider our own contemporary moment, and what the current discourse of radicalization might reveal about the ideology underwriting the endless war on terror.

Over the past decade, I have received support from many individuals and institutions. My advisers at New York University cultivated my appreciation for the necessity and challenges of critical historical thinking: first and foremost Harry Harootunian, whose generosity and critical acumen remain a source of inspiration. Rebecca Karl constantly pushed me to refine my questions and ideas. Tom Looser taught me how to read texts with attention to the political and theoretical demands of the contemporary moment. At Waseda University, Umemori Naoyuki provided invaluable support over the years. I thank him and his graduate students for their suggestions and criticisms on this project as it developed. I also thank my undergraduate teachers at UC Berkeley for nurturing my interest in both interwar radical politics and East Asian history, including Margaret Anderson, Andrew Barshay, Alan Tansman, and, in particular, Irwin Scheiner.

I have many people to thank for helping me refine and improve the manuscript. Takashi Fujitani, Katsuya Hirano, and Louise Young offered sharp criticisms of the manuscript at a workshop sponsored by the President's Office and the Rohatyn Center for Global Affairs at Middlebury College in January 2017. Colleagues who participated, including Maggie Clinton, Darién Davis, Joyce Mao, Tamar Mayer, Sujata Moorti, Jacob Tropp, Linda White, and Don Wyatt, deserve special thanks. Over the years, friends have kindly read portions of this manuscript and supported my work more generally, in particular Brian Hurley, Phil Kaffen, Namiko Kunimoto, Matsusaka Hiroaki, Nakano Osamu, Mark Roberts, Viren Murthy, and Robert Stolz. Constructive feedback offered at conferences, workshops, and reading groups have helped shape my thinking about many of the problems pursued in the book. I especially thank Catherine Ashcraft, Michael Bourdaghs, Adam Bronson, Kyeong-Hee Choi, James Dorsey, Mark Driscoll, Robert Eskildsen, Erik Esselstrom, Clinton Godard, Tom Fenton, Irena Hayter, Reto Hofmann, Ken Kawashima, Aaron S. Moore, Ryan Moran, Alexis Peri, John Person, Leslie

Pincus, Stefan Tanaka, Robert Tierney, Gavin Walker, and Mark Williams. Over the years I have also benefited from conversations with Emily Anderson, Noriko Aso, Deokhyo Choi, Jeff DuBois, Ellery Foutch, Kawamura Satofumi, Robin Kietlinski, Takeshi Kimoto, Elena Lange, George Lazopoulos, Ricky Law, Joyce Liu, Ethan Mark, William Marotti, Wendy Matsumura, Shota Ogawa, Jonas Prida, Yukiko Shigeto, Ken Shima, Kunihiko Terasawa, Brian Tsui, Nori Tsuneishi, Benjamin Uchiyama, Christian Uhl, and Jack Wilson. I am especially grateful for the generous comments and suggestions provided by the reviewers for Duke University Press, which have helped shape this book in significant ways.

Ken Wissoker and Olivia Polk at Duke University Press supported and shepherded me through the publication process. I thank them and others at Duke University Press who helped prepare the manuscript for publication, including Sara Leone, Julie Thomson, Christopher Robinson and, for copyediting, Karen Fisher. Carol Gluck and Ross Yelsey of the Weatherhead East Asian Institute believed in this project in its early stages. Research for this book has been supported by an Advanced Social Science Research Fellowship from the National Endowment for the Humanities, Japan-US Friendship Commission, a research fellowship from the Japan Foundation, the Northeast Asia Council of the AAS, Fulbright IIE, and by Middlebury College. I thank the various forums that provided me the opportunity to present my research as it developed, including the School of Languages, Cultures and Societies at the University of Leeds, East Asia Center at the University of Virginia, Institute of Japanese Studies at The Ohio State University, the Rohatyn Center for Global Affairs at Middlebury College, Center for Japanese Religions and Cultures at University of Southern California, Center for East Asian Studies at the University of Chicago, Center of Japanese Studies at University of Michigan, the University of Tokyo Center for Philosophy, Center of East Asian Research at McGill University, as well as the Association of Asian Studies, American Historical Association, Asian Studies Conference Japan, British Association of Japanese Studies, Social Science History Association, the Modern Japanese History Workshop at Waseda University and the Kyoto Asian Studies Group, among others. I would also like to thank the faculty at the Inter-University Center for Japanese Language Studies, and in particular Kushida Kiyomi for her patience and dedication to my language learning. The majority of the materials used in this study are archived in the Japanese National Diet Library in Tokyo, Waseda University Library, and the Ōhara Institute for Social Research at Hosei University. I would like to thank these libraries and their staff, as well as Rachel Manning and the staff of Middlebury College's Interlibrary Loan office, for their assistance in acquiring materials during the final stages of revising the manuscript.

I am fortunate to have supportive and generous colleagues in the History and Japanese Studies departments at Middlebury College, and I thank my friends and colleagues for welcoming me into their homes, including Jamie McCallum, Erin Davis and Asa, Febe Armanios, Boğaç Ergene, Maggie Clinton, Roger White and Lenni, Adam, Elana and Naomi Dean, Steve Snyder, Linda White, Jonas Prida, Marshall Highet, Kian and Brylea, and in Burlington, Haley Renwick, Julian Hackney, Joy Snow, and Samantha van Gerbig. In Tokyo, I thank Osamu, Aya, and Riko-chan, as well as the Yoshida family. I especially look forward to taking many walks with Motoko Jumonji now that this manuscript is complete. I thank John at Carol's Hungry Mind and Haley at Speeder and Earl's for keeping me caffeinated. Thanks also to Hayakawa Yugo of Okinawa Shokudō for the delicious food and engaging conversation over the years.

During my time in New York City, I was encouraged and supported by a number of teachers and students at NYU and beyond, including Ramona Beltran, Sasha Disko, Feng Miao, Manu Goswami, Greg Grandin, Jane Hayward, Franz Hofer, Marilyn Ivy, Jennifer Lee, Soonyi Lee, Andy Liu, Patrick Noonan, Lisa Onaga, Hyun Ok Park, Janet Poole, Moss Roberts, Paul Roquet, Nate Shockey, Dexter Thomas, Christophe Thouny, Keith Vincent, Lorraine Wong, Timothy Yang, Marilyn Young, and Qian Zhu. On the picket line I was inspired by my comrades of GSOC/UAW 2110, members of Faculty Democracy, and the wider graduate student union movement that supported us during our strike in 2005–2006.

Last, I thank my mother, Nancy, and late father, William, for unconditionally supporting my endeavors over the past four decades including music, activism, and academia; my sister Michele for inspiring me with her strength and resilience; and to the international DIY punk scene, including my prior bandmates, for continuing to demonstrate that alternative forms of community are possible. Up the punks.

Parts of chapters have been published elsewhere: portions of the introduction and chapter 3 pertaining to Louis Althusser's theory of Ideological State Apparatuses are derived from "Ideology and Subjection in Ōshima Nagisa's *Kōshikei* (1968)" in "Perspectives on Ōshima Nagisa," UTCP-*Uehiro Pamphlet*, no. 7 (2015). Sections on the idea of thought war in chapter 5 come from

"Displaying the Worldview of Japanese Fascism: The Tokyo Thought War Exhibition of 1938," *Critical Asian Studies* 47, no. 3 (Sept. 2015); "Crisis Ideology and the Articulation of Fascism in Interwar Japan: The 1938 Thought War Symposium," *Japan Forum* 26, no. 4 (December 2014).

The Ghost in the Machine: *Emperor System Ideology*
and the Peace Preservation Law Apparatus

In early 1938, Hirata Isao, the director of the newly established Tokyo
Thought Criminal Protection and Supervision Center (Tōkyō shisōhan
hogo kansatsu sho), stood before a group of military officers and other officials to promote the Japanese Justice Ministry's decade-long effort to suppress domestic communists. Hirata was a key architect of the imperial state's
anticommunist policies: he helped organize the first major roundups of suspected communists under the 1925 Peace Preservation Law (Chianijihō) in
1928 and 1929, assisted in the prosecution of central committee members of
the Japanese Communist Party (JCP) in a high-profile trial in 1931–1932, and
experimented with urging incarcerated communists to defect from the JCP
in the early 1930s with some success.[1] This latter experiment developed into
the official policy of ideological conversion (*tenkō*) in 1936, which Hirata
and others were now implementing in the empire-wide network of Protection and Supervision Centers. Hirata most likely recognized that many in
the audience were ardent anticommunists and thus would be suspicious of
any leniency toward incarcerated or paroled political criminals. Indeed, in its
1927 Theses, the JCP advocated to "abolish the emperor system" (*kunshusei
haishi*)—that is, the essence of the imperial state—as a central objective for
communist revolution in Japan.[2] However, Hirata not only defended the rehabilitation of communists but he also argued that their ideological conversion provided a model for the spiritual purification and mobilization of the

Japanese Empire, particularly after Japan's invasion of China in July 1937 (the so-called China Incident).

In his speech, titled "Overcoming Marxism" ("Marukishizumu no koku-fuku"), Hirata tailored his comments to the military officials in the audience by equating the swift arrests of domestic communists with the Imperial Army's sweeping military victories in China, and compared the political reform policies he was overseeing in the Tokyo Protection and Supervision Center with the Imperial Army's pacification of the Chinese population in occupied territories. In what he referred to as a thought war (shisōsen) raging through-out East Asia and the world, Hirata explained that he and his fellow thought reform officials were doing work similar to the pacification units (senbun-han) in occupied China. He emphasized that instead of punitive repression and punishment, thought reform officers were benevolently guiding detain-ees through the conversion process toward a self-awakening (jikaku) as true Japanese (hontō no nihonjin). He celebrated the fact that many of the com-munists who reformed under the guidance of the Protection and Supervi-sion Centers were now demonstrating their loyalty to the empire through productive labor in society. The underlying principle of these centers, Hirata argued, was imperial benevolence, which exemplified how criminal reform was the institutional expression of the unique "Japanese spirit within the Jus-tice Ministry system," a spirit that was also guiding the military campaigns in China.[3] Hirata concluded his lecture by presenting the ex-communist ideo-logical convert, or tenkōsha, as a model for a renovated and mobilized Japan, arguing, "The people who should effect tenkō are not only those defendants from the Communist Party, that is, the thought-criminals, but we—this may be rude to say—we, from here forward, must [also] carry out a grand tenkō."[4] Indeed, Hirata was attempting to refigure a policy initially developed to suppress and eradicate communism and anticolonial nationalism from the Japanese Empire into a general principle for the spiritual mobilization of the empire for the war effort in China.

A decade earlier, such a claim would have been unthinkable. In the 1920s, state officials warned about the infiltration (sennyū) of dangerous foreign ideologies into the empire and the need to eradicate such ideologies before they poisoned the national polity (kokutai) from within. For them, domestic communists and other political radicals embodied this foreign ideological threat, a threat that needed to be extracted from society and imprisoned so as to contain its spread.[5] Now, in 1938, one of the key architects of the state's anticommunism campaign presented reformed ex-communists as exem-plars for all imperial subjects to follow. In this refiguring, Hirata portrayed the parole of reformed ex-communists as a means to purify the local community from dangerous Western influences. This vision of using converts to shore up the nation's spiritual resolve dovetailed with and informed wartime campaigns such as the National Spirit Mobilization Movement (Kokumin seishin sōdōin undō) that were created to mobilize the general populace for total war.[6]

What allowed Hirata Isao and other justice officials to promote the reformed ex-communist as a model for all imperial subjects to emulate in the late 1930s? How did state policies targeting communists and other political radicals evolve from suppression and incarceration in the 1920s, to include rehabilitation, conversion, and parole in the 1930s? Most important, what do these transformations reveal about imperial state ideology and its relationship to the transforming modes of state power during the interwar period? *Thought Crime* explores these questions by reading the interwar Japanese state's political crime policies as an index of imperial state ideology—first and foremost, the ideology of imperial sovereignty and the relationship between sovereign and subject—and how this ideology informed and transformed within the expanding apparatus to police political crime in the 1930s. I recuperate what English-language scholars once referred to as Japan's prewar emperor system (*tennōsei*) and will read the Peace Preservation Law as an extensive security apparatus that formed one important component of that system, both institutionally and ideologically.[7] I utilize the metaphor of the ghost in the machine to emphasize the dynamic relationship between the ideology of the imperial sovereign (the ghost as it were) that both informed, and was itself refined and disseminated through, the expanding institutional apparatus (the machine) to police political criminals in the Japanese Empire during the 1930s. Before elaborating this metaphor, however, it is first necessary to review previous scholarship on the Peace Preservation Law in order to clarify the critical-theoretical intervention that I hope to make in our understanding of the interwar period in Japan.

The Peace Preservation Law as History

The Japanese state's thought reform policy developed from a notorious antiradical law called the Peace Preservation Law (Chianijihō).[8] Passed in 1925, this law was utilized to arrest over seventy thousand people in the Japanese metropole and tens of thousands more in Japan's colony of colonial Korea, until repealed by Allied Occupation authorities in October 1945.[9] The law was initially proposed as a legal instrument to suppress domestic communists and anticolonial activists that were said to be threatening imperial sovereignty, but in the 1930s the law was extended to other academic, political, and religious groups who were seen as challenging imperial orthodoxy. Not only was the purview of the law expanded, but the policies that were developed for administering the law transformed and intensified. By the late 1930s, the law had become a complex institutional apparatus for the continuing surveillance, assessment, reform, and ultimately ideological conversion—or tenkō—of political criminals, informed by the ideology of the loyal imperial subject.

For these reasons, the law's extension and increasing institutional complexity provides a unique archive in which to study the prewar imperial state and its transformations in the 1930s. In conventional scholarship, the Peace Preservation Law is commonly portrayed as an explicit instrument of repression used by the prewar emperor system against progressive social forces.[10] That the law was an instrument of repression is, of course, undeniable, but such a characterization implies that the law was clearly understood by state officials and implemented in a uniform manner across the Japanese Empire over its twenty-year history. As I demonstrate in *Thought Crime*, officials continually questioned how to interpret the law's central categories and experimented with different policies based on the changing political circumstances in the Japanese Empire.[11] Nor does the conventional repression thesis adequately explain the logic that informed the later rehabilitation policies such as ideological conversion. To be sure, in the early 1930s a detainee's rehabilitation was initiated with political defection from the JCP, and thus officials understood recantation as one weapon in their arsenal to suppress communism. However, as I explore in later chapters, such experiments moved well beyond urging a detainee to merely defect, to encompass welfare services, spiritual guidance, employment training, family counseling, and the prolonged assessment of imperial loyalty for years after parole. Officials continually explained this expanded rehabilitation system as reflecting the majesty of the august emperor and the benevolence of his imperial state toward wayward subjects, even as arrests continued.

By the 1970s, scholars such as Okudaira Yasuhiro and Richard Mitchell recognized the complexity of the law, and started to reveal the interministerial debates between the Home and Justice Ministries, as well as how the law included both repressive and reform measures, what Mitchell referred to as an expression of Japan's unique "Janus-faced" form of justice.[12] Okudaira approached this complexity through a normative understanding of modern jurisprudence, explaining that, by including the term "kokutai" (national polity or essence) in the Peace Preservation Law (wherein the central infringement of the law was joining or forming an organization that sought to "alter the kokutai"), legislators had contaminated (*konkō*) the realm of legal rationality with an extra-juridical term with sentimental (*jōchoteki*) associations.[13] Area studies scholars translated this binary into the modernization theory paradigm, in which this juridical excess was explained as a vestige of traditional Japanese culture continuing into, and conflicting with, modern Western institutions.[14] Consequently, in the area studies literature, the Peace Preservation Law was explained as having incorporated specifically Japanese cultural elements (symbolized in the term kokutai), forming a uniquely Japanese way of dealing with the political tumult that attends modernization.[15] Such cultural explanations of the Peace Preservation Law reinforce a more general characterization that the modern imperial state implemented a particular Japanese form of governance dating back to the Tokugawa period (1603–1868), what Sheldon Garon has identified in the discourse of "moral suasion" (*kyōka*).[16]

Certainly, the imperial state legitimated the suppression of political activists as protecting Japan's timeless cultural traditions or, later, celebrated its rehabilitation policies as expressions of Japan's unique imperial benevolence toward wayward subjects. However, we should not confuse the rhetoric of these cultural claims with the ideological forms through which the imperial state exercised its power, for when we do, our analytical explanations replicate the very claims that officials used to legitimize these policies.[17] As I argue in *Thought Crime*, in essence, the Japanese campaigns to suppress and rehabilitate political criminals were based on modes of power that various modern states utilize in periods of political crisis, including attempts to guide social morality and behavior.

Emphasizing the ideological forms and modes of state power that constituted the interwar security apparatus, *Thought Crime* argues that the complexities of the Peace Preservation Law need to be understood, not as cultural or extrajuridical effects, but as articulations of the ideological foundations of the imperial state within the realm of law and penal policy—first and foremost, of the august emperor, which grounded the logics of both repression and rehabilitation. Imperial sovereignty was the penultimate object to be defended from ideological threats and, at the same time, the benevolent source from which to reform political criminals as loyal imperial subjects. The ideological nature of such campaigns becomes particularly apparent when we recognize that the Peace Preservation Law was applied simultaneously across the different legal systems of Japan's colonial empire, raising questions about the extension of imperial sovereignty to the colonies, particularly to colonial Korea, as well as how to later reform colonial activists as imperial subjects.[18] *Thought Crime* draws upon the recent work conducted by Mizuno Naoki, Hong Jong-wook, and others in order to reveal the different articulations of imperial ideology and modalities of state power between the Japanese metropole and colonial Korea.[19]

In this regard, *Thought Crime* reads the Peace Preservation Law as an index of the aporias of imperial state ideology and their different articulations across the Japanese Empire during the 1920s and 1930s. Following Fredric Jameson's distinction between contradiction and aporia, I am using the term "aporia" in order to emphasize the unresolvable nature of the paradoxes that constituted imperial sovereignty (both in theory and practice) as well as how these aporias were generative within the field of state ideology and its institutionalization.[20] As an index of the aporias of imperial ideology, the conceptualization and implementation of the Peace Preservation Law provides an important window into the ideological transformations of the imperial state in the 1930s.

The nature of the prewar state has been a central question for scholars of Japan: from Maruyama Masao's early thesis that in prewar Japan all value was exteriorized into the emperor, allowing for the state to spread a "many-layered, though invisible, net over the Japanese people," to Fujita Shōzō's analysis of the emperor system as a dialectic between the particular institutional forms of the imperial state and the principles with which it ruled society, to Takeda Kiyoko and Walter Skya's respective analyses of the double structure of the emperor system in which the Meiji oligarchs presented the emperor as both divine, mythical and absolute, and at the same time as a constitutional monarchy, what Takeda calls the enduring "dual image" of the emperor, and what Skya finds as the grounding problematic that informed prewar constitutional theory.[21] While these studies focus largely on developments at the state or constitutional level, other scholarship has explored how the emperor system was disseminated and reproduced at the level of society: from Carol Gluck's groundbreaking work on the circulation of Meiji ideology at the local level, to Takashi Fujitani's study of the symbolic construction of the emperor through public pageantry and the circulation of imperial imagery, to Yoshimi Yoshiaki's thesis of popular "imperial consciousness" and "grassroots fascism" in the 1930s and 1940s, to Sheldon Garon's research on how social elements reciprocated, if not actively collaborated, with the state to manage certain social behaviors and practices.[22] And finally, recent scholarship has sought to understand the new modalities of power emerging in the mid-Meiji-period prison and police systems, including Umemori Naoyuki's pioneering research on the "colonial mediations" during the formation of the modern penal system, and Daniel Botsman's study of the radical break that occurred in punishment between the late Tokugawa and mid-Meiji periods.[23] *Thought Crime* engages with this research by reading the Peace Preservation Law apparatus as indexing the transformations of imperial state ideology across the interwar period, as combining multiple modes of power in order to police political crime, and how the apparatus functioned to reproduce and circulate imperial ideology to the wider community through its later ideological conversion policy.[24]

My intervention in the historiography on the Peace Preservation Law and the prewar imperial state begins by drawing upon critical theories of state power and ideology in order to analyze the material practices through which imperial ideology was reproduced, transformed, and circulated in the 1930s. I contend that this type of critical-theoretical approach reveals the general forms of state power operating in the particular historical circumstances of interwar Japan, and thus qualifies earlier studies that have portrayed the interwar state as manifesting traditional characteristics unique to Japanese statecraft. Toward this end, each chapter of *Thought Crime* is framed by a theoretical question related to state power and ideology, which informs an analysis of a specific development within the Peace Preservation Law over its twenty-year history. At the same time, the Peace Preservation Law provides a rich historical archive in which to reflect on the limits or lacunae in specific theories of state power and ideology.

Before outlining the chapters of *Thought Crime*, it is necessary, first, to explain the metaphorical through line of the ghost in the machine in regard to the prewar Japanese imperial state and, second, to elaborate how my analysis of the Peace Preservation Law is informed by critical theories of ideology, subjection, and state power.

The Tennōsei as Ghost in the Machine

The sovereign power of reigning over and of governing the State, is inherited by the Emperor from His Ancestors, and by Him bequeathed to His posterity. All the different legislative as well as executive powers of State, by means of which He reigns over the country and governs the people, are united in this Most Exalted Personage, who thus holds in His hands, as it were, all the ramifying threads of the political life of the country, just as the brain, in the human body, is the primitive source of all mental activity manifested through the four limbs and the different parts of the body. For unity is just as necessary in the government of a State, as double-mindedness would be ruinous in an individual. —ITŌ HIROBUMI, commenting on the Meiji Constitution in 1889

I utilize the metaphor of the ghost in the machine in order to analyze how the ideology of the emperor system (tennōsei) was articulated in, and transformed through, the institutional efforts to suppress and reform political criminals. The metaphor of the ghost in the machine derives from Gilbert Ryle's classic text *The Concept of Mind* (1949), in which Ryle attempted to subvert the Cartesian distinction/conjunction of mind and body, in which the mind, Ryle argued, is assumed to be a "spectral machine" inside the physical body, an "interior governor-engine" that animates the body, but obeys "laws . . . not known to ordinary engineers."[25] Ryle's target was the concept of mind in philosophy, but tellingly, he made passing mention of Thomas Hobbes's Cartesian conception of sovereignty in *Leviathan* (1651), in which the sovereign was to the commonwealth as the mind was to the parts of the body.[26] Indeed, in the epigraph above, we see the recognized author of the 1889 Meiji Constitution, Itō Hirobumi, drawing upon this Cartesian analogy in order to explain imperial sovereignty as outlined in the 1889 Constitution and the supposed unity it brought to the new Meiji state.[27] Ryle's intention was not to reduce mind to matter or vice versa, but to free philosophy of the ideology of mind so that philosophy could elaborate a "correct logic of mental-conduct concepts" appropriate to the "facts of mental life."[28] And yet, in the judgment of A. J. Ayer, although Ryle had "succeeded in reduc[ing] the empire of the mind over a considerable area" of philosophical inquiry, the "ghost . . . still walks, and some of us are still haunted by it."[29] Indeed, the metaphor of the ghost in the machine was popularized by Arthur Koestler, who, in a 1967 book that took the metaphor as its title, argued that in "the very act of denying the existence of the ghost in the machine," Ryle and others may "incur the risk of turning it into a very nasty, malevolent ghost."[30] Evidently, exorcising the ghost from philosophy proved to be more difficult than Ryle originally imagined, a paradox that was replicated as the metaphor was extended to other disciplines in order to exorcise their own respective assumptions.

Scholars in political theory have deployed the ghost in the machine metaphor in order to discard what they believe to be the analytical ambiguities produced by terms such as "sovereignty" and the "state." In one well-known example, David Easton critiqued state theory, which, in his estimation, figured the state as "some kind of undefined and undefinable essence, a 'ghost in the machine,' knowable only through its variable manifestations."[31] The issue for Easton was that the various proponents of the state, whether liberal, conservative, or Marxist, were all assuming that there was a single, "easily identifiable" locus of authority or power that could be discerned in the wider field of political practice. He countered that his concept of "political system" took into consideration the complexity and diversity of the political field without having to rely on the assumption of a ghostly essence (i.e., the state) determining the field of political practice.[32] However, Timothy Mitchell has countered that Easton and one could say by extension Ryle were asking the wrong question: before exorcising the ostensible ghost from their respective fields, they must first account for why the machine operates as if there was a ghost animating it.[33] Mitchell argues that criticisms such as Easton's "ignore the fact that this is how the state very often appears in practice. The task of a critique of the state is not just to reject such metaphysics, but to explain how it has been possible to produce this practical effect, so characteristic of the modern political order."[34] *Thought Crime* is an attempt to understand how this metaphysics was produced through and animated the particular policies and practices of the Peace Preservation Law apparatus.[35]

By using the metaphor of the ghost in the machine, I seek to illuminate how the "practical effect" (Mitchell) of the sovereign emperor and the radiant Japanese spirit (*nihon seishin*) were reproduced, transformed, and disseminated through the institutional practices of the Peace Preservation Law. As a kind of ghostly presence that was both ostensibly transcendent of secular politics and simultaneously their sovereign origin, the august emperor was invoked in, firstly, the Diet deliberations over the use of kokutai (national polity or essence) in the 1925 Peace Preservation Law as something under existential threat from foreign ideologies, and then in the day-to-day interrogations, court decisions, and rehabilitation programs that constituted the administrative application of the Peace Preservation Law. In fact, two corollary ghosts were conjured in the operations of the Peace Preservation Law: the imperial sovereign that the law was protecting, and the imperial subject (*shinmin*) that reformed ex–political criminals were to manifest during their rehabilitation.[36] By the late 1930s, justice and police officials continuously invoked the Japanese spirit as animating their institutional practices: as a 1940 thought police manual explained, the "prime mover of police power" (*keisatsuryoku no chūshin dōryoku*) was the "spirit of the police" which "elucidates [*tōtetsu*] the fundamental principles of our kokutai."[37] Rather than dismissing them, *Thought Crime* approaches such claims as revealing the imperial ideology that informed, and was transformed through, the institutional practices of the Peace Preservation Law apparatus in the 1930s.

To be clear, I am not arguing that hidden behind the operations of the security apparatus was the active monarch at the helm of the state; rather, I am arguing that the security apparatus and, by extension, the imperial state, functioned as if the august sovereign was animating the security apparatus since he was continually referenced as the ostensible sovereign source of all imperial law as well as the object to be protected from political-ideological threats. Nor am I arguing that detained communists were rehabilitated back to an original imperial subjectivity. Rather, I am arguing that, as so-called ideological converts (tenkōsha) set out to confirm their conversions and find purposeful work in their communities, they drew upon established tropes of the Japanese spirit and imperial loyalty to give their activities meaning. This shifts the problematic away from conventional questions such as "Did communists really convert and embrace imperial ideology?" to understanding how their practices made it appear as if they had become loyal imperial subjects. In other words, I am interested in how the ideology of the emperor was inscribed in the practical, institutional, and juridical operations of the prewar Peace Preservation Law apparatus, and how this ideology informed and was disseminated through the practice of ideological conversion in the 1930s.

As I explore in chapter 1, state officials initially infused the expanding institutional apparatus to suppress political radicalism with the sovereign ghost by using the term "kokutai" (national polity or essence) in the Peace Preservation Law, identifying a political crime as anyone who formed or joined an organization with the intention to "alter the kokutai" (kokutai o henkaku).[38] Legislators defined their use of kokutai in the law as signifying that sovereignty resided in the "line of Emperors unbroken for ages eternal" as stipulated in Article 1 of the Meiji Constitution, and thus political crime was identified as the intention to alter imperial sovereignty. Consequently, in their continuing legislative debates over the use of kokutai in the law, officials were not only arguing about how the term defined an infringement to be punished, but were simultaneously and inadvertently addressing the ostensible sovereign essence of the Japanese Empire itself. Then later, in the emerging rehabilitation policies of the Peace Preservation Law apparatus, officials and detainees ruminated on imperial subjectivity as criminal reform was measured by the degree to which a political criminal (re)identified as an imperial subject, the spectral cognate to the imperial sovereign. Indeed, throughout the 1930s, officials such as Hirata Isao and reformed political activists continuously wrote on the significance of ideological conversion and, in the process, reflected on the essence of imperial subjectivity. As I will explore in chapter 5, this was a particularly vexed endeavor in colonial Korea, where anticolonial activists, although not ethnically Japanese (*minzoku*), were urged to reform as loyal nationals (*kokumin*) of the Japanese Empire.

Despite these challenges, by the late 1930s, officials in metropolitan Japan abstracted the policy of ideological conversion from the Protection and Supervision Centers and re-presented it as an imperative for all imperial subjects to practice, effectively turning tenkō into an ideology in its own right. In chapter 5, I demonstrate how tenkō became a generalized ideology of thought purification and spiritual mobilization, which provided a model for the total-war mobilization campaigns of the late 1930s and early 1940s. If the imperial ghost initially animated the machine to repress political threats against the sovereign in the 1920s, and if political criminals invoked their own subjective ghost as they converted as loyal subjects of the emperor in the mid-1930s, then the spiritual mobilization campaigns modeled on the tenkō policy in the late 1930s and 1940s envisioned imperial Japan as a war machine animated by the ghost of the Japanese spirit (*nihon seishin*).

The Peace Preservation Law as Combined Repressive and Ideological State Apparatus

Power would be a fragile thing if its only function were to repress.
—MICHEL FOUCAULT, "Body/Power"

In order to illuminate the ideological and institutional transformations of the Peace Preservation Law in the 1930s, *Thought Crime* draws upon the theoretical investigations of Louis Althusser, Michel Foucault, and, to a lesser extent, Nicos Poulantzas concerning the differing modalities of state power and the effective operations of ideology.[39] Although Althusser and Foucault are conventionally read as theoretical adversaries, there have been recent attempts to read them together, opening new, productive lines of inquiry into the complex processes of state power and subjection.[40] Poulantzas's later state theory serves to mediate between Foucault and Althusser, for, as Bob Jessop has explored, Poulantzas attempted to bring aspects of Foucault's theory of power as dispersed at the microlevel of society into a structural-Marxist theory of the state and how the state intervenes and reproduces the relations of capitalist production.[41]

To begin with, both Althusser and Foucault reject the conventional theory of ideology, since this is predicated upon the assumption of, as Foucault explains, a preconstituted liberal "human subject . . . endowed with a consciousness which power is then thought to seize on."[42] In contrast, as Warren Montag has summarized, for both Althusser and Foucault "the individual was not given, but constituted or produced as [a] center of initiatives, an effect, not a cause of the conflictual processes of ideology or power."[43] Furthermore, although Foucault did not use the term "ideology," both he and Althusser rejected idealist theories of how power or ideology seize upon or mystify the consciousness of an individual, what Althusser deemed "the ideology of ideology."[44] We can find this ideology informing prior studies of the tenkō phenomenon in interwar Japan, whereby tenkō is explained as when the state, through external force, coerced an individual to change his or her internal ideas. Most studies of tenkō thus track the ostensible change in thought of an individual, overlooking the extensive institutional apparatus that provided the models through which the individual experienced and practiced conversion. Tellingly, converts described their conversion as a uniquely personal experience of introspection, even though their experiences followed a predictable sequence and produced almost identical biographical forms. Althusser and Foucault, each in his own way, shift our attention to the mechanisms or diagrams of power (Foucault) and practices ritualized within specific apparatuses (Althusser) through which the subject is constituted as such. My objective in *Thought Crime* is to elaborate the logic at work in the ensemble of apparatuses that the imperial state developed to reform political criminals as loyal and productive imperial subjects.

In the prewar Japanese context, this entails, as Harry Harootunian reminds us, that we recognize how these apparatuses worked to interpellate individuals "as subjects (not primarily imperial subjects—shinmin—even though this was obviously included in the formulation, but as subjects—shutai or shukan)."[45] Indeed, as I will demonstrate, it was through the tropes of imperial subjectivity that a reformed political criminal would, in Althusser's terms, "*(freely) accept his subjection* . . . in order that he shall make the gestures and actions of his subjection 'all by himself.'"[46] *Thought Crime* analyzes how various modalities of power combined within the Peace Preservation Law, transforming it into an apparatus that functioned to reform political criminals as imperial subjects that would work "all by themselves" (Althusser) without threat of reprimand. Indeed, by the mid-1930s we find justice officials and converts alike celebrating the practice of "indirect rehabilitation" (*kansetsu hogo*) in the Peace Preservation Law, in which detained thought criminals converted ostensibly on their own volition and continued to demonstrate their loyalty after parole with only minor oversight by the state.[47]

From Foucault, I explore the transformations of the Peace Preservation Law apparatus through his tripartite schema of sovereign-juridical power, disciplinary power, and governmentality.[48] In the 1930s, the Peace Preservation Law apparatus transformed from its initial function as a law to juridically repress political threats to imperial sovereignty in the mid-1920s, to establishing semiofficial organizations that experimented with disciplinary methods to safely release reformed political criminals back into imperial society in the early 1930s, to finally codifying and intensifying the earlier reform experiments into a multistage process of ideological conversion (tenkō) so that released ex–political criminals would morally govern themselves in the late 1930s. Foucault's tripartite schema allows us to distinguish the various modalities of power that combined within the Peace Preservation Law by the mid-1930s, while at the same time allowing us to understand these modes of power, not as unique vestiges of premodern Japanese statecraft but as general forms of power that modern states exercise to some degree and combination in particular moments of political crisis.[49] Moreover, the Peace Preservation Law provides a unique example through which to reconsider Foucault's threefold schema of power, not as a series of three unique historical forms (which is sometimes how Foucault is read), but rather as the simultaneous configuration of three modes of power—"sovereignty-discipline-government" (Foucault)—into a single security complex that had important influences and effects in interwar Japanese society.[50]

I engage with Althusser's theory of Ideological State Apparatuses (ISAs) in order to analyze how the Peace Preservation Law apparatus, by the mid-1930s, included particular reform procedures that functioned to rehabilitate individuals as loyal and productive imperial subjects. Althusser distinguished between a (single) state apparatus—the Repressive State Apparatus (RSA), which primarily functions by violence—and the plural apparatuses that function primarily by ideology, including schools, family, law, and so on, which Althusser calls the (plural) ISAs. Althusser contends that all "State Apparatuses function both by repression and by ideology," with one element predominating over the other in the last instance.[51] Poulantzas qualified Althusser's functional distinction, arguing that, depending on the situation, "a number of apparatuses can slide from one sphere to the other and assume new functions either as additions to, or in exchange for, old ones."[52] Indeed, we will see how, as a fully elaborated apparatus in the 1930s, the Peace Preservation Law combined both repressive and ideological functions, and "slid" (Poulantzas) between one function over the other depending on location and changing political conditions. According to Althusser, however, it is ideology that secures the internal coherence between the apparatuses, and thus presumably the state apparatus itself. And while the repressive function of the RSA may serve as the ultimate horizon of state power—dealing with what Althusser called "bad subjects" (*mauvais sujets*) or those rare occasions when the local police are overwhelmed by events—repression alone cannot explain how the relations of the social formation are reproduced, or the coherence between the multiple state apparatuses.[53]

As we see here, Althusser expands the ideological function of the state—and thus the state itself—beyond the conventional state/society divide, finding educational institutions, churches, families, religious groups, and other entities functioning to interpellate individuals as subjects. In this way, Althusser provides an important corrective to Foucault and others who reject the analytical purchase of the state as a critical category. Indeed, as Nicos Poulantzas has noted, Foucault and others rejected the term "state" specifically because they retained a surprisingly "narrow, juridical definition of the State" that was "limited to the public kernel of army, police, prisons, courts, and so on." Poulantzas argues that this allowed Foucault and others to argue "that power also exists outside the State as they conceive it. But in fact, a number of sites of power which they imagine to lie wholly outside the State (the apparatus of asylums and hospitals, the sports apparatus, etc.) are all the more sites of power in that they are included in the strategic field of the State."[54] In *Thought Crime*, I reveal how the Japanese state collaborated with Buddhist temples, municipal employment agencies, family members, and other community groups in order to rehabilitate political criminals and secure their ideological conversion. Each institution had its own unique function, what Althusser would call their respective "secondary ideologies," whereby temples provided spiritual guidance, schools educated students, training centers provided industrial reskilling to workers, and so on. But when taken together and overseen by the imperial state, they functioned to reconfigure political criminals as loyal imperial subjects, what Althusser would see as their "primary" ideological function.[55]

Disregarding Althusser's more problematic theory of interpellation, I will focus specifically on Althusser's concept of ISAs in order to explore the operations of the Peace Preservation Law apparatus.[56] In his approach to ISAs, Althusser argues that ideology is not ideational, but rather "always exists in an apparatus, and its practice, or practices. This existence is material."[57] Subverting the causality of the ideational thesis, Althusser argues that "the 'ideas' of a human subject exist in his[/her] actions" and that these actions themselves are "inserted into *practices*" that "are governed by the *rituals* in which these practices are inscribed, within the material existence of an *ideological apparatus*."[58] Althusser's theory of ISAs requires that we move beyond the conventional problematic regarding to what degree did ideological converts truly come to believe in imperial ideology in the 1930s, and to focus on the forms and practices ritualized within political reform groups through which thought criminals acted as if they were loyal imperial subjects.

Attentive to the important theoretical differences that exist between Althusser and Foucault, as well as the lacunae that exist in their respective theories of ideology and power, each chapter of *Thought Crime* reflects on a specific question posed by one of these theorists and pursues this question through an analysis of a particular development in the Peace Preservation Law apparatus.

Chapter Outline

Chapter 1 begins by exploring the Japanese state's efforts to pass antiradical laws earlier in the 1920s, and then conducts an in-depth analysis of the drafting and legislative debates that led to the passage of the Peace Preservation Law in 1925. I demonstrate that while most officials and politicians agreed on the need to pass measures that would suppress radical political movements, they struggled to define the object that was threatened by such movements. Officials ultimately decided upon the term "kokutai" to identify the bill's object of protection, defining a political crime as forming or joining an organization that had the intention to "alter the kokutai" (*kokutai o henkaku*). Whereas existing scholarship portrays the inclusion of kokutai in the law as the contamination of juridical rationality by the irrational and ambiguous category of kokutai, chapter 1 shows how lawmakers continually referred to kokutai as signifying imperial sovereignty as stipulated in the 1889 Meiji Constitution. Drawing upon critical theories of sovereignty, I argue that if the inclusion of kokutai in the law was irrational or ambiguous, it was an irrationality that emerged from the concept of sovereignty and the particular form that this took in the prewar Japanese Empire. Consequently, by utilizing the term "kokutai," legislators inadvertently brought questions related to the form and content of imperial sovereignty into debates over the law, infusing the law's emerging institutionalization with the ghostly specter of the sovereign emperor. This chapter reveals how these kinds of issues are most clearly seen in the discussions over how to implement the Peace

Preservation Law in colonial Korea, where, at least initially, colonial courts defined kokutai as referring largely to the territorial integrity of Japan's colonial empire.

Chapter 2 traces the process of how reform and rehabilitation protocols slowly emerged from a law that was initially intended as a legal instrument to repress threats to imperial sovereignty. Drawing upon Foucault's theoretical distinction between sovereign and disciplinary power, I argue that, by the early 1930s, the initial repressive application of the Peace Preservation Law was so successful in metropolitan Japan that justice officials were faced with the problem of how to manage thousands of detained political criminals. Through a contingent process of trial and error, officials in Tokyo arrived at the solution of reforming repentant political criminals, drawing upon disciplinary measures that were developed earlier to reform delinquent youth. While prior scholarship has recognized this complex combination of repression and reform in the law, it does not consider the functional relationship between these two modes of state power, explaining it simply as the schizophrenic, Janus-faced justice unique to prewar Japan.[59] In contrast, chapter 2 reveals how imperial ideology mediated the functional relationship between repression and rehabilitation: for example, repression was legitimated as protecting the imperial sovereign, while reform was increasingly portrayed as an expression of the unique benevolence of the Japanese imperial house. And although reform was institutionalized in colonial Korea as well, repression continued to constitute the primary application of the law in the colony into the mid-1930s, demonstrating how the colonial articulation of imperial sovereignty differed from the metropole. This functional but differential combination of repression and disciplinary reform in the Peace Preservation Law apparatus provides a historical example through which to reconsider Michel Foucault's logical and historical distinction between sovereign-juridical and disciplinary power.

In chapter 3, I explore the oft-overlooked network of semiofficial rehabilitation groups that facilitated the ideological conversion (tenkō) of ex-communists and their reintegration into society. This chapter focuses on the most important group in this network—the Tokyo-based Imperial Renovation Society (Teikoku Kōshinkai)—and the early contributions of one of its staff members, the ex-communist convert Kobayashi Morito. Originally established in 1926 as a semiofficial support group for detainees awaiting criminal indictment, by the mid-1930s the Imperial Renovation Society oversaw the ideological conversion of hundreds of ex-rank-and-file JCP members, establishing protocols for other thought crime reform groups throughout the empire. Tenkō is commonly defined as when a political criminal spontaneously changed his or her thought under the coercion of state power. This overlooks the fact that an institutional network predated the phenomenon referred to as tenkō. Drawing upon Louis Althusser's theory of ISAs introduced above, this chapter argues that it was in such semiofficial support groups that the corollary ghost of the imperial subject was starting to take shape, who, once paroled would, to paraphrase Althusser, make the gestures and actions of his or her continuing subjection all by him or herself.[60] Groups such as the Imperial Renovation Society enlisted Buddhist chaplains, family members, employers, educators, and civic leaders in assisting with the rehabilitation of political criminals, thereby serving as important sites of ideological mediation between the imperial state and the wider community.

Chapter 4 traces how, following a wave of defections from the JCP in 1933–1934, the Justice Ministry attempted to formalize and extend administrative policies for reforming detained and paroled political criminals, culminating in the 1936 Thought Criminal Protection and Supervision Law (Shisōhan hogo kansatsu hō). This chapter focuses on two important developments within this process between 1934 and 1936. First, I explore how as justice officials and reformed ex-communists ruminated on the significance and practice of political rehabilitation, they increasingly drew upon the tenets of imperial ideology to define ideological conversion, thereby refining the figure of the ghost of imperial subjectivity informing these conversions. I understand this development through Louis Althusser's distinction between primary and secondary ideologies at work in ISAs: in this case, the mandate to reform criminals (secondary ideology) guiding groups like the Imperial Renovation Society was increasingly yoked to imperial loyalty and national veneration (the primary ideology). The second development I focus on in chapter 4 is the emerging concern for securing a political convert's conversion after he or she was released. With an increasing number of converts being released, counselors and justice officials sought a new ethic, most often in Buddhist self-negation, for converts to return to and function in society without constant state oversight. I contend that this objective introduced a new complementary mode of power to the Peace Preservation Law apparatus— what Foucault theorized as governmentality—a mode of power whereby the population of converts would govern themselves in their everyday practices as productive subjects of the imperial polity.[61] This addition of governmentality complemented the sovereign and disciplinary modes of power that converged earlier in the 1930s. And as the state codified these practices in the 1936 Thought Criminal Protection and Supervision Law, we can understand this development as "the 'governmentalization' of the state" (Foucault).[62] The chapter also points to how, although there had been far fewer cases of ideological conversion in colonial Korea than in the metropole before 1936, once established, the Protection and Supervision Center apparatus facilitated a sudden increase of conversion in Korea in the latter half of the decade, raising new questions about how Korean colonial subjects, although not ethnically Japanese, could ideologically convert as nationals of the Japanese imperial nation-state.

The fifth and final chapter analyzes the transformation in ideological conversion during the early years of the China Incident. Immediately after Japan's invasion of China in 1937, tenkōsha mobilized in support of war as a means to demonstrate their rehabilitation as patriotic imperial subjects. This was a natural extension of the practices taking place in the newly established Protection and Supervision Centers. At the same time, reform officials abstracted from the practices within the centers and presented tenkō to the general public as a model for how all subjects—not just political criminals—could purify their thoughts and spiritually mobilize for war. The convergence in the changing practices and representation of tenkō refigured ideological conversion as an ideology—what I call the ideology of conversion—applicable to the general population. The ideology of conversion was most explicit in the portrayal of reformed ex-communists and anticolonial nationalists as the vanguard of an empire-wide spiritual awakening, presaging later war mobilization campaigns. However, in colonial Korea, where conversion started to become a more widespread phenomenon in 1937, officials ruminated on the inherent limitations of colonial conversion, thus revealing specific aporia in imperial ideology and its articulation in the colony.

Chapter 5 concludes by reviewing the passage of an extensive revision to the Peace Preservation Law in 1941, which demoted the earlier emphasis on reform with a policy of indeterminate detention called preventative detention (yobō kōkin), returning the function of the law to an emphasis on repression of suspected threats against the state during wartime. By this time, however, the notions of thought purification and spiritual mobilization that were developed within the Peace Preservation Law earlier in the 1930s had become general principles to mobilize society, most clearly exemplified in the National Spirit Mobilization Movement (Kokumin seishin sōdōin undō). In the epilogue, I reflect on the transwar legacies of the Peace Preservation Law and ruminate on possible lines of inquiry for further research into the revived rehabilitation practices in the early postwar period.

Before beginning, three qualifications are necessary. First, *Thought Crime* does not address the individual experiences of activists who underwent the practice of conversion, or the effect the Peace Preservation Law had on the interwar socialist, communist, and anticolonial movements. There are volumes of research on these aspects of interwar history, to which I refer in the endnotes. Rather, my analytical focus is on what the Peace Preservation Law reveals about imperial state ideology and how this ideology was inscribed in state apparatuses to police so-called thought crime.[63] Second and relatedly, my objective is not to inquire into the Peace Preservation Law's success or failure in policing thought per se, but rather the legal, institutional, and ideological conditions within which the discourse of thought crime and ideological conversion emerged and transformed. For those interested in criminological approaches to the interwar law, I refer to many secondary sources in the endnotes. Last and most importantly, although *Thought Crime* touches upon the ways in which the Peace Preservation Law was interpreted and implemented differently in colonial Korea, the complexity of the colonial institution and the different experience of colonial tenkōsha require much further research. Where necessary, I refer to scholarship in the endnotes that has started to illuminate these complexities, including the groundbreaking work of Mizuno Naoki and more recently Hong Jong-wook's excellent study of tenkō in colonial Korea. I hope that by illuminating the complex logic and institutional operations of the Peace Preservation Law, *Thought Crime* will inspire new research into these areas as well as a broader reconsideration of the complex political and ideological transformations across the Japanese Empire during the 1930s.

Kokutai and the Aporias of Imperial Sovereignty:
The Passage of the Peace Preservation Law in 1925

Law is always present from the beginning in the social order: it does not arrive post fes-
tum to put order into a pre-existing state of nature. For as the codification of both prohi-
bitions and positive injunctions, law is a constitutive element of the politico-social field.
—NICOS POULANTZAS, *State, Power, Socialism*

The Japanese state's thought reform policy developed from a notorious
antiradical law called the Peace Preservation Law (Chianijihō). Passed in 1925,
this law was utilized to arrest or detain over seventy thousand people in the
Japanese metropole and colonial Korea, until it was repealed by Occupation
authorities in October 1945, two months after Japan's surrender in World
War II. The law was initially envisioned as a legal instrument to suppress
domestic communists and anticolonial activists, but in the 1930s the law was
extended to other political and religious groups, as well as academics, writers,
lawyers, and others who were seen as posing an ideological threat to imperial
state orthodoxy. Not only was the purview of the law extended, but the policies
that developed for administering the law were also intensified in the 1930s, as
the Peace Preservation Law became a complex institutional apparatus for the
interrogation, surveillance, and rehabilitation of political criminals throughout
the empire. It is therefore necessary to begin our analysis by returning to the
early legislative debates over the law in order to understand how it was originally conceptualized and the interpretive questions that it generated.

Engaging with the extensive literature on the Peace Preservation Law, this chapter proposes a new interpretation that turns the law against itself and reads its early conceptualization not only as an instrument to suppress dangerous political ideologies, but as also articulating some of the constitutive ideological aporias of the imperial state and its colonial empire.[1] This chapter argues that in order to respond to the threat posed by domestic communism and anticolonial nationalism, state officials crafted a law that inadvertently revealed ambiguities in the state's own foundational ideology of imperial sovereignty. Specifically, in order to identify someone as a threat to the imperial state, officials were compelled to legally define the essence of imperial sovereignty as well as the unique relationship between sovereign and subject that was threatened by such political ideologies. Furthermore, because this law was to be applied simultaneously in Japan's colonies—most intensively against the anticolonial movement in Korea—it forced colonial administrators to clarify how imperial sovereignty extended to the colonies and how to police anticolonial activism as political crime. As we will see, these questions crystallized in the central category of the law, kokutai (national polity, or essence).

This chapter explores how bureaucrats and legislators struggled to legally define kokutai in the initial deliberations over the Peace Preservation Bill in 1925, and what kind of questions these debates produced regarding the nature of imperial sovereignty. Kokutai's categorical ambiguity did not hinder the application of the law but became the condition for its expansion into various domains of everyday life in imperial Japan. And as we will explore in later chapters, not only did kokutai continue to be debated every time a revision to the law was proposed, but it was also discussed by officials who were charged with facilitating the increasing population of detained political criminals in the 1930s. By this time, the categorical function of kokutai in the Peace Preservation Law apparatus was shifting from repression to rehabilitation, and by the late 1930s it informed ideological conversion protocols in an empire-wide parole system for political criminals. In this way, we can say that kokutai indexed the ghosts that animated an ever-expanding institutional apparatus to combat political crime in the interwar Japanese empire.

The Category Kokutai in the Peace Preservation Law

Although everyone understands what kokutai is, when asked to clearly explain it, this becomes something extremely difficult to do, and there is certainly no one who can speak of it precisely. —MATSUDA TAKECHIYO, deliberating a proposed revision to the Peace Preservation Law in the Imperial Diet in 1934

Conventionally translated as "national polity," kokutai was initially defined by proponents of the Peace Preservation Bill as signifying the location of sovereignty in the "line of Emperors unbroken for ages eternal" (*bansei ikkei no tennō*).[2] In order to juridically legitimate this definition, proponents of the bill consistently referred to Articles 1 and 4 of the Meiji Constitution of 1889, which stated that the "Empire of Japan shall be reigned over and governed by a line of Emperors unbroken for ages eternal" and that the "Emperor is the head of the Empire, combining in Himself the rights of sovereignty, and exercises them, according to the provisions of the present Constitution" respectively.[3] It is important to note that, although legislators cited the Meiji Constitution to legally define kokutai, the term itself does not appear in the text of the Constitution; it was only after the promulgation of the Constitution in 1889 that constitutional theorists started using the term "kokutai" to interpret the juridical form of the new imperial state.

Rather, kokutai was best known for its use in the 1890 Imperial Rescript on Education (Kyōiku ni kansuru chokugo, or Kyōiku chokugo), which was memorized by schoolchildren throughout the Japanese Empire. This Rescript translated the neo-Confucian ethics of loyalty and filial piety into a modern form of civic morality that all imperial subjects were to embody.[4] The Rescript reads in part: "Our Imperial Ancestors have founded Our Empire on a basis broad and everlasting and have deeply and firmly implanted virtue; Our subjects ever united in loyalty and filial piety have from generation to generation illustrated the beauty thereof. This is the glory of the fundamental character of our Empire [*waga kokutai no seika*], and herein also lies the source of our education."[5] Note that here kokutai did not signify imperial sovereignty per se, but rather the purportedly timeless ethical values mediating the relationship between emperor and subject from time immemorial. We will see how this ethical significance is periodically invoked in discussions over the Peace Preservation Law, thus complicating the attempt to define kokutai in purely constitutional terms.

How then should we understand the choice to use kokutai in this criminal law? Clearly, the drafters from the Home and Justice Ministries of the original Peace Preservation Bill did not choose the term "kokutai" to resolve ongoing debates in constitutional theory.[6] Rather, they chose kokutai to signify something essentially Japanese that was being threatened by radical foreign ideologies such as communism. In other words, kokutai was used to identify the foreign ideological threat, not to clarify the nature of imperial sovereignty. However, when pressed, proponents of the law argued that this object of protection was imperial sovereignty, and continually referred to the

Meiji Constitution to validate its usage. By doing so legislators inadvertently exposed fundamental questions about imperial sovereignty and sovereign power and continued to stage these questions every time a revision was proposed to the Peace Preservation Law. In this way, the functional definition of kokutai in the law opened into interpretive questions related to the foundation of the imperial state. This requires that we follow two lines of analysis when exploring the Peace Preservation Law: one in regard to the categorical function of kokutai in the law, and another in regard to the different interpretive definitions of kokutai, which open into broader questions related to imperial state ideology.[7]

Kokutai and Constituent Power

Prior studies of the Peace Preservation Law have sought to explain the law's increasing expansion and intensification in the 1930s as the result of the slow contamination of external, mystical, or affective meanings associated with kokutai, such as those expressed in the Imperial Rescript on Education. For instance, Okudaira Yasuhiro has argued that although kokutai functioned as a "fixed frame-like thing" (*ittei no waku no yō na mono*) for the ensemble of subsidiary laws, regulations, and institutions that were related to the Peace Preservation Law, at the same time, kokutai harbored sentimental (*jōchoteki*) intimations about the sanctity of the imperial household.[8] Okudaira argues that the law was increasingly "contaminated" (*konkō*) by this sentimental meaning of kokutai, ultimately rendering the Peace Preservation Law "a mysterious thing completely unrelated to modern law."[9] From a similar perspective, Richard Mitchell has argued that it was kokutai's sentimental excess that made it such an effective legal instrument to suppress communism and integrate Japanese society during a period of tumultuous modernization. Mitchell argues that lawmakers had "picked a term which aroused a strong emotional response in the emperor's subjects. . . . They could not have devised a better term; '*kokutai*' in one word symbolized everything worth protecting."[10] As we see here, both Okudaira and Mitchell derive their evaluations of the law from an assumed opposition between legal rationality and the external cultural excess of kokutai, an assumption that informs many subsequent studies, including those that explore the application of the law in the colonies.[11] Implied in many of these studies—particularly those written from an earlier area studies paradigm—is an analogous distinction between Western rationality manifest in modern legal forms and traditional culture harbored in ambiguous terms such as kokutai, which renders the Peace

Preservation Law as a symbol of Japan's vexed attempt to translate its traditional culture into the forms of Western legal rationality.[12]

More recently, Ogino Fujio has argued that it was through "the 'spell' [*maryoku*] of kokutai" that the Peace Preservation Law was able to apply to an ever-expanding list of groups, including the Korean national independence movement, as well as Christians and new religions such as Ōmotokyō.[13] Similar to Okudaira, Ogino contends that when officials turned to the Imperial Rescript on Education in order to provide a definition for kokutai, the term "attained an unconditional inviolability in law." Defined in this way, kokutai came to have an "omnipotent 'power'" (*bannō no 'mashō'*), and as the Peace Preservation Law was used against ideological threats to the imperial state, kokutai's "omnipotent 'power'" cleared the way for the "idea that the emperor was a 'living deity'" (*arahitogami*) to become ideological orthodoxy by the late 1930s.[14] Although more nuanced than Okudaira and Mitchell's assessments, Ogino reproduces the assumption that over time kokutai shed any relation to constitutional rationality and came to inject the ideology of imperial divinity into the realm of law.

Even if we retain the language of sentimentality or spiritual excess when analyzing kokutai, however, we still need to account for how this excess could be articulated within the domain of law, particularly since kokutai was consistently defined by reference to the Meiji Constitution. I contend that it is not a question whether a clearer, less sentimental term could have been used, since this assumes that a pure realm of legal rationality is possible by calibrating clearly defined legal categories.[15] Rather, as this chapter argues, the deployment of kokutai indicates a problem immanent to sovereignty and how it was inflected in the particular imperial form of the prewar Japanese state. From this perspective, we can recast the distinction Okudaira, Mitchell, and others have assumed between modern law and the cultural or spiritual excess of kokutai as a problem emerging internal to the question of sovereignty that kokutai was said to signify. While the particular and often contradictory attributes associated with the term "kokutai" need to be interrogated in their own right, we must first recognize the aporic form through which these attributes became articulated within the realm of law. It was, in fact, through this spectral excess—that is, the imperial sovereign and the legal field that his sovereignty constituted—that the machinery of the Peace Preservation Law's security apparatus came to life.

Rather than contrasting the constitutional rationality of sovereignty with the sentimentality or ambiguity of kokutai, we should begin by noting the constitutive ambiguity of sovereignty itself. In one sense, the elements of sovereignty and how it defines the modern political order seem straight-forward enough. To cite one introductory definition of the concept: "Sovereignty is an idea of authority embodied in those bordered territorial organizations we refer to as 'states' or 'nations' and expressed in their various relations and activities, both domestic and foreign."[16] However, questions immediately arise. As Hent Kalmo and Quentin Skinner have asked in their review of theories of sovereignty: "what is the nature of the authority invoked in the name of sovereignty? Is it legal or political in nature?" Kalmo and Skinner summarize that "sovereignty appears as the very guarantor of the unstable union of politics and law—the afterlife of the original *coup de droit* that grounds every legal order."[17] In many ways, the legislative debates that took place concerning the Peace Preservation Bill in 1925 were based on this indetermination between the legal or political nature of imperial sovereignty, particularly as the law was being envisioned to identify and suppress political criminals.

Moreover, if the nature of sovereignty is an open question, it is also unclear how sovereignty is bounded. For instance, Jens Bartelson has argued that "particular claims to authority only make sense in a world in which mankind already has been divided into distinct and bounded communities."[18] Drawing upon Kant's idea of the parergon, Bartelson argues that sovereignty acts as a kind of parergonal frame to a bounded nation-state: "A *parergon* does not exist in the same sense as that which it helps constitute; there is a ceaseless activity of *framing*, but the frame itself is never present, since it is itself unframed."[19] In this regard, sovereignty neither signifies an a priori essence internal to the territorial state, nor is it defined solely from external relations with other states. As a "composite of inside and outside" of the state, sovereignty is a line of demarcation or frame that is continually reposed and redrawn in and through political practice.[20] We will see this kind of problem expressed in the debates over how to identify the external threat that the Peace Preservation Law was said to target, as well as how the law would be applied throughout the differentiated legal space of the Japanese empire.[21]

These questions concerning the nature and demarcations of sovereignty point to an even more fundamental aporia of sovereignty, as revealed in the theoretical investigations into the duality of constituent and constitutive power. Following Carl Schmitt's writings on the constitutional exception and the sovereign decision, recent theorists have reflected on the paradox wherein an established constitutional order (constituted power) demarcates the sovereign authority that is its purported source (constituting power), thus blurring the direction of which power is determinative in the last instance.[22] When explicated, the location of the subject of sovereignty entails a folding back of the constitutional norm into the figure of that subject, leading to the paradox wherein the sovereign both designates the constitutional order, and is also necessarily designated by it.[23] Constituent power appears as what Martin Loughlin and Neil Walker have called "an authorizing moment" of the constitutional order.[24] William E. Connolly describes the historico-temporal paradox of this assumed authorizing moment this way: "the paradox of sovereignty is asserted with respect to the founding act of a state, but those who locate a paradox in the founding act typically discern its echoes and reverberations in the state that results as well."[25] One could trace such "reverberations" in the other direction, in which the imperative to recognize the authority of constituted power will always necessarily revert back to the purported authorizing moment.

One such example of this authorizing moment can be found in the preamble to the Meiji Constitution, which reads in part, "The right of sovereignty of the State, We have inherited from Our Ancestors, and We shall bequeath them to Our descendants. Neither We nor they shall in the future fail to wield them, in accordance with the provisions of the Constitution hereby granted."[26] Beyond the mythical nature of this claim, the origin that the Constitution is invoking for itself is not, of course, a historical-empirical event but rather can only be articulated within the framework of an already constituted constitutional order, resembling what Jean-Jacques Rousseau once described as when "the effect would have to become the cause."[27] The recognized author of the Meiji Constitution, Itō Hirobumi, explained the above passage in the following manner: "At the outset, this Article states the great principle of the Constitution of the country, and declares that the Empire of Japan shall, to the end of time, identify itself with the Imperial dynasty unbroken in lineage, and that the principle has never changed in the past, and will never change in the future, even to all eternity."[28]

In other words, the promulgation of the Constitution merely reflected what has always been, and what has always been was the condition for the Constitution to be promulgated, a declaration that utilizes the particular myth of the imperial household to fill the (atemporal) conditions for sovereignty to be posited.[29] And as Takashi Fujitani has shown, the myth of imperial origin was not only inscribed in the text of the Meiji Constitution but also performed in the elaborate ceremonies that attended the Constitution's promulgation in 1889, in which the heir of the unbroken imperial lineage was presented to the public in a series of newly invented ceremonies that were to be experienced as timeless and recognizable rituals authorizing the promulgation.[30]

This tension between constituent and constituted power does not produce a constitutional crisis in itself. Rather, this tension becomes the space in which politics or a political crisis is rearticulated in juridical discourse—a space that Giorgio Agamben has called a "zone of indistinction."[31] In other words, in times of emergency, the question of constituted/constituent power allows for the political to most explicitly appear within the ostensible purity of legal rationality: for example, in the political decision to suspend the constitution or to take extraconstitutional measures in order to protect the legal order.[32] In these moments, sovereign power suspends that which gives it the power to do so, and any legal scrutiny of this decision can only take place once the constitutional norm returns and replaces the state of exception.[33]

Although the Japanese Peace Preservation Law did not suspend the Meiji Constitution, it was presented as a legal response to a purported existential threat to imperial sovereignty. Consequently, the questions outlined above concerning sovereignty and constituted/constituent power were inadvertently staged by legislators who used the term "kokutai" to signify that imperial sovereignty was under existential threat from imported "dangerous thought" (kiken shisō). They chose kokutai for they believed it to be a concrete term (gutaiteki no moji), and proponents repeatedly returned to the explanation that kokutai signified the location of sovereignty in the "line of Emperors unbroken for ages eternal" as stipulated in Article 1 of the Meiji Constitution. This reference inadvertently forced the question of the nature of this sovereign subject and its relationship to the national polity every time revisions were proposed to the Peace Preservation Law. Not only was this problem concerning sovereignty and the national polity never settled, but as I explore in later chapters, it was the basis for the law to be continually reconceptualized and transformed over time.

These questions become even more complicated when we focus on how officials struggled to interpret and apply the law in the colonies. Most studies of the Peace Preservation Law have analyzed its application in the Japanese metropole, overlooking the fact that the law was applied simultaneously in the colonies, including the sovereign colonies of Korea, Taiwan, and Karafuto (southern Sakhalin), as well as the Kwantung Leased Territory and the South Sea Islands, without any changes to its wording.[34] This was new, for prior antiradical laws or ordinances applied only to a particular region and its unique political situation at the time. In contrast, the Peace Preservation

Law was envisioned as coextensive with the Japanese empire, and kokutai identified the primary infringement across imperial space. Consequently, the interpretive challenges that lawmakers faced in applying the law in Japan became even more explicit when we turn our attention to the colonies.

We can find intimations of these interpretive challenges in an earlier attempt to pass an antiradical law in 1922, challenges that the 1925 Peace Preservation Law would inherit and amplify.

Identifying the Threat: Dangerous Foreign Thought and the 1922 Antiradical Bill

In 1921 a junior economics professor at Tokyo Imperial University, Morito Tatsuo, was charged with violating Article 42 of the 1909 Newspaper Law for publishing an analysis and partial translation of the anarchist Peter Kropotkin's social thought in the Tokyo Imperial University Economics Department's journal *Keizaigaku kenkyū* (*Research in Economics*).[35] In a sensational decision, Morito, along with the publisher of *Keizaigaku kenkyū*, Ōuchi Hyōe, were found guilty of publishing matter that "subverts the laws of the state" (*chōken o binran*). Ōuchi and Morito both lost their jobs at Tokyo Imperial University and Morito served a three-month jail sentence at Sugamo Prison.[36]

The prosecution of Morito and Ōuchi was symptomatic of the increasing fear in the Japanese state that foreign ideologies such as anarchism and communism were spreading amid the social, economic, and political tumult following World War I. In the wake of the domestic Rice Riots of 1918 (at that time, the largest uprising in Japan's modern history), the Korean anticolonial movement that emerged in 1919 (the March First Movement), as well as the successful Bolshevik Revolution of 1917 and the establishment of the Communist International, state officials began to consider antiradical measures along the same lines as those in Europe and the United States.[37] In this increasingly tense political context, the Home Ministry published a report in September 1921 summarizing antiradical laws that were in effect in Europe, the United States, and South America.[38] Officials feared that existing Japanese laws were insufficient to deal with the new threat posed by international communism, both in the metropole and, as I review below, in colonial Korea.[39] These anxieties inspired the Home Ministry, with the collaboration of the Justice Ministry, to propose a security bill to the Imperial Diet in 1922 called the Kageki shakai undō torishimari hōan, literally the Draft Bill to Control Radical Social Movements (hereafter, Antiradical Bill).[40]

A Home Ministry report published in 1923 detailed the process by which the bill was drafted and explained the need for such a law as follows: "Recently in our nation there are those who, working with their foreign counterparts, have spread extremism, and together with lawless Koreans and Chinese, have attempted to Bolshevize [*sekka*] our country."[41] As we see here, the threat was conceived as coming from outside the borders of the empire (with colonial Korean and Chinese activists agitating outside imperial borders). The task was to protect the Japanese Empire from the new threats posed by so-called foreign radicalism (*kagekishugi*).

Furthermore, there is some indication that officials were beginning to entertain the idea of a single antiradical law to apply in both the metropole and the colonies. Up until this time, the Government-General in Korea had relied on the 1907 Security Law (Hoanhō)—established when Korea was still a protectorate of Japan—to prosecute political crimes. Later, in addition to this 1907 Security Law, other ordinances were issued in response to changing conditions in Korea, for example, the Public Peace Police Ordinance (Chian keisatsu rei) issued soon after annexation in 1910, and later, Ordinance No. 7, "On the Punishment of Political Crime" (Seiji ni kansuru hanzai no ken), in response to the widespread anticolonial March First Movement that began in 1919.[42] The first clause of this latter ordinance (*seirei*) stated that "those who disturb, or intend to disturb the public peace, by acting collectively with the intention to change the political order" would face up to ten years of imprisonment. Korean activists who were charged under this ordinance were found to have disrupted the public peace (*chian*) and to have disturbed the laws of the state (*kokken*).[43] However, it is important to note that this 1919 ordinance was issued specifically in response to the March First Movement, and thus limited to the colonial administration of Korea.[44] In contrast, preparatory reports reveal that the drafters of the 1922 bill expected that, if passed, the law would apply in both the metropole and colonies.

The Home and Justice Ministries began working on the Antiradical Bill in late 1921 and delivered the bill to the House of Peers of the Forty-Fifth Imperial Diet in 1922.[45] Vice Justice Minister Yamanouchi Kakusaburō, the head of the Criminal Affairs Bureau, Hayashi Raizaburō, and other proponents of the bill explained its necessity by arguing that, unlike current ordinances such as those contained in the 1898 Civil Code (Minpō), or the 1900 Public Peace Police Law (Chian keisatsu hō), which only covered violent acts of civil disturbance or the formation and assembly of political groups, this antiradical bill would "recognize, capture, and imprison" elements that "are poisoning society" through ideological dissemination.[46] As noted above, the poison was not homegrown, but originated abroad and was already infiltrating (sennyū) Japanese society.[47] Hayashi Raizaburō, who would later become chief procurator in 1932, urged Diet members to recognize that current laws were insufficient against this new threat since they did not apply to those planning to harm the empire through ideological subversion.[48] He urged legislators to recognize that current laws only covered civil disturbances when they reached a level of violence, not "the slow infiltration of dangerous thought into the hearts and minds [of the people]" which would eventually "destroy the national structure from within."[49]

Proponents argued for the necessity of the emergency law through a binary logic, one in which "our state" (waga kokka) and "the fundamental structure of our country" (waga kuni no konpon soshiki) was being threatened by "foreign thought" (gairai shisō) that had infiltrated the borders of the empire. Article 1 of the 1922 bill read, "Anyone who propagandizes, or attempts to propagandize, in order to subvert the laws of the state in matters connected with anarchism, communism, and others, shall be liable to imprisonment with or without hard labor for a term not exceeding seven years." In addition, the bill stated, "Anyone who encourages [kanyū] others, or anyone who responds to such persuasion, to execute the above matters, will receive the same punishment mentioned above."[50] Though "communism" and "anarchism" are stated to be the primary targets of the law, these were both generalized under the infringement "to subvert the laws of the state" (chōken o binran suru), and qualified by the addition of "and others."

Furthermore, Article 3 of the bill read, "Anyone who propagandizes [senden], or attempts to propagandize, in order to alter the fundamental structure of society [shakai no konpon soshiki] by means of riot, violence, intimidation, or by other illegal methods, shall be liable to imprisonment with or without hard labor for a term not exceeding five years."[51] Thus the identification of a crime was defined largely against what it was ostensibly threatening—that is, "laws of state" (chōken) and "the fundamental structure of society" (shakai no konpon soshiki). These were ambiguous terms and remained unclear to even the bill's advocates during the legislative discussions.

Almost immediately debate began on the meaning of these terms. The concern for many legislators was that terminological ambiguity could allow for the law to apply to a number of accepted activities, restricting the boundaries of academic writing, political debate, or other forms of speech. When first introducing the bill to the House of Peers on February 21, Yamanouchi used both "national polity" (kokutai) and the "national laws" (kokka no kokken) in order to define chōken, demonstrating the difficulty in specifying what chōken signified.[52] At a later meeting in the House of Peers, Yamanou-chi repeated this definition, arguing that "to subvert the laws of the state" was to "repudiate our country's kokutai" (*waga kuni no kokutai o hinin suru*) and to "destroy the foundation of the kokutai" (*kokutai no kiso o hakai*).[53] It is important to note that Yamanouchi attempted to clarify the phrase "laws of state" by referring to an even more enigmatic term—kokutai—one that had, as noted earlier, spawned long and intense debates in prewar Japanese con-stitutional theory.[54] As we will see below, this issue would become explicit in the later debates over the 1925 Peace Preservation Bill.[55]

Debates raged over the term "fundamental structure of society" as well. After Yamanouchi passed on a question over the designation of "fundamen-tal structure of society," Okada Ryōhei, a member of the Kenseikai Party, asked, "[If this] is not clearly understood, then won't there be difficulty in applying the law?" He pressed the bill's proponents to clearly explain its cov-erage, saying, "It is still unclear [how to determine] if something fits within the boundaries of this term."[56] The future education minister, Matsuda Genji, rose to the challenge and defined the fundamental structure of Japanese soci-ety as consisting of both the "family system" (*kazoku seido*) and the "private property system" (*shiyūzaisan seido*).[57] Although "fundamental structure of society" was taken out of the bill by the time it reached the Lower House on March 14, it is important to note that one of the terms Matsuda used to explain this phrase—"private property system"—would reappear in the later Peace Preservation Bill.[58]

What exactly constituted anarchism and communism was unclear to leg-islators as well. Earlier, in the second committee meeting in the House of Peers on March 1, Yamanouchi himself admitted to not fully understanding the specificities of communism and anarchism, completing the circuit of confusion between both polarities of the bill's binary structure. He lamented, "Although I have heard of anarchism, I am unclear of its meaning" and then went on to incorrectly explain that anarchist activities included contacting the Soviet Union and receiving money in order to "import so-called 'Bolshe-vism,' and with this, to destroy our kokutai." He admitted that perhaps they should have used the term "Bolshevism" rather than "anarchism."[59] However, proponents and critics alike remained uncertain of what the exact differences were between anarchism and communism, and how to fine-tune the law so it would apply to all versions of revolutionary social movements without curtailing acceptable political discourse and practices. By the time the draft arrived on the floor of the Lower House on March 14, the terms "anarchism," "communism," and "and others" were taken out, leaving "to subvert the laws of the state" and "fundamental structure of society" to stand by themselves without any explicitly defined threat.[60] Additionally, "or to attempt to propagandize" was also stricken due to its vagueness, compared with the more explicit act, "to propagandize."[61]

The general ambiguity of all the terms, and the failure to reach a consensus over what these terms designated, forced proponents to simply insist on the necessity for the law in a time of foreign ideological assault against Imperial Japan. They tried to calm fears that this bill would infringe upon freedom of speech and academic research by stressing that the law would be applied only to those who were in contact with foreign agents, receiving money from outside the country, or importing and spreading dangerous ideas from abroad. By the time the bill returned to the House of Peers on March 24, the foreignness of the ideological threat became more explicit in the bill's text.[62] In place of "anarchism, communism and others," Article 1 now read, "Anyone who has contact with foreign nationals, or any others who are outside of the jurisdiction of this law, and propagandizes in order to subvert the laws of the state, shall be liable to imprisonment with or without hard labor for a term not exceeding three years."[63] This emphasis on the foreign source of subversion was probably inspired by revelations that, the year before, Japanese radicals had met with Soviet agents in China and were attempting to establish a communist party in Japan.[64] Additionally, the foreignness of the crime was also indexed by the addition of "outside of the jurisdiction of this law" (*honpō jigyō kuikigai*), indicating that nationals of the empire would be prosecuted for political crimes carried out abroad once they returned or were extradited.

A review of preparatory Justice and Home Ministry documents reveals that officials were envisioning this law to be implemented in Japan's colonies, which would have made it the first security law to apply simultaneously in both the Japanese metropole and colonies. This would have presented an interesting legal challenge, since Japan's formal colonial empire—including Taiwan, Korea, Karafuto, Kwantung Leased Territory, and the South Sea Islands—were acquired after the promulgation of the Meiji Constitution in 1889 and constituted their own respective legal domains. The Japanese Empire consisted of two different legal spaces; *naichi*, or inner territory, including the four main islands and Okinawa, and *gaichi*, or outer territories, referring to Japan's formal colonies.[65] As Edward I-te Chen explains, "*Gaichi* literally meant areas *outside* the jurisdiction of laws and regulations enforced in the *naichi*. It implied that the special ordinances issued by the colonial governors of all *gaichi* were temporary in nature, to be replaced gradually by laws and regulations of the *naichi*. From the legal point of view, integration would be considered as completed when all the territories within the empire were brought under the uniform jurisdiction of the Meiji Constitution and Japanese law."[66] Furthermore, each colony had its own legal structure; for example, ordinances in Taiwan were issued as *ritsuryō* while in Korea as *seirei*. In this regard, drafters had to address both how this law would be instituted in these different legal systems and how colonial independence could be interpreted as "subvert[ing] the laws of the state" or "alter[ing] the fundamental structure of society."

We find a hint of how this may have been defined in the February 1922 Home Ministry document "An Explanation of the Antiradical Bill" ("Kageki shakai undō torishimari hō shakugi") drafted by Kawamura Teishirō, in which Kawamura outlines a definition of "subvert[ing] the laws of the state." Kawamura explained this as including any attempt "to illegally overthrow [*funkō*] the location of sovereignty, the extent [*han'i*] of this sovereignty, or the outline of the state structure; an act that subverts [*jūrin*] the constitution (in both its form and substance); to overturn the government, to seize a part of the realm, or to align a part or the entire empire to a foreign country; to alter the imperial kokutai, to limit imperial rule, to abolish the Imperial Diet, or to alter such powers; to destroy the system of military conscription."[67]

As Mizuno Naoki has argued, Kawamura's examples "to seize a part of the realm [*hōdo sensetsu*]" and "to align a part or the entire empire to a foreign country" can be interpreted as applying to those activists agitating solely for colonial independence, not necessarily for communist revolution.[68] This is further substantiated by Kawamura's use of "the extent of sovereignty" since this defined subversion as threatening the territorial composition of the Japanese Empire.

Furthermore, when Kawamura defined the phrase "outside of the jurisdiction of this law," he explained that the law would apply to those carrying out the outlined crimes not only in Japan and "the colonies of Korea, Taiwan, Karafuto, Kwantung, and the South Sea Islands" but also in "other foreign countries" (*sono hoka shogaikoku*).[69] This latter application, however, was of course in relation to the criminal act, not the legal prosecution of such a crime in the colonial legal systems. The only discussion of the formal application of this law in the colonies occurred in passing in a March 6 House of Peers committee, in which Justice Ministry officer Miyagi Chōgorō, responding to a question about where the law would apply, answered that the content of this law would be issued as ordinances according to the specific legal systems of the various colonies; for instance, as a seirei in Korea and ritsuryō in Taiwan.[70] This indicates that drafters were planning that this Antiradical Bill would be implemented simultaneously through the different legal systems of Japan's colonies.

However, in the end, the Antiradical Bill was pulled from Diet consideration by members of the Seiyūkai party for fear that it would obstruct other important bills being deliberated at the time.[71] The general consensus was that the bill had "not been adequately prepared for," as exemplified by the inadequate explanations provided by officials from the Justice and Home Ministries.[72] Up to the last deliberations, critics continued to maintain that the terms "laws of state" and "fundamental structure of society" were too ambiguous, and questioned why earlier security ordinances such as the Public Peace Police Law would not already apply to those calling "to subvert the laws of the state."[73]

Although the 1922 bill was not passed, it serves as an early example of how officials believed that the Japanese Empire faced an ideological threat from abroad. Throughout its many revisions, the underlying logic of the 1922 bill remained a binary opposition between foreign ideological threats and domestic objects requiring protection. The Peace Preservation Bill would inherit this logical structure three years later, and many of the terms that were used to explicate the 1922 bill would reappear in the 1925 debates. The challenge for lawmakers in 1925 was to present this binary in terms that could either answer, or override, concerns about restricting political debate, speech, assembly, or thought. And in the context of increasing alarm over political radicalism in the empire and the intensifying geopolitical situation after 1922, officials redoubled their efforts to pass a new security bill.

Increasing Fears of Dangerous Foreign Thought in the mid-1920s

The fear of ideological infiltration and political subversion felt by state officials in 1922 was heightened by a number of alarming incidents in 1923. First, authorities learned in the spring of 1923 that a Japanese Communist Party (Nihon kyōsantō; hereafter, JCP) had formed illegally in 1922 and began arresting suspected members in Japan and Korea in June. Twenty-nine suspected communists were subsequently charged for violating the Public Peace Police Law. With most of its central committee members facing trial or under state surveillance, the JCP decided to dissolve itself in February 1924.[74] Even with this victory, state officials remained concerned about domestic communism for a few reasons: for one, Japan was planning to establish diplomatic relations with the Soviet Union (which took effect in February 1925), and they believed this would increase the possibility that Bolshevik ideas would infiltrate the Japanese Empire.[75] Second, the campaign for universal male suffrage gained traction in 1924, leading to the passage of the General Election Law (Futsū senkyo hō) in 1925. Officials were concerned that communists would infiltrate legal political parties and use these to foment revolution.[76] Third, colonial administrators in Korea were alarmed at the increased labor and tenant activism in 1924 and were equally concerned that communists would infiltrate these movements and use them for anticolonial activities.[77]

Other events exacerbated these fears of radicalism. On September 1, 1923, a 7.9-magnitude earthquake struck the Tokyo-Yokohama region, starting multiple fires that spread over the next forty-eight hours. It is estimated that over 100,000 people perished in the earthquake and subsequent fires.[78] Fearing that dangerous elements would take advantage of the chaos following the earthquake, the government declared martial law on September 2, mobilizing military reserves, police, and civilians to patrol affected areas. In this state of emergency, the police and military reservists rounded up political activists and held them in protective detention (hogo kensoku), brutalizing hundreds. For instance, in what came to be known as the Kameido Incident, ten socialist labor activists were rounded up in eastern Tokyo and killed on September 4.[79] In another incident, the anarchist Ōsugi Sakae, his six-year-old nephew, and feminist activist Itō Noe were killed by the Military Police (kempeitai) under the command of Lieutenant Amakasu Masahiko on September 16 (the so-called Amakasu Incident).[80]

Officers of the state carried out these murders under martial law. More disturbing was the mass killings of Koreans by vigilante groups in the days after the earthquake. On September 2, rumors spread that Koreans were setting fires, poisoning wells and planning insurrection.[81] With martial law announced later that day, police began to detain Koreans under protective detention, while at the same time civilian vigilante groups—often with direct or indirect support of the police and reservists—carried out a vicious pogrom against Koreans. Historians estimate that anywhere from four thousand to over six thousand Koreans were killed in the weeks following the earthquake. We may be inclined to distinguish these two acts of violence as manifesting two different motivations or logics: one, calculated executions carried out by state officers against their political enemies; the other, a racist, mass hysteria expressed by nonstate vigilantes in the wake of a disaster. However, Sonia Ryang and Takashi Fujitani have, from different theoretical perspectives, persuasively argued that these two cases of violence were predicated upon the logic of imperial sovereignty.[82]

In response to this chaotic situation, the government issued an Emergency Ordinance No. 403, titled "On Penalties for Securing the Peace" (Chian iji no tame ni suru bassoku ni kan suru ken) on September 7, and ordered colonial administrations to institute similar emergency ordinances on September 9. The objective of this ordinance was to prevent the distribution of any dangerous materials following the disaster, including the spread of rumors such as the kind that inspired the pogroms against Koreans. While this emergency ordinance is not directly related to the later Peace Preservation Law, there were extensive debates in the Forty-Seventh Imperial Diet in December 1923 concerning whether to extend the duration of this emergency law. These debates reintroduced questions concerning the adequacy of existing security laws and further stoked anxiety about foreign ideological influences inside the empire.[83] Moreover, the emergency ordinances of September 7 and 9 indicated that state officials were once again considering security on an empire-wide scale.

Finally, one of the more sensational political incidents following the failed Antiradical Bill was the attempted assassination of Prince Regent Hirohito (later Shōwa emperor) on December 27, 1923, outside the Imperial Palace: the so-called Toranomon Incident. The would-be assassin, Namba Daisuke, came from an elite family, and his father was then serving as a representative in the Lower House of the Imperial Diet (his father subsequently resigned after Namba's assassination attempt). In preparing for the trial, justice officials learned that Namba was influenced by translations of foreign revolutionary texts, including writings by Lenin, Sorel, and Kropotkin. This confirmed officials' fears that foreign ideologies could corrupt even an elite youth like Namba. Namba was found guilty of violating Article 73 of the Criminal Code—attempting to cause bodily harm to the emperor or a member of the imperial family—and was executed on November 13, 1924.[84]

In this context, officials in both the Home and Justice Ministries redoubled their efforts to create a security bill in 1924, cooperating more closely than they had for the 1922 bill. These contextual factors also help explain why politicians were more receptive to the 1925 Peace Preservation Bill than to the earlier Antiradical Bill.[85]

The 1925 Diet Debates: Staging the Aporias of Sovereignty

Whereas preparations for the 1922 Antiradical Bill largely took place in the Home Ministry, it was the Justice Ministry that took the initiative with the Peace Preservation Bill (Chianijihōan).[86] In 1924, Justice Minister Suzuki

Kisaburō advised the head of the Criminal Affairs Bureau, Yamaoka Manno-suke, to begin work on a new antiradical law.[87] Yamaoka assembled a team of officials and began drafting a new security law in January. Early drafts of this bill continued to define the danger as those who wished to "subvert the laws of the state" (chōken o binran), similar to the earlier 1922 bill. But in contrast to the earlier bill, it was no longer subversion through propaganda activities (senden) but now by means of "secretly organizing societies [himitsu ni kessha o soshiki] with the intent to subvert the laws of the state."[88]

Moreover, these early drafts more explicitly elaborated how "to subvert the laws of state" would apply to the colonies. For instance, in a 1924 Home Ministry document, examples of "subverting the laws of the state" are listed:

> To alter the basis of the state structure; to alter the kokutai or seitai [state form]; to revise the constitution or elements that are determined by the constitution; to revise the seitai or to disrupt the laws of the state; to deny state authority; to repudiate the existence of the state; to repudiate or negate the location of sovereign authority [tōchiken]; to proscribe the scope of sovereign authority; for example, to overthrow the government; to seize part of the realm; to plan for colonial independence, or; to combine [a part of the empire] with a foreign country.[89]

As we see here, agitating for colonial independence was explicitly identified as an infringement: that is, to "proscribe the scope of sovereign authority." Additionally, it is important to note that at the very same time this bill was taking shape in Tokyo, the Police Bureau of the Korean Government-General was also reviewing their security ordinances and apparently began drafting an ordinance called the Public Peace Police Ordinance (Chian keisatsu rei).[90] Ultimately, the ordinance was not put into effect, but we can understand it as one further aspect contributing to the development of the Peace Preservation Law.

Another important development came in November 1924, when the Police Bureau of the Home Ministry, working in response to the earlier Justice Ministry drafts, produced its own Peace Preservation Bill draft. It is worth citing the first article from this Police Bureau draft: "Anyone who forms a society with the intention to destroy the national polity [kokutai o henkai], to deny the state or its laws, or to seize a part of the realm, or knowingly joins such a society, shall be liable to imprisonment with or without hard labor for a term not exceeding three years."[91]

As Ogino Fujio has shown, from this point forward every draft produced by the Justice and Home Ministries contained the term "kokutai."[92] And as

Mizuno Naoki has argued, the earlier association of colonial independence as threatening the laws of the state was now defined as an infringement against the kokutai.[93] In subsequent versions, drafters focused their attention on revising terms other than kokutai, such as state (*kokka*), state authority (*kokken*), constitutional system (*kenpō ni sadameru seido*), and constitutional organization of rule (*kenpōjō no tōchi soshiki*). And after multiple drafts were shared between the Justice and Home Ministries, and then reviewed by the Cabinet Legislation Bureau (Naikaku hōseikyoku), these other terms became encapsulated in the single term "state form" (seitai).[94]

The three terms designating the objects to be protected in the first draft of the Peace Preservation Bill submitted to the Diet were national polity (kokutai), state form (seitai), and private property system (*shiyūzaisan seido*). The first version of Article 1 read, "Anyone who forms an organization with the intention of altering the kokutai or seitai [*kokutai mata ha seitai o henkaku shi*], or rejecting the private property system, or anyone who knowingly joins such an organization, will be liable to imprisonment for no more than ten years."[95] The first two terms, seitai and kokutai, had appeared in constitutional theory before, but it is important to note that they formed an inseparable categorical dyad—wherein kokutai signified the location of sovereignty, and seitai designated the means or form through which that sovereignty was expressed.[96] In other words, kokutai did not have its own constitutional designation divorced from its pairing with seitai; constitutional theorists merely differed in how they theorized the juridical and historical relationship between the two. While the choice to use these terms may indicate that the bill's drafters were familiar with ongoing debates in Japanese constitutional theory, by using these terms, they inadvertently brought these debates into the discourse of criminal law.

Before the bill was delivered to the Diet for deliberation, the Home and Justice Ministries published explanations in February 1925 defining the terminology and logic behind the first draft of the Peace Preservation Bill. In the Home Ministry's explanation, to "alter the kokutai" was defined as "changing such things as the location of sovereignty (Article 1 of the constitution) or the procedure of imperial succession [*kōi keishō no junjo*] (Article 2)."[97] In another Home Ministry document published at the same time, it was explained that to "alter the kokutai (Staatsform) is to attempt to change our imperial kokutai [*waga kunshu kokutai*]; that is, to even slightly alter the locus of sovereignty in the reign of Emperors ages eternal of our Empire." In regard to altering the state form, the Home Ministry document explained that "to alter the seitai (Regierungsform) would be to fundamentally change our constitutional and representational state form [*rikken seitai soku daigi seitai*]."[98] The Justice Ministry reiterates these two definitions in their own official explanation, stating that kokutai refers to the "reign of Emperors ages eternal" and seitai to the "form in which sovereignty is exercised" (*shuken kōshi no keishiki*), including the elected representatives of the Imperial Diet.[99] Furthermore, both the Home and Justice Ministry documents explain "the private property system" as signifying the system in which individuals or groups have ownership rights (*shoyūken*), which, as the Home Ministry document posits, "is the current basis of our socioeconomic life."[100]

Justice Minister Ogawa Heikichi and Home Minister Wakatsuki Reijirō delivered the bill to the Lower House of the Fiftieth Imperial Diet on February 19, 1925.[101] Similar to the failed 1922 Antiradical Bill, they explained that the objective of the new Peace Preservation Bill was to "suppress . . . anarchism and communism" (figure 1.1).

Home Minister Wakatsuki introduced the bill by pointing to the urgency of the contemporary moment—emphasizing the danger posed by the restoration of diplomatic relations with the Soviet government the month before, which, Wakatsuki warned, would increase "opportunities for extremist activists."[102] He reminded the Diet that current laws were ineffectual against this new threat, since compared to other social movements, communism was composed largely of "dangerous ideological activities" (*kiken naru shisō kōdō*).[103] To whatever degree Diet members were persuaded that Japan faced an external ideological threat, debate immediately began over the terminology of the bill and what effect the bill would have on public speech, academic research, and other reforms that were being debated at the time, particularly in regard to the Universal Male Suffrage Act also under deliberation at the time.

The lawyer and politician Hoshijima Nirō issued the first volley of criticism, lamenting that this "extremely oppressive policy" would indicate that the government "did not trust the Japanese people."[104] However, when he turned his critique toward the juridical indeterminacy of the bill's categories, he focused on seitai rather than kokutai. He began his investigation of the categories by declaring, "I cannot believe there is one person in the nation who would wish for something akin to altering the kokutai." He then justified his liberal reform agenda by invoking the timelessness of kokutai, asking drafters if someone wanted "to build a better state form [seitai] with human and social progress as its necessary principles . . . one based upon Japan's kokutai as the foundation, a kokutai that has not changed for three thousand years," would this not be proscribed by the ambiguity of the term "seitai"?[105]

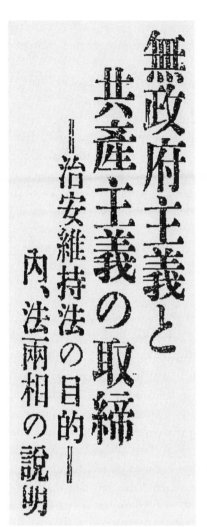

無政府主義と共産主義の取締
＝＝治安維持法の目的＝＝
内、法両相の説明

Figure 1.1. "To Suppress Anarchism and Communism: The Objective of the Peace Preservation Law, the Home and Justice Ministries Explain," *Yomiuri Shimbun*, February 13, 1925.

Here we see Hoshijima referring to kokutai as an absolute (*zettai no mono*)— one, moreover, that was seemingly conducive to his reform agenda. Critics of the bill like Hoshijima were concerned that seitai would apply to anyone calling to reform the Diet or to abolish the extraconstitutional Privy Council. However, we should note that Hoshijima's distinction between something transcendent/absolute and secular/historical would continue to frame the debates over the bill's categories, in which state form and private property system were repeatedly contrasted to kokutai.[106] What we find then is that while critics were concerned about protecting the scope of political criticism and social reform from falling under the category seitai, the effect was that the category kokutai was isolated as something unquestionable and projected outside of legislative scrutiny.

Similarly, Arima Yoriyasu asked how kokutai—if it was absolute—could be paired with such secular forms as seitai and private property.[107] Arima pressed further and wondered if the mere implication that the kokutai could be altered would not cause anxiety among the people. More important than the issue of social anxiety, however, was that Arima's question turned the logic of the bill back on itself by asking whether kokutai was something that could be altered or under threat. Here Diet members were being asked to understand kokutai as both something ostensibly absolute (*zettai no mono*) and something seemingly under existential threat from foreign ideologies. To extend Arima's inquiry further, we could also ask: how could something that is the transhistorical source of the imperial state require protection by a criminal law from such an ideological threat?

Responding to these kinds of criticisms, Wakatsuki repeatedly argued that drafters chose terms that did not lend themselves "to vague interpretations."[108] To demonstrate the concreteness (*gutaiteki*) of the bill's terms, Wakatsuki cited Article 1 of the Meiji Constitution, arguing that kokutai signified that the Japanese empire is ruled by a "line of Emperors unbroken for ages eternal" (*bansei ikkei no tennō*), and added that "if someone is planning to alter our glorious kokutai, then we must use the law to suppress this."[109] Wakatsuki continued to refer to imperial sovereignty in order to define kokutai in the law, thus invoking the sovereign ghost of the state apparatus. That a criminal regulation was necessary in order to protect the sovereign origin of law expressed the paradox of constituent/constituted power.

In regard to state form, Wakatsuki did not elaborate seitai as a general category of constitutional theory but rather explained the concept by listing the supposed varieties of state formations, including the "aristocratic state form" and the "parliamentary state form." He added, "If it is asked what kind of seitai we have in Japan, it would be a constitutional state form, a representative state form" (*rikken seitai, daigi seitai*).[110] Wakatsuki did not explain how the constitutional state form was based on the location of sovereignty in the eternal unbroken line of emperors as symbolized in the term kokutai. He merely declared that if someone intended to "destroy this state form," then it was necessary to "control this with this law."[111]

Following this first round of discussions, the bill was sent into committee consideration, which began on February 23. The committee focused on how to revise the bill in order to answer the myriad questions related to the terms kokutai and seitai, with special emphasis on quelling fears that the law could apply to those who were calling for legitimate political and social reforms.[112] Interestingly, however, these committee debates focused on the category seitai rather than the overdetermined concept of kokutai. The result was that when the bill returned for Diet deliberation on March 7, seitai was excised from the bill, leaving kokutai and *shiyūzaisan seido* as the two objects under threat from foreign ideologies.[113] Furthermore, although kokutai came under more scrutiny with seitai's erasure, the debates continued to note how, in constitutional theory, kokutai was theorized in relation to seitai. And behind the questions that framed these debates was the paradox of constituted/constituent power.

For instance, in the March 7 Diet meeting, Tabuchi Toyokichi asked, if kokutai signified the location of sovereignty and seitai the "objective and subjective aspects" of this sovereignty, was not then "the monarchy [*kunshu*] itself the kokutai?"[114] Kiyose Ichirō then asked if the law was directed toward those planning to "harm the emperor himself." If so, Kiyose asked, was this not already covered by existing laws?[115] Justice Minister Ogawa retorted that to alter the kokutai was "not related to doing physical harm to the Emperor" but rather the various ways in which imperial sovereignty could be "impinged upon [*sawaru*]."[116] More directly, Kikuchi Kenjirō inquired into the decision to delete seitai while retaining kokutai. He asked, if "the constitution determines our state form as a constitutional monarchy [*rikken kunshu seitai*]" and if kokutai refers to the "line of Emperors unbroken for ages eternal" as stipulated in Article 1 of that very same constitution, then "kokutai is included in seitai" and there is no need to distinguish them. This line of questioning demonstrates how the debates continued to be framed by the constituent/constituted power paradox even after seitai had been deleted from the bill.[117]

Indeed, Justice Minister Ogawa responded to these kinds of questions by explaining that kokutai was "absolute" and thus not "something that begins with the constitution."[118] Ogawa urged the Lower House not to confuse seitai with kokutai, arguing that no matter the various state forms in Japanese history—whether absolute monarchy or representative government—"sovereignty is not altered" by these forms. Ultimately, to equate "the location of sovereignty's operation [*taiken no hataraku tokoro*]" with the "form of its exercise" was to "confuse the two [*kōdō suru*]."[119]

After three rounds of deliberations in the Lower House, the revised bill was delivered to the House of Peers by Home Minister Wakatsuki Reijirō on March 11. As with the kinds of questions Justice Minister Ogawa faced in the

Lower House, Wakatsuki fielded many questions that gestured toward the duality of constituent/constituted power. The most explicit critique came from the liberal reformer and education bureaucrat Sawayanagi Masatarō. Sawayanagi reminded his peers that in the 1890 Imperial Rescript on Education, kokutai had a much different significance than the constitutionally derived definition given by Wakatsuki and others.[120] As mentioned earlier, in the 1890 Rescript the term "kokutai" referred to the ethical values of imperial loyalty and filial piety that mediated the relationship between emperor and subject. Sawayanagi declared that educators had "painstakingly labored and dutifully cultivated this concept's resilience and depth in the nation" and that the implied instability of Japan's kokutai in the bill was an affront to the work of educators, who had taught that kokutai was "clear and unmovable."[121] Sawayanagi rhetorically asked proponents of the bill, "Does the government think that our kokutai, as inscribed in Article 1 of the constitution, that has been demonstrated for 2,600 years of history, and cultivated under the glorious virtue of the Meiji Emperor, that our kokutai is disturbed [dōyō], and that we are now facing a danger from outside movements?"[122] As with Arima's questions back in February, this line of questioning was a rhetorical move to expose a contradiction implied in the proponents' argument—that kokutai was absolute, yet facing an existential threat.

Sawayanagi's rhetorical move worked, for in his response, Justice Minister Ogawa ultimately collapsed the distinction: "The Emperor founded the country, and through morality governed the people, and the people in turn were filial and pious. . . . This is the glory of our kokutai. And I believe this does not change Article 1's [meaning], nor does it change what this is grounded upon." Collapsing the "location of sovereignty" designation into the ethics of imperial loyalty, Ogawa argued that kokutai was "the deep and profound morality" as explained in the Imperial Rescript on Education as well as "what constitutes the governance of our country" as defined in the Meiji Constitution.[123] Despite the efforts of Sawayanagi and others to emphasize the terminological indeterminacy of the bill's main concept of kokutai, it was apparent in these mid-March deliberations that there was enough support to pass the bill.

In the very last meeting on the bill in the House of Peers, on March 17, the topic of the law's applicability to the colonies was finally discussed. This meeting opened with questions about how to interpret the language in Article 7 of the bill, which stated that the law would apply to those committing these infringements "outside of the jurisdiction of this law" (honhō shikō kuiki gai). It was explained that this law would be issued through each particular colonial legal system and would apply to any national who committed crimes outside of the imperial realm.[124] This then led to further questions about what exactly would constitute "rejecting sovereign rule" (*tōchiken o hinin*) as symbolized in the term "altering the kokutai" in the colonial context. Justice Minister Ogawa Heikichi explained, "To separate one part of the Empire, for instance, all of Korea, or let's say half of Korea, from imperial rule [*heika no tōchiken kara hanareru*]" would thus constitute a case of "altering the kokutai."[125] This territorial emphasis of sovereignty would become one of the distinguishing aspects of how the law would be interpreted differently between metropole and colony.

Although debates over the meaning of kokutai continued into the final deliberation of the bill, there was enough support to pass it on March 19. The Peace Preservation Law was issued on April 22 (Law No. 46) and went into effect in the Japanese metropole on May 11, 1925. On May 8, the government issued two imperial decrees announcing that the Peace Preservation Law would be issued in the particular legal systems of Korea, Taiwan, and Karafuto (No. 175) as well as the Kwantung Leased Territory and the South Sea Islands (No. 176).[126] The final version of the bill that went into law read as follows:

> Article One: Anyone who has formed a society with the objective of altering the *kokutai* or rejecting the private property system, and anyone who has joined such a society with full knowledge of its objective, shall be liable to imprisonment with or without hard labor for a term not exceeding ten years.
>
> Any attempt to commit the crime in the preceding clause will be punished.
>
> Article Two: Anyone who has discussed [*kyōgi*] the execution of matters specified in Paragraph One of Article One with the objective mentioned therein shall be liable to imprisonment with or without hard labor for a term not exceeding seven years.
>
> Article Three: Anyone who has instigated [*sendō*] the execution of the matters specified in Paragraph One of Article One with the objective mentioned therein shall be liable to imprisonment with or without hard labor for a term not exceeding seven years.[127]

Article 4 stipulated penalties for those causing violence or property damage in relation to the crimes listed in Article 1, while Article 5 penalized those who supported or who received material support to commit such crimes. Article 6 concerned the reduction of sentence for those who cooperated with authorities, while the last article stipulated that the law would apply to those committing such crimes outside of the law's jurisdiction. In regard to this last article, it is important to note that when the Peace Preservation Law was issued by colonial governments in their respective legal systems, the law's terminology was left unchanged. Consequently, we can understand the Peace Preservation Law as a security measure that, in its implementation, was largely coextensive with the territory of the Japanese Empire itself. Furthermore, when crimes were committed by imperial nationals outside of the formal jurisdiction of the Japanese Empire, these nationals could be prosecuted when they returned or were extradited.

Coming to Terms with the 1925 Law: Early Explications and Criticisms

As the debates reviewed above demonstrate, the Peace Preservation Law's categories of protection were anything but clear to legislators. The capacity for their wide interpretation and application not only was a source of objection by the bill's opponents, but now became a particular problem for those who had to implement the law. By the early 1930s, procedural precedents were slowly established, along with a standardized interpretation of the law's categories. Additionally, in this process an increasing amount of literature was published by the Home Ministry, the Justice Ministry, and the Governor-General in Korea as well as district courts, which discussed the meaning and methods for suppressing what was increasingly being called thought crime (*shisō hanzai*). But at first, this literature was sparse, and the first task was to explain the basic contours of the new law so it could be applied to suspected communists and anticolonial activists.

One of the earliest interpretative explanations was a police training pamphlet by justice official Furuta Masatake published in 1925.[128] In this pamphlet, Furuta moved through each article of the law, explaining its underlying objective and drawing out the distinguishing characteristics in contradistinction to other criminal and civil regulations. As expected, Furuta focused on explicating Article 1 and the significance of its two objects of protection. Regarding the category kokutai, Furuta repeated arguments from the recent legislative debates, noting that although the term was used in the Imperial Rescript on Education, this was different from kokutai's designation in the Peace Preservation Law.[129] Rather, Furuta explained that kokutai as used in this law designated the location of sovereignty as stipulated in Articles 1 and 4 of the Meiji Constitution. Here Furuta touched upon the constituent/constituted paradox when he emphasized that imperial sovereignty was a "historical fact since the founding of our nation," and not something "first established with Articles 1 and 4 of the Constitution."[130] In regard to "altering" this historical fact, Furuta explained that this applied to an intention "directly toward sovereign authority, as well as toward the location of sovereignty"; in other words, an intention to alter either the emperor or the very principle of imperial sovereignty.[131] As we see here, Furuta's explanation to those charged with now implementing the law reiterated the same constituent/constituted paradox that framed the legislative deliberations earlier that year.

In Japan, newspaper editorials and lawyer groups voiced criticism of the new law. For instance, in the metropole, many newspapers—and in particular the *Tokyo Asahi Shimbun*—published scathing critiques of the law, demonizing it as a bad law (*akuhō*) that would impinge upon academic research and public speech.[132] The lawyer and reform politician Kiyose Ichirō of the Kakushin Party published a critical review of the law from a legal perspective in 1926.[133] However, Kiyose's critique was based on a liberal interpretation of the Meiji Constitution, in which he accepted the designation of kokutai in the law as signifying the location of sovereignty in the line of Emperors unbroken for ages eternal and supported the notion that criminal laws were necessary to protect this sovereignty. Rather, Kiyose's critique was focused more on issues related to judicial discretion and procedure.[134] In addition to these critiques in the metropole, Mizuno Naoki notes that there were also criticisms of the law in colonial Korea. However, since colonial Koreans did not have the same rights as Japanese—in particular, lacking representation in the Imperial Diet—these criticisms did not carry the same legal weight as those voiced by Japanese nationals.[135]

Conclusion: The Birth of the Peace Preservation Law Apparatus

This chapter has explored how state officials in Tokyo attempted to craft an antiradical law in order to safeguard the empire against imported ideologies such as communism. In order to criminally identify this foreign threat, officials were required to define what exactly was being threatened. They chose the term "kokutai" for its apparent concreteness and consistently defined it as signifying the location of sovereignty in the "line of Emperors unbroken for ages eternal" (*bansei ikkei no tennō*) as defined in Articles 1 and 4 of the Meiji Constitution. However, this opened into legislative debates over the nature of imperial sovereignty as well as the relationship between sovereign and subject, which continued up to the very last deliberations over the proposed bill.

With the passage of the bill in the spring of 1925, however, these interpretive questions were transposed into the institutional procedures that would come to constitute the Peace Preservation Law apparatus into the 1930s. In this way, the sovereign ghost breathed life into the emerging criminal apparatus designed to police political crime. Chapter 2 explores how these interpretive problems with the term "kokutai" continued into the institutional implementation of the Peace Preservation Law throughout the empire in the late 1920s and early 1930s. And while the law was initially implemented to suppress threats to imperial sovereignty as originally intended, by the early 1930s procurators and prison officials started to experiment with reforming political criminals so they could be safely reintegrated into society. Chapter 2 analyzes the emerging functional relationship between repression and reform in the Peace Preservation Law apparatus in the early 1930s, and how the spectral ghost of the imperial sovereign informed both modalities of state power.

Transcriptions of Power: *Repression and Rehabilitation in the Early Peace Preservation Law Apparatus, 1925–1933*

The "delinquency" effect produced by the prison becomes the problem
of delinquency to which prison has to provide a suitable response.
—MICHEL FOUCAULT, *The Punitive Society*

Following its passage in 1925, the Peace Preservation Law was used in the late
1920s to arrest thousands of communists in metropolitan Japan and anticolonial activists in Korea for threatening imperial sovereignty and the socioeconomic foundation of Japanese society. As I explored in chapter 1, these two
threats were defined in the law as anyone forming or joining an organization
with the objective to "alter the kokutai" (*kokutai o henkaku*) or "reject the
private property system" (*shiyū zaisan seido o hinin*), respectively. Supporters of the law understood these intentions as stemming from the "infiltration" (*sennyū*) of dangerous foreign ideologies into the empire and attacking
it from within. Consequently, those arrested under the law were said to have
committed thought crime (*shisō hanzai*) and were labeled thought criminals
(*shisō hannin*). After a nationwide roundup of suspected Japanese Communist Party (JCP) members in March 1928, the government revised the Peace
Preservation Law through an Emergency Imperial Order, in which the offense of "alter[ing] the kokutai" was separated into its own clause and made
punishable by death (*shikei*). With this revision, and a further round of arrests in April 1929, it appeared that the Peace Preservation Law was being

implemented as proponents had initially intended: namely, as a legal instrument to suppress threats against imperial sovereignty. Consequently, we can understand the Peace Preservation Law in the late 1920s as consolidating the various components of what Louis Althusser would theorize as the Repressive State Apparatus (RSA)—including the legislature, police, courts, colonial administrations, and prison networks—into a new configuration in order to more intensely protect the ghost of the imperial state: that is, the imperial sovereign.[1]

In the early 1930s, however, the Peace Preservation Law apparatus started to slowly transform in the metropole. To be sure, repression continued: arrests increased in the early 1930s—according to some estimates reaching as high as 18,387 in the metropole in 1933 alone—and the purview of the law expanded, first to suspected affiliated or outside groups (*gaibu dantai*) of the JCP, then later to educators, religious groups, leftist intellectuals, or anyone who was believed to be threatening imperial orthodoxy.[2] Moreover, there were many cases in which the police brutalized detainees during interrogation, the murder of proletarian writer Kobayashi Takiji in 1933 being the most famous example.[3] Furthermore, arrests and indictments increased in colonial Korea, surpassing the relative rate of cases advancing to criminal indictment in the metropole.[4] However, even with this continued repression, by the late 1930s the policy for administrating the majority of those arrested under the law in the metropole was not imprisonment, capital punishment, nor even criminal prosecution, but to reform and reintegrate detainees back into society before they were formally tried in court.[5] The remaining chapters of *Thought Crime* will explore the changing dynamics and complex logic of this transformation in the Peace Preservation Law during the 1930s.

The main architects of this emerging reform policy were district court procurators (*kenji*), who were charged with interviewing detained political criminals in preparation for their prosecution.[6] Procurators assisted in organizing arrests with the police and, after an initial police interrogation, were responsible for investigating a detainee, preparing the state's case, and, if a case advanced, working with the trial judge to prepare the prosecution. Importantly, they had the discretion to decide if a suspect was going to advance to trial or if the indictment would be suspended until further notice.[7] In the late 1920s, with the increasing arrests of so-called thought criminals under the Peace Preservation Law, procurators such as Ikeda Katsu, Moriyama Buichirō, Hirata Isao, and others became specialists in dealing with political detainees and were appointed to the new position of thought procurators (*shisō gakari kenji*, or shisō kenji for short).[8]

Based on their experiences with thought crime and armed with adminis-trative discretion, thought procurators began to experiment with inducing what they called repentance (*kaishun*) in recently arrested JCP members as early as 1928, even as legislators were revising the Peace Preservation Law to include the death penalty. One procurator in particular—Hirata Isao of the Tokyo District Court—urged detainees to recognize the error of JCP policies and to reconsider their position on Japan's imperial kokutai. In later chapters I examine how Hirata went on to become one of the main archi-tects of the policy to rehabilitate thought criminals, developing procedures for ideological conversion (tenkō) for a nationwide network of Thought Criminal Protection and Supervision Centers established in 1936. However, well before his promotion to this position, Hirata was experimenting in the late 1920s and early 1930s with different methods to have JCP members defect from the party.[9]

This chapter explores how a rehabilitation policy emerged from a law that was originally intended to explicitly suppress a threat to imperial sover-eignty. I argue that, similar to Michel Foucault's observation in the epigraph that begins this chapter, the initial application of the Peace Preservation Law against thought crime produced the problem of an increasing popula-tion of detained thought criminals to which it had to respond. With fears of ideological recidivism as well as the isolated but successful experiments with inducing suspects to defect from the JCP, rehabilitation slowly and contingently emerged as a method to facilitate the increasing population of thought criminals arrested under the Peace Preservation Law. Although this chapter explores the institutional and legal particularities of the Peace Pres-ervation Law, its unique combination of repression and rehabilitation opens into larger questions related to the complex modalities of state power more generally. Consequently, whereas earlier studies have approached the Peace Preservation Law as a uniquely Japanese way to control political criminals, this chapter considers the law in relation to general theories of modern state power, with specific emphasis on Michel Foucault's distinction between sovereign-juridical power and disciplinary power.

Transcription of Sovereign and Punitive Power in the Peace Preservation Law

In many postwar studies, the Peace Preservation Law is portrayed as a straightforward legal instrument used by the emperor system (tennōsei) to repress progressive social movements.[10] That the law was an instrument of state repression is, of course, undeniable. However, what is overlooked in these studies is not only the interpretive ambiguity of the Peace Preservation Law's categories related to imperial sovereignty that were reviewed in chapter 1, but also the institutional complexities that emerged when the law was implemented, including the development of the rehabilitation policy in the 1930s.[11] Other scholars have recognized this institutional complexity, explaining it as a tension arising between the judicial practices of the Justice Ministry and the administrative procedures of the police in the Home Ministry.[12] Here repression is most often linked to the procedures of the police in the Home Ministry and, in particular, the Special Higher Police (Tokubetsu kōtō keisatsu, or Tokkō), including the extrajudicial torture of detainees.[13] Many of these studies are based on a normative understanding of law and legal protection and are thus concerned with assessing the degree to which legal oversight protected a detainee's procedural rights while in police detention.[14]

In this framework, the 1930s rehabilitation policy is portrayed as a uniquely gentle administrative measure developed by the Justice Ministry, in contrast to the instances of extrajudicial brutality practiced at times by the Home Ministry's Special Higher Police. For instance, Richard Mitchell assesses the later ideological conversion, or tenkō, policy as a "humane method of handling communist political criminals" that reflected Japanese "traditional values."[15] For Mitchell, this humaneness represented one face of what he calls Japan's prewar "Janus-faced justice."[16] However, this does not explain the functional dynamic between these two modes of power, ultimately rendering the Peace Preservation Law as a kind of schizophrenic apparatus, moving randomly between humaneness and cruelty depending on which ministry was dealing with the detainee.

In order to shift the terms of analysis, I would like to consider the twin functions of the Peace Preservation Law through Michel Foucault's distinction between penal and putative power—what he later elaborated as the historical distinction between the modes of sovereign-juridical power and disciplinary power.[17] Foucault's theory of power helps illuminate the functional relationship between repression and reform in the Peace Preservation Law apparatus, as well as to situate the particular history of the Peace Preservation Law in a wider conversation about modern forms of state power. At the same time, the historical example of this apparatus will allow us to clarify some of the enduring questions concerning Foucault's nuanced theory. And once disciplinary policies were accepted and implemented by Japanese procurators in the early 1930s, we will explore in later chapters how discipline provided a framework for a form of moral guidance to emerge that resembled the logic that Foucault later theorized as governmentality.

As is well known, Foucault subverted the repressive hypothesis informing conventional theories of power, in which power was approached as something exercised by the state in order to repress, reprimand, or prohibit.[18] Foucault countered that modern power is dispersed throughout society through a series of relations and techniques that are productive in nature—in the sense that they produce subjects that fulfill certain social functions, what Foucault called "docile bodies."[19] Through these productive modalities of power, individuals assume dispositions, behaviors, and practices that constitute them as active subjects functioning without threat of reprimand or punishment by the state.[20]

In order to elaborate this theory, Foucault posited a logical and historical distinction between earlier repressive forms of sovereign/juridical power in seventeenth-century Europe and the productive and normalizing technologies of modern disciplinary power that emerged in the eighteenth and nineteenth centuries. In regard to the distinct logics of these modes of power, Foucault argued that juridical power responds to a transgression of sovereign law and is thus predicated on a binary logic of legality/illegality. In contrast, disciplinary power is based on a norm, which, by its very nature of infinite gradations, allows for the constant intervention of disciplinary mechanisms.[21] In books such as *Discipline and Punish* (1975) and *History of Sexuality*, Volume 1 (1976), Foucault formulated these distinctions through a historical narrative in which new normalizing technologies of disciplinary power colonized and then superseded an earlier modality of sovereign-juridical power.[22] Consequently, scholars have focused on Foucault's characterization of the modern period as a "phase of juridical regression," in which sovereign law is demoted to an ideology that merely serves to mask the determinate operations of disciplinary power.[23]

Foucault's work provides numerous examples in which he is arguing such a position, and Nicos Poulantzas was not incorrect to argue that in his major works Foucault was "led to underestimate . . . the role of law in the exercise of power within modern societies" and thus also "the role of the State itself."[24] However, in his lectures at the Collège de France in the early to mid-1970s, we find Foucault working through a more nuanced distinction between these two forms of power, which open new ways to consider the multiple modalities of power as well as reinterpreting Foucault's theory of power in relation to the state.[25] In these lectures, Foucault outlines an almost dialectical relationship—what he refers to as a "double movement"—in which sovereign-juridical power harnesses the "corrective and penitentiary" functions of an emerging disciplinary power.[26] In this formulation, disciplinary power becomes what Jan Goldstein has called in another context "framed" by law: that is, although these two modalities are distinct and cannot be subsumed within each other, they work together in maintaining the modern state.[27] Considering the functional relationship between these two modes of power, Foucault elaborated:

> We have in modern societies, on the one hand, a legislation, a discourse, and an organization of public right articulated around the principle of the sovereignty of the social body and the delegation of individual sovereignty to the State; and we also have a tight grid of disciplinary coercions that actually guarantees the cohesion of that social body. Now that grid cannot in any way be transcribed in right, even though the two necessarily go together. A right of sovereignty and a mechanics of discipline. It is, I think, between these two limits that power is exercised.[28]

Notice that Foucault locates the nexus of power between the limits of the two irreducible modes of sovereignty and discipline. Furthermore, although he elaborates his theory of sovereign-juridical power from a notion of popular sovereignty (not imperial sovereignty as was the case in prewar Japan), he was not interested in debates about the purported origins or essence of sovereignty per se, but rather sovereignty as a particular logic and modality of power, one that policed a social body constituted through disciplinary modes of power. In the Japanese context, we might read Foucault's social body as the national body, or kokutai that was constituted through disciplinary mechanisms.

Elsewhere, Foucault considered the process through which an individual moved between these two modes, theorizing it as a process of "transcription":

> On the one hand . . . a discourse of pure penality, which knows only the positivity of the law and not the immorality of the crime, the universality of the law and not the moralization of individuals, the inevitability of the law and not the correction of individuals; and, on the other hand, mixed with the texts, with the institutions, a kind of research claiming to correct, to regenerate the individual. These two elements

are fundamental in the penal system, and at the point of their articulation is the place where the transcription of one into the other takes place, a kind of psycho-juridical discourse the function of which is to retranscribe the juridical elements of penality in terms of correction, regeneration and recovery, and conversely, to recodify moral notions into penal categories.[29]

Thus, in contrast to what he would describe elsewhere as two distinct historical modes of power, here Foucault is considering the complex way in which sovereign-juridical and disciplinary forms configure modern power without one being reduced or displaced by the other.

Informed by Foucault's theory of the transcriptions of sovereign and disciplinary power, this chapter analyzes the functional relationship and institutional arrangement between repression and rehabilitation in the emerging Peace Preservation Law apparatus in the late 1920s and early 1930s. Within this apparatus, juridical-sovereign power functioned to identify someone as a threat to imperial sovereignty and to punish this transgression, whereas disciplinary power, couched in terms of imperial benevolence, aimed to reform political criminals based on the norm of the productive and loyal subject. The former mode of power was exercised at the time of the arrest and, in a few cases, the court decision that punished the "illegalism" (Foucault) of threatening the sovereign, while the latter mode of power was based on the gradated norm of an ideal loyal subject, which authorized the endless intervention of disciplinary mechanisms to observe, record, guide, and reform the individual thought criminal into a productive imperial subject.[30] Note that the institutional and functional relationship between sovereign and disciplinary power in the Peace Preservation Law apparatus provided the institutional framework for the two spectral cognates of imperial ideology to be articulated simultaneously, that is, the sovereign ghost of the state machine and the loyal imperial subject who, once reformed, would work "all by themselves" (Althusser). In later chapters, I explore the increasing disciplinary intervention that this norm of imperial subjectivity authorized, as well as how sovereign-juridical and disciplinary power were further complemented by what Foucault would theorize as governmentality, combing three logics of power—sovereign, disciplinary, and governmentality—in the fully elaborated Peace Preservation Law apparatus of the late 1930s. This chapter seeks to locate the conditions in which disciplinarity first emerged in the Peace Preservation Law apparatus in the early 1930s, opening the way for the technologies of governing the self to emerge later.

To be sure, the particular logics of these two modes of power in the Peace Preservation Law—that is, sovereign and disciplinary—were irreducible to each other: reforming thought criminals was not informed by constitutional theories of sovereignty, although reform was one way to neutralize the threat against the imperial sovereign. Similarly, the moralizing rhetoric of reform and rehabilitation did not figure into the initial legal deliberations over the Peace Preservation Law, or how to define the location of sovereignty in the imperial line, although by the mid-1930s, many officials argued that the rehabilitation policy exemplified the benevolence of imperial justice.

In this articulation between sovereign and disciplinary power, the thought criminal functioned similarly to what Foucault finds in the nineteenth-century delinquent: as an "exchanger element" between two different modes of power. At the level of the individual political criminal, a substitution occurred as the thought criminal was emerging as both a target of suppression through the exercise of juridical power and, at the same time, a potentially reformable subject through disciplinary mechanisms.[31] At the level of state power, this substitution appears as the transcription in which judicial categories and logics were articulated in the discourse of disciplinary reform, and vice versa. This was not simply a transition, or a unidirectional transcription, from repression to reform, for as I explore in later chapters, not only did a mode of power emerge similar to what Foucault has called governmentality, but also, sovereign law returned later with the 1936 Thought Crime Protection and Supervision Law to "frame" (Goldstein) the expanded rehabilitation system.[32] Consequently, the thought criminal was continually moved back and forth between juridical forms of sovereign power that assessed the criminal's potential to transgress imperial orthodoxy and, simultaneously, disciplinary forms of power that continually worked to reform him or her as a loyal and productive imperial subject, and later, to assess the degree in which ex-criminals were governing themselves. Nor was this process even across the empire, for as I explore below, the functional relationship between repression and rehabilitation developed very differently in colonial Korea.

The initial intention of the law, however, was not to reform or rehabilitate, but rather to suppress communists and anticolonial activists. Before analyzing the emerging duality between repression and rehabilitation that we find in the early-1930s, it is first necessary to account for how the Peace Preservation Law was implemented in the late 1920s and how, through a contingent process of experimentation, reform became one of the main policies of the Peace Preservation Law apparatus.

THE FIRST APPLICATIONS OF THE PEACE PRESERVATION LAW

The first application of the Peace Preservation Law in the Japanese metropole was the prosecution of members of the Student Federation of Social Science (Gakusei shakaikagaku kenkyūkai, or Gakuren) from campuses primarily in the Kansai region.[33] Starting as a study association in 1922, by 1925 Gakuren had become a nationwide student federation that cited Marxism-Leninism for its guiding principles.[34] Arrests were made in the winter of 1925–1926, and the first trials took place in Kyoto District Court in the spring of 1927. Thirty-eight students, many of whom were from the elite Kyoto Imperial University, were tried for having discussed "altering the kokutai" and "rejecting the private property system" as defined in the new Peace Preservation Law.[35]

Already in this early application of the Peace Preservation Law against Gakuren members, certain unique procedural features of the law's application were becoming established. Most important was that procurators from district courts facilitated the arrest, investigation, and prosecution of the students, after the local Special Higher Police had bungled the first round of arrests in early December 1925.[36] Procurators and the Justice Ministry would continue to manage the implementation of the Peace Preservation Law into the 1930s. However, one unique aspect of this first episode in metropolitan Japan was that the Gakuren defendants were ultimately found guilty of infringing the "reject the private property system" clause, rather than the kokutai clause. This was one of the few times that this clause was applied in the Japanese metropole.[37]

Mizuno Naoki has revealed that the first application of the Peace Preservation Law was actually against suspected communists in Korea (the so-called Chōsen kyōsantō jiken, or Korean Communist Party Incident), challenging the conventional claim that Gakuren members were the first victims (*giseisha*) of the Peace Preservation Law.[38] Arrests of suspected communists in Korea were carried out in November 1925 (one month earlier than the Gakuren arrests), and defendants were later tried and sentenced for forming an organization with the objective of "altering the kokutai." Additionally, similar to cases in Japan, courts in Korea had to at first distinguish between the Peace Preservation Law and other antiradical ordinances at their disposal when indicting a suspect.[39] However, one immediate difference exemplified between the metropole and colonial Korea was that, in June 1925, only one month after the Peace Preservation Law was implemented in Korea, the head procurator of the Chōsen High Court issued a directive in which he directly connected the new law to the Korean independence movement: "It has been determined that the Peace Preservation Law will be applied to those organizing a society with the objective of Korean independence, joining such a society knowingly, or assisting in implementing this objective, or agitating for its implementation."[40] As many scholars have noted, this direct association of altering the kokutai with national independence signaled an important difference in how the law would be interpreted in the colony, opening the way for many noncommunist national independence groups to be charged with intending to alter the kokutai.[41]

Moreover, up through the end of the 1920s, Korean communists were often prosecuted for infringing both the "alter the kokutai" and "reject the private property system" clauses—something that, despite a few early exceptions such as the 1925 Gakuren Incident, did not occur in the Japanese metropole.[42] In February 1928, the Keijō District Court handed down a decision against suspected Korean Communist Party members explaining that "a kind [isshu no] of communist movement was carried out that blended [konwa] communist thought with the idea of Korean national liberation." It was explained that this "kind of" communist movement "had the objective of repudiating the private property system in Chōsen and actualizing a communist system as well as seceding Chōsen from the bonds [kihan] of our empire."[43] In another important case that same year, the Keijō District Court handed down a guilty verdict predicated on a similar combination of the two clauses, stating that "Our Japanese Empire celebrates [ōka] the private property system," which the defendants "repudiated and planned to realize a communist system in Chōsen." Additionally, it was argued that the defendants were also planning to have "Chōsen secede [ridatsu] from the bonds of our Japanese Empire, and become an independent nation."[44] In early trials in colonial Korea, courts interpreted the Peace Preservation Law in such a way as to encapsulate the objectives of colonial independence as well as overthrowing capitalism.[45]

As we see in these examples, officials in both the metropole and colonial Korea were experimenting with applying the Peace Preservation Law in these early cases. It was not until the end of the decade that legal and procedural precedents were established in both Japan and colonial Korea that would define the application of Peace Preservation Law apparatus in their respective areas into the 1930s.

Apart from a few early cases such as the Gakuren prosecutions, from 1927 onward suspected communists in the Japanese metropole were prosecuted solely under the "alter the kokutai" clause. This was made much easier with the publication of the Communist International's (Comintern) 1927 Theses, which described the emperor system as the nexus between finance capitalism and large landowning feudal remnants, calling upon communists to "abolish the monarchy" (*kunshusei no haishi*) as an important step in the revolutionary struggle.[46] Recall that in the debates over the Peace Preservation Bill in 1925, some proponents argued that the "alter the kokutai" clause would apply to anarchists, while the "private property system" clause would apply to communists. However, following the publication of the 1927 Comintern Theses, to join or support the JCP was interpreted as falling under "alter the kokutai."

Then on March 15, 1928, one month after the first general elections were held, there was a nationwide roundup of suspected communists, what came to be known as the 3.15 Incident. Based on information obtained in this first roundup, more arrests continued throughout the year, with another coordinated roundup on April 16, 1929. In total, over eight thousand suspected communists were netted in this empire-wide arrest campaign.[47] The increasingly powerful procurators of the Tokyo District Court led the organizational planning of this nationwide campaign.[48] From these arrests, detailed information was gathered concerning the activities and organizing of the communist movement, which spurred procurators and police to redouble their efforts to study the movement in closer detail. Within a few years, this produced a massive amount of information on thought crime and the figure of the thought criminal.

Although the JCP was relatively small at the time, these arrests confirmed conservative fears of a communist conspiracy inside the empire, leading to new efforts to suppress political radicalism. The cabinet of Prime Minister Tanaka Giichi quickly went on the offensive. The result was the dissolution of many labor and student organizations, as well as the new proletarian political parties that formed for the 1928 general election.[49] Additionally, the Ministry of Education ramped up efforts to monitor campus activism, while the Home Ministry increased the staff as well as funding for police agencies.[50] In regard to the Justice Ministry, although a thought section had been established in the procuracy of the Tokyo District Court in 1927 (Hirata Isao was its first chief), in 1928 thought procurators were established in the Supreme

Court and important district courts, as well as in the Korean Government-General that August.[51] A directive in May 1928 outlined the mandate for thought procurators: to review all cases related to the Peace Preservation Law, political crimes, publication crimes, violent political acts, and rioting inspired by political motives, among other politically inspired crimes.[52] In this manner, the repressive power of the state apparatus against dangerous thought was expanded.

At the center of the state's attempt to strengthen its ability to suppress communists and other radicals was a proposed revision to the Peace Preservation Law in spring 1928.[53] Suzuki Kisaburō, now home minister in the Tanaka government, introduced the bill to the Fifty-Fifth Imperial Diet in April 1928, but the bill failed to go to the floor before the Diet adjourned.[54] In an extraordinary move, the Tanaka government introduced the bill as an emergency imperial ordinance to the extraconstitutional Privy Council on June 27, which passed the ordinance (Ordinance No. 129).[55] The Diet formally approved the revision in February and March the following year.[56]

In the revised Peace Preservation Law, the kokutai and private property system clauses were separated and assigned different punishments. While the punishment for forming or joining a society with the intention of rejecting the private property system remained the same (up to two years imprisonment), the punishment associated with forming or leading an organization with the objective of altering the kokutai became punishable by death (*shikei*). These changes signaled that altering the kokutai represented the primary infringement of the Peace Preservation Law, evidenced by the fact that from the late 1920s until its repeal in 1945, almost all of the arrests under the Peace Preservation Law (over seventy thousand total in the metropole and thousands more in colonial Korea) were based on this clause.[57] Furthermore, based on the complexity of processing thousands of suspected communists after the March arrests, justice officials added a clause concerning "persons who commit acts in order to further the aims" (*mokuteki suikō*) of an organization intending to alter the kokutai or reject the private property system.[58] Thus in this revision's form (emergency imperial ordinance) and content (capital punishment as well as expanding the purview to cover furthering the aims), we see in this revision the most explicit example of the original sovereign-juridical function of the law: namely, to suppress supposed ideological threats against the imperial sovereign.

In both the Privy Council and Diet debates, proponents of the revision cited the unique dangers facing Japan at the time. For example, on June 27, 1928, Hiranuma Kiichirō and Prime Minister Tanaka Giichi presented the revision to the Privy Council by portraying the arrests of communists earlier in the year as evidence of the extensive dangers that Japan faced both domestically and abroad.[59] Proponents defined these dangers by contrasting it to the term "kokutai," as when Home Minister Mochizuki Keisuke argued that the threat posed by foreign thought (*gairai shisō*) such as communism was to undermine "the spirit of our national foundation" and the "glory of our kokutai" (*kokutai no seika*).[60] In addition to focusing on the supposed threat to the kokutai, proponents now clearly defined the foreignness of such threats. For instance, Prime Minister Tanaka explained that Soviet representatives were operating inside the country and that Moscow was trying to ideologically infiltrate Japan through the Comintern.[61] For Justice Minister Hara Yoshimichi, this external threat was clearly expressed in the Japanese Communist Party's 1927 Theses, which, as noted above, called for "abolishing the monarchy."[62]

Most of the debate in the Privy Council centered on the format of the proposed revision as an emergency imperial ordinance and the significance of including the death penalty, although Eki Kazuyuki, Kubota Yuzuru, and Matsumuro Itasu did voice direct opposition to the law itself. However, the Privy Council passed the revision on June 28. For almost eight months, the revision existed as an emergency imperial ordinance, until the Diet was able to deliberate the revision in early February the following year.[63]

In the Fifty-Sixth Imperial Diet of 1929, Justice Minister Hara Yoshimichi repeated his warning that Japan's "pure kokutai" was under threat from communist ideology with "international revolution as its aim."[64] Additionally, Hara emphasized that unlike the criminal acts covered in Japan's regular Criminal Code, the threat posed by communism was unique since it was largely one of ideas, explaining, "we should say that these are crimes of an ideological foreign threat" (*shisōteki gaikanzai*).[65] Opponents in the Diet focused their critiques on the same concerns as were voiced earlier in the Privy Council; namely, the inclusion of the death penalty and the form of the revision as an emergency imperial ordinance.[66] Yet Hara continued to argue that the Meiji Constitution allowed for such imperial ordinances to be issued in times of emergency and emphasized that the addition of the death penalty was intended as a preemptive deterrent only.[67] Apparently convinced by such reasoning, the Lower House ratified the revision, with the Upper House following suit in March.[68]

Then, on April 16, procurators and the Special Higher Police carried out a second wave of arrests, known as the 4.16 Incident. Combined with the arrests the year before, most of the JCP's central committee were arrested or had gone underground.[69] In total, Okudaira Yasuhiro estimates that 3,426 people were arrested in 1928 and 4,942 in 1929. The annual number of arrests would continue to increase into the 1930s.[70]

Thus, by the end of the decade, the Peace Preservation Law had become what proponents had originally intended: a legal instrument used to suppress threats to imperial sovereignty in both metropole and colony.[71] By 1930, the police and various justice departments had their finances and personnel increased in order to combat thought crime—including the Korean Government-General—and thousands of suspected communists were detained and/or under investigation. Additionally, the text of the Peace Preservation Law had been revised, elevating the offense of altering the kokutai to be punishable by death. In the same year that this revision was ratified (1929), the Sapporo Court of Appeals confirmed the legal definition of kokutai in the law as signifying the location of sovereignty in the "line of Emperors unbroken for ages eternal" as stipulated in the Meiji Constitution. The Supreme Court confirmed this interpretation in decisions in 1929 and 1931, thus establishing this definition as legal precedent in the metropole.[72] With the sovereign ghost confirmed by the courts, the security machine began the decade of the 1930s with renewed life.

SECURING TERRITORIAL SOVEREIGNTY IN COLONIAL KOREA

Territory and people are the two elements out of which a State is constituted. A definite group of dominions constitutes a definite State, and in it definite organic laws are found in operation. A State is like an individual, and its territories, resembling the limbs and parts of an individual, constitute an integral realm. —ITŌ HIROBUMI, *Commentaries on the Constitution of the Empire of Japan* (1889)

The developments that took place in the metropole in the late 1920s had influence in the colonies as well. Recall that up until the 1928 revision, colonial administrators and judges in Korea had prosecuted suspected communists with infringing both the "alter the kokutai" and "reject the private property system" clauses. In 1929, however, prosecutors and courts started to emphasize the kokutai infringement by equating it with the territorial integrity of Japan's sovereign empire. Around this time, communists in Korea were increasingly charged with pursuing "the objective to secede from the bonds of our empire." This colonial interpretation of kokutai as territorial sovereignty became legal precedent in 1930–1931 through Keijō High Court decisions.[73] This was largely in response to challenges and appeals that had been brought by defendants charged under the law. In one such case in 1930, the High

Court recognized the applicability of Article 1 to the Korean independence movement this way: "To try to establish Korean independence is to usurp [*sensetsu*] one part of our empire's territory, to substantially reduce the content of sovereignty [*tōchiken no naiyō*] and thus is nothing more than violating this sovereignty. Therefore, it is appropriate to understand this as planning to alter the kokutai [as proscribed in] the Peace Preservation Law."[74]

Citing this earlier ruling, a later 1931 High Court decision added a further explanation, stating that "the kokutai is not simply in reference to the location of sovereignty, but is to be understood as a concept that also includes the content of that very sovereignty," which we can interpret here as meaning the territorial integrity of the Japanese Empire.[75] Such interpretations extended Itō Hirobumi's anatomical analogy in the epigraph above to cover the territorial breadth of the Empire of Japan, even with the legal distinction between the metropole (*naichi*) and the outer colonies (*gaichi*).[76] Also, an imperial national who carried out one of the acts criminalized in the law outside the borders of the empire could be arrested and tried once he or she returned. Mizuno Naoki argues that it was paradoxical for kokutai to be used to prosecute independence activists in Korea since it was not used during the initial incorporation of Korea into the Japanese Empire.[77] In other words, kokutai was not initially identified in Japan's sovereign claims over Korea. Only now, almost twenty years since Korea was formally annexed in 1910, were courts interpreting kokutai as the basis of Japan's sovereign authority over its colonial territory and peoples.

Arrests continued into the 1930s, both in the metropole and in the colonies. In Japan, 6,124 persons were arrested in 1930, 10,422 in 1931, 13,938 in 1932, and 14,622 in 1933.[78] As Nakazawa Shunsuke has argued, this increase in arrests in the early 1930s was due to the expansion of arrests to affiliated groups (*gaibu dantai*) whom authorities suspected of trying to reorganize the JCP after the arrest campaigns of the late 1920s.[79] In colonial Korea, 2,661 activists were arrested in 1930, 1,708 in 1931, 4,481 in 1932 and 2,007 in 1933.[80] Beyond Korea, Ogino summarizes that up to 1934 there were 701 arrests in Taiwan and 420 in the Kwantung Leased Territory.[81]

In addition to these arrests in the formal boundaries of the Japanese Empire, Erik Esselstrom has shown that the Foreign Ministry Consular Police also applied the Peace Preservation Law when policing ideological threats in Chinese port towns and the Japanese settlement in Shanghai in the early 1930s.[82] Furthermore, Louise Young has revealed how, following Japan's seizure of Manchuria in 1931, the rhetoric used by the Imperial Army to justify their continuing military actions shifted from defending against external military provocations to now internal "pacification" and "suppression," which discursively "transformed the Manchurian Incident from a battle between two national armies to a matter of internal police work."[83] Indeed, soon after the puppet-state of Manchukuo was established in spring 1932, security laws were passed in September 1932 that aimed to preserve the new quasi-sovereign Manchukuo state within the Japanese imperium.[84] This included passage of Manchukuo's own Public Peace Police Law (Chian keisatsu hō, Ordinance No. 86) in 1932 modeled on the Japanese law, as well as other provisional securities law, which replicated familiar terminology such as criminalizing organizations that intended to "disrupt the laws of the state or threaten the foundation of the state's existence" (*kokken o binran shi kokka sonritsu no kiso o kitai*).[85] As I explore in chapter 5, following Japan's invasion of China in 1937 and the expansion of the war in the mainland, a revised version of the Peace Preservation Law was applied for the first time in Manchukuo in 1941.[86]

Back in the early 1930s, however, officials in the Japanese metropole soon found themselves responsible for interrogating, investigating, and surveilling an ever-increasing population of so-called thought criminals. Ironically, it was the repressive application of the Peace Preservation Law in the late 1920s that inspired procurators in the metropole to experiment with reform and rehabilitation as a means to deal with this large population of thought criminals. Here, we find the pioneering efforts of Hirata Isao.

Transformations in the Peace Preservation Law in the Early 1930s

PROSECUTION AND DEFECTION: HIRATA ISAO AND THE LABOR FACTION

Immediately following the mass arrests in March 1928, the Special Higher Police and newly created thought procurators began investigating detainees. Hirata Isao was at the forefront of this effort. As chief procurator of the newly created Thought Division in Tokyo District Court, Hirata helped organize the mass arrests of 1928 and 1929, and once the Special Higher Police concluded their initial criminal investigations, Hirata and his fellow procurators oversaw the more intensive interviews of suspects in Tokyo.[87] From these initial interrogations the state was able to build cases against the captured JCP leaders as well as collect a large amount of information that led to further arrests in 1929, including remaining JCP leaders Sano Manabu (arrested in Shanghai) and Nabeyama Sadachika, among others.[88] In this way, we can interpret these interrogations as an extension of the repressive application of the Peace Preservation Law; that is, as a means to prosecute those who threatened imperial sovereignty. The state decided to prosecute the leadership of the JCP and other party members in an open, collective trial in Tokyo District Court, which the JCP leadership agreed to since this gave them a platform to openly declare their revolutionary platform.[89] Hirata Isao, assisted by fellow procurator Tozawa Shigeo, prepared the state's case against the defendants, which was then taken up by Chief Justice Miyagi Minoru, who presided over the trials. Defendants were divided into three groups, and after 108 sessions between June 1931 and July 1932, 181 JCP members were given sentences ranging from life imprisonment (four JCP leaders—Sano Manabu, Nabeyama Sadachika, Ichikawa Shōichi, and Mitamura Shirō) to multiyear prison sentences for other defendants depending on their organizational affiliations and the purported depth of their dangerous thought.[90]

At the same time as procurators were investigating communists for possible indictment, they were also researching the causes and contextual factors for why individual detainees became involved in thought crime. Thus under the rubric of a criminal investigation, thought procurators began constructing a detailed archive of personal histories, motivations, and opinions by having detainees sketch memoirs (*shuki*) in their own hand, which would often be included in official reports (*jōshinsho*) in their case. Through this process, the state's ostensible target of repression—the thought criminal— was coming into focus.[91] Moreover, in these extensive interviews with detained thought criminals, individual procurators began to experiment with "morally persuading thought criminals" (*shisōhannin kyōka*) to express repentance (*kaishun*), hoping that some disaffected JCP members would defect from the party.[92] These kinds of experiments had two important effects: first, they started to construct an archive of thought crime, and second, while still based on the repression of thought crime, they revealed new possibilities that would later become the rehabilitation policies of the 1930s. And as we will soon see, negotiating between the repressive application of the Peace Preservation Law and the emerging reform efforts were thought procurators such as Hirata Isao.

As early as 1928, arrested JCP members were individually voicing discontent with the Comintern and JCP policies, and calling for the dissolution of the party. By spring 1929, a group had coalesced around Nagano organizer Kawai Etsuzō and chief of the JCP secretariat Mizuno Shigeo. From his jail cell in Osaka, Kawai was the first to outline in an official report his dissatisfaction with the JCP and his willingness to cooperate with the authorities. Soon after, Mizuno, held in Ichigaya Prison in Tokyo and under the supervision of Hirata Isao, followed suit, drafting a scathing critique of the Comintern and the JCP leadership.[93] In his report, Mizuno argued that the Comintern did not understand the unique conditions in Japan and, in particular, the sentiments of the Japanese population toward the emperor.[94] Mizuno critiqued the JCP's slogan "abolish the monarchy," which he argued reflected the leadership's "tactical formalism" (*senjutsuteki kōshikishugi*) as out of touch with conditions in Japan and ignorant of Japan's mission in its colonial empire. In contrast, Mizuno rejected the premise outlined in the 1927 Theses that the emperor was a "fetter" (*shikoku*) to the liberation of the Japanese masses and thus that a communist transformation in Japan required abolishing the emperor system.[95] Additionally, Mizuno critiqued the theory of violent overthrow modeled on the Bolshevik Revolution, the Comintern's internationalism that equated Japan's colonial project in East Asia to Western imperialism, and sacrificing Japan's national interests in order to defend the Soviet Union. All of these, Mizuno argued, alienated the party from the Japanese masses and would lead to the JCP's defeat.[96] He concluded by calling for the "dissolution" (*kaitō*) of the JCP and the formation of a "true mass labor party." After procurators distributed Kawai and Mizuno's respective letters to their comrades, a dozen party members similarly declared criticisms of the JCP.[97]

The bureau of the struggling JCP critiqued these defectors, calling them the Dissolutionist Faction (Kaitō-ha). This did not stop Mizuno from organizing a new party called the Japanese Communist Party Labor Faction (Nihon kyōsantō rōdōsha-ha) in June 1930.[98] The Labor Faction was based on the tenets outlined in Mizuno's earlier critique, namely that a successful communist movement required recognizing, first, the unique political conditions in Japan; second, the deep historical and cultural ties between the emperor and the people; and third, the liberatory potential immanent in Japan's colonial empire in East Asia. These positions conveniently placed the Labor Faction outside the purview of the Peace Preservation Law's kokutai infringement. As expected, the JCP leadership critiqued the Labor Faction from jail, calling for communists to "Smash the Social Fascist Dissolutionist Faction!"[99] As a political party, the Labor Faction remained small and relatively ineffective in its short existence, disbanding in 1933, but it provided an early precedent—if not also an ideological victory—to procurators who hoped to sow the seeds of division among the communist movement.

Many historians have explained these early defections as a particularly Japanese expression of the national question that has plagued communist internationalism more generally.[100] The national question was clearly one aspect of the defections in 1929, for what many Labor Faction members first understood as a tactical break from the Comintern quickly turned into their proactive embrace of Japan's historical and cultural uniqueness symbolized by the emperor.[101] However, to explain these defections as solely a manifestation of the national question unique to Japanese Marxism ignores not only how the national question was, and continues to be, an important question in Marxist theory but, more importantly, the central role of state officials in inducing and structuring these defections along nationalist lines.[102] Moreover, by guiding these defections, state officials' own understandings of the meaning of the imperial kokutai was changing, indicating how the imperial sovereign remained an elusive ghost even as it animated this expanding and changing justice apparatus.

Here, the example of Hirata Isao is instructive. As thought procurator of Tokyo District Court, Hirata oversaw Mizuno, who was held in Ichigaya Prison.[103] Mizuno first hinted at critiquing the JCP and defecting from the party in conversations with Hirata; soon afterward he started drafting an official report (jōshinsho) of his critique with Hirata's close assistance.[104] It appears that Hirata's objective at this early stage was not the wholesale eradication of anticapitalist socialism, but something much more humble: namely, that communists could continue to agitate for the overthrow of capitalism as long as they discarded their antiemperor position.[105] For example, the Labor Faction member Asano Akira recounted later that when he spoke with Hirata Isao in Ichigaya Prison, Hirata exclaimed, "If you are able to retain the emperor [tennō goji], then I can say I agree with you." According to Asano, Hirata demonstrated that he was familiar with Marxist theory and agreed that, in the interwar crisis of global capitalism, a major renovation (daikaikaku) of Japanese society must occur. The only issue Hirata had with the communists under his supervision at the time was apparently the kokutai question (kokutai no mondai).[106] Many incarcerated JCP members who were considering defecting from the party understood Hirata as willing to accept their continued dedication to overthrowing capitalism, only as long as they recognized the emperor.[107] Upon reflection, Asano admitted that he did not believe that the Kaitō-ha defections would have taken place without Hirata's intervention and guidance.[108] Importantly, Itō Akira has argued that there was a kind of "ideological resonance" (shisōteki kyōei) between the Kaitō-ha's tactical critique of the JCP slogan "abolish the monarchy" and Hirata's willingness to accept a breakaway communist party as long as it recognized the emperor. This "resonance," Itō contends, became a "narrow ideological passage" (*semai shisōteki tsūro*) for communists to leave the JCP and identify with the emperor system in the early 1930s.[109] Furthermore, we can understand Hirata's emphasis on the kokutai question and his disregard for anticapitalism as strategically correlating to the revision of the Peace Preservation Law in 1928 in which altering the kokutai became a greater offense than rejecting the system of private property.

Later in 1936, Hirata reflected on his earlier work with the Labor Faction and lamented that their defection was insufficient, signifying a shift in political tactics rather than a true return to Japanese consciousness. For Hirata, the Labor Faction's continued dedication to communist revolution rested on a naïve passion (*junshin netsuretsu*).[110] But as we saw above, Asano recounted that Hirata expressed similar opinions about the need for Japan to undergo a socioeconomic transformation. In other words, Hirata's own understanding of the significance of the imperial kokutai was changing, if only in terms of its categorical function in the Peace Preservation Law. In other words, the national question that historians have isolated to a problem afflicting the JCP was also, ironically, a question for state officials attempting to apply the Peace Preservation Law to ostensibly defend imperial sovereignty from communism.

Hirata's early administrative experiment with the Kaitō-ha was successful in further fracturing the beleaguered Japanese communist movement and reveals how, at this stage, such experiments were linked to the original intention of the Peace Preservation Law as a means to repress the JCP. Within a short time, such ad hoc experiments would soon be formalized within a pretrial parole policy that procurators used to induce such defections from the communist movement. And it is within this formal structure that the rehabilitation of detained thought criminals began to take on a dynamic of its own.

THE CHARGES WITHHELD SYSTEM AND THE FIGURE OF THE THOUGHT CRIMINAL

Nothing exists for the capitalist State unless it is written down.
—NICOS POULANTZAS, *State, Power, Socialism*

In addition to the political defections of Mizuno and the Labor Faction in 1929–1931, there were other arrested JCP members who were reassessing their political affiliations, most often as a spiritual awakening to Buddhism or through love for their families (and the shame their arrest had brought them). As we will see in chapter 3, Kobayashi Morito was one such rank-and-file JCP member who, under the guidance of Buddhist prison chaplain Fujii

Eshō, was saved (*kyūsai*) and, through his Buddhist studies, experienced a self-awakening (*jiko no jikaku*) as a Japanese imperial subject.[111] By 1931, at national meetings procurators were sharing their diverse experiences with detained thought criminals and began to consider a formal policy to nurture and facilitate these kinds of isolated defections and reassessments.

As noted earlier, very few thought criminals arrested under the Peace Preservation Law were brought to trial. Richard Mitchell reports that out of the 66,000 persons arrested between 1925 and 1941 in Japan, only 8 percent were actually prosecuted.[112] The vast majority of those arrested were either released without being charged once it was determined they did not pose a political threat, or were administered through a Suspended Indictment policy. The Japanese criminal code allowed for a suspect—political or otherwise— who showed potential for reform to be granted a Suspended Indictment (Kiso yūyo), at which time the suspect was temporarily released to a family member or reformatory. These policies were designed for the suspect to reflect on his or her crime, while at the same time the state was able to monitor the suspect's activities.

This policy was left to the discretion of district court procurators who, after conducting their preliminary investigation, decided whether to advance a case to trial, activate a Suspended Indictment or, once a suspect was tried and sentenced, confer with the district court judge to temporarily issue a Suspended Sentence (Shikkō yūyo) before a convict was sent to prison. Although the criminal code contained these provisions, it was not until the 1920s that reform-minded officials in the Justice Ministry started to see them as the cornerstone of the criminal justice apparatus.

There were earlier reform efforts dating back to the turn of the twentieth century, including local parolee-support programs coordinated by the Justice Ministry that operated under the rubric of *hogo* (lit. "protection," which I refer to as rehabilitation), as well as public reformatories (*kanka-in*) for youth delinquents established by the Home Ministry in Tokyo and Osaka.[113] In the 1910s, the Justice Ministry began to experiment with releasing juvenile offenders to private rehabilitation groups before they were officially indicted or sentenced, consequently moving into the Home Ministry's domain of juvenile reform. Then in the 1920s, the Justice Ministry largely took over the administration of juvenile delinquents (*hikō shōnen*) with the implementation of a new, expanded Juvenile Law (Shōnen hō) on January 1, 1922, which overhauled the entire juvenile justice system, bringing a variety of institutions and private groups under the direction of the Justice Ministry.[114] This law consisted of seventy-four articles outlining procedures for, among other things, establishing juvenile courts in Tokyo and Osaka, outlining specific procedures for adjudicating juvenile cases, and, most importantly, coordinating welfare services for juvenile delinquents who were released before being officially indicted or sentenced.[115] A Youth Reform Association (Shōnen hogo dantai kyōkai) was established that May to coordinate between the juvenile courts and various organizations that worked to reform youths. The director of the Youth Reform Association in Tokyo was Miyagi Chōgorō, the future director of the Imperial Renovation Society that I analyze in chapter 3.[116] These welfare and reform efforts came under the general rubric of delinquent protection (hogo) and hinged on providing procurators with the discretion to assess if a juvenile had the potential to be reformed under the supervision of newly commissioned probation officers (*shokutaku hogoshi*) while working with guardians (*hogosha*)—often family members—and reform groups (*hogo dantai*), which would evaluate the juveniles' progress.[117]

The 1922 Juvenile Law symbolized the increasing influence of reform-minded officials in the Justice Ministry who espoused a new approach to criminal justice under the rubric of *hogoshugi* (protectionism or rehabilitationism).[118] Justice officials quickly set out to extend rehabilitation to other areas of the criminal justice system, experimenting with applying suspension policies to adult detainees.[119]

In a later 1935 article addressing a foreign audience, Judge Miyake Masatarō described the centrality of these reform programs in the Japanese criminal justice system this way:

> The idea [has] gained ground that reformation and not retaliation is the purpose of punishment; and the Japanese Criminal Code early provided for the system of suspension of execution [i.e., Suspended Sentence], which allows an offender who is sentenced to imprisonment or penal servitude for a period of less than two years, a certain time for reflection before beginning to serve his term. If the order for suspension is not revoked the sentence itself becomes void at the expiration of the period and the offender escapes not only the hardship of a prison term but also the humiliation of being branded as an ex-convict.[120]

By the late 1920s, these juvenile programs had been extended to adult offenders and coalesced into a system called protection and supervision (*hogo kansatsu*). For example, in 1926, justice officials established the first semiofficial rehabilitation organization for adult offenders in the Suspended Indictment

Figure 2.1. "The First Rehabilitation Organization for Those with Suspended Indictments, Sentences: The Imperial Renovation Society Is Formed," *Osaka Mainichi Shimbun*, November 21, 1926.

or Suspended Sentence programs called the Imperial Renovation Society (Teikoku kōshin kai) in Tokyo (figure 2.1).

As I explore in chapter 3, this society would soon play a central role in the ideological conversions (tenkō) of political criminals, as many detained political criminals increasingly received a form of Suspended Indictment in the early 1930s. The juvenile reform experiments of the mid-1920s provided an immediate example for thought procurators who were facilitating the growing population of thought criminals arrested under the Peace

Preservation Law in the late 1920s. For instance, Okudaira Yasuhiro notes that procurators in Tokyo started to apply the Suspended Indictment policy to a few cases involving students who were arrested in the 3.15 Incident.[121] By 1931, this policy was formalized for thought crime cases by the Justice Ministry in Instruction No. 270, titled "Applying Charges Withheld to Peace Preservation Law Cases Related to the Communist Party" (Nihon kyōsantō kankei chianijihō ihan jiken ryūho shobun no ken).[122] Similar in form to a Suspended Indictment, Charges Withheld (Ryūho shobun) quickly became the primary procedure for administering thought crime cases in the early 1930s, before it was replaced by the conventional policy of Suspended Indictment in the Thought Criminals Protection and Supervision Law of 1936 (discussed in chapter 4).[123] As with the earlier reform policies in the 1922 Juvenile Law, procurators in Tokyo and Osaka took the lead in experimenting with the Charges Withheld policy in thought crime cases.[124] Between 1931 and 1936, Charges Withheld allowed procurators to investigate suspects without officially charging them. In this state of legal limbo, procurators could record the subjective and objective conditions of the suspect's life and past political activities, and determine if he or she should be officially charged. This was normally a period of six months. Additionally, rather than being held in a detention facility, thought criminals were released through a guarantor system (mimoto hikiuke) in which family members, civic leaders, or a host of other nonstate actors served to oversee the reform of the thought criminal.

In this system, thought crime and the thought criminal were constituted through an array of reports to assess a suspect's potential for reform. Recalling Poulantzas's observation in the epigraph above, the amount of paper that was produced on the thought criminal paralleled only the amount expended earlier to clarify the meaning of kokutai in the law, discursively configuring both ghosts of the Japanese Empire. Already in 1928, directives were sent to procurators to collect data on those detained since the March arrest campaigns, including information on employment, education, family situation, marital status, income and standard of living, life experiences, health, "development of [political] thought" (shisō suii katei), which organizations or movements suspects belonged to (e.g., laborer, farmer, outcast, student, etc.) and if their indictment had been suspended.[125] A review of procurator directives related to thought crime during this period reveals how the Justice Ministry intensified its effort to gather information on thought crime suspects and their lives.[126] The next major step in this process occurred in 1932, with a Charges Withheld protocol (Directive No. 2006) which stated that a procurator would implement this policy after a detailed assessment of, among other things, the suspect's character, prior criminal record, history in the movement, depth of political consciousness, and "whether or not [the suspect] can effect a thought conversion [shisō tenkō] and maintain a conventional daily life."[127] This was the first time the term "tenkō" was officially used to signify a thought criminal's purported change in political or ideological disposition.[128] During the Charges Withheld policy period, both the probation official (kansatsukan) and the guarantor were required to submit monthly reports on the suspect's "thoughts and activities," "acquaintances and contacts," "family relationship and life condition," "physical health," "the conditions of the guarantor's supervision" (mimoto hikiukenin no kantoku no jikkyō), and "degree of repentance" (kaishun no jōkyō), among other things.[129] The guarantor system extended surveillance responsibilities from procurators to the community—primarily family members—effectively bringing nonstate actors into the state's expanding thought crime apparatus.[130] From the massive amount of data collected by officials, families, and community members, the object of thought crime in the Japanese metropole was constructed, and the silhouette of the thought criminal became legible.[131]

SOVEREIGN POWER AND JAPANESE EMPIRE

While procurators in metropolitan Japan were increasingly relying on suspension policies such as Charges Withheld, thought crime was being handled very differently in colonial Korea in the early 1930s. Although the Justice Ministry extended the Charges Withheld protocol throughout the empire, Korean colonial procurators emphasized prosecution over reform. According to Hong Jong-wook, out of the 12,271 suspected thought criminals arrested in colonial Korea between 1925 and 1932, 3,561 individuals, or nearly 30 percent, were formally indicted.[132] In Japan, 38,852 people had been arrested during the same period, with only 5.9 percent or 2,278 individuals indicted.[133] However, this disparity between indictments in Japan and colonial Korea became even more acute as procurators in Japan began to invoke Charges Withheld more frequently in thought crime cases from 1931 onward.[134] To anticipate a question I explore in chapter 5, once reform was institutionalized with the passage of the Thought Criminal Protection and Supervision Law in 1936, justice officials began to take closer notice of the disparities between metropolitan Japan and colonial Korea, and attributed the relatively fewer cases of conversion to the particular "complexity" and "unique quality" of thought crime in Korea.[135]

For most of the 1930s, the repressive mode of juridical power took precedence in the thought crime policies of the Korean Government-General. In the name of protecting Japan's claims on Korea from anticolonial activists (not just communist anticolonialists), procurators largely relied on punishing transgressions of sovereign law rather than expanding efforts to guide activists to reform as loyal subjects. Furthermore, while historians have debated whether or not executions were carried out under the provisions of the Peace Preservation Law, Mizuno Naoki has noted that in Korea, there were cases in which suspects were charged under a variety of laws—including the Peace Preservation Law—and executed.[136] However, we should recognize that, even if not invoked to the same degree as in the metropole, suspension policies such as Charges Withheld were implemented in the colony, thus allowing us to consider the significance of the disparities between metropole and colony. I explore these disparities in the use of reform and repression between the Japanese metropole and colonial Korea further in the following chapters.

Conclusion: The Curious Substitution of the Thought Criminal

When analyzing the emergence of the delinquent in nineteenth-century penal discourse, Michel Foucault observes a "curious substitution" that takes place within the penitentiary, as a sentenced criminal offender became the target of programs to observe and study the inmate as well as to reform him or her to "be of use to society."[137] Foucault argues the penitentiary brings about

> a curious substitution: from the hands of justice, [the penitentiary] certainly receives a convicted person; but what it must apply itself to is not, of course, the offence, nor even exactly the offender, but a rather different object, one defined by variables which at the outset at least were not taken into account in the sentence, for they were relevant only for a corrective technology. This other character, whom the penitentiary apparatus substitutes for the convicted offender, is the *delinquent*. . . . The delinquent is to be distinguished from the offender by the fact that it is not so much his act as his life that is relevant in characterizing him.[138]

In this chapter we have seen how a similar substitution started to take place in the Peace Preservation Law in Japan in the early 1930s, whereby the thought criminal, once apprehended, passed from being an offender to punish for the transgression of threatening the imperial kokutai to becoming a target of observation, study, and ultimately disciplinary reform. In Foucault's terms, state power shifted from punishing the thought criminal's act to his or her life and what had led him or her to become influenced by dangerous foreign thought in the first place. This substitution was also the mediation between the sovereign ghost of the state apparatus and the corollary ghost of the ideal imperial subject who was being discursively formed as detainees were being documented and assessed in a series of official reports. With the increasing population of thought criminals managed in the Peace Preservation Law apparatus in Japan in the early 1930s, procurators increasingly utilized the Suspended Indictment and, after its formalization in 1931 and 1932, the Charges Withheld administrative procedures to process these individuals. As I argue in this chapter, this was not a unilinear transition from repression to reform, but rather their dual configuration of repression with reform within the Peace Preservation Law apparatus.[139] The statistics for metropolitan Japan in the early 1930s for arrests, indictments, and suspended indictments reveal this relationship: of the almost forty thousand people arrested in Japan during 1931–1933, three-quarters were released, and of the remaining suspects, only 2,235 individuals were indicted, while 4,499 individuals were placed in either the Suspended Indictment or Charges Withheld programs.[140]

Once placed in Charges Withheld status, the thought offender served as a kind of "exchanger element" (Foucault), allowing for a transcription between sovereign-juridical and disciplinary power to take place. Furthermore, the guarantor in the Charges Withheld policy and the volunteers who assisted in reforming criminals extended the state's thought crime campaign into the wider community. Such policies mediated between the state's imperial ideology that defined thought crime and the general population, which increasingly took on the responsibility of assisting reformed parolees. In chapter 3, I explore the practices of a semiofficial rehabilitation group based in Tokyo, the Imperial Renovation Society, and how this society took on the responsibility of guiding the rehabilitation of hundreds of ex-communists as they transitioned back into society. It was in such groups that political rehabilitation— or what would soon be called ideological conversion (tenkō)—was first experimented with, establishing the practical forms and ideological content that would come to frame the mass tenkō phenomenon of the mid-1930s. Similar to how the imperial sovereign appeared as the ghost animating the apparatus to suppress political crime, another, corollary ghost—the loyal imperial subject—was inscribed in the reform practices of groups like the Imperial Renovation Society. To understand how this ghost was conjured in the forms and practices of such groups is the topic of chapter 3.

Apparatuses of Subjection:

The Rehabilitation of Thought Criminals in the Early 1930s

The [incarcerated] man . . . whom we are invited to free, is already in himself the effect of subjection much more profound than himself. A "soul" inhabits him and brings him to existence, which is itself a factor in the mastery that power exercises over the body. The soul is the effect and instrument of political anatomy; the soul is the prison of the body. —MICHEL FOUCAULT, *Discipline and Punish*

Ideology does not exist in the "world of ideas" conceived as a "spiritual world." Ideology exists in institutions and the practices specific to them. We are then tempted to say, more precisely: ideology exists in apparatuses and the practices specific to them. This is the sense in which we said that Ideological State Apparatuses realize, in the material dispositives of each of these apparatuses and the practices specific to them, an ideology external to them, which we called the primary ideology and now designate by its name: the State Ideology, the unity of the ideological themes essential to the dominant class or classes. —LOUIS ALTHUSSER, *On the Reproduction of Capitalism*

While Hirata Isao and other thought procurators (shisō kenji) were experimenting with inducing repentance in detained thought criminals (shisō hannin) and urging them to defect from the Japanese Communist Party (JCP) in the late 1920s, a corollary component was emerging: the effort to assist suspects as they reflected on their political crimes while awaiting indictment, returned to their families, and looked for employment.[1] As the number of arrested thought criminals increased in the early 1930s, so too did efforts to reintegrate political suspects deemed reformable back into society upon being paroled or released before indictment. The first and most important group in this effort was the semiofficial Imperial Renovation Society (Teikoku kōshinkai) in Tokyo. Established in 1926, the Imperial Renovation Society was the first reform group (*kōsei hogo dantai*) designed specifically for adult detainees released through the Suspended Indictment (Kiso yūyo) or Suspended Sentence (Shikkō yūyo) programs. As reviewed in chapter 2, these programs started to be applied to a few thought-crime cases in the late 1920s and early 1930s. Then, as the Charges Withheld (Ryūho shobun) policy became protocol for dealing with repentant political criminals after 1931–1932, the Imperial Renovation Society advised hundreds of thought criminals every year, guiding them through the process of rehabilitation while also maintaining surveillance so as to protect against ideological recidivism. In this way, the Imperial Renovation Society became a laboratory for experimenting with and developing the procedures that would come to define the state's policy of ideological conversion (tenkō). And although ideological conversion was a phenomenon largely limited to the Japanese metropole at this time, in the next chapters I explore how these early protocols would come to be applied in colonial Korea later in the decade.

This chapter explores the Imperial Renovation Society as a historical example of Louis Althusser's theory of Ideological State Apparatuses or ISAs: that is, apparatuses that function to interpellate individuals to be productive subjects in capitalist society without the continuing threat of state reprimand.[2] As an ISA that coordinated the resources of the wider community for criminal reform, the Imperial Renovation Society mediated between the imperial state, the community, and criminal parolees so that the latter would reform as loyal imperial subjects. Indeed, it was in and through such ISAs that the spectral images of the benevolent sovereign emperor and the ideal imperial subject were reproduced and further disseminated into local communities. Therefore, this chapter has two objectives: first, it presents a new way of understanding the phenomenon of ideological conversion by challenging many of the theoretical assumptions that have informed previous scholarship on tenkō in the 1930s. Toward this end, the chapter begins with a review of the foundational scholarship on tenkō and then elaborates Louis Althusser's theory of ISAs in order to propose a new framework to understand the tenkō phenomenon in the 1930s. The second objective is historiographical: to reveal the important but oft-overlooked role of semiofficial rehabilitation groups such as the Imperial Renovation Society in the development and institutionalization of ideological conversion in the 1930s.

I focus on the important contributions made by one of its members, Kobayashi Morito, an ex-communist convert who joined the society in early 1932 and guided his fellow comrades to defect from the JCP and reform. As these two interventions—theoretical and historiographical—converge in tenkō, it is first necessary to discuss the conceptual issues surrounding the term "tenkō" and the importance of the phenomenon in the historiography of the interwar Japanese Empire.

Understanding the Interwar Tenkō Phenomenon

TENKŌ AS HISTORICAL AND THEORETICAL PROBLEM

No other term has come to symbolize the vexed decade of the 1930s more than tenkō. The combination of its two characters (転向) means something to the effect of "to change direction," but in the historiography of interwar Japan, tenkō takes on a much more convoluted significance. There the term refers to the ideological apostasy of thousands of political activists throughout the 1930s, beginning with JCP members who publicly defected from the party earlier in the decade, and later to socialists, leftist writers, and intellectuals who either abandoned political activism or began to explicitly identify with the emperor and the aims of the imperial state.[3] With few exceptions, tenkō has largely been portrayed as a phenomenon of intellectual history, in which metropolitan and colonial intellectuals—party affiliated or otherwise—shifted from political opposition to nonpolitical endeavors or to actively supporting the imperial state.[4] Generalizing from this ostensible intellectual shift, many scholars have represented tenkō as a more general turning point (*tenkanki*) in Japanese history in which earlier forms of cultural and political experimentation from the 1920s were suppressed or rechanneled to support nationalism and militarism—in other words, the shift from so-called Taishō democracy to Shōwa fascism.[5] Indeed, many historians refer to the mid-1930s as the period of conversion (*tenkō no jidai*).[6]

The term "tenkō" came to be widely understood as signifying an act of political or ideological conversion in the summer of 1933, when it was reported that two incarcerated JCP leaders, Sano Manabu and Nabeyama Sadachika, had renounced the policies of the Communist International (Comintern) as ill-suited to the realities of Japan and condemned the JCP's slavish adherence to Moscow's directives (figure 3.1).

In a joint letter titled "A Letter to Our Fellow Defendants," Sano and Nabeyama announced a "significant change" (*jūyō na henkō*) in their political

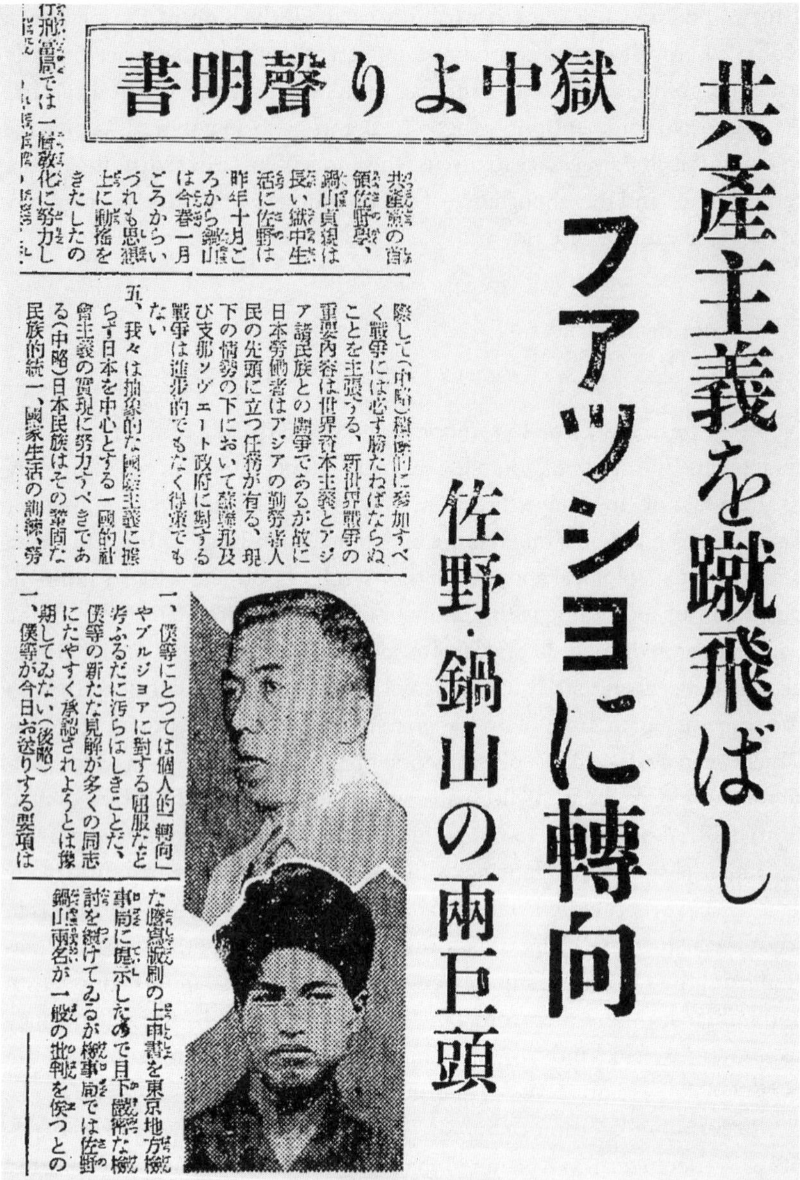

共產主義を蹴飛ばし ファッショに轉向

佐野・鍋山の兩巨頭

獄中より聲明書

共產黨の首領佐野學、鍋山貞親は長い獄中生活に佐野は昨年十月ごろから鍋山は今春一月ごろからいづれも思想上に動搖をきたしたの

行刑當局では一層敎化に努力し

際して(中略)積極的に參加すべく戰爭には必ず勝たねばならぬことを主張する、新世界戰爭の重要內容は世界資本主義とアジア諸民族との鬪爭であるが故に日本勞働者はアジアの勤勞者人民の先頭に立つ任務が有る、現下の情勢の下において蘇聯邦及び支那ソヴエート政府に對する戰爭は進步的でもなく得策でもない

五、我々は抽象的な國際主義に據らず日本を中心とする一國的社會主義の實現に努力すべきである(中略)日本民族はその鞏固な民族的統一、國家生活の訓練、勞

一、僕等にとつては個人的「轉向」やブルジョアに對する屈服など考ふるだに汚らはしきことだ、僕等の新たな見解が多くの同志にたやすく承認されようとは豫期してゐない(後略)

一、僕等が今日お送りする要項は

な謄寫版刷の上申書を東京地方檢事局に提示したので目下嚴密な檢討を續けてゐるが檢事局では佐野鍋山兩名が一般の批判を俟つとの

Figure 3.1. All the daily newspapers ran the sensational story of the JCP leaders' defection from prison. "A Declaration from Jail: Leaders Sano and Nabeyama Discard Communism and Convert to Fascism," *Yomiuri Shimbun*, June 10, 1933.

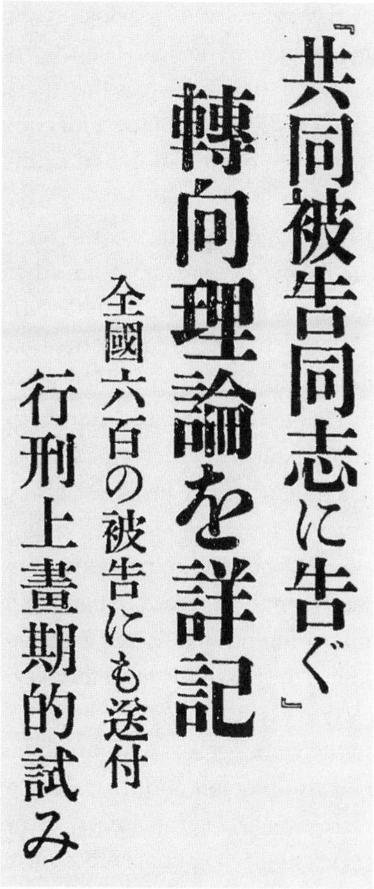

「共同被告同志に告ぐ」
轉向理論を詳記
全國六百の被告にも送付
行刑上畫期的試み

Figure 3.2. Many newspapers reprinted detailed excerpts from the Sano and Nabeyama letter soon after their so-called tenkō, informing the public of the rationale guiding the defections as well as introducing the term "tenkō" to the general public. "'A Letter to Our Fellow Defendants': A Detailed Description of the Theory of Tenkō/Distributed to 600 Defendants Nationwide," *Tōkyō Nichi Nichi Shimbun*, June 14, 1933.

position and urged their comrades to break with the Comintern, reconnect the revolutionary vanguard to the Japanese masses, and harness the national-ist sentiments of the working class in order to carry out a socialist transfor-mation in Japan.[7] The authorities released the letter to the press on June 10 and distributed it to six hundred other incarcerated JCP members through-out the country on June 13 (see figure 3.2).[8]

In the weeks following the Sano-Nabeyama announcement, procura-tor Hirata Isao, chief procurator Miyagi Chōgorō, chaplain Fujii Eshō, and other justice officials met in Tokyo to take stock of these conversions, explain their significance, and consider methods to urge other incarcerated thought criminals to convert.[9] By the end of summer, hundreds of incarcerated JCP members similarly declared their defection from the JCP and renounced the Comintern.[10] Some detainees had their indictments or sentences suspended, while the more famous leaders of the JCP who were already serving prison sentences, including Sano and Nabeyama, remained in jail. Defections continued into the following year and have come to be known as the "mass tenkō" (tairyō tenkō) of 1933–1934.[11] These conversions, combined with continued police repression, eliminated the JCP as an organization and extinguished any hope of its reformation.[12]

It is important to note that Sano and Nabeyama did not use the term "tenkō" in their sensational "Letter to Our Fellow Defendants."[13] In other words, in the text that is conventionally understood as initiating the phenomena of tenkō, the term is curiously absent.[14] Rather it was the authorities that used the term "tenkō" when they informed the press of Sano and Nabeyama's defection on June 10.[15] As I explore in this chapter, the state had started to use tenkō to signify something to the effect of a political or ideological apostasy as early as the fall of 1932.[16] This was at a time when the Justice Ministry made a concerted effort to increase its efforts to prevent so-called thought crime (shisō hanzai) and explore ways to reform thought criminals who were starting to be released after serving their sentences.[17] In regard to Sano and Nabeyama's use of tenkō elsewhere, in a longer but not publicized explanation of their critique of the JCP and Comintern they used the term this way: "We recognize our responsibility for the party [i.e., the JCP], and believe it is absolutely necessary at this time to turn to the working class and reveal the correct path forward. We believe it would be dishonorable and shameless to secretly turn inward and individually convert [kojinteki ni tenkō suru]. Now we must take the initiative and have the responsibility to publicly recognize the errors [we have made] to our comrades up until now, and, based on our new consciousness, to reveal to the public a [new] course of action."[18]

As we can see here, Sano and Nabeyama mention tenkō only in passing and portray it in a largely negative sense: that is, as an individual process of introspection and conversion.[19] In other words, they use tenkō as a foil against which to represent their own political transformation as a bold reconsideration of revolutionary politics. Although Sano and Nabeyama came to use the term "tenkō" more regularly later, this does not mean that they were the first to use it in regard to an ideological transformation, or that they developed a theory of tenkō, as has been conventionally argued.[20] We can assume they merely borrowed the term from officials overseeing their cases, including Hirata Isao, Miyagi Chōgorō, and prison chaplain Fujii Eshō. Indeed, chaplain Fujii set out to explain the process by which Sano and Nabeyama came to "convert" in a four part series of articles in the Yomiuri Shimbun only four days after their conversion was announced (see figure 3.3).

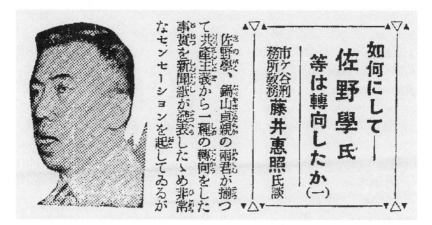

Figure 3.3. In a four-part series, Ichigaya prison chaplain and Imperial Renovation Society Vice Director Fujii Eshō explains the process through which the JCP leaders converted. "How Did Sano Manabu and the Others Tenkō? (Part 1)," *Yomiuri Shimbun*, June 14, 1933, morning edition.

However, with the mass defections of 1933–1934, state officials categorized all expressions of repentance or political defection as tenkō, and, as I explore in chapter 4, codified the term in 1936 with the Thought Criminal Protection and Supervision Law (Shisōhan hogo kansatsu hō), making tenkō the official policy for dealing with thought criminals arrested under the Peace Preservation Law. By the late 1930s, it was not uncommon for officials to anachronistically apply the term tenkō to any prior defection or change of political stance that occurred before 1933, including those of the Labor Faction analyzed in chapter 2.[21] This practice continues in postwar scholarship, where tenkō is applied not only to any political change enacted by a leftist intellectual or activist during the interwar period, but is generalized and applied to all the supposed shifts in modern Japanese intellectual or cultural history.[22]

The increasing ubiquity of the term "tenkō" in the mid-1930s did not mean that it was clearly understood, either by those announcing a break from the communist movement or by the state officials who were facilitating these recantations. From the perspective of incarcerated thought criminals, it was only after the publication of autobiographical essays on the conversion experience in 1934–1935 that tenkō came to be defined within a fixed range of motivations, including a general sense of political defeat, theoretical or political differences with the Comintern and/or Marxism, health concerns, a spiritual awakening, a return to national consciousness, or the most commonly cited reason, love and concern for one's family.[23] On the other side of the interrogation table, many state officials were surprised by the tenkō boom of 1933–1934, and procurators like Hirata Isao soon found themselves having to explain these conversions to skeptical colleagues.[24] In 1933–1934, most officials understood tenkō as merely an extension of the initial repressive function of the Peace Preservation Law reviewed in chapter 2: that is, as signifying a defection from party affiliation and thus the organizational destruction of the communist movement.[25] However, as concerns over ideological recidivism arose in the wake of the mass conversions of 1933–1934, tenkō morphed into an intellectual renunciation of Marxism as an ideology (i.e., beyond one's organizational affiliation with the JCP), and soon thereafter a process that required an explicit declaration of imperial loyalty and one's embrace of Japan's imperial kokutai. Following the codification of tenkō as state policy in 1936, officials continued to revise and refine the categories indexing a supposed act of conversion as they implemented the policy in the Thought Criminal Protection and Supervision Centers.

Interestingly, then, tenkō was used in the 1930s by a number of different people to signify a number of different practices and experiences—from communists reflecting on the failed policies of the JCP, to proletarian writers narrating their experience of betraying their earlier ideals, to justice officials who continually redefined what constituted an act of tenkō, to nationalist activists in colonial Korea who, in the late 1930s and 1940s, understood tenkō as yoking Korea's destiny more closely to the Japanese Empire. This semantic ambiguity is, I believe, the very condition for the term to be as ubiquitous as it was in the 1930s, and subsequently allowed tenkō to serve as a symbol of the entire interwar intellectual and political milieu in postwar scholarship. For our purposes, tenkō's combined semantic ambiguity and ubiquity provides a unique window into the myriad articulations of imperial ideology in the 1930s and how groups like the Imperial Renovation Society mediated between the sovereign ghost of the imperial state and individual imperial subjects.

THEORIES OF TENKŌ AND THE ABSENCE OF IDEOLOGY

In the early postwar period, tenkō became a lens through which many intellectuals, writers, and activists theorized and debated over ethics, subjectivity, and political praxis.[26] Through these kinds of debates about the political possibilities in the immediate postwar period, the interwar tenkō phenomenon became an important historical question in its own right. The exemplary work in this regard was conducted by Tsurumi Shunsuke and the Shisō no kagaku kenkyūkai (Science of Thought).[27] Between 1959 and 1962, Science of Thought published a three-volume study of tenkō, which established the methodological framework for many later studies. The study consists of roughly three dozen individual biographies of intellectuals, writers, and political activists who supposedly committed tenkō in the interwar period (whether the individual used the term tenkō or not). The study approached tenkō as largely a phenomenon limited to intellectuals or party theoreticians, overlooking that thousands of rank-and-file activists and organizers also underwent so-called conversion. The individual entries were organized under four categories—radicals, liberals, conservatives, and nationalists—which, taken together, ostensibly provided a snapshot of the various trajectories in interwar Japanese intellectual history.

Toward this end, Tsurumi proposed a general definition of tenkō that, he believed, would account for the variety of motivations, experiences, and degrees of ideological conversion while remaining objective so as not to pass judgment on those who converted. Tsurumi defined tenkō as "a change of thought under the coercion of state power" (*kokka kenryoku ni yotte kyōsei sareta shisō no henka de ari*).[28] Tsurumi elaborated that tenkō had two essential components: "the compulsion exercised by the state, and the response chosen by the individual or group. The use of force and the existence of spontaneity are the two essential elements."[29] Tsurumi's dualistic definition of tenkō as a phenomenon produced between coercion and spontaneity— between external state power and the internal thoughts and decisions of an individual—was hugely influential and continues to inform many studies today.[30]

There have been critiques of Tsurumi's definition of tenkō, but, tellingly, these criticisms have emphasized either state coercion or individual spontaneity, consequently reinforcing the duality of Tsurumi's original theory of tenkō. From one direction, Okudaira Yasuhiro has argued that intellectual histories such as those of the Shisō no kagaku kenkyūkai "limit their subject to the re-examinations of the thought content, and the way of undergoing 'tenkō'" and thus "fail to analyze . . . state power." For Okudaira, these studies have "not yet comprehended the mechanism and operations of . . . thought suppression . . . much less the systematic and organizational state control."[31] From the other direction, Nabeyama Sadachika argued in the 1970s that by supposedly emphasizing "only the external conditions for tenkō," Tsurumi failed to adequately reflect on the "internal spontaneity" (*naiteki jihatsusei*) that led many JCP members such as himself to ideologically convert.[32] Nabeyama then proceeded to outline his reasons for defecting from the JCP in

1933, including the misguided directives of the Comintern at the time, the difficulty in organizing a mass base under the JCP's slogan of "abolish the monarchy" (*kunshusei haishi*), and the increasingly petit bourgeois character of the JCP in the early 1930s, among other reasons.[33]

As we see here, both of these approaches emphasize one polarity or the other of Tsurumi's original definition of tenkō—either external state power (Okudaira) or internal spontaneity (Nabeyama). What is missing in all these theories of ideological conversion is, paradoxically, a theory of ideology. For instance, while many studies recognize the role of state power, it is unclear if the coercion that the state exerted was itself of an ideological nature or, as Tsurumi's definition implies, was merely an external force that acted upon the ideological disposition of an individual. Does the state exist outside of ideology, or is it the locus through which ideology is reproduced and disseminated throughout society? Or, from the other direction, it is also unclear whether the new disposition or activities of a convert were, more than merely informed by a new set of ideas, themselves ideological. In many studies of tenkō, "ideology" is used to refer to the ideas that exist in the mind of an individual before and after a supposed conversion. Indeed, these approaches to tenkō reflect what Louis Althusser has called "the ideology of ideology"; that is, a theory of ideology that rests upon idealist dualities of mind and body, ideas and reality, rather than the material practices in which ideology is itself inscribed and reproduced.[34] If interwar tenkō was an explicitly ideological phenomenon nurtured and guided by the imperial state, it is first necessary to propose a theory of ideology that is able to reflect on the various practices that inflected imperial ideology and how these practices were inscribed in specific institutions. This will allow us to move beyond the conventional duality between external state coercion and internal ideas that have informed postwar scholarship on tenkō.

ALTHUSSER'S THEORY OF IDEOLOGICAL STATE APPARATUSES

In his essay "Ideology and Ideological State Apparatuses (Notes Towards an Investigation)" published in the journal *La Pensée* in June 1970, Louis Althusser proposed a provocative, but admittedly partial, theory of ideology and state power.[35] In this essay, Althusser presents two theses: that ideology functions to "interpellate individuals as subjects" and that this process of interpellation occurs through the ritualized practices inscribed in what he called Ideological State Apparatuses (Appareils Idéologiques d'État, ISAs). I focus on the latter thesis in order to analyze how the tenkō phenomenon was produced in groups like the Imperial Renovation Society.[36]

In contrast to the conventional emphasis on distorted ideas, Althusser emphasizes that ideology resides in the specific set of practices guided by the rituals inscribed within a particular apparatus, whether the apparatus is juridical, educational, cultural, and so on. In this manner, Althusser extends the conventional boundary of the state to encompass such elements (apparatuses) as labor unions, medical institutions, and, most importantly, the family, which, along with the educational apparatus, are the two central ISAS of the capitalist social formation.[37] Moreover, Althusser's unique theorization of apparatuses (*appareils*) may have more in common with what Foucault called a *dispositif* (often translated as "apparatus" as well) than has been previously recognized.[38]

For Althusser, the state not only maintains the power of a ruling class through the legitimate exercise of violence, but also functions to reproduce the relations of production through ideologization.[39] Here Althusser distinguishes between a (single) state apparatus—the Repressive State Apparatus (RSA) that primarily functions "by violence"—and the plural ISAS that function primarily "by ideology," including schools, family, and law, among others.[40] Althusser contends that all "State Apparatuses function both by repression and by ideology," with one element predominating over the other in the last instance. It is ideology, however, that secures the internal coherence between the apparatuses—a "sometimes teeth gritting . . . 'harmony'"—and thus presumably of the state itself.[41] And while the repressive function of the RSA serves as the ultimate horizon of state power, called upon in those moments when the police are "'overwhelmed by events,'" repression alone cannot explain how the relations of the social formation are reproduced, or the coherence between the multiple state apparatuses.[42]

In order to explicate the material practices of ideology within the ISAS, Althusser points to Pascal's formula "Kneel down, move your lips in prayer, and you will believe" in order "to invert the order of the notional schema of ideology" in which our actions are based on predetermined ideas.[43] Rather, for Althusser, ideas (or in his reading of Pascal, faith) are produced in ritualized practices: Althusser argues that "ideology exist[s] in a material ideological apparatus, prescribing material practices governed by a material ritual, which practices exist in the material actions of a subject acting in all consciousness according to his [or her] belief."[44] We act as if our actions are predetermined by our ideas, when in fact our ideas are materially inscribed in the practices themselves. This is the necessary misrecognition (*méconnaissance*) at work in ideology—not a mystification, but in the "obviousness" that we all, "of course," act upon our own volition.[45] This then shifts the emphasis from a subject being mystified by ideology to the formation of the subject through ideological interpellation, or what we will explore as the subjective ghost— the Japanese spirit (*nihon seishin*)—that animated the reformed offender as an imperial subject (*shinmin*) in interwar Japan.[46] Althusser argues that there is no ideological operation that is not already "for subjects"; that is, the subject is the "destination" of ideology, and thus "there are no subjects except by and for their subjection" through/in ideology.[47] Ultimately, the subject is itself the primary ideological effect, and while "bad subjects" (*mauvais sujets*) may periodically arise and "provoke the intervention of one of the detachments of the (repressive) State apparatus," Althusser notes that the "vast majority of (good) subjects work all right 'all by themselves,' i.e. by ideology (whose concrete forms are realized in the Ideological State Apparatuses)."[48]

Of course, Althusser's partial notes on ideology and state apparatuses leave many questions unanswered; first and foremost, how a so-called bad subject could emerge within a society in which ISAs are functioning to reproduce the relations of production.[49] As the example of the rise of the JCP in the 1920s and its slogan "abolish the monarchy" demonstrates, thousands of workers, activists, and intellectuals disidentified with imperial ideology and understood the overthrow of the emperor system as a necessary step toward international communist revolution—what Ernesto Laclau in his early writings (following Nicos Poulantzas) would call a politics of "disarticulation."[50] Furthermore, activists in colonial Korea resisted imperial identification in the name of national liberation, and it was not until later in the decade, when colonial nationals were mobilized as imperial subjects (i.e., the *kōminka* policy) that policies like ideological conversion became widespread among Korean thought criminals.[51]

However, for our purposes, Althusser's theoretical intervention complicates a number of the assumptions that have informed the study of tenkō in interwar Japan. First and foremost, Althusser's emphasis on the material operations of ideology within an ISA undermines the dualist understanding of tenkō as a phenomenon produced between internal ideas and external coercion. Rather, we can consider the ISAs as dispersed sites of ideological mediation between the imperial state, individual detainees, and the wider community. Consequently, a whole series of related assumptions are called into question, including that there is a moment outside of the determinations of ideology in which an individual spontaneously decides to convert.[52] Following Althusser, this would be the attribution of a subjective decision to the material practices ritualized within an institution such as the Imperial Renovation Society. As we will see, this is in fact one of the primary tropes of conversion in which a number of incarcerated activists retroactively narrated their conversion as a spontaneous epiphany (often religious), although such (individual) conversions followed a recognizable form and occurred under the guidance of a group like the Imperial Renovation Society. Similarly, Althusser's theory deflates the debates about who truly converted, or if someone performed a fake conversion (*gisō-tenkō*) in order to escape imprisonment.[53] If anything, the very notion of a fake conversion was an important component animating the further elaboration of ideological subjection: for state officials, such fears legitimated increasing state surveillance and interventions into a convert's life, while for the converts themselves, this fear was internalized and informed their increasing determination to prove the authenticity of their conversion, thereby intensifying the practice of conversion.[54]

Recalling Michel Foucault's theory of disciplinary power discussed in chapter 2, Althusser's thesis more explicitly links the subjectivization that takes place through ideological apparatuses to the productive capacities of the subject.[55] As I discuss in chapters 4 and 5, while on one level the ideologization that took place in ISAs like the Imperial Renovation Society invoked the timeless relationship between the emperor (capital S Subject) and his loyal subjects (small s subjects), conversion was measured through the convert's productive capacity. Following Althusser then, in the process of eliminating the ideological threat against the imperial state, the Imperial Renovation Society and groups like it served to also relink individual subjects to their labor capacities in specific social stations, whether as rural farmers, industrial laborers, educators, or journalists. In these and many other ways, Althusser's theory of ideology provides a lens through which to understand the material practices and institutional forms in which the phenomenon of ideological conversion was generated and managed in interwar Japan.

The Imperial Renovation Society and the Early Contributions of Kobayashi Morito

DEVELOPING THE FORMS AND CONDITIONS FOR CONVERSION

Although Sano Manabu and Nabeyama Sadachika are rightly credited for initiating the mass tenkō of 1933–1934, and so-called tenkō literature, or *tenkō bungaku*, continues to be analyzed to reveal the complexities and anguish of the tenkō experience, the important role played by Kobayashi Morito in the Imperial Renovation Society in the development of tenkō is often overlooked.[56]

Figure 3.4. Soon after the sensational defections of June 1933, newspapers were reporting that the Imperial Renovation Society and its director, Miyagi Chōgorō (pictured), were working to assist thought criminals to convert. "Rehabilitation for Released Thought Criminals: For Converts or Partial Converts," *Yomiuri Shimbun*, August 13, 1933, morning edition.

Kobayashi was a local organizer in Shinano who had joined the JCP in January 1928 and was arrested just two months later in the 3.15 Incident. Through a series of events, he came to occupy a central position within the state's thought rehabilitation apparatus, developing many of the early forms and practices of what later would be called tenkō. Indeed, along with Tokyo thought procurator Hirata Isao, discussed in chapter 2, Kobayashi Morito became the impromptu expert on ideological conversion by the mid-1930s. As the head of the Imperial Renovation Society's Thought Section (Shisōbu) established in 1934, Kobayashi guided hundreds of political detainees to ideologically convert and wrote extensively in official journals explaining the conversion phenomenon and advocating for ideological converts (tenkōsha). In this way, the Imperial Renovation Society and its Thought Section functioned in an intermediary position between political criminals, the state, and the wider community, one that does not fit in the conventional dualistic approach of tenkō as a confrontation between external state coercion and an individual's internal ideas. Indeed, as this chapter argues, it was in such ISAs as the Imperial Renovation Society that the phenomenon of ideological conversion was first developed and refined before becoming official policy in 1936 (see figure 3.4).

Kobayashi Morito was born in northern Nagano Prefecture (Shinano) in 1902, where, as he recounted later in various biographical essays, he became acutely aware of rural poverty and persisting social discrimination.[57] By his own account, Kobayashi's introduction to social activism started in the late 1910s when, in response to the social prejudice he witnessed in his village against Japan's outcaste community (*burakumin*), he started to work with local members of the Zenkoku Suiheisha (Levellers Society) for outcaste rights. Kobayashi's initial concern about social discrimination turned into a wider concern over the increasing impoverishment of small agricultural cultivators in rural Japan, which became particularly severe during the economically turbulent years following World War I. In this context, Kobayashi noted that his localized concerns expanded into a general social consciousness, one wherein the liberation of the outcaste community and rural improvement were inextricably linked to the socioeconomic transformation of Japan in general. After a brief period serving in the Imperial Army, Kobayashi returned to Nagano in the mid-1920s and soon joined various political and labor groups, including the All-Japan Proletarian Youth League (Zennihon musan seinen dōmei). By the late 1920s he was active in the proletarian party movement, heading the local office of the Labor-Farmer Party (Rōdōnōmintō) in preparation for the first general election in 1928.[58] Upon reflection, Kobayashi reported that the more deeply he became involved in social activism, the more he believed that "Marxism was the ultimate truth," portraying his arrival at Marxism (retroactively) in terms of a kind of search for salvation.[59] He officially joined the JCP in January 1928, only to be arrested two months later in the nationwide arrest campaign known as the 3.15 Incident.[60]

Kobayashi later recounted that he "manifested signs of tenkō" during his pretrial investigation in a detention center in Nagano in September 1928, in which he experienced a conflict between his love for his family and his loyalty to his political comrades.[61] These contradictions led Kobayashi to suffer from insomnia and other psychological and physical ailments, which only worsened in prison. In December he was sentenced to a prison term of three and a half years, and was transferred to Ichigaya Prison in Tokyo in January 1929, where his case came under the direction of Miyagi Chōgorō and where he first met Buddhist chaplain Fujii Eshō.[62] Just a few years earlier, Miyagi and Fujii had founded the Imperial Renovation Society in 1926 and served as the society's director and vice director, respectively.[63] Due to his ongoing psychological and physical distress, Kobayashi was transferred to

Toyotama Prison in April, where he started to be more closely counseled by Chaplain Fujii for his psychological distress.[64] As the arrest and prosecution of suspected communists continued into the 1930s, Kobayashi began to meet many other members of the beleaguered JCP in prison. It was also at this time that Kobayashi started studying Pure Land Buddhism texts given to him by Chaplain Fujii. Through such studies he slowly healed his spiritual torment and overcame his physical ailments.[65] Kobayashi was released early for his expression of repentance in December 1931 and, through the invitation of Chaplain Fujii, joined the Imperial Renovation Society in January 1932.[66] He worked for the society until the end of the war in 1945.

As mentioned above, the Imperial Renovation Society was established in 1926 to specifically reform criminal detainees released through the Suspended Indictment and Suspended Sentence policies.[67] The director of the society was Miyagi Chōgorō, who, as section chief of the Rehabilitation Division created by the Justice Ministry in 1921, was an early proponent of rehabilitation (hogo).[68] Chaplain Fujii served as vice director and initiated the reform of thought criminals at the Imperial Renovation Society in 1932.[69] Soon after its formation, the Imperial Renovation Society was heralded as exemplifying the Justice Ministry's emphasis on reform and rehabilitation over punishment and imprisonment. The society was funded by private donations—it was established with funds from Consolidated Electric Company Ltd. (Daidō denryoku) and Tokyo Electric Light Company Ltd. (Tokyo dentō kabushiki gaisha)—and periodically received gifts from the Imperial Household to expand its reform work.[70] Although directed by justice officials and funded through donations from the Imperial Household, the society was staffed by volunteers drawn from the Justice Ministry and assisted by community members and organizations; hence its semiofficial status.

Pursuing its reform mandate, the Imperial Renovation Society provided psychological, spiritual, and material support to criminal detainees in suspension programs, finding them employment, counseling them in family disputes, and serving as their legal guarantors (mimoto hikiuke), among many other services. As we will analyze more closely in chapter 4, although on one level the society was guided by the principles of criminal reform and assistance, it increasingly drew upon imperial ideology to define its work as it took on more ex–thought criminals in the early 1930s. Miyagi explained that the society was organized under the principle of "familyism" (kazokushugi)—a common term among rehabilitation circles at that time—in which all members, whether reformed ex-criminals or guidance counselors, assisted each other, raised funds for the society, and worked together under the benevolent stewardship of Director Miyagi. Portrayed in this way, the Imperial Renovation Society invoked the form and benevolence of the sovereign ghost, becoming a kind of microcosm of the larger Japanese family-nation-state (*kazoku kokka*) and imperial kokutai.

Kobayashi started working at the Imperial Renovation Society in January 1932, just one year after procurators had instituted the Charges Withheld policy for handling thought crime cases. Consequently, the Imperial Renovation Society quickly took on hundreds of ex–political criminals and, following the mass tenkō of 1933–1934, became the center of a nationwide but still loosely organized network of groups working to reform and reintegrate ex–thought criminals into society.[71] In 1934, Kobayashi was named the head of the Imperial Renovation Society's newly established Thought Section (Shisōbu), at which time he became the principal theoretician and expert on tenkō, writing extensively on the subject and advocating for converts in Justice Ministry publications.

"Move Your Lips in Prayer, and You Will Believe": Kobayashi's 1932 Biography

During his first year at the Imperial Renovation Society, Kobayashi made an important contribution to what would later be called ideological conversion by publishing a semiautobiographical book, *Up until Leaving the Communist Party* (1932; *Kyōsantō o dassuru made*).[72] Written under the pen name Ono Yōichi, this text established one of the main forms through which conversion was practiced in ISAs such as the Imperial Renovation Society: namely, introspective autobiography. In other words, beyond what it tells us about Kobayashi's reasons for leaving the JCP, the text is significant for establishing the primary narrative forms for practicing tenkō. Indeed, within a few years, hundreds of other ex-communists would replicate Kobayashi's narrative as they published biographical accounts of their ideological conversions under the auspices of the Imperial Renovation Society.[73]

In this text, Kobayashi utilizes a variety of literary modes such as third-person observation, inner monologue, and historical reportage to weave together a narrative that contrasts his longings for family and his rural origins (*furusato*) with the psychological and physical hardship of prison life as a political criminal. This combination of past and present punctuates the story at key moments, creating a sequence of inversions that ultimately culminates with Ono (Kobayashi) arriving at national consciousness as a Japanese imperial subject, mediated through tropes of Buddhist self-negation and salvation.

At this time, the category tenkō was not used to encompass the various motivations and practices of defection. Consequently, we find Kobayashi using other terms to signify his spiritual transformation and eventual defection from the JCP. Interestingly, Kobayashi's choice of terms changes throughout the text, mirroring the process of his spiritual conversion. For instance, early in the text Kobayashi uses terms with a political connotation such as "a change in direction" (hōkō tenkan)—a common phrase in socialist circles in the 1920s—but then later, he begins to use terms such as revived (sosei), reborn (saisei), total salvation (zettai kyūsai), and self-awakening (jiko no jikaku), which invoke a much more spiritual significance.[74] The performative act of conversion is initiated, at least as Kobayashi retroactively narrated here, in a moment of tortured psychological grief, reflection, and spiritual self-contemplation in a detention center in Nagano. Kobayashi's arrival at imperial consciousness, anticipated at the very outset, invests the various narrative inversions throughout the text with meaning and, recalling Althusser's theory of ideological misrecognition, reflects the retroactive temporality that many conversion narratives of the 1930s share.[75]

THE SPLITTING OF THE SELF: NARRATIVE OF SELF-NEGATION

Kobayashi begins Up until Leaving the Communist Party by briefly describing his arrest (chapter 1), which prompts him to reflect on his activities in a variety of social and political movements (chapters 2 through 5).[76] But the story, so to speak, does not begin until Kobayashi declares that, once in prison, he "gradually had the opportunity to reflect upon himself."[77] Notice here that the intervention of the RSA—that is, Kobayashi's arrest, prosecution, and imprisonment—does not figure prominently into his reflection, rendering the RSA as a kind of vanishing mediator between Kobayashi's participation in the communist movement and his self-reflection in the solitude of a prison cell.[78] At this point, Kobayashi (as Ono) begins to worry that his arrest has impacted others—not just his family but other Nagano activists who might have been arrested because of their affiliation with him. Kobayashi then recalls his village, remembering events with his family and noting nostalgically how the mountains that enveloped his village were where "dreams" and "utopia are born," a nostalgic longing that "instilled in him a sense of beauty."[79] These reflections on origins produce a conflict between Kobayashi's twin loyalties: one to his comrades, the other to his family and origins.[80] This division in loyalties—between the Soviet Union and the Japanese Empire, mediated by the Communist Party and his family respectively—is inflected into Kobayashi's own being, producing what he calls a "splitting of the self" (*jiko bunretsu*).[81]

Recalling the metaphor of the ghost in the machine that guides our analysis, Kobayashi's splitting of the self does not remain limited to his antagonistic loyalties but rather soon manifests as a fissure between his own spirit and body. The sequence begins with a psychological (*seishinteki*) dilemma: political commitments are tested by antagonistic loyalties, which then manifest physically in insomnia, weight loss, blackouts, and declining physical health.[82] As his condition worsens, Kobayashi worries that there are only two conclusions to such a split: his spirit falling into madness (*kyō*) or the death of his body (*shi*). At this point Kobayashi contemplates suicide, which, if carried out, would be the culmination of his existential split. He is soon saved, however, when, as "by fate," he meets the Buddhist chaplain Fujii Eshō at Ichigaya Prison, who "guided Ono [Kobayashi] toward rebirth."[83] Later in 1929, when Kobayashi is transferred to Toyotama Prison due to his declining health, he comes under Chaplain Fujii's direct counseling. It is through Chaplain Fujii's teachings of Pure Land Buddhism and the books he recommends that Kobayashi further mends his twin ailments.[84] Kobayashi reports that he (Ono) starts to focus on finding a balance between mind and body: Kobayashi begins to meditate and regulate caloric intake (body), and, through Chaplain Fujii's guidance, he delves further into Buddhist texts (spirit).[85] Although he makes great strides in healing his psychological and physical ailments, it is only with the ideological "erasure of Marxism" (*marukishizumu no seisan*), through Buddhist reflection, that his spiritual and physical health are finally restored and brought back into harmony (*gacchi*).[86] Here, health is equated with the correspondence between mind and body (not to mention defection from his communist affiliations), and, with this, Kobayashi arrives at a new basis of Buddhist faith. From this position, Kobayashi sets out to explain Ono's journey through the communist movement into his new appreciation of Japan's unique imperial kokutai.

SUBLATION OF THE WILL AND THE ETHICS OF SELF-SACRIFICE

Reflecting back on his political activism from his jail cell, Kobayashi explains that the deeper his political commitments, the more he came to believe that "Marxism was the ultimate truth." Thus by entering the party, Kobayashi admits he felt more "powerful."[87] In hindsight, he realizes that this was false: his sense of empowerment was only his ego led astray by the pride that came with identifying himself with the proletarian movement. Through his study of Shinran and True Pure Land Buddhism, Kobayashi came to realize that only by "discarding his pride as a prior member of the proletarian movement" could "the total salvation of his ego" occur, rendering defection a necessary step toward healing his spiritual-psychological distress.[88] In Kobayashi's narrative of self-negation, then, his prior politics are retroactively reduced to false pride. Described in these terms, the only solution open to Kobayashi was to "discard with the ego [*jiko*]"—and, by implication, the politics that served as a vehicle for false pride—in order to be sublated (*shiyō*) back into the world, informed by a new Buddhist ethics of selfless commitment to others.[89]

In contrast to the vulgar Marxist critique of religion, wherein religion is reduced to false consciousness that obscures social reality, Kobayashi counters that Buddhist inspired self-negation is necessary for one to be sublated into, and active in, society. He explains that human beings' awareness of secular imperfection and the longing for salvation that this produces is what makes humans, however limited, strive for self-improvement and ethically committed to society. Kobayashi believes it necessary for humans to desire to enter "the world of salvation"—the world of Buddha—in order to give their lives meaning.[90] He rhetorically asks: although religion "negates the self, one that is imperfect in reality . . . is this not the ceaseless advance to the world of Buddha, in other words . . . to the world of perfection?"[91] Through such reasoning, Kobayashi's earlier attention to society as the site of class contradiction and social discrimination, knowable through social analysis and political activism, is here converted into a religious ontology of the self that, prior to any social praxis, must be negated through the Other-Power (*tariki*) of Buddhist grace.[92] This radically alters Kobayashi's understanding of society and social praxis: religion was no longer the obstacle to social awareness as communists would argue—that is, false consciousness—but became the very basis for social praxis through self-negation and the resulting ethos of self-sacrifice. And, as mentioned earlier, such an understanding retroactively portrayed his Marxist commitments simply as a failed search for salvation.[93]

Although Kobayashi continues to refer to the unavoidable social dislocations in Japan, which had only become more acute following the Shōwa Financial Panic in 1927 and the subsequent worldwide Great Depression, he now believes class struggle to be the illusory effect of Marxism's "ideology of struggle" (*tōsōshugi*).[94] Consequently, Kobayashi refers to his defection and conversion as a departure from the "world of struggle" (*tōsō no sekai*) to the "world of religion" (*shūkyō no sekai*), initiated by the question, "As humans, do we only exist in a world of daily struggle?"[95] Kobayashi's new standpoint is no longer immanent within the social field of capitalist contradiction and exploitation, but rather from a presumed transcendent domain of religious universalism that, before any ethical praxis could take place in society, began by emphasizing human imperfection and self-negation.

SPIRITUAL DEPOLITICIZATION AND THE REIDENTIFICATION WITH THE IMPERIAL STATE

Once Kobayashi had outlined his newly found religious ethics, the next step in the narrative was to erase any remaining remnants of Marxism that might influence his view of the world. Tellingly, Kobayashi delivers the final blow to Marxism through an analysis of the state, which necessarily requires him to articulate the basic tenets of imperial state ideology. Kobayashi had touched on this earlier in the text when he reflected on his family and village, inspiring the "first step" in his "change of direction."[96] There, Kobayashi began to contemplate his commitment to Marxism-Leninism and came to believe that his political and ideological errors converged in his disposition toward "the state process" (*kokka katei*).[97] The important displacement that takes place in this section is between what Kobayashi refers to as the "world state" posited by communism (*sekai kokka*) and the "family state" of Japan (*kazoku kokka*). At a general level, Kobayashi's critique of revolutionary communism is that an international socialist state was impossible, both in the current global situation of the early 1930s and due to its discrepancy with Japan's unique national essence (kokutai). He is inspired to consider such questions, he writes, when nostalgically reflecting on his family and rural village: "Ono's sentimental world of his past made him reflect on recent incidents. Beyond the question of whether materialism was good or bad, Ono was troubled by the problem related to the state process. A world state! Although this is . . . a grand ideal, in reality this is nothing but a fantasy [*kūsō*]. If the present Japanese nation is based on the simple economic position of the proletariat, does this make it similar [*kyōtsū*] to Soviet Russia? [He] came to wonder, is not Japanese national consciousness stronger [than the ideal of a world state]?"[98] Such doubts lead Kobayashi to ruminate on the particularity of the Japanese nation-state later in the text, where he draws upon the mythos of a three-thousand-year relationship between the state (i.e., the imperial household) and the people of the nation, which had been nurtured and solidified by geography and climate.[99] Mediated by his family ancestry, the effect is that Kobayashi's sociopolitical analysis leads to a political disassociation from internationalism: "Ono considered that, as humans continue to confront the process of the world state . . . [they] must also grasp the Japanese state, the bounded society [*shūdan shakai*] of the Japanese nation. Ono knew that the blood in his own body flowed along with the masses of contemporary Japan."[100]

This dissociation then leads Kobayashi to reidentify with the Japanese nation: "Ono lived as one with this flow. No matter how he may try, Ono could not become a European or an American. In other words . . . the blood of the Japanese nation, which has a three-thousand-year history, moves through Ono's veins. Therefore, first, one had to affirm [kōtei] that one was Japanese. No, it is not to affirm oneself as Japanese, one is Japanese."[101] As we see here, Kobayashi's displacement of the world state with the family state necessarily leads to the displacement of class by nation, which he portrays as the descent from abstract idealism (communism) to the objective ground of national belonging (nativism).[102] Later in the text, Kobayashi connects his new appreciation of the nation to the imperial state, arguing that the state is "something that makes territory and blood coterminous" (ittei no tochi ittei no chi o onajifu suru mono) and is "organized to secure life and property" of each member of the nation.[103] Ironically, we could read these two state operations summarized in the two objects that the Peace Preservation Law was to protect: that is, kokutai and the private property system. Kobayashi extrapolates that, as such, the state "thus expresses the total unification of social relations." He concludes, "in a territory without a state, social life cannot be established"; it is the state itself "which must integrate the nation."[104] In this respect, Kobayashi reasons that a purely social existence, that is, the socialist future in which the state would eventually wither away, could not possibly exist.

Attempting to undermine a vulgar base-superstructure dichotomy, Kobayashi notes that economic relations are merely one aspect of national life:

> Of course, the fact that economic relations are extremely important is not wrong, but for the nation [kokumin], are economic relations more important than the state [kokka]? By calling, "workers of the world, unite!" Marx said that "workers have no country," but do the various economic relationships transcend the state process? Are they the basis of [national society]? Are the people reducible to economic relations? Do these relations condition the state? It was not just that Ono felt doubts about this, but that he knew that national consciousness was the one thing that transcended these economic relations.[105]

With Kobayashi's affirmation of the imperial state and his newly found national consciousness, the social dislocations that first brought Kobayashi to the socialist movement are recast as a predicament afflicting the imperial polity (kokutai). Kobayashi's social praxis is predicated on harnessing his new imperial subjectivity in order to confront the social issues afflicting the imperial kokutai.

THE NARRATIVE FORM OF RELIGIOUS TENKŌ

This 1932 text is an early example of what would later be classified by the state as a "religious tenkō" (shūkyō tenkō), in which spiritual faith replaced Marxism as a new ethos for social praxis.[106] As we saw above, Kobayashi constructed his narrative of religious salvation through a series of ideological displacements—internationalism by nationalism, class by culture, social contradiction by spiritual sublimation, political activism by self-negation—that lead to the ultimate displacement of his earlier belief in the ultimate truth (zettai no shinri) of Marxism with a total faith (zettai na shinkō) in Buddhist compassion. However, what Kobayashi fails to confront in this text is that, in such a narrative, Buddhism is reduced to merely a means or method to reidentify with the imperial state and its founding ideology. Ironically, Kobayashi's religious conversion did not culminate in him expounding a religious universalism nor entering into monastic life, but rather served as a means for him to reidentify with imperial ideology in order to assist the state to reform other political criminals. The eclipse of Buddhist universalism by Kobayashi's reidentification with the imperial state is most clearly exemplified in the conclusion of this 1932 text.

Here, Kobayashi celebrates the "creation of a new Manchuria" (i.e., Japan's seizure of Manchuria in September 1931), which, he believes, will allow Japan "to break through the deadlocks" of its current socioeconomic conditions.[107] Kobayashi calls for the eradication of "big-monopoly capital" and the creation of a "communal society" (kyōdō shakai) with small farmers and workers at its core. This, Kobayashi concludes, would accord with "Japan's national character" (Nippon no kokuminsei). In these new circumstances, Kobayashi explains that it was his (Ono's) "personal destiny" to take up his "national duty" and assist with the creation of a "new Japan" (shin Nippon), consisting of an expanded national state extending to Manchuria. Only by securing Manchuria and fortifying the imperial state could the national economy be restored, thus relieving the suffering of the laboring masses.[108]

While not denying Kobayashi's religious morality or his sincerity in helping others, we must recognize that such sincerity became a vehicle for Kobayashi to reidentify with the imperial state and to proactively assist the Justice Ministry to reform ex-political criminals as loyal and productive imperial subjects.

One has to make a choice and, even when one does not choose (consciously, after the 'crisis of conscience' that is one of the sacred rituals to be observed in such cases), the choice makes itself. —LOUIS ALTHUSSER, *On the Reproduction of Capitalism*

DEVELOPING THE RITUALS OF AN EMERGING IDEOLOGICAL STATE APPARATUS

Kobayashi published *Up until Leaving the Communist Party* in November 1932, only seven months before the sensational defections of Sano Manabu and Nabeyama Sadachika in June 1933. In addition to this biographical account, Kobayashi also began writing articles in the journal *Hogo Jihō* (*Aid and Guidance*), a monthly bulletin in which wardens, justice officials, ex-convicts, prison chaplains, and reform advocates regularly published articles on their experiences with criminal rehabilitation.[109] *Hogo Jihō* was the successor of an earlier publication produced by the Hoseikai, a parolee aid group established in 1912 that had pioneered criminal reform efforts in the 1910s.[110] Throughout the 1920s, the *Bulletin of the Hoseikai* (*Hoseikai Kaihō*) and its successor, *Hogo Jihō*, carried many articles celebrating the rehabilitation of delinquent youths and other criminal parolees. By 1931, *Hogo Jihō* started publishing articles addressing the rehabilitation of thought criminals, which was becoming a pressing question for justice officials who were overseeing the cases of communists completing their prison sentences or recently arrested communists placed in the newly established Charges Withheld program. In this context, Kobayashi was solicited to address the unique challenges and early successes with reforming thought criminals in the Imperial Renovation Society.[111]

In June 1933, the same month that the Sano-Nabeyama letter was issued, Kobayashi published an important article for *Hogo Jihō*, titled "How We Must Reform Thought Criminals: Based on the Experiments in the Imperial Renovation Society," in which he outlined the challenges and emerging forms for rehabilitating political criminals.[112] This article is revealing, for it provides a summary of how political rehabilitation was conceived on the eve of the mass tenkō of 1933–1934. Additionally, Kobayashi names the conversion process "tenkō" in this article, requiring that we recognize that officials and criminal reformers were already categorizing a political or ideological conversion as tenkō that spring.[113] Indeed, the month before this article was published in the June issue of *Hogo Jihō*, Tokyo District Court procurators had already outlined new "rehabilitation" procedures for "thought criminals who ideologically convert" (*tenkō shisō hannin*) at a May 12 meeting.[114] In other words, on the eve of the sensational Sano-Nabeyama defection, the state was already formulating a set of procedures to assist and facilitate what they were increasingly referring to as tenkō.

Kobayashi begins by noting that by this time in 1933, hundreds of thought criminals that were arrested in the 1928–1929 roundups had either served their full prison sentences or had been granted suspended sentences. While many of these ex-offenders were living as normal citizens (*shakaijin to shite no seikatsu*), they were also under the combined surveillance of local police as well as the Special Higher Police, which distinguished their postparole experiences from those of regular parolees. In reference to the process of tenkō, Kobayashi emphasizes that there were a number of distinctions within the phenomenon. Importantly, Kobayashi distinguishes between five types of tenkō:

1 Democratic socialist: Those who simply move from an illegal movement [communist movement] to a legal movement.
2 National socialist: Those who recognize Japanese particularity and thus convert from internationalism to a socialism based on nationalism.
3 Those who truly break [with politics]: Those who come to feel a fundamental difference with Marxism's worldview of dialectical materialism, and convert to the world of religion based on a spiritual life.
4 The so-called dissolutionist faction: Those who revise their [political] strategy in recognition of Japan's particularity.
5 Others: Those who did not fully believe in Marxism and, without [replacing Marxism] with another, applicable worldview, simply break with the movement.[115]

Anticipating his readers' concerns over a convert's continued political commitments, Kobayashi admits that the democratic socialist, national socialist, and dissolutionist faction types do pose challenges: in particular, by remaining in the "realm of the political movement," such converts are susceptible to dangerous political influences.[116] Yet Kobayashi argues that officials should not overlook the other types of conversion, that is, the nonpolitical converts. In the latter cases, Kobayashi notes that although these converts have come to recognize "our kokutai" and have returned to the Japanese nation, he argues that "religious reflection" (*shūkyō hansei*) is necessary to guard against this reidentification becoming a "narrow-minded, exclusionary nationalism" (*henkyō na haitateki kokuminshugi*).[117] This is particularly necessary for those converts who never fully accepted Marxism as a "guiding principle" (*shidō seishin*) to begin with; that is, Category 5. Interestingly, Kobayashi is arguing that such a principle—although not Marxism—was necessary for converts to return to society, so they could face the various problems afflicting Japanese society in the mid-1930s. In this light, reform was a "movement of moral suasion" (*kyōka undō*) in which officials needed to instill moral principles in ex-convicts so that they could function in society.[118] We will see in chapter 4 how Kobayashi's concern for locating a new social ethics for reformed criminals will transform in the years ahead and become one of the primary endeavors of the burgeoning thought rehabilitation system mid-decade.

Although Kobayashi provides some details on current reform efforts in this 1933 article, he uses this forum to urge justice officials to grasp the importance and underlying principles of reforming thought criminals. In this regard, Kobayashi outlines three main principles guiding reform work (*hogo jigyō*). First, he stresses that rehabilitation—political or otherwise—takes place between people and as such is a product of human bonds. Recalling Althusser's theory of ISAs, Kobayashi notes that although "material facilities" such as the Imperial Renovation Society are important, it is the "spiritual connections" (*seishinteki tsunagari*) that are produced in such sites that are most important.[119] Second, he contends that guidance must not extinguish a convert's "sense of justice" (*seigishin*). He explains that the appeal of Marxism is that it counters the atomization and the "ideology of individualism" (*kojinshugiteki shisō*) of capitalist society with an ethic of social concern and commitment, implying that this sense of justice can be rechanneled toward endeavors that do not threaten the imperial state.[120] Third, Kobayashi argues that in order to develop "clear principles for guidance" (*meikaku ni shidō seishin*), officials must truly understand the "consciousness of conversion" (*tenkō no ishiki*).[121] These principles reveal how the administration of the Peace Preservation Law was combining new disciplinary procedures for the production of imperial subjectivity with the original intention of the law to suppress communists as threats to the imperial sovereign.

With these fundamental principles established, Kobayashi writes about other elements of the reform effort, including the particular challenges related to employment, as well as the potential role for families and other outside groups to foster and support defection and/or conversion.[122] Taken together, this article provides a unique window into the policies and practices that were being developed in ISAs like the Imperial Renovation Society, and how such policies were already in formation before the sensational defection of Sano Manabu and Nabeyama Sadachika.

FORMALIZING TENKŌ AS REHABILITATION POLICY

As we saw above, procurators and reformers were already discussing administrative protocols for thought criminals who were converting before Sano and Nabeyama's letter was issued in June 1933. Immediately following the publication of this letter, hundreds of other incarcerated party members followed suit, publishing their own "tenkō declarations" (*tenkō seimei*). As sensational media reports of the Sano-Nabeyama defection introduced the term "tenkō" to the wider public, state officials were busy trying to assess the significance of this development and what further protocols were needed to sustain the wave of conversion. Furthermore, many conservatives expressed skepticism about these conversions and critiqued the Justice Ministry's liberal treatment of such dangerous threats against the imperial kokutai.

As the conversions of JCP members continued, procurators and reformers were busy establishing the significance of the conversion phenomenon. For instance, Hirata Isao wrote an article in *Hōritsu Shimbun* (*Legal Times*) that August, in which he explained how justice officials persuaded thought criminals to convert. Recalling Althusser's claim that the family was one of the most important ISAs functioning in capitalist society, Hirata explained, "The foundation for performing tenkō is love for one's family. This is the unique characteristic of Japan's family system [*kazoku seido*]. To consider this more generally, Japan's national spirit is as a large family with the emperor at its center, and, as such, is unshakable. This unmovable national spirit is the source of the sentiments we use to have a thought criminal ideologically convert."[123]

Additionally, *Hogo Jihō* published multiple essays on thought crime following the Sano-Nabeyama defection, attempting to situate this sensational event within the wider work of criminal rehabilitation. Only one month after the Sano-Nabeyama defection was publicized, the July issue of *Hogo Jihō* included multiple articles related to thought crime, including general articles explaining the thought problem (*shisō mondai*), a report from a recent convert who was released from jail, and a critique of Sano and Nabeyama's continuing commitment to socialist politics after their tenkō, as well as a record of an important weeklong conference addressing the theme of the significance and methods for rehabilitating thought criminals throughout the empire.[124]

This conference, held between June 24 and 30 in Tokyo, was attended by over fifty procurators, chaplains, guidance counselors, and other officials from throughout the empire, including Keijō Korea.[125] Officials from the Tokyo District Court and the Justice and Education ministries as well as private national culture research groups lectured on such topics as the existing laws regulating thought crime, the history of the JCP, the recent "change in direction" witnessed in thought criminals, the Japanese spirit, thought crime policies in other countries, critiques of Marxism-Leninism, and moral guidance (kyōka) of political criminals.[126] Lectures such as "The Singular Truth of the Japanese Nation" ("Nippon kokumin no shinri tokuisei"), given by Justice Undersecretary Minagawa Haruhiro, and "The Return to Japan" ("Nihon e no fukki"), by literature professor Kihira Tadayoshi, demonstrate that rehabilitation was increasingly infused with the ideology of the imperial state. Indeed, in his lecture "The Japanese Spirit and the Contemporary Social Movement," the ex-socialist-turned-nationalist Akamatsu Katsumaro argued that the rise of "dangerous thought" (kiken shisō) such as communism in Japan should be attributed to the "liberal education" and its notions of "individualism" (liberalism) and "classism" (socialism). Akamatsu called for the instruction of "Japanism" as a "third ideology" (daisanshugi) that could overcome the dichotomy of capitalist individualism and socialist classism.[127] In addition to lectures on these themes, materials were passed out that provided procurators with examples of recent conversions, including copies of the Sano-Nabeyama letter, statistics related to the radicalization of students, a report on the ideological transformation of a Korean communist, and copies of Kobayashi Morito's conversion biography, Up until Leaving the Communist Party, published the year before.[128] Through such gatherings, reform officials were organizing the practice of converting thought criminals on a wider scale.

Narratives of Religious Tenkō: Tenkōsha Memoirs (1933)

SITUATING TENKŌ BETWEEN REPRESSION AND REHABILITATION

Soon after the Sano-Nabeyama defection, ex-communist "ideological converts" (tenkōsha) would also reflect on the significance of their apostasies and write about their own experiences. For instance, a collection titled Tenkōsha Memoirs (Tenkōsha no shuki) was published in November 1933, only six months after the Sano-Nabeyama defection.[129] This volume collected essays by recent converts, many of whom had received guidance from Kobayashi, Chaplain Fujii, and others at the Imperial Renovation Society in Tokyo. Consequently, the various essays in this volume represented the conversion experience as a religious transformation and followed the narrative template that Kobayashi had developed in his own 1932 conversion biography analyzed earlier. Indeed, this collection established biography as one of the primary ritualized practices of conversion—religious or otherwise— overseen by the Imperial Renovation Society.

Tenkōsha Memoirs is prefaced by a short essay written by the head of the Justice Ministry's Corrections Department, Shiono Suehiko, who connected tenkō to efforts to suppress communism in the Japanese Empire.[130] Shiono oversaw the 3.15 and 4.16 arrest campaigns as justice minister, and thus began his essay by recounting the alarm over the appearance of communism in Japan: "How can we prevent this troubling thought crime from emerging from our own homes? How can we extinguish [*tatsu*] the trace of the turbulent and radicalized red students in our universities and vocational schools? And how will we be able to eradicate once and for all [*kaijo sōmetsu*] the ideological activists from among the national people?"[131]

This latter effort begins, Shiono explained, by recognizing that thought criminals were still members of the national polity, and thus the eradication of communist ideology could be accomplished through a reform policy that emphasized excavating the thought criminal's essential Japanese spirit: "In my opinion, these communists, i.e., those who have dangerous, extreme thought [*fuon kageki naru shisō*], were born from this land [*tsuchi ni sei o uketa*] and as such are members of the Japanese nation. The Japanese spirit, a spirit cultivated for three thousand years, flows through their veins. Naturally, then, they are of the Japanese nation [*nihon no kokumin*]."[132]

Thus, he explained, the essays collected in this volume detail how communists, once in jail, can begin the process of "deep self-reflection, awaken to religious faith, eradicate their past crimes [i.e., ideas] and be reborn through the truth of the traditional Japanese spirit."[133] Along with Kobayashi's 1932 semiautobiography, this collection was to be read as a manual on how to convert.

Shiono's preface was followed by an introduction by the editor of *Tenkōsha Memoirs*, Saotome Yūgorō. Saotome took this opportunity to critique Sano and Nabeyama's political conversion to national socialism as "simply a politico-practical change in direction" (*tan ni seijiteki, jissenteki hōkōtenkan*). Such a conversion—what he called "a lateral tenkō" (*yoko no tenkō*)—lacked the deep self-reflection, sincere repentance, and spiritual conversion exemplified in *Tenkōsha Memoirs*.[134] For Saotome, the deficiencies of Sano and Nabeyama's new national socialism revealed a much deeper spiritual crisis afflicting Japan in 1933: "Japan is facing simultaneously emergencies abroad and an ideological emergency [shisōteki hijōji] at home. Some intellectuals see this ideological emergency as arising from the deficiencies in the structure of society [shakai-sōshiki], but this is to see only one side of the problem. As a result of the loss of [our] religious spirit due to the Westernization of thought [ōka shisō], [we overlook] the issue of materialism and self-centeredness, wherein one emphasizes one's own interests and desires."[135]

Indeed, Saotome was implying that the social crisis that Japan faced was, at its core, a crisis of spirit; only after the Japanese spirit was recuperated and fortified could social reform efforts then begin. By anchoring objective social deficiencies to materialism and self-centeredness, Saotome inverted the objective dislocations witnessed throughout Japanese society at the time as resulting from ideas and moral dispositions, effectively masking the constitutive social contradictions of capitalism. Saotome argued that reformed ex–thought criminals expressed a passion for social issues and reform, a passion that had been misdirected into communism: "Communists are searching for truth. They are promising young men and women who have a burning passion. If Marxists redirect [tenjite] their search and their passion onto the path of religion, they will be able to find . . . the one source of power for social reform. This means that they must completely purify themselves, look deeper into themselves, and return to their own true inner essence [jiko honrai no shinmenmoku]."[136] This essence, of course, was as an imperial subject who, having returned to the fold of the imperial kokutai, could labor to reform the deficiencies afflicting Japanese society.[137]

The contributors to Tenkōsha Memoirs were not leaders or theoreticians in the JCP, and thus we can read the book as addressing rank-and-file communists.[138] The different social backgrounds and statuses of the contributors encompassed all sectors of Japanese society, ranging from farmers and rural organizers (Yamaguchi Hayato) to a college student (Nagai Tetsuzō), a female activist involved in the women's liberation movement (Kojima Yuki), and an industrial laborer (Uchimura Shigeru), among other variants.[139] The cumulative effect was that, although their respective class positions continued to determine their choices upon being released from jail, they all shared a similar conversion experience informed by Buddhism, which returned them to being loyal and productive imperial subjects.[140] In this way, the nine biographical essays largely followed the template established by Kobayashi in his earlier Up until Leaving the Communist Party, as the authors recount their story by following the established narrative structure: from youthful idealism to participating in the communist movement, their arrest, a moment of self-criticism inspired by love and shame for one's own family, harnessing religion to quell one's psychological torment, an epiphanic religious conversion, and finally their discovery of imperial consciousness and a return to the national polity. Each essay has a discrete terminus, a narrative conclusion, which, at this early point in tenkō's conceptualization, implied that the conversion process concluded when one returned to the national polity. With this return, each person could now fulfill his or her respective imperial duties as wife, laborer, farmer, or intellectual.

Kojima Yuki's narrative was typical in this regard.[141] Her essay, titled "Before Receiving Buddha's Grace" ("Daihi no ote ni sugaru made"), begins with Kojima reflecting on her "ideals of youth" (*wakaki hi no risō*), which were cultivated when she studied at a women's school in Tokyo. At this time, Kojima recounts, she sought a principle upon which to live her life, and found this in the Meiji ideology of "good wife, wise mother" (*ryōsai kenbō-shugi*).[142] However, upon reading social-tragedy novels (*shakai higeki*) and contemplating the inequality and contradictions of modern society, Kojima began to question the principle of good wife, wise mother. This led her to read socialist literature that directly addressed the inequalities that she saw around her. In socialist and Marxist theorists such as Babel, Engels, Lenin, Luxemburg, and Marx, Kojima recounts that she discovered a "theory to transform the irrational social structure."[143] Kojima found in Marxism "a logical explanation of the world," and it was at this time that she decided to join the communist movement in order to put this theory into practice.

Similar to Kobayashi, Kojima explained her decision to join the movement in terms of self-determination. She explained that at the time she believed that her "power as one individual was insignificant," but that if she joined the communist movement, her "own power would merge with this group and become grand."[144] After joining, she committed all her time and energy to political activities. She worked tirelessly "for the new society to come," but in the process she had sacrificed her friends, family, and her own health. She lamented, "My mother, my brother, my family—I sacrificed it all for the party, for the movement. . . . My total existence was for the party."[145] Upon her arrest, Kojima was held at a detention center in which her psychological and physical health declined. It was at this moment that she started receiving letters from her mother, which spurred Kojima to nostalgically reflect on her life with her family in contrast to the cold detention center. This reflection led Kojima to realize she had sacrificed her family for the movement.[146] Upon reflection, her "ideals of youth" were nothing but the "ignorance of youth" (*wakage no itari*): "When I think about it now, I have come to consider it as the ignorance of youth. Drunk with the brilliance of revolutionary theory and the beauty of the label of 'militant,' I had lost sight of my true self. Now, I have returned to my position as an ordinary woman [*heibon na ichijosei*] and decided I need to start over again from this basis."[147]

Although she resolved to break with the movement, Kojima was tormented by the prospect of betraying her comrades. Similar to Kobayashi's biography, Kojima explains that her dilemma was resolved when she accepted the love and mercy of Buddha, which was symbolized by her mother's "eternal love."[148] The result was that Kojima accepted her limitations and ultimately blamed thought crime on "humans' insufficient understanding of their own weaknesses."[149] Upon being released from jail early for expressing repentance, she returned to Akita Prefecture and married.

Kobayashi Morito contributed two essays to *Tenkōsha Memoirs*, one essay written under the pen name Ono Yōichi, titled "How a Marxist Had a Religious Experience in Prison," and a concluding essay under his own name, titled "Where the Tenkōsha are Going," forecasting the future role of tenkōsha in Japanese society. The first essay was a summary of Kobayashi's earlier biography, *Up until Leaving the Communist Party*, in which he described his (Ono's) conversion as "a Copernican shift [*koperunikusuteki na kaiten*]" wherein more than his "worldview changing in an opposite direction," his "self was situated within the realm of Buddha" (*jiko o nyorai no ichi ni tenchi shita*).[150] Kobayashi concludes the volume with another essay—this time written under his own name—in which he contemplates the future of ex-communists who have ideologically converted.[151] Here Kobayashi celebrated tenkōsha for reforming themselves and returning to the national polity with renewed determination, exclaiming, "Although these people have broken with the Communist Party, this is not their downfall [*botsuraku*], but the essential sublation of their selves [*jiko o honshitsuteki ni shiyō*]. Without losing their concern for social justice, they are living new lives with determination and vigor."[152] Whereas Shiono Suehiko introduced *Tenkōsha Memoirs* by defining the significance of tenkō within the larger effort to eradicate communism from the national polity, here Kobayashi was providing a more affirming and positive content to the phenomenon: that is, as reformed imperial subjects, tenkōsha were working diligently in their respective social stations for the imperial nation.[153] Within a few years, the figuration of reformed tenkōsha would become increasingly ideological, as they became models for the proactively loyal and productive imperial subject working tirelessly for the nation.

Consolidating the Mass Tenkō of 1933–1934

THE EXPANSION OF IDEOLOGICAL CONVERSION IN JAPAN IN 1934

The publication of *Tenkōsha Memoirs* in November 1933 was part of the state's larger effort to encourage and expand conversion among the population of detained communists.[154] This effort was extremely successful: it was reported that by 1935, of the 650 communists sentenced and in jail, 505 (almost 78 percent) had or were in the process of declaring tenkō.[155] This was in addition to the hundreds who had already declared tenkō while in the Charges Withheld or Suspend Sentences programs, or once paroled. These successes led to an ever-expanding typology of ideological conversion. For instance, in 1936 the state reported the following types and motivations among 324 cases of tenkō in the Japanese home islands: love and concern for one's family (42.6 percent), national self-consciousness (22.5 percent), discarding Marxist theory (12.4 percent), regret (7.7 percent), health or psychological issues (7.4 percent), religious faith (6.2 percent), and other (1.2 percent).[156] Within a few years, the innocuous motivations classified would slowly be overshadowed by more ideological classifications of tenkō, particularly following Japan's invasion of China in July 1937.

It is important to note, however, that none of the contributors to *Tenkōsha Memoirs* were from colonial Korea or Koreans working or studying in metropolitan Japan. This is despite the fact that Koreans were active in the JCP, with many colonial activists seeing communist revolution in Japan as the first step in the liberation of Korea.[157] It was only in 1935 that Kobayashi and other reform counselors started to address the particular issues facing Korean converts, which I explore further in chapter 4.[158] In contrast to its successful implementation in the Japanese metropole, tenkō did not become a widespread phenomenon among activists in colonial Korea until much later in the decade.

Returning to the activities of the Imperial Renovation Society, one official source cites that almost one thousand parolees had received assistance from the society by mid-1934, and we can surmise that many of the more recent parolees were ideological converts.[159] Recall that the society officially established a Thought Section in 1934 and named Kobayashi as its head. Kobayashi recounted later that in the midst of the mass tenkō, thirty ex–thought criminals per month came to the Imperial Renovation Society looking for assistance, turning the society's Thought Section into what he called later "a kind of large rest stop" (*ōkina teishajō no yō na mono*) for released thought criminals.[160] Moreover, at this time, regional tenkōsha support groups and research groups on national culture and thought started to form across the empire, as I explore in chapter 4. These groups expanded the coverage of political rehabilitation ISAS beyond Tokyo, replicating the forms and practices first developed in the Imperial Renovation Society.

The increasing population of paroled converts and the establishment of regional reform associations led to increased calls for the state to provide more support for such reform efforts. Such funding would support a range of welfare services to released converts, including employment counseling, industrial skill training, assisting students to return to school, temporary housing and medical treatment, marriage mediation, legal assistance, and finally providing resources such as library facilities, lecture series, study groups, and a publishing house so that tenkōsha could write about and fortify their ideological conversions. Additionally, this funding would enable reform groups to advocate for tenkōsha, making sure that local police and society at large understood that, as Kobayashi would write in 1935, "yesterday's enemy has become today's ally."[161] As we will see in the next chapter, this increasing attention to reintegrating political criminals into society inspired the state to establish an empire-wide network of official centers to oversee the conversion and social reintegration of political activists.

Conclusion: Ideological State Apparatuses and the Mass Tenkō of 1933–1934

As I have explored in this chapter, Kobayashi Morito and the Imperial Renovation Society developed the early forms and categories that the Justice Ministry would utilize to direct the mass tenkō of 1933–1934. In this way, we can understand the Imperial Renovation Society as what Louis Althusser theorized as an Ideological State Apparatus, in which political criminals were guided to reidentify as imperial subjects—whether through religious, familial, or other means—thus manifesting the ghost of imperial subjectivity. Having been reformed, ex–political criminals returned to their respective social stations and demonstrated their reform by being productive laborers for the nation.

In the wake of the mass tenkō of 1933–1934, we see the Imperial Renovation Society and other newly established reform groups increasingly defining their reform efforts through imperial state ideology. Of course, this ideological element had guided the Imperial Renovation Society since it was established in 1926 (as its name suggests). However, as I explore in chapter 4, as the state worked to expand and formalize the rehabilitation apparatus for thought criminals, such efforts were infused with the tenets of imperial state ideology, invoking the corollary ghost of the imperial subject who would be loyal to the sovereign and his imperial state. In the coming years, tenkōsha would increasingly interpret and narrate their personal experiences of defection and/or ideological apostasy through the tenets of imperial ideology.

Similar to how the mass arrest campaigns of the late 1920s led to the reform efforts of the early 1930s, the mass tenkō of 1933–1934 produced its own unique administrative problems. These problems inspired many officials within the Justice Ministry to campaign for expanding and streamlining the rehabilitation system for the hundreds of thought criminals who were at various stages of conversion. Approached in this way, such a process reveals how the Peace Preservation Law was a dynamic apparatus, transforming and manifesting different modalities of power in order to respond to changing circumstances. As I will explore in the next chapter, by the mid-1930s, the challenge for justice officials was to find ways to nurture morals in tenkōsha in order to guard against ideological recidivism and secure their conversion (*tenkō no kakuho*) without constant state oversight.

Nurturing the Ideological Avowal:
Toward the Codification of Tenkō in 1936

Their concrete, material behavior is simply the inscription in life of the admirable words of the prayer: "*Amen—So be it!*" —LOUIS ALTHUSSER, *On the Reproduction of Capitalism*

The Expansion of Political Rehabilitation in the Mid-1930s

By the mid-1930s, tens of thousands of suspected communists and other thought criminals had been arrested under the Peace Preservation Law, while ideological conversion (tenkō) swept through the population of detainees in the Japanese metropole.[1] Although the Japanese Communist Party (JCP) had been effectively eliminated as an organization by 1935, and while there were imprisoned communists who refused to declare tenkō—the so-called nonconverts or *hi-tenkōsha*—the more pressing challenge that justice officials faced was tracking the rehabilitation of the large and varied population of thought criminals, including those who had yet to be indicted and others serving prison sentences, as well as those who had been released back into society upon declaring tenkō.[2] Thus following the mass tenkō of 1933–1934, justice officials looked to groups like the Imperial Renovation Society and began to consider establishing a system that could support conversion and monitor thought criminals. What we find emerging at this time are officials considering, more than simply extending and intensifying surveillance, how to develop methods and practices for ex-political criminals to govern themselves as loyal and productive imperial subjects, the corollary ghost of the Peace Preservation Law apparatus.

This chapter explores how justice officials responded to this administrative challenge by proposing revisions to the Peace Preservation Law in 1934 and again in 1935. When these revision attempts failed, officials began to develop an administrative protection and supervision system (*hogo kansatsu seido*) in 1935, which was then formalized and expanded by a 1936 law titled the Thought Criminal Protection and Supervision Law (Shisōhan hogo kansatsu hō), which codified tenkō as one of the central policies of the Peace Preservation Law. To facilitate tenkō, this 1936 law established a network of twenty-two Thought Criminal Protection and Supervision Centers (Shisōhan hogo kansatsu sho) in the Japanese home islands, seven centers in colonial Korea and one center in Dalian in the Kwantung Leased Territory. This system effectively streamlined and extended the political rehabilitation practices first developed in semiofficial groups like the Imperial Renovation Society on an empire-wide scale.[3]

In this chapter I trace two key developments within this emerging protection and supervision system between 1934 and 1936. The first development is how the practices of groups like the Imperial Renovation Society increasingly drew upon the ideological tenets of the imperial state. This ideologization of rehabilitation took place on two levels, what Louis Althusser distinguishes as the secondary and primary ideologies at work in all Ideological State Apparatuses (ISAs).[4] First, political reform efforts were informed by the secondary ideologies of reform (*kōsei*) and protection (hogo)—for example, counseling detained criminals and providing welfare services to assist in their reintegration into society. However, this subordinate ideology was, in the years after 1934, increasingly complemented by what Althusser calls the primary ideology: imperial state ideology in which the goal of rehabilitation was specifically to return the detainee to imperial subjectivity, the corollary ghost to the imperial sovereign animating the state machinery.[5] Of course, the primary ideology of imperial sovereignty was operative from the very beginning, evidenced by the name of the Imperial Renovation Society and by the periodic donations the society received from the Imperial Household—an expression of the emperor's benevolence toward even his bad subjects (*mauvais sujets*, Althusser). However, as we started to see in chapter 3, this primary ideology was becoming more explicit in criminal reform efforts as political criminals were released under the new Charges Withheld program in the early 1930s. By the mid-1930s, criminal reform efforts were increasingly defined through the tenets of imperial state ideology—whereby imperial subjectivity became the explicit measure of reform—demonstrating how imperial ideology increasingly defined the secondary ideology of criminal rehabilitation. And, at the same time, the secondary ideology of criminal reform functioned as what Althusser theorized as the "material functions specific" to reform ISAs, "anchoring" the primary ideology of the imperial state, serving as its "'support.'" It was in this way that imperial ideology "was realized" in criminal reform ISAs such as the Imperial Renovation Society and later the Protection and Supervision Centers.[6]

The second development I explore in this chapter is connected to the first: as the ideology of the imperial subject came to define the practice and meaning of criminal reform, a new mode of power was forming that complemented the combined juridical-disciplinary modes already at work in the Peace Preservation Law apparatus, what Foucault later theorized as governmentality. Foucault explains that governmentality is a "very specific albeit complex form of power, which has as its target [a] population" and which deploys disciplinary and security apparatuses in order to govern a population (here the population of thought criminals).[7] Similar to how we saw rehabilitation policies emerging from, and complementing, the repressive application of the Peace Preservation Law earlier in the 1930s, the emergence of governmentality did not entail the displacement of sovereign or disciplinary power, but rather, as Foucault explains, governmentality "renders all the more acute the problem of the foundation of sovereignty . . . and all the more acute equally the necessity for the development of discipline," thus forming the "triangle, sovereignty-discipline-government, which has as its primary target the population and as its essential mechanism the apparatuses of security."[8] We can understand the emerging protection and supervision system in 1935 in this manner, as officials attempted to oversee and govern a growing population of thought criminals at various stages of conversion, including paroled converts and thought criminals in some stage of conversion, as well as recalcitrant communists who were serving their full sentences in jail.

Within this emerging system, officials sought to cultivate an ethic so that converts would govern themselves, thereby guarding against ideological recidivism (saihan) and function on their own as productive members of the imperial polity. One important ethical source that officials like Chaplain Fujii Eshō and converts like Kobayashi Morito turned to was True Pure Land

Buddhism, which in its emphasis on self-negation functioned as what Foucault called a "technology of the self" in that it supplied "a set of conditions and rules of behavior for a certain transformation of the self."[9] The objective was that, through self-governance and the cultivation of a new ethical disposition, converts' psychological and social well-being would be secured, thus protecting them against ideological recidivism and sustaining them as productive and loyal subjects of the imperial polity. In this way, while the emerging protection and supervision system would oversee the diverse population of thought criminals at various stages of conversion, it was also simultaneously nurturing practices so that this differentiated population would work toward its own self-improvement; as Foucault explains, "the means that the government uses to attain these ends [the welfare of the given population] are themselves all in some sense immanent to the population."[10] In this way, the protection and supervision system merely "direct[ed] . . . the flow of the population" toward "certain . . . activities" that the converts would pursue on their own.[11] And as I argue in the introduction, such an approach counters the argument that these reform efforts represent a culturally specific way of Japanese governance, allowing us to reconsider the Japanese protection and supervision system and its emphasis on "moral suasion" (*kyōka*) as a particular articulation of a mode of power—governmentality—that other modern states have deployed in their own way to manage and mobilize their respective polities.

This chapter explores how these two developments—the increasing ideologization of political rehabilitation and the governmental strategies to manage the expanding and varied population of tenkōsha—were taking shape following the mass tenkō of 1933–1934, and how they converged in the 1936 Thought Criminal Protection and Supervision Law. This law formalized the isolated reform experiments cultivated earlier in groups like the Imperial Renovation Society at the level of the imperial state, a process Foucault theorized as the "governmentalization of the state."[12] And, as I explore in chapter 5, this convergence laid the groundwork for ideological conversion to become an ideology in its own right later in the decade, as reform officials translated tenkō into the rhetoric of what I have called elsewhere the "crisis ideology" that coalesced at the beginning of the Second Sino-Japanese War (1937–1945).[13] The objective of this chapter is to understand the institutional and practical conditions for justice officials to reconceptualize tenkō as a general principle for the mobilization of Japanese society for total war.

The Increasing Ideologization of Political Rehabilitation in
1934–1935

As mentioned above, there were two intertwined developments in the Justice Ministry's political reform policies in 1935: first, efforts to institutionally expand and streamline the procedures to reform political detainees, and second, the increasing articulation of imperial ideology in these reform efforts. Indeed, the mass tenkō was seen as marking an important success for the Justice Ministry's policy of rehabilitation. In Althusser's terms, we can understand the increasing ideological representation of political rehabilitation as an effect of this success: that is, the mass tenkō validated reform (kōsei) and rehabilitation (hogo, both being the secondary ideology) and was explained as an expression of Japan's unique imperial kokutai (primary ideology).[14]

Already by 1934, study groups and journals were created for recent ideological converts to connect their conversion experiences to national culture and imperial mythology. For instance, in February 1934 Justice Undersecretary Minagawa Haruhiro established a short-lived center called the Loyalty Research Center (Taikōjuku kenkyūsho) in the Shibuya District of Tokyo for reformed thought criminals to conduct studies of national culture and imperial history.[15] The center quickly gathered over twenty thousand books related to national history, among other topics. Many of the thought criminals receiving assistance from the Imperial Renovation Society were active at this center. Then in August 1935, a larger research center for ex–thought criminals was established in Tokyo called the Research Center for National Thought (Kokumin shisō kenkyūsho).[16] The Research Center for National Thought had its own monthly journal, first named Rebirth (Tensei) and then aptly retitled National Thought (Kokumin shisō). This journal documented the efforts of tenkōsha to explore national culture and substantiate their reform as a process of recuperating their imperial subjectivity. The articles published in these centers' journals were a mix of personal stories about challenges facing converts upon their parole, critiques of Western political thought, and more esoteric tracts on the glorious Japanese spirit and Japan's unique kokutai as the basis for criminal reform.[17]

While converts were recasting their defections from the JCP through imperial ideology and national culture, officials were busy assessing the recent mass tenkō and considering ways to formalize conversion within the Peace Preservation Law apparatus.

As we explored in chapter 3, justice officials at this time were busy explaining the recent tenkō phenomenon to other bureaucrats and politicians. Part of this effort was to confirm the importance of their reform efforts and to establish conversion protocols for other justice officials to apply in their local prisons and courts. These discussions took place in regional and national reform conferences attended by procurators, wardens, and reform advocates as well as in the pages of the monthly journal *Hogo Jihō* (*Aid and Guidance*), which carried an increasing number of essays on political—not just criminal—rehabilitation and ideological conversion in late 1934 and early 1935.[18] In this context, members of the Imperial Renovation Society took a leading role in explaining the importance and methods of political rehabilitation.

For example, in the January 1935 issue of *Hogo Jihō*, vice director and prison chaplain Fujii Eshō wrote an article titled "Reform Methods for Paroled Thought Criminals," in which he reviewed the objectives, types, and methods of reforming political criminals.[19] Fujii pointed to recent statistics related to thought crime in order to establish the importance of reform: although 56,000 individuals had been arrested under the Peace Preservation Law by this point, only 3,800 had been indicted, implying that the vast majority had been released or placed in Charges Withheld (Ryūho shobun) so they could contemplate their illegal political activities and repent before going to trial. Furthermore, half of those indicted had their indictments suspended (Kiso yūyo). Of the remaining incarcerated thought criminals, many of them were completing their jail terms.[20] Fujii argued that, as thought criminals were being released back into society either through Suspended Sentences (Shikkō yūyo) or parole, it was critically important to escalate reform efforts in order to "protect against recidivism."[21]

Here Fujii drew upon his experiences with reform at the Imperial Renovation Society, arguing that it was necessary to establish groups and procedures that answered the specific needs of thought criminals. Fujii posited that thought crime was not an "individual crime" but rather related to one's membership in or relation to a political party or organization. Therefore, unlike conventional crime, the reform of political criminals needed to be a group endeavor, requiring the establishment of many local groups to nurture ideological conversion and support among peers.[22] In such groups, local comrades, family members, and the wider community would assist in the process of reform, with state officials providing indirect (*kansetsu*) guidance.

Fujii warned that direct intervention by state officials could produce negative results. Therefore, he urged the formation of smaller thought criminal reform groups—aided but not directly managed by local officials—that could guide the reform with a lighter hand.[23] In Fujii's vision, small semiofficial reform ISAs would be dispersed throughout the empire, embedding criminal reform into local communities and working to cultivate principles that would allow tenkōsha to govern themselves.

In addition to budgeting for welfare and employment services similar to regular criminal reform, Fujii warned that such reform groups needed to budget for the unique requirements of "thought guidance" (shisō o shidō) and "instruction expenses" (kyōka-hi).[24] He argued this was the most important aspect of thought rehabilitation since, at their core, communists were "criminals of conviction" (kakushin hannin), and once they had discarded their faith in Marxism, they needed to construct a new belief system so as not to fall (botsuraku) into moral nihilism. Echoing themes we saw in Kobayashi Morito's writings reviewed in chapter 3, Fujii explained that this was because communists believed in Marxism as a kind of religious faith (shūkyōteki shinnen); Marxism had been "their blood, their body, their life."[25] Consequently, converts could not return to society and "just live idly" (yūseimushi). Rather, Fujii argued that their relationship and view of society needed to be reoriented. Expectedly, Chaplain Fujii presented religious faith as the path for such a reorientation and the source of a new self-governing morality.[26]

This is why, Fujii explained, morally informed guidance policies (shidō hōshin) were of the utmost importance. Reformers needed to instruct thought criminals with ideological analogues to the principles of Marxism, and since Marxism was "one aspect of Western thought," reformers needed to find analogues in Eastern thought. For example, if Marxism and other Western belief systems are based on the principle of equality (byōdō), then reformers could present the Pure Land Buddhist principle of "equal yet distinct, distinct yet equal" (byōdō soku sabetsu, sabetsu soku byōdō). Similarly, as Marxism and other Western systems are predicated on materialism, then it is necessary to instruct converts in the "world of spirit" (kokoro no sekai), and so forth. Through such analogues, Fujii believed that an activist's ideological disposition could be recalibrated toward Eastern thought and the Japanese spirit, a process in which thought criminals would realize that their prior leftist thoughts were ultimately antisocial, isolating them from their loved ones and the imperial polity. Armed with their new self-awareness, they could now return to the fold of Japan's kokutai and would be able to actively participate in society as reinvigorated imperial subjects.[27]

Fujii's article is one example of the changes that were taking place within the Peace Preservation Law apparatus in the wake of the mass tenkō of 1933–1934.[28] Fujii and others were hoping to expand the kind of work the Imperial Renovation Society was conducting in Tokyo to various locales throughout the empire. Parallel with these calls for expanding the institutions of rehabilitation was the increasing ideologization of reform work.

THE IDEOLOGICAL AVOWAL: THOUGHT AND LIVES
OF TENKŌSHA (1935)

The increasing ideologization of reform can be found in Kobayashi Morito's writings in the wake of the mass tenkō of 1933–1934. As we saw in chapter 3, Kobayashi published his own defection biography in 1932. By 1934, Kobayashi had assisted hundreds of his comrades through the process of defection and apostasy, and, following the mass tenkō of 1933–1934, he was promoted to head the Imperial Renovation Society's Thought Section (Shisōbu). Therefore we can read his writings from the years 1934 and 1935 as revealing the changing conceptualization and practice of political rehabilitation taking place in the Imperial Renovation Society.

In a series of writings from this period, Kobayashi explained that the pressing issue was no longer the political criminal's decision to defect as we saw earlier. Rather, by 1935 the challenge had become to secure the conversions of political criminals and to find ways for them to demonstrate their new imperial subjectivity and national consciousness. We might understand this pivot—a pivot that links disciplinary reform and the technologies for self-government—through the couplet of wrongdoing/truth telling that Michel Foucault finds at work in the penal avowal. Foucault argues that the avowal should be situated "in the broader history of what could be called 'technologies of the subject,'" by which he means "the techniques through which the individual is brought, either by himself or with the help or the direction of another, to transform himself and to modify his relationship to himself."[29] In regard to the avowal, Foucault explains that through the avowal the "subject affirms who he is, binds himself to this truth, places himself in a relationship of dependence with regard to another, and modifies at the same time his relationship to himself."[30] Indeed, the avowal was the initial invocation of the ghost of the self-governing imperial subject that would be conditioned and formed in ISAs such as the Imperial Renovation Society. By 1935, Kobayashi Morito and hundreds of other tenkōsha had already admitted to their prior thought crimes; now it was imperative for them to yoke their new disposition to imperial ideology in order to develop a new moral basis for their everyday lives.

In this process, the tenkōsha affirmed themselves as ex–thought criminals requiring reform, binding themselves more closely to the truth as reawakened subjects of the emperor.

We can see the avowal at work in a second collection of conversion biographies that Kobayashi edited, *The Thought and Lives of Tenkōsha* (*Tenkōsha no shisō to seikatsu*), published in 1935.[31] This collection largely followed the format of the earlier *Tenkōsha Memoirs* (1934) analyzed in chapter 3. However, whereas the earlier collection represented conversion as a personal and spiritual process that concluded with the detainee defecting from the party and discarding Marxism, the essays contained in this 1935 collection emphasized the reinvigorated imperial subjectivity that tenkōsha were manifesting after defecting. In other words, tenkō was shifting from signifying the moment of apostasy to a durational process in which the tenkōsha increasingly confirmed their new subject position in and through daily practice.

Kobayashi prefaced the collection with a sweeping, ninety-five-page introduction in which he proposed a definition of tenkō and contextualized the phenomenon within the larger changes taking place in Japan and East Asia.[32] In this introduction, titled "Upon One's Self-Awareness as a Member of the Japanese Nation," Kobayashi covered many different aspects of the tenkō phenomenon, but here I would like to focus on three new distinct aspects: first, Kobayashi's increasing reliance on the tenets of imperial state ideology to define tenkō; second, his attempts to situate tenkō within larger historical phenomena such as the interwar crisis of global capitalism; and last, his discussion of tenkō in relation to Korean activists and the wider colonial question. These three aspects reveal the changing conceptualization of tenkō within the political rehabilitation system in 1935.

CONVERSION AS IDEOLOGIZATION: FAMILY-NATION-EMPEROR

Kobayashi begins by reiterating his earlier, religious definition of tenkō as "being reborn [*saisei*] in the religious sense, of a new life [*shinsei*], of rebirth [*tensei*]," in which tenkōsha "returned to their essential figure" as members of the Japanese national polity.[33] However, this required a further elaboration of the particular substance of the Japanese nation and imperial kokutai. Kobayashi explained that what moved a political criminal to convert was, first, familial love, but since "the Japanese nation emerged and developed from the family," Kobayashi extended this into a more elaborate consideration of the relationship between the family and Japan's unique kokutai, further exemplifying the ideologization of conversion through the trope of the family.[34]

As we noted in chapter 3, Louis Althusser theorized that, along with educational institutions, the family was one of the most important ISAS functioning in capitalist society. By 1935, we find Kobayashi theorizing the Japanese family system not only as an ideal to guide one's tenkō, but also a form that contained the seeds of a new society. Here Kobayashi posits a kind of sociological notion of the family as mediating between the individual subject and imperial society, whereby the family served as a conduit through which the tenkōsha could reidentify with the imperial kokutai. From the initial moment of self-analysis, spurred by familial love while isolated in prison, the tenkōsha must then recalibrate their connection to society through the family: "only when one first considers the issue of their own spirit [*tamashii*], then, extends this to the family and then to society, only this standpoint is correct"(10). In Kobayashi's theory of tenkō, the family functioned as a sort of ideological conduit to reenter society.

Kobayashi expands this notion of the family as a model for social renovation against the excesses of materialist individualism. For Kobayashi, the Japanese household (*ie*) is not predicated on "individual property" relations, but is rather "a communal effort, of communal ownership" in which "both those above and below must labor" for the family. For Kobayashi, if the remaining "feudal edifice" of familyism (*kazokushugi*) could be overcome and "received anew" in the present, familyism could then serve as a model for a renovated Japan. Kobayashi argued that the Japanese family system was a reflection of Japan's unique kokutai, and as such it approximates "the kind of society dreamed of by communists."[35]

Expanding upon his theory of tenkō, Kobayashi extends this relation between familial love and the Japanese kokutai to the imperial state. He begins by rejecting the Marxist understanding of the state as a class instrument. Drawing upon the friendly relations that he had with his captors, Kobayashi reflects, "I became aware of the love of fellow Japanese through the police, jailors, judges and procurators. This was more than an issue simply of these people's humanity; I came to realize that the Japanese state apparatus is certainly not a bourgeois thing, but that it was for all people [*zentai no minshū*]. We were fellow countrymen [*dōhō*], and I realized that we loved the same nation."[36] From this personal experience Kobayashi located a guiding principle that purportedly "flows at the core of the Japanese state": the balance between the "sword of justice [*jasei no katana*]" and "the beads of mercy [*jihi no tama*]." This was demonstrated to Kobayashi by such figures as his prison chaplain, Fujii Eshō.

In a subtle shift in emphasis compared to his earlier writings, Kobayashi here argues that his tenkō was an expression of the unique principles of the imperial kokutai, thereby linking the sovereign ghost animating the state with his recuperated imperial subjectivity. He explains that it was "the Japanese state [nihon kokka] that naturally sprouted the seeds of tenkō—its three thousand years of history, its actual figure, which exists unyielding before us."[37] Extending this idea beyond the practice of tenkō, Kobayashi argues that "we feel that we originated from the imperial household" and, as such, that tenkōsha and indeed all Japanese recognize that Japan is "a single family based on the identity between emperor and subject" (kunmin ittai no ichi-dai kazoku).[38] As such, Kobayashi explains that the emperor is "the center that expresses the total unification of the masses."[39] Later in the essay, Kobayashi elaborates that the emperor "does not represent the interest of just one class, but, as a totality [zettai no mono to shite] unifies the state and exists as the total embodiment of the state's mercy [kokka no daijihi]."[40] According to Kobayashi, such characteristics derived from the unique, organic (yūki teki) nature of the Japanese state, which "is not a conceptual entity, but is a thing of conviction and concreteness" (shinnenteki, gutaiteki na mono).[41] Here Kobayashi was implying that tenkō was the articulation of this conviction in the organic and singular quality of the Japanese imperial state.

In his earlier writings, Kobayashi explained conversion as an individual experience in which one, through religious awakening, returned to national consciousness. By 1935, however, this individual experience had been over-shadowed by Kobayashi's ontological claims about the singularity and histori-cal mission of imperial Japan and the divinity of the emperor as the symbolic center of the imperial state. Kobayashi's increasing ideological investment in tenkō is particularly evident when he discusses the current crisis of global capitalism and Japan's historical mission in East Asia.

TENKŌ AND THE RENOVATION OF CAPITALISM

The reality in question in this mechanism, the reality which is necessarily *ignored* [*méconnue*] in the very forms of recognition . . . is indeed, in the last resort, the repro-duction of the relations of production and of the relations deriving from them. —LOUIS ALTHUSSER, *On the Reproduction of Capitalism*

As with most social commentaries at the time, Kobayashi situated the topic of tenkō within the context of the deepening crisis of global capitalism and the urgent need for domestic social reforms. Here, many tenkōsha used Sano Manabu and Nabeyama Sadachika's new "socialism in one country" (*ikkoku-shakaishugi*) as a foil against which to elaborate a vision of social reform that they believed was in accordance with Japan's imperial kokutai. Recall that, as incarcerated leaders of the JCP, Sano and Nabeyama inspired the wave of apostasies with their sensational defection in June 1933. At that time, Sano and Nabeyama declared their new appreciation of "Japanese realities" and attempted to reconsider socialist praxis through nationalism, one that would harness the masses' patriotic sentiments toward the emperor and what they believed to be the liberatory possibilities of Japan's colonial empire. Sano and Nabeyama strategically called their new politics "socialism in one country", appropriating the Soviet slogan and turning it into a kind of national socialism.[42] For many tenkōsha, however, Sano and Nabeyama did not go far enough, for they continued to see Japanese society as divided by class, called for a workers' government, and ultimately yoked a Western-derived socialism to Japanese nationalism. Ultimately, for many tenkōsha, Sano and Nabeyama failed to understand the singularity of Japan's imperial kokutai and remained inspired by Western notions of socialism.

In his introductory essay, Kobayashi developed an extended critique of Sano and Nabeyama's new politics of socialism in one country.[43] While he recognized the inherent contradictions in capitalist society, Kobayashi countered Sano and Nabeyama's sociopolitical critique by presenting the transformative power of the Japanese spirit. For instance, whereas Sano and Nabeyama grounded their analysis in the productive forces of the Japanese working class, Kobayashi located the power to transform and overcome capitalism in the Japanese spirit emanating from the emperor: "our nation and the imperial household's resilience is everlasting [*eien*], and in opposition to this, capitalism as it stands, is not eternal; for it to develop, it must be modified. And the more we become self-aware as Japanese, it is only natural that present society will have to be improved [*yoriyoku*]. The Japanese spirit is not something that can be contained; rather, I believe it is able to assimilate [various elements] and provides the path for creative activity [*sōzō shi ikashite iku michi*]."[44] In other words, for Kobayashi social renovation must be predicated upon the Japanese spirit, wherein to recuperate one's purportedly latent imperial subjectivity compels one to strive for social improvement. In this political reconfiguration, "one spirit connects above and below" (*jōge sono kokoro o hitotsu nishite*) becomes the ideal for social praxis.[45] And by awakening to such a spirit, tenkōsha provided an exemplary model for such a necessary awakening.

Indeed, in Kobayashi's new theorization in 1935, tenkō was no longer limited to ex–thought criminals; rather, Kobayashi explicitly titles one of the essay's sections "Every Person Will Tenkō: Our Conversion as One Link in National Self-Awareness."[46] Here, he presents tenkō as a national imperative for all imperial subjects to perform, wherein the conversion of ex-communists was but "one link in the total conversion of Japan" (*nihon no zentaiteki tenkō no ikkan*).[47] He explains that no longer was the "tenkō phenomenon ... a question limited to communists, but today signifies a major turning point in which all domains [of the Japanese Empire] are being thoroughly evaluated and reanalyzed."[48]

Kobayashi proposed tenkō as a model for a nonrevolutionary, gradual overhaul of society based upon the Japanese spirit. The contradictions that Marxists identify in the constitutive class relations of capitalism were, for Kobayashi, the result of a disjuncture between Western capitalism (*ōbei-ryū shihonshugi*) and Japan's unique kokutai.[49] Kobayashi lamented that "up until today, capitalist [development] has certainly not been perfect" and that since "the essence of Western capitalism itself is something different [*sōi*] from the Japanese spirit ... social anxieties have arisen."[50] However, this disjuncture between Western capitalism and the Japanese spirit was also the space within which capitalism could be transformed: its un-Japanese character was the very possibility from which to renovate it. In this essential difference, Kobayashi argues that capitalism itself was "going through a total, Japanese tenkō," becoming in effect Japanese. This implied that in addition to the ghosts animating the imperial state and individual imperial subjects, the economy too was being reformed and infused with the Japanese spirit.[51] For Kobayashi, this reform required that the imperial state intervene and control all sectors of production so that capitalist society would be transformed along Japanese lines: "I do not think this will be a revolutionary transformation. Although currently there are many things that should be corrected, these can be renovated and developed harmoniously [*wakyō no uchi ni*]. State regulation of production and the necessity of state management are [now] being considered. ... To advance and harness [*juyō*] our nation's capitalism, we have to control production throughout all sectors in order to push this initiative [*sōi*] forward."[52]

With the state guiding production, the tenkōsha provides the model of a productive laborer guided by the imperial spirit. Kobayashi declares that today's workers and farmers, based on "their self-awareness as Japanese" are ready to cooperate in "advancing our nation's industry."[53] No longer inspired by the communist slogans "Abolish the emperor!" and "Destroy capitalism!," tenkōsha formulated the new slogan "Renovate capitalism!" (*shihonshugi zesei*). This was a national effort, since "capitalists and laborers reside within one nation," whereby competing "class interest" would be overcome by the "Japanese spirit," integrating society into a national economic unit without social contradiction.[54] In these terms, tenkō heralds an epochal turning point in Japanese history:

> It is said that the development of Japan's national destiny was spurred on [*motarashita*] by its connection to Western civilization; receiving the baptism of liberalism, developing [through] the capitalist mode of production, and currently within the trend of Marxism. Now, all of these have to be analyzed, filtered and developed from the true Japanese standpoint. Our tenkō is nothing more than one link in this process. From this new standpoint, a new movement for the strengthening of the Japanese nation-state must emerge. A movement must be created that, while rejecting revolutionary theories, will overcome domestic contradictions and will grasp the international position that Japan occupies.[55]

Tenkōsha embody this new standpoint, thus providing a model for all Japanese to return to national consciousness and begin to renovate society.[56] Importantly, Kobayashi believes that this new standpoint necessarily includes the "awareness of Japan's new mission" (*nihon kokumin no shin-shimei no jikaku*) in East Asia, which, for him, begins with Japan's mission in its colonies.

TENKŌ AND JAPAN'S HISTORICAL MISSION IN ITS COLONIES

The ideological violence that necessarily attends Kobayashi's changing conception of tenkō comes to the fore when, through a series of asides, he comments on the issue of Korean tenkōsha and their role within Japan's empire.[57] As noted in chapter 3, tenkō did not become a widespread phenomenon among detained activists in colonial Korea until later in the decade. However, there were a few celebrated cases of conversion among Korean communists living in Japan, discussed by officials and reported in the media (see figure 4.1).[58]

Indeed, unlike the earlier *Tenkōsha Memoirs* (1933), the 1935 *Thought and Lives of Tenkōsha* volume contains a short essay from a reformed Korean communist, Sim Kil-bok, who was receiving guidance from Kobayashi in the Imperial Renovation Society at the time.[59]

Kobayashi notes that Korean tenkōsha in the metropole face a double bind; that is, they face the stigma of being both thought criminals and colonial subjects living in the metropole. In this regard, Kobayashi urged acceptance and compassion toward Korean tenkōsha, arguing that "to extend

朝鮮人の轉向者がある──それは
去る七月初めから本富士署に檢束留
置取調中であつた中央大學專門部

轉向者續出の
昨今これは珍
しくも警視廳
では始めての

二年で朝鮮平安北道江界郡高山面
浦上洞一五四屈指の資産家金善玉
長男李熙東(二こ)で

彼は昭和六年廣島縣吳市の大正
中學四年に入學したが同校に社
會學研究會を造り退校、次で岡
山市の岡北中學に轉校卒業し昨
年三月中大に入學するや左運動を繼

Figure 4.1. The news that Korean activists living in Japan were among the population of converts was big news for the Justice Ministry and national media. "The First Korean Convert Emerges," *Tokyo Asahi Shimbun*, September 10, 1933, evening edition.

a helping hand of salvation to fellow Korean tenkōsha" was "the task of our nation."[60] While not denying the sincerity of Kobayashi's empathy toward his Korean brethren, we must recognize the imperialist function of his discourse of empathy.

Following his discussion of "Japan's new mission," Kobayashi recounts a conversation he had with a "Korean-born comrade" (*Chōsen shusshō no dōshi*) who exclaimed that, although Korean converts "have awoken to familial love and recognize that communism is unrealistic, we are unable to have . . . the Japanese spirit," hindering Korean converts from achieving a full conversion. Kobayashi's interlocutor thus questioned what the essence of ideological conversion is, proclaiming that "tenkō not only entails the eradication of communism" but must "also subsume national prejudices" (*minzokuteki henken mo yōki shi*).[61] What Kobayashi's advisee was pointing to was the subtle but important difference that although Koreans were said to have the potential to ideologically convert as nationals (kokumin) of the Japanese Empire, they were, of course, not ethnically (*minzokuteki*) Japanese, thus complicating their relation to Japan's imperial kokutai and the Japanese spirit that would inform and measure their tenkō. By extension, this problem reveals a contradiction between the two ideologies—secondary and primary—at work in the Imperial Renovation Society, in which Korean converts were successfully reforming as ex-criminals (the secondary ideological function) and yet struggling to confirm their reform in terms of the state's primary ideology of Japanese kokutai and imperial subjectivity.

These kinds of questions prompt Kobayashi to consider tenkō through the ideology of the Japanese Empire. He responds that the "Japanese spirit is not something as narrow" as his interlocutor implies. Rather, those who are able to grasp this Japanese spirit—that is, the colonial tenkōsha—can advance Korean development and culture. For this to occur, Kobayashi argues that distinctions such as "Korean" and "Japanese" must be done away with since, "we form a totality" (*minna zentai no mono da*).[62] Those who emerged from the social movement and converted are uniquely positioned to "be leaders of their Korean brethren."[63] Similar to how Kobayashi saw Japanese tenkōsha as models for the spiritual renewal of Japanese society, Kobayashi hoped that Korean converts would return to the colony and serve as examples of loyal colonial subjects. Indeed, Kobayashi declares that Korean tenkōsha embody the possibility of the "fusion of Japan and Korea" (*naisen no yūgō*), emerging as the veritable vanguard of colonial integration.[64] The shared tenkō experience between Japanese and colonial Koreans provides the first step in this direction: the bonds forged earlier within the communist movement could serve as a basis from which to reconstruct and strengthen the bonds between Japanese and Koreans to further the imperial project.[65] The first step in such a project is, Kobayashi tells us, to support reform efforts in colonial Korea.[66] Kobayashi celebrates a plan to establish a tenkōsha support group in Keijō Korea called the Kōfūkai (Wind of Light Society), arguing that it was Japan's "national mission" to support such efforts in the colonies.[67]

Later in the essay, Kobayashi defines a Korean tenkōsha as someone who has realized that the path for Korean development (*hatten*) is not through "national liberation" but rather by "assimilating with the Japanese people."[68] Clearly, Kobayashi has grafted the colonial divisions of the Japanese Empire into the figure of the colonial tenkōsha. For example, Korean tenkōsha were simultaneously within the imperial kokutai and without: they were objects within the embrace of the "Japanese spirit"—a spirit that would drive their historical advancement—but simultaneously external to this spirit as colonial subjects, as Kobayashi's interlocutor so clearly exposed. The imperative for the colonial tenkōsha to more closely identify with the emperor was a version of Japan's colonial policy to assimilate (dōka) the populations in the colonies in the 1930s and prefigures the later policy to mobilize Koreans as imperial subjects (kōminka).[69]

IDEOLOGIZATION OF CONVERSION AND ITS INSTITUTIONAL EXPANSION

Related to Kobayashi's ideologization of conversion in this 1935 essay was his celebration of the institutional expansion of reform efforts directed toward thought criminals. *Thought and Lives of Tenkōsha* was published at a time when officials were attempting to revise the Peace Preservation Law in order to elevate reform as one of the central policies of the state's policy against thought crime. In this regard, Kobayashi draws upon his experience in the Imperial Renovation Society, pointing to the various programs that were developed after the mass tenkō in 1933–1934. Echoing themes that we saw elaborated by his colleague Chaplain Fujii, Kobayashi emphasizes that employment is one of the most important components for fortifying an ideological conversion. Here he notes how the Imperial Renovation Society was collaborating with municipal employment agencies to find work for converts as they transitioned back into society as well as working with the Ministry of Education in order to return reformed students and teachers to schools.[70] In addition to industrial labor and education, Kobayashi reports that in 1933 the Imperial Renovation Society received a plot of land in Ibaraki Prefecture with the assistance of the Imperial Household Agency, which became the Imperial Renovation Society's Imperial Memorial Farm (Teikoku kōshinkai onshi kinen nōjō).[71] As many as thirty members of the society at a time worked on the farm to cultivate rice, barley, and vegetables and care for a host of farm animals.[72] Similar to Chaplain Fujii, Kobayashi is presenting labor—industrial and agricultural as well as intellectual—as central to fortifying ideological conversion and reforming detainees so they can return to society as productive subjects.

Kobayashi reported that these kinds of efforts were not limited to the Imperial Renovation Society in Tokyo, but were being implemented in unofficial tenkōsha support groups that had formed in various locales, including the Friendship Society (Dōyūkai) in Osaka, the Illustrious Virtue Association (Meitokukai) in Nagoya, the Honor and Harmony Society (Keiwakai) in Nagano, the White Light Society (Hakkōkai) in Kyoto, and, as mentioned earlier, the soon-to-be-established Wind of Light Society (Kōfūkai) in Keijō Korea.[73] Kobayashi urges the state to support these unofficial groups, while also respecting their independence: state support would allow these groups to provide support to local families of tenkōsha who were still in prison, as well as funding a series of services upon their parole, including employment counseling, skill training, and temporary accommodations. In addition to these material services, funding would also support library facilities, lecture series, study groups, and publishing projects similar to those taking place in the Research Center for National Thought in Tokyo, so that tenkōsha could similarly connect their rehabilitation to imperial ideology and cultivate their new imperial subjectivity.[74] These groups also advocated for tenkōsha in their local areas, making sure that local police and society at large understood that, Kobayashi writes, "yesterday's enemy has become today's ally."[75] As I explore further below, this dispersed network of independently run, local support groups would be brought under state control over the next two years—formalized with the passage of the Thought Criminal Protection and Supervision Law in 1936.

Kobayashi's ideological investment in conversion as well as his call for its institutional expansion across the empire demonstrates the degree to which criminal rehabilitation had become intertwined with imperial state ideology. As one of the leaders in guiding ideological conversion, Kobayashi's 1935 writings exemplify how criminal rehabilitation and ideological conversion were being reformulated in 1934–1935.

Recalibrating the Peace Preservation Law Apparatus in the Mid-1930s

THE 1934 AND 1935 PEACE PRESERVATION LAW REVISION PROPOSALS

Although Fujii and Kobayashi drew upon their experiences in the Imperial Renovation Society, their writings inflect a larger rethinking by justice officials and reform workers about how to manage political crime cases in 1935. As noted in earlier chapters, this rethinking drew upon earlier reform efforts targeting youth delinquents in 1922 that was then expanded to adult parolees later in the 1920s. By the mid-1930s, a well-established archive of reform practices was available to procurators who oversaw thought crime cases. Now, following the mass tenkō in 1933–1934, justice officials in the metropole recognized that the Peace Preservation Law was advancing into a new stage, what Procurator Ikeda Katsu described in 1936: "[Having] passed through the period of arresting communists and [their] reform in prison [gyōkei kyōka], [we] are now advancing into the period of protection and guidance."[76] Indeed, by 1935 the Justice and Home ministries recognized that the JCP had been effectively crushed as an organization by the earlier repressive measures of the Peace Preservation Law.[77] Now, with thousands of ex-communists having either been released or assessed in the Charges Withheld program, or still in prison, justice officials were considering ways to formalize and expand the reform experiments taking place in groups like the Imperial Renovation Society on a wider scale.

The increasing commitment to reform in relation to thought crime cases was exemplified in the budget for supporting thought criminal reform groups and policies: between 1933 and 1934, the year in which the mass tenkō took place, the Justice Ministry increased the budget earmarked specifically for "thought crime prevention" (shisō hanzai bōatsu tokubetsu shisetsu hi) from 116,657 yen in 1933 to 190,929 yen in 1934. This jumped again in 1936 to 310,643 yen, reaching over one million yen annually after 1938.[78] Particularly after the mass tenkō of 1933–1934, rehabilitation and ideological conversion became core aspects of the Justice Ministry's commitment to rehabilitationism (hogoshugi) in regard to political crime cases, seeing it as the best method to prevent ideological recidivism (saihan) and reverse tenkō (gyaku-tenkō). One part of rehabilitationism was, of course, monitoring political criminals who refused to convert but had served their full sentences.[79] By late 1934, these developments were translated into two distinct proposals for administering arrested thought criminals: for those who had declared tenkō, officials envisioned an official system of protection and supervision (hogo kansatsu), which would ostensibly support tenkōsha as they returned to society. For those who refused to convert but were completing their prison sentences, officials proposed preventative detention (yobō kōkin), which would extend detention for unrepentant political criminals beyond their formal prison sentences.[80]

Officials from a variety of government ministries discussed these kinds of issues in a new government committee—the Shisō jimuka kai—established in April 1933 and charged with formulating a coordinated thought policy (shisō taisaku) between government ministries. With Sano and Nabeyama's defection a few months later, this committee became the main forum for officials to discuss ideological conversion in relation to thought crime. Over the next year, the Home and Justice ministries delivered reports to this committee in which they explored how to expand the state's efforts to control or suppress groups that ostensibly threatened the state as well as to administer the large population of detained thought criminals.[81] By December 1933, these efforts culminated in a Justice Ministry proposal—supported by the Home Ministry—to revise the Peace Preservation Law.[82] After further committee deliberations, this proposal, along with supporting reference materials, advanced to the Diet in February 1934.[83]

The proposed revision expanded the Peace Preservation Law into thirty-seven separate articles, divided into five sections addressing (1) the application of the law—including its retroactive application to those already charged and/or paroled under previous versions of the law; (2) new punishments in which the kokutai and private property infringements were further distinguished, and clarifying how the purview of the law would extend to so-called communist affiliated groups (gaibu dantai); (3) the elaboration of new penal procedures for the various infringements; (4) stipulations for the new system of protection and supervision (hogo kansatsu) for those undergoing conversion; and (5) an outline of the preventative detention (yobō kōkin) policy for recalcitrant thought criminals.[84] Justice Minister Koyama Matsukichi delivered the proposal to the Lower House on February 7, and deliberations continued in the Lower House and House of Peers through the end of March, producing further revisions to the original proposal.[85]

As with the 1925 and 1928 Diet deliberations over the Peace Preservation Law, the 1934 revision bill was scrutinized from a number of standpoints.[86] Some questioned the constitutionality of preventative detention, while others asked for a clearer explanation of how tenkō would be defined and administered.[87] A more pressing concern for politicians, however, was the applicability of the Peace Preservation Law—revised or in its current state—to ultranationalists, who had recently carried out a spate of violent attacks against industrialists, bankers and politicians. Diet members expressed concern over recent incidents such as the League of Blood Incident (Ketsumeidan jiken) and the May 15 Incident (Goichigo jiken)—both carried out in the spring of 1932—in which industrialists, bankers, and heads of political parties were violently attacked, including the mortal wounding of Prime Minister Inukai Tsuyoshi.[88] Recognizing that the Peace Preservation Law was originally issued to suppress leftist radicals, many politicians asked if this revision would allow the law to be applied to ultraright groups as well.[89]

As Nakazawa Shunsuke has summarized, questions related to the nationalist right wing followed three lines of inquiry: first, in regard to groups planning to carry out assassinations and other violent acts (bōryoku kōi); second, some politicians, such as Soeda Kenichirō, asked how, if at all, the Peace Preservation Law's categories of kokutai and private property system would apply to rightist movements that rejected parliamentary government and capitalism, similar to Italian fascism or German Nazism; and last, members of the House of Peers hoped to revise the bill so it would apply to national socialist (*kokka shakaishugi*) groups that, although not calling for violent revolution, advocated renovating the state and capitalism.[90]

These questions about the Peace Preservation Law's applicability to rightists were not purely technical. Rather, as John Person has argued, such debates point to the underlying ideology informing the Japanese security apparatus and the contradictions that arose when it was applied to ultranationalists.[91] As explored in previous chapters, such debates centered on how to juridically define the term "kokutai" and, in the new political circumstances of the mid-1930s, how to specify its categorical function in the law. For example, in deliberations in the House of Peers, Iwata Chūzō posed doubts about the difference between the kokutai and private property infringements outlined in the law, connecting both to the family form. Since Kobayashi and others emphasized the centrality of the family in the practice of conversion at this time, it is worth citing Iwata's question in full:[92]

> In my view, the Japanese kokutai has an inseparable relationship with the private property system. As you know, there is an inseparable relationship between the family system and Japan's kokutai—no one would doubt this—and the private property system is a system that maintains [*yashinau*] the family system, with the head of the household [*koshu*] at its center. If the family system was separated from the private property system, it would cease to exist. Therefore, to reject the private property system, to destroy it and then establish a communistic system of production similar to Russia, the family system could not be sustained, and Japan's kokutai could not be preserved. Addressing this from Japanese circumstances, we should say that Japan's kokutai rests on the family system, which itself rests on the private property system. Should we not see the private property system as the ground [*dodai*] upon which Japan's kokutai is constructed [*kensetsu*] and preserved [*iji*]?[93]

Iwata argued that when radical nationalists attack the private property system, this "threatens the foundation of our kokutai" and thus clearly has "the intention to alter the kokutai."[94] Other Diet members posed similar questions about whether the law's private property clause would apply to anticapitalist ultranationalists.[95] Beyond the problem of suppressing ultranationalists, such questions revealed deeper concerns about the relationship between capitalism—a historical social formation—and Japan's purportedly timeless kokutai.

Responding to such questions, Justice Minister Koyama Matsukichi did not ruminate on the relationship between capitalism and Japan's kokutai but rather focused on the technical definition of crime in the law. He explained that "so-called right-wing groups are not, as such, illegal"; rather, it was "the disturbing activities of individuals within the group" that were illegal, and thus their crimes did not fall within the purview of the Peace Preservation Law.[96]

Due to concerns over preventative detention and the applicability of the Peace Preservation Law to right-wing activists, this first proposal failed to gain support before the Sixty-Fifth Imperial Diet adjourned. However, officials in the Justice and Home ministries began preparing for a second revision proposal to be submitted next year.

THE 1935 PEACE PRESERVATION LAW REVISION BILL

After the failure of the 1934 revision bill, the Justice Ministry, in cooperation with the Home Ministry, began preparing a new revision bill in September 1934.[97] They responded to the two main concerns expressed in the 1934 deliberations—that is, preventative detention and right-wing activism—by erasing the former from the bill, and offering a separate bill designed to apply to rightist groups that were planning assassinations or other violent acts, the Bill Related to Punishments for Illegal Conspiracies Etc. (Fuhō danketsu nado shobatsu ni kansuru hōritsuan).[98] Recall that drafters of the 1934 bill envisioned the protection and supervision system to administer the detainees who were in the process of converting, while preventative detention would apply to recalcitrant political criminals who refused to convert, the so-called hi-tenkōsha. In the new 1935 bill, the protection and supervision system would oversee hi-tenkōsha as well, in which recalcitrant communists would be urged to convert while remaining under close ideological supervision in prison.[99] In preparation for the new revision, officials collected a large amount of data on thought crime in Japan, Korea, and Taiwan, which revealed the empire-wide importance that justice officials saw in these revisions.[100] The revision bill and reference materials were presented to the Sixty-Seventh Imperial Diet in March 1935.[101] Unfortunately for the Justice Ministry, the deliberations were overshadowed by the controversy over the professor of constitutional law and House of Peers member Minobe Tatsukichi's interpretation of the Meiji Constitution, what came to be known as the Emperor Organ Theory Incident (Tennō kikan setsu jiken).[102] Although nuanced, Minobe's theory posited that the state was sovereign and the emperor was a part or organ (kikan) of this sovereign entity, albeit one of the most important since the emperor symbolized the state. This came to be known as Minobe's Emperor Organ Theory. In the 1930s, rightists singled out Minobe for sullying Japan's glorious kokutai by demoting the emperor to a mere organ of the state. Minobe was critiqued in the House of Peers, and, after much debate, he stepped down as a member of the House of Peers as well as resigning his professorship at Tokyo Imperial University.[103] This incident inspired the government to form a committee charged with the task of clarifying the kokutai (*kokutai meichō*), culminating in the infamous Ministry of Education text, *Fundamental Principles of the Kokutai* (*Kokutai no hongi*, 1937).[104] Therefore, it can be argued that the earlier legislative debates over kokutai in the Peace Preservation Law reviewed in previous chapters anticipated the later movement to clarify the kokutai.

The debates concerning Minobe's constitutional theory dominated the deliberations over the revised Peace Preservation Bill in 1935, further revealing issues concerning the relation between sovereignty, law, and kokutai ideology.[105] For example, in the Lower House on March 20 a heated exchange occurred over the definition of kokutai between Makino Shizuo of the Seiyūkai Party, Justice Minister Ohara Naoshi, and Home Ministry official Gotō Fumio. Makino began this debate by quoting Minobe, wherein Minobe claimed that kokutai was not a legal concept but rather a historical and ethical concept.[106] Minobe argued that the concept of the kokutai cannot be fully equated with "the current constitutional system" but rather signified "the ethical [*rinri*] particularity of the history of the nation and the state as its historical result."[107] By citing Minobe, initially without attribution, Makino was attempting to set a trap for his interlocutors.[108] However, Justice Minister Ohara asked Makino whom exactly he was citing, and he and Home Minister Gotō wittily dodged the confrontation by noting the excessive amount of time it would have taken to study such complex theories as Minobe's constitutional interpretations.

However, this did not end the discussion of the revision in the context of Minobe's theory. Two days later on March 22, the minister of education, Matsuda Genji, came under specific attack in the Lower House by Nakatani Sadayori of the Seiyūkai Party.[109] Nakatani and others chastised Matsuda for his vague responses to Minobe's organ theory as well as for the Ministry of Education allowing Minobe to teach for decades at Tokyo Imperial University. In this exchange, Nakatani argued that if the Minister of Education himself could not clarify what the kokutai was, how could they determine a national education policy, let alone deliberate on a revision to the Peace Preservation Law with the kokutai as its main object of protection? As in the problem of constituent and constituted power discussed in chapter 1, Nakatani argued, "If the concept of the kokutai is not clarified, then it is impossible to continue deliberations. . . . In the case of someone scheming . . . to construct a system that restricted [kōsoku] the emperor's authority [taiken] . . . how would the law apply to this? I think that this is the fundamental problem. Deliberations cannot continue concerning a law protecting the kokutai by only referring to Article One of the Constitution."[110]

Inadvertently echoing Minobe's contention that the kokutai was a historical and ethical concept, Matsuda responded that he had said all along that "Japan's kokutai has not changed for three thousand years" and that "it is on this basis [gen] that our state [kokka] exists."[111] Nakatani, unsatisfied, retorted, "[To say] only that it has existed for three thousand years, this has no meaning. In regard to sovereignty and its actual content [tōchiken sono mono ni kanshite no naiyō], there are those who claim that sovereignty resides in the state, that is, that it does not reside in the hands of the Emperor [tennō no te ni arazu]. This is a question quite different from the idea of the kokutai existing for three thousand years."[112] Nakatani's aggressive questioning of Matsuda continued, with Nakatani asking if he, like Minobe, believed that sovereignty did not reside solely with the emperor. This line of questioning provided one of the most explicit statements concerning the unresolved issues related to the ambiguity of kokutai in the Peace Preservation Law.

These kinds of exchanges did not bode well for the passage of the revision. As with the 1934 attempt, this 1935 revision bill failed to pass before the Sixty-Seventh Imperial Diet concluded, and the Peace Preservation Law continued in its 1928 form.[113] As in 1925, no one denied that imperial sovereignty needed to be defended against supposed threats, but when asked to juridically define the central category of the law—kokutai—officials struggled to supply an adequate definition that could clarify how kokutai would be used to arrest rightist activists (1934) or could be clarified in the context of the Emperor Organ Theory Incident (1935).

Securing Tenkō in 1935–1936

CONSTRUCTING THE PROTECTION AND SUPERVISION SYSTEM IN 1935

The failures of the 1934 and 1935 revision proposals dismayed many justice officials who had hoped to organize and streamline the effort to reform the large and diverse population of thought criminals at various stages of ideological conversion.[114] By the end of 1935, 58,000 people had been arrested under the Peace Preservation Law in the Japanese metropole, the vast majority of whom were never charged—that is, they were either released after being interrogated or placed in a temporary disposition of Suspended Indictment or Charges Withheld.[115] However, as Ogino, Okudaira, and other historians remind us, while officials implemented suspension policies in an attempt to guide communists through ideological conversion, the repressive application of the Peace Preservation Law expanded to other groups in the Japanese metropole, including new religions such as Ōmotokyō in December 1935, as well as socialist and Marxist study groups from 1936 to 1938, including popular-front cultural groups and the Labor-Farmer Faction (Rōnō-ha).[116] In other words, by the mid-1930s the Peace Preservation Law apparatus was a dynamic security apparatus that combined repression of newly identified threats to the imperial state, disciplinary rehabilitation for suspects showing signs of repentance, and governmental moral guidance for converts who were transitioning back to society.

In colonial Korea, around sixteen thousand people had been arrested under the Peace Preservation Law by 1935, with 2,137 (or over 13 percent) of suspects having committed tenkō. Although this number may appear like a success for colonial administrators, they were concerned with the relatively higher number of cases of ideological recidivism in the colony: 221 cases, or 10 percent of all tenkōsha at this point.[117] Keongil Kim has suggested that, unlike the metropole where officials described their reform experiments as expressions of imperial benevolence, in Korea colonial officials implemented thought rehabilitation policies as a method to counter the high rate of recidivism among political criminals who had been released after serving their full sentences.[118] In other words, in the colony disciplinary power was applied for specifically repressive ends. Moreover, as explored in chapter 3, there was a higher ratio of criminal indictments in the colony compared to the metropole.[119] Rehabilitation and ideological conversion would not become a widespread phenomenon in colonial Korea until later in the decade.

In response to these challenges, throughout 1935 officials continued to share rehabilitation protocols with their colleagues at conferences and in the pages of journals such as Hogo Jihō with increasing frequency.[120] In these discussions, officials related the hardships that tenkōsha faced upon returning to society, which translated into further calls for the streamlining of local rehabilitation efforts and the creation of a state-managed, empire-wide thought rehabilitation system.[121]

In addition to the Imperial Renovation Society's Thought Section in Tokyo, there were only four thought criminal reform groups in Japan recognized by the Justice Ministry: a Christian home for women in Yokohama, the Mutual Love Society (Kyōaikai) in Mie, the Friendship Society (Dōyūkai) in Osaka, and the Illustrious Virtue Association (Meitokukai) in Nagoya. Recall that the groups Kobayashi mentioned in *The Thought and Lives of Tenkōsha* reviewed above were unofficial support groups taking on the task of reforming political criminals upon their release. Such a small number of official support groups was clearly insufficient to meet the needs of the over five thousand thought criminals that were placed in the Suspended Indictment and Charges Withheld systems in the metropole between 1931 and 1934.[122] Moreover, whereas the high-profile Imperial Renovation Society received donations from the Imperial Household and industrial businesses, other regional groups relied on support from temples, private donations, the goodwill of community volunteers, and, in some cases, support from local courts.

To meet these challenges in the metropole, and despite the failure to pass revisions to the Peace Preservation Law in 1934 and again in 1935, the Justice Ministry began to develop a protection and supervision system for ex–thought criminals in 1935, incorporating a new organization to serve as its flagship, called the Virtuous Brilliance Society (Zaidan hōjin shōtokukai). As the Virtuous Brilliance Society's 1936 mandate outlines, its mission was to "guide, assist and oversee the nation-wide effort to rehabilitate thought criminals" by coordinating the efforts between the procuracy, courts, prisons, local reform groups, the police, and local governments.[123] In addition to working with already established rehabilitation groups like those listed above, the Virtuous Brilliance Society was mandated to establish new rehabilitation groups in areas without such groups and provide protocols for thought guidance (*shisō shidō*), including employment counseling and serving as a place for "consultations on the thought problem" (*shisō mondai sōdan sho*). Similar to Miyagi at the Imperial Renovation Society, court procurators would head these local groups, working closely with prison officials and others to coordinate thought rehabilitation efforts. In this way, the Justice Ministry took the initiative to establish an institutional basis from which to manage their ideological reform efforts. At the same time as officials established this institutional basis, they were also considering ways to legally formalize this developing rehabilitation system.

THE 1936 THOUGHT CRIMINAL PROTECTION AND SUPERVISION LAW

As the Justice Ministry was constructing the protection and supervision system, they were simultaneously working on a bill to legally formalize this reform effort. This task fell to the Justice Ministry's new chief of rehabilitation, Moriyama Takeichirō. Interestingly, Moriyama presented protection and supervision not in terms of the benevolent guidance and imperial compassion that other reform advocates were using at the time, but rather as a matter of protecting the imperial state against dangerous ideological threats in a moment of crisis.[124] As Uchida Hirofumi has noted, the term "protection" (hogo) rarely appeared in the Justice Ministry's official explanation for the reform bill presented to the House of Peers and Lower House in May: rather, the Justice Ministry emphasized the necessity for supervision (*kansatsu*) in order to both "prevent recidivism" and "to secure ideological conversion."[125] Justice officials most likely assumed that politicians would be more receptive to the new proposal when explained in terms of security and surveillance.

Moriyama's proposal and the resulting 1936 Protection and Supervision Bill represents how the Justice Ministry was attempting to bring the disciplinary practices of reform and moral guidance of governmentality back under the purview of sovereign law, a process that Foucault theorized as the "governmentalization of the state," in which sovereign-juridical and disciplinary apparatuses were harnessed for the governing of a population.[126] In other words, as we have reviewed in previous chapters, moral guidance emerged from the disciplinary practices taking place in unofficial or semi-official groups that were responding to the immediate needs of thought criminals released into the Charges Withheld programs in the early 1930s. Only later did the imperial state absorb and formalize these initiatives in terms of securing the empire and protecting the imperial sovereign. For example, in a November 1935 meeting, Moriyama explained to his colleagues the need for such a law in the context of the "present crisis" (*hijō jikyoku*) in East Asia and the kinds of dangerous ideas that find purchase in such a context, including "liberalism" as well as Sano and Nabeyama's post-tenkō "socialism in one country."[127] The central point of the bill, Moriyama explained, would be to "prevent" (*bōshi*) a tenkōsha from backsliding to such ideologies in such unstable times, as well as to try to convince recalcitrant political activists to convert.[128] A thought criminal would be placed in protection and supervision status for a maximum of two years, with a variety of officials working together to assess his or her ideological progress, including thought guidance counselors (*shisō shidōkan*), thought guidance officers (*shisō hogoshi*), members of newly created thought guidance examination committees (*shisō hogo shinsa kai*), and center secretaries.[129]

Building from Moriyama's original proposal, the Justice Ministry produced an outline of the Thought Criminal Protection and Supervision bill in January 1936, and, after some editorial revisions, submitted the bill for Diet review in April 1936.[130] Justice Minister Hayashi Raizaburō presented the bill to a Diet committee in May. Hayashi explained that this law would apply to those who, arrested under the Peace Preservation Law, had their indictments or sentences suspended (Kiso yūyo and Shikkō yūyo respectively), as well as those still in prison or who had been either paroled or had served their full sentences.[131] In other words, the administrative procedures of protection (hogo) and supervision (kansatsu) could be applied to everyone who had not been immediately released after their initial interrogation. Furthermore, as we saw with the 1934 Peace Preservation Law revision bill, this 1936 law would apply retroactively to all arrested thought criminals who fell into one of these categories earlier in the decade.[132]

Hayashi explained that tenkō had taken many different forms: while there were those "who effected a real tenkō" and those who demonstrated "the eradication of illegal thought [*futei shisō*]," there were also many converts whose "dispositions were extremely ambivalent" and cases in which it was not certain whether detainees had "converted their thought" or, if they had, how "stable" (*kengo*) their new ideological dispositions were.[133] Noting this varied population of thought criminals at different stages of conversion, Hayashi argued that this law would allow the government to "supervise the thought and actions" of converts as well as "promote conversion among nonconverts."[134] Ultimately, Hayashi argued, in such unstable times it was necessary to "secure tenkō" (*tenkō o kakuho*) by passing this law. As with Moriyama's earlier explanation, Hayashi was using the rhetoric of sovereign power to legitimate the use of disciplinary and governmental measures in order to protect the imperial state.

The Imperial Diet passed the bill on May 29 (Law No. 29), which went into effect in the Japanese metropole on November 14, 1936. This was the first time the categories thought criminal (*shisōhan*), ideological conversion (tenkō), and ideological convert (tenkōsha) were codified in law, demonstrating how the reform practices developed in semiofficial groups like the Imperial Renovation Society were now brought back under the purview of imperial law. With the passage of this law, the earlier Charges Withheld policy employed by procurators in thought crime cases since 1931 was replaced by the conventional Suspended Indictment (Kiso yūyo) policy. At the same time the law went into effect, its various institutional and procedural components were also enacted, including the establishment of twenty-two Thought Criminal Protection and Supervision Centers (Shisōhan hogo kansatsu sho) in the metropole, and their constitutive Examination Committees (Hogo kansatsu shinsa kai) attached to district courts that would review thought criminal cases and judge the degree to which a political criminal had converted.[135]

Although by this point the Charges Withheld and Suspended Sentence programs had produced far fewer cases of tenkō in colonial Korea than in the metropole, the new law and its institutions were enacted in colonial Korea on December 12, 1936.[136] It was also enacted later in the Kwantung Leased Territory (Kantōshū) in December 1938 with a Thought Criminal Protection and Supervision Center established in Dalian.[137] The Korean Government-General established seven Protection and Supervision Centers, including those in Keijō (Seoul), Heijō (Pyongyang), and Taikyū (Taegu).[138] Unlike metropolitan Japan, where in 1935 the Justice Ministry had already started to organize and coordinate the independent and semiofficial tenkōsha support groups into a protection and supervision system, the phenomenon of tenkō in colonial Korea took shape only after this "formal conversion system was established," as Hong Jong-wook has argued.[139] Moreover, as Ogino Fujio has noted, while officials in the metropole understood the first objective of the new system as "preventing recidivism" (saihan bōshi), this objective was coupled in colonial Korea with the explicit objective, as the chief of legal affairs of the Korean Government-General, Masunaga Shōichi, explained, "to clarify the kokutai and positively strengthen the Japanese spirit" among colonial subjects.[140] In chapter 5, I analyze the differences between metropole and colony, but it is important to recognize that the 1936 Thought Criminal Protection and Supervision Law institutionalized ideological conversion beyond the Japanese metropole.[141]

Some converts as well as reform officials expressed reservations about the new Protection and Supervision Law. While on the one hand, tenkōsha and reformers welcomed the increased support for rehabilitation, they were concerned that the state would take over the reform effort, with detrimental effects.[142] As Fujii, Kobayashi, and others had argued earlier, reform required a certain degree of freedom from police or governmental oversight in order that conversion emerge naturally between comrades.[143] They repeatedly argued that the state's presence in such a process should be as "indirect" (kansetsu) as possible. There were critiques of the new law in colonial Korea as well. For instance, articles in the June 11 and 14 editions of the Chōsen Nippō questioned if the new law could meet its mandate to "correct thought and stabilize the daily life" (shisō no kansei, seikatsu no kakuritsu) of colonial thought criminals. In particular, one article questioned how these mandates could be met if resentful parolees had their freedoms restricted under supervision, while another article questioned how effective thought guidance would be without also "renovating the social system" that such radical ideologies were aiming to transform.[144] Last, as Itō Akira has analyzed, there were other independently organized tenkōsha groups who feared losing their independence as well as having to compete with state-sponsored reform groups that would be established under this law.[145] However, these kinds of concerns quickly faded as the Protection and Supervision network was put into place.

By 1938, Protection and Supervision Centers in metropolitan Japan had reviewed the cases of thirteen thousand thought criminals, and officials were celebrating a purported ideological recidivism rate of around 1 percent.[146] As explored in chapter 5, not only did justice officials actively celebrate the apparent successes of their rehabilitation programs but, following Japan's invasion of China in 1937, they started to represent ideological conversion as a model for the total renovation of Japanese society during wartime. Recalling Kobayashi Morito's earlier claim that tenkō signaled a historical turning point for the Japanese Empire, the 1936 Thought Criminal Protection and Supervision Law and its extensive network of centers provided the conditions for ideological conversion to be envisioned as a model for general mobilization.

Conclusion: The Governmentalization of the Imperial State in 1936

With the passage of the Thought Criminal Protection and Supervision Law in 1936, the disciplinary reform practices and moral injunctions developed earlier by reform groups like the Imperial Renovation Society were brought back under the sovereign rule of the imperial state, a process that Foucault has theorized as "the governmentalization of the state."[147] The 1936 corollary law elevated the policy of ideological conversion to the center of the Peace Preservation Law apparatus, expanding political rehabilitation across Japan as well as to colonial Korea and the Kwantung Leased Territory. The new Protection and Supervision Centers oversaw a vast network of volunteers from the community to assist with guiding thought criminals who were released from detention, and collaborated with various reform groups to assist in supervising the ideological dispositions of parolees. Additionally, in metropolitan Japan, the number of privately funded support groups now overseen by their local Protection and Supervision Center rose to about 130 groups nationwide.

The Protection and Supervision Law was thus the institutional culmination of a tendency traced in previous chapters, wherein rehabilitation arose out of the successes of repression in the early 1930s, and how, following the mass tenkō of 1933–1934, governmental techniques emerged to secure these ideological conversions. Through the twin thematics explored in this chapter, this new network of Protection and Supervision Centers institutionalized the ideologization of criminal rehabilitation as well as the "techniques of government" (Foucault) that were developed in groups like the Imperial Renovation Society. Protection officers would draw upon the tenets of imperial state ideology to assess the degree to which a detainee had converted and, at the same time, would attempt to cultivate a new ethical position for tenkōsha to govern themselves upon parole, thereby protecting them from ideological recidivism and guiding them toward being loyal and productive imperial subjects.

In chapter 5, I trace how, following Japan's invasion of China in 1937, the practices and ideologization of rehabilitation taking place in the Protection and Supervision Centers were translated into a general principle for the spiritual mobilization of the general public, as well as how officials sought to understand the differences in administering political crime cases in the metropole and colonial Korea.

The Ideology of Conversion:
Tenkō on the Eve of Total War

Conversion in a Period of Global Intellectual Disorder

In December 1936, the director of the Tokyo Thought Criminal Protection and Supervision Center (Shisōhan hogo kansatsu sho), Hirata Isao, explained the threefold mission (*shimei*) of the newly established network of Protection and Supervision Centers to an assembly of his colleagues from the justice ministry.[1] "Our task," Hirata claimed, "is first to implement and spread the Japanese spirit through penal policy," adding that recently, "the meaning of the term Japanese spirit has become extremely narrow and . . . misunderstood." However, the new centers would rectify this error by establishing the "true Japanese spirit in an expansive sense." For reform advocates like Hirata, this true Japanese spirit was symbolized in the benevolence of the imperial state and its willingness to reform dangerous political criminals.[2] In turn, thought criminals would be re-produced as loyal imperial subjects and returned to society, consequently fortifying the spiritual resolve of the imperial polity through their example. Recalling the ghost in the machine metaphor that frames my analysis of the Peace Preservation Law (Chianijihō), Hirata envisioned the new centers as the institutional conduit through which the benevolence of the imperial sovereign would nurture the imperial subjectivity of his wayward subjects, thereby providing an example for the rest of imperial society to fortify their own Japanese spirit.

The second task, Hirata explained, was to establish these centers as the "cornerstone" and "standard" of a new, wider "state system for general parolee reform." Hirata believed that the rehabilitation of political criminals provided the model par excellence for all criminal reform and envisioned an empire-wide reform system modeled on the new Protection and Supervision Center network.[3] Indeed, as Hirata hoped, the Justice Ministry passed a sweeping Judicial Protection Services Law (Shihō hogo jigyō hō) in 1939, which established an extensive criminal reform apparatus modeled in part on the Thought Criminal Protection and Supervision system. This new Protection Services Law built upon and oversaw the 1,200 already operating support groups for adult criminal parolees.[4] The third and most pressing task, Hirata argued, was to link criminal reform to the wider campaign "for national thought defense [shisō kokubō] in [this] turbulent period of global thought [sekaiteki shisō konran jidai]."[5] As the institutional embodiment of the Japanese spirit, the Protection and Supervision Centers would fortify the imperial nation against external ideological threats.

Hirata delivered this speech only a few weeks after the Protection and Supervision Centers were opened in Japan in November, and eight months before the start of the Second Sino-Japanese War in July 1937.[6] Thus from the very beginning, and well before Japan started mobilizing for war in mainland China, officials like Hirata Isao envisioned these centers and their thought reform policies in terms of "national thought defense" and the spiritual renovation of the Japanese Empire. With the start of hostilities in 1937, other officials, such as Hirata's colleague at the Tokyo Center, Nakamura Yoshirō, joined the campaign and published articles in which they presented the new rehabilitation apparatus as the domestic bulwark in a so-called thought war (shisōsen) against dangerous ideologies assailing the Japanese Empire and East Asia.

This more urgent and renovationist formulation of political rehabilitation was not simply an image presented to other bureaucrats and the public. This formulation was glossed from the recently codified policy of ideological conversion (tenkō) being implemented in the new Protection and Supervision Center network.[7] As explored in chapter 4, tenkō became official policy with the passage of the 1936 Thought Criminal Protection and Supervision Law (Shisōhan hogo kansatsu hō). In addition to establishing an institutional apparatus for the implementation of conversion, this law officially codified the increasingly ideological formulations of conversion that had emerged in semiofficial reform groups after the mass tenkō of 1933–1934. For example, in a 1937 Justice Ministry manual, the chief of rehabilitation in the Justice

Ministry, Moriyama Takeichirō, outlined the five stages of ideological conversion that would be used in the centers to assess and guide political criminals:

1 One who accepts and advocates the correctness of Marxism.
2 One who, although uncritical of Marxism, rejects a liberal-individualist position.
3 One who is in the process of developing a critical position toward Marxism.
4 One who recognizes and grasps the Japanese Spirit.
5 One who has mastered [*taitoku*] the Japanese Spirit and is able to actively put it into practice [*jissen kyūkō*].[8]

As we see here, Moriyama's outline indexes the increasing ideologization of conversion that took place since the early 1930s, beginning with the initial emphasis that a detainee defect from party affiliation and reject Marxist theory (Stages 1 through 3) and culminating in a detainee's proactive identification with the Japanese spirit and the active manifestation of this spirit in their daily lives (Stages 4 and 5). This also indexes the combination of various modes of power within the Peace Preservation Law apparatus over time, including repression, disciplinary power, and governmental techniques. Finally, notice that Moriyama's schema figures Marxism as a particular inflection of a wider intellectual inheritance from the West, with its basis in liberalism and individualism. Based on this new index, the Protection and Supervision Centers were to guide political criminals not only to reject Marxism but to question the entire liberal legacy from the Meiji period from the standpoint of a restored Japanese spirit. Armed with this mandate, the centers would coordinate with employment agencies, Buddhist temples, research groups, and the local community so that parolees would become able to master and actively practice the Japanese spirit in their daily lives. Such mastery was, at the same time, the means through which ex–thought criminals came to govern themselves without direct state supervision. In this way, the Protection and Supervision Center network functioned as a machine to cultivate the ghost of imperial subjectivity in the population of parolees and, by extension, strengthen the Japanese spirit across the imperial polity.

THE IDEOLOGY OF CONVERSION IN THE LATE 1930S

This chapter analyzes the formation of what I call the "ideology of conversion" in Japan in the late 1930s, when the myriad developments explored in previous chapters converged and coalesced to render tenkō an ideological trope in its own right. This convergence took place both within and outside the Protection and Supervision Centers, elevating the image of the reformed thought criminal as the model of the imperial subject for all to follow.

Within the Protection and Supervision Centers, the practice of criminal reform and ideological conversion was now officially defined through the tenets of imperial state ideology. And following the Japanese invasion of China in 1937, the war provided a context in which tenkōsha could demonstrate their degree of conversion by supporting the military campaigns. This produced a new set of challenges for officials in colonial Korea, who were now tasked with converting anticolonial activists arrested under the Peace Preservation Law into loyal subjects of the Japanese emperor. As I explore in this chapter, although tenkō cases increased in Korea after the establishment of seven Protection and Supervision Centers in the colony, justice officials began to express doubts about the potential of colonial thought criminals to convert as completely as their Japanese comrades, thereby articulating underlying problems in the ideology informing Japan's sovereign claims over the colony in the discourse of criminal rehabilitation.

Outside of the Protection and Supervision Center network, officials started to represent ideological conversion as a model for the spiritual mobilization of the general population, particularly in the context of Japan's invasion of China in July 1937—what was referred to as the China Incident (Shina jihen). In these campaigns, which included lectures, articles, and public exhibitions, justice officials represented ideological conversion as a general imperative for all Japanese to follow in wartime. Tenkōsha within the Japanese metropole as well as in colonial Korea were presented as exemplars of the mobilized imperial subject, the ostensible vanguard in Japan's thought war with foreign ideologies threatening the Japanese spirit (nihon seishin). Thus, at the same time as the China Incident provided tenkōsha an opportunity to demonstrate their degree of criminal reform by proactively supporting the war effort, the notion of ideological conversion was repackaged as a model for spiritual mobilization of the general population during wartime.

This chapter begins by exploring the formation of the ideology of conversion within the institutional practices of the Protection and Supervision Centers, in both the metropole and colonial Korea. I focus on how the new conversion policy presented particular challenges to colonial officials in Korea, rearticulating the aporias of imperial ideology explored in earlier chapters into the new discourse of ideological conversion after the codification of tenkō in 1936. Then the chapter turns to exploring how officials presented tenkō to the wider public in the early years of the Second Sino-Japanese War, not as a policy targeting thought criminals but as a principle for the spiritual mobilization of the empire. The period between 1936, when the Protection and Supervision Law was issued, and 1941, when the Peace Preservation Law was extensively revised, marked the culmination of the various developments explored in previous chapters, elevating ideological conversion to the central policy of the Peace Preservation Law apparatus.

This elevation of ideological conversion was short-lived, however. This chapter concludes by analyzing how, with an extensive revision of the Peace Preservation Law in 1941, reform and rehabilitation were overshadowed by a stricter policy of preventative detention (yobō kōkin). To be sure, the Protection and Supervision system continued to operate into the 1940s alongside the Preventative Detention system. However, since tenkō had been generalized into the national spiritual mobilization (kokumin seishin sōdōin) campaigns for the wider population, this allowed the Peace Preservation Law to return to its original repressive function, used to indefinitely detain those considered ideological threats during a time of war. This final chapter in the Peace Preservation Law's development further exemplifies how the thought crime apparatus "slid" (Poulantzas) back and forth between repression and rehabilitation depending on the changing political conditions and institutional needs of the interwar imperial state.[9]

Institutionalizing Conversion: The Protection and Supervision Network

AN OUTLINE OF THE REHABILITATION APPARATUS

After their establishment in late 1936, the funding and staff of the Thought Criminal Protection and Supervision Centers were expanded annually, peaking in 1941.[10] In addition to the twenty-two centers in metropolitan Japan, seven centers were established in colonial Korea. Additionally, in January 1939 a center was opened in Dalian in the Kwantung Leased Territory to oversee thought criminals apprehended in areas controlled by the Japanese in northern China.[11] As reviewed in chapter 4, the centers were established to "promote and secure ideological conversion" (shisō tenkō o sokushin shi mata ha kore o kakuho suru) among those arrested under the Peace Preservation Law and who either had served their complete sentences, were paroled early, or were in one of the suspension policies: Suspended Indictment (Kiso yūyo) or Suspended Sentence (Shikkō yūyo).[12]

Overseeing each Protection and Supervision Center was an Examination Committee (Hogo kansatsu shinsa kai) that would assess the degree to which a detainee had converted, and would determine if the detainee required further supervision by a guidance counselor (*hogoshi*) and/or assignment to one of the recognized thought criminal rehabilitation groups (*hogo dantai*). Directors of the Protection and Supervision Centers would produce a report (*tsūchi*) for each detainee that, in addition to recording their age, employment, marital status, criminal record, current penal status, and guarantor, also measured their "development of thought," their "current state of mind," and in particular whether or not they had "converted" or "semiconverted" as well as their motivations for doing so.[13] Thought criminals were classified into three basic categories: converted (tenkō), semiconverted (*juntenkō*), and not converted (*hitenkō*).[14] The second category—juntenkō—applied to anyone who was assessed as in the process of converting, and thus applied to a large number of thought criminals in the system.

In a 1937 handbook published by the Aomori Protection and Supervision Center, Head of Rehabilitation Moriyama Takeichirō explained the standards for defining the three classifications for tenkō and the unique counseling approach each required as follows: nonconverts (*hitenkōsha*) were those who continued to embrace "illegal thought" (*futei shisō*), which required officials to exert their efforts "from the position of correct thought guidance" (*shisō zendō teki tachiba yori*). Next, semiconverts (*jun-tenkōsha*) were those thought criminals who were considering whether to "extinguish their illegal thought" and thus required officials to act from the "standpoint of promoting tenkō" (*tenkō sokushin no tachiba*). Last, the classification of tenkō would apply to those who had "stated that they have renounced [*hōki*] illegal thought" and thus "do not pose the same kind of danger as a nonconvert" while under supervision.[15] However, Moriyama warned that one of the conditions for "securing conversion" was a "stable life" built on employment and the "beautiful customs of the family system." Thus although a thought criminal might have discarded illegal thought, Protection and Supervision officials would assist with securing employment, family stability, and so on, so that the convert could master and fortify their newly restored imperial subjectivity in daily life.

The standard time set for administering a detainee through a center was two years, although this could be altered depending on the detainee's degree of progress.[16] The earlier guarantor system (*mimoto hikiuke*) was replaced by a new set of community relations managed by the Protection and Supervision Centers and reviewed by the Examination Committees. Thus groups like the Imperial Renovation Society, analyzed in chapter 3, came under review of the Examination Committees. Furthermore, there was closer coordination between state officials—procurators, prison wardens, police—as well as reform groups such as those under the umbrella of the Virtuous Brilliance Society (Zaidan hōjin shōtokukai), discussed in chapter 4.[17] The overall result was that the various and isolated reform experiments taking place since the early 1930s—including in public and private parolee welfare organizations, self-organized tenkōsha support groups, as well as in families, Buddhist temples and community organizations—were brought under the purview of, and now closely coordinated by, the Protection and Supervision Centers.

Throughout 1937, justice officials discussed the new mandate of rehabilitation work (hogo jigyō) in forums such as the journal Hogo Jihō as well as lectures and conferences. For instance, the January 1937 issue of Hogo Jihō carried multiple essays that contemplated the objectives and methods for the newly codified work of rehabilitating ideological converts. One essay written by Yamagata Jirō reminded readers that the work of thought reform entailed not only consolidating conversion, but also assisting thought criminals with securing employment and a stable daily life.[18] Other issues reprinted the ordinances establishing Protection and Supervision Centers in colonial Korea, as well as attendance and transcripts of lectures at meetings of reform officials.[19]

Within a few years there were efforts to assess the success of the new ideological conversion policy, focusing specifically on the rate of recidivism (saihan) among thought criminals. The most extensive and in-depth study was conducted in 1938 by the Tokyo District Court procurator Tokuoka Kazuo. In this study, *Research on Recidivism among Peace Preservation Law Cases* (*Chianijihō ihan jiken no saihan ni kansuru kenkyū*), Tokuoka reviewed the conventional explanations for converting, including love of one's family, a restored national identity, health or psychological distress, the duress of imprisonment, the theoretical critique of Marxist thought, and (religious) faith, among other motivations.[20] Furthermore, Tokuoka explained that some political criminals convert for personal reasons (kojinteki genin), including awakening to familial love due to long-term detention, appreciation for the benevolence shown by the state, or religious instruction provided by a prison chaplain, as well as for social reasons (shakaiteki genin) including the international situation and the errors of the Communist International, the emergence of an active right-wing nationalist movement in the 1930s, and international incidents such as the 1931 Manchurian Incident, the 1932 Shanghai Incident, or Japan's decision to exit the League of Nations in 1933.[21] These distinctions were important if officials were to monitor a suspect's varying motivations and degrees of commitment to conversion.

Issues of *Hogo Jihō* in the second half of 1937 clearly demonstrate the impact of the China Incident on the practice and conceptualization of reform work. For example, three months after Japan's invasion of China, a special issue of *Hogo Jihō* in October addressed the theme "The Current Crisis and Crime Prevention" ("Jikyoku to hanzai bōshi"), which carried such articles as "Joining the National Spirit Mobilization Movement" and, echoing Hirata's lecture which started this chapter, "National Thought Defense and Protection and Supervision."[22] In this new context, reformed thought criminals could demonstrate their criminal reform by supporting Japan's war effort.

Reports from various Protection and Supervision Centers reveal the various activities organized in support of the war, including roundtable discussions of the significance of the conflict, tenkōsha collecting donations for the war, and organized trips to Manchukuo and Korea, among many other activities.[23] Consequently, right when the Protection and Supervision system was being consolidated, the China Incident provided an opportunity for officials to further yoke the meaning and practice of tenkō to imperial state ideology.

MOBILIZATION AS CONFIRMATION OF CONVERSION

It is not surprising that almost immediately after Japan's invasion of China in July 1937, converts rallied in support of the Imperial Army, for this was one very clear way to demonstrate that they had mastered the Japanese spirit and were proactively practicing it in their daily lives. Thus, contrary to some explanations that imply that the incentive to mobilize tenkōsha for the war effort derived from outside the Protection and Supervision apparatus, it is important to recognize Hirata and others were already conceptualizing their work inside the Protection and Supervision Centers in terms of spiritual mobilization for the imperial state.[24] And while the China Incident prompted many officials to reconsider criminal rehabilitation—not just of political criminals—ideological conversion was uniquely positioned to serve as a model for national mobilization for war.[25]

Officials began to reconsider criminal reform almost immediately after the Japanese military invaded China in July 1937. For instance, reports on the activities of Protection and Supervision Centers in late 1937 announced that tenkōsha across Japan had formed the National Committee in Response to the Current Crisis (Jikyoku taiō zenkoku iinkai). This was to be the tenkōsha contingent of the larger National Spirit Mobilization Movement (Kokumin seishin sōdōin undō) established by Prime Minister Konoe Fumimaro and the renovationist bureaucrats the same year.[26] This national committee of tenkōsha would collect donations, organize roundtable discussions on the current crisis, and organize support for the Japanese Imperial Army, among other activities.[27]

In November 1937 the Seimeikai (Illustrious Sincerity Society), a tenkōsha group formed in the Osaka Protection and Supervision Center, published a pamphlet detailing their activities within the National Committee in Response to the Current Crisis. The pamphlet is prefaced by a call for tenkōsha to join the "movement for donations in support of national defense" (kokubō kenkin undō).[28] The Seimeikai urged tenkōsha to realize that unlike the violent persecution of political criminals in Germany, China, and elsewhere, Japan had benevolently granted them the opportunity to become "children of his majesty" (heika no akago), thus directly linking their renewed imperial subjectivity to the sovereign ghost animating the imperial state.[29] Consequently, in this moment when the Japanese Empire was under ideological threat, the Seimeikai exclaimed that tenkōsha, as the "pioneers of national thought defense," must "join hands and defend the nation!"[30]

In such campaigns, ideological conversion and national mobilization converged: tenkōsha confirmed their conversion through such campaigns while also going out into the community to collect donations in defense of the imperial polity. Indeed, the 1937 Seimeikai pamphlet listed the exact amount individual tenkōsha donated "for the defense of their native Japan": here, a specific monetary value reflected the degree to which they were manifesting their newly recuperated Japanese spirit.[31] With chapters formed in every Protection and Supervision Center, the national committee mobilized tenkōsha and provided a method for them to confirm their rehabilitation as patriotic imperial subjects.

At this time, justice officials also linked their successful efforts to convert political criminals in the Protection and Supervision Centers to the war effort. A flurry of pamphlets were published that described tenkōsha as constituting the front line of a wider "domestic anticommunist" effort (bōkyō naikoku).[32] In such pamphlets, the very existence of tenkō was portrayed as exemplifying the unique benevolence of the imperial state, once again invoking the imperial ghost in order to explain how these institutions functioned to restore the imperial subjectivity of wayward subjects.[33] In one pamphlet, the activities of the National Committee in Response to the Current Crisis was described as exemplifying how the "Japanese spirit is the spirit of anti-communism" (*bōkyō seishin soku nihon seishin*).[34]

This link between rehabilitation, converts, and the China Incident was not just metaphorical: justice officials organized tenkōsha to travel to occupied areas of China in order to support the war effort. In 1939, the Zen Nihon Shihō Hogo Jigyō Renmei (All Japan Justice Rehabilitation Alliance) published a pamphlet titled *Cornerstone of Asian Development* (*Kōa no soseki*) that reported on the various experiences and contributions tenkōsha made during a recent visit to China.[35] Many of the tenkōsha travel essays followed the established form of blending biographical reflection on past crimes and how, following their individual conversion, tenkōsha were ready to be mobilized in defense of the Japanese Empire.

Similar to their Japanese tenkōsha comrades, Korean converts also mobilized for the war effort. For instance, an association called the All-Korean Emergency Patriotic Thought League (Jikyoku taiō zenchō shisō hōkoku renmei) was formed in July 1938, declaring the following three principles:

1 As imperial subjects, we strive to cultivate the Japanese Spirit, and to strengthen the integration of Korea and Japan.

2 On the battlefront of national thought defense, we strive to become foot soldiers to eradicate antistate thought [*hankokkateki shisō*].

3 We will serve to the utmost, executing national policy, and strengthening the patriotic efforts on the home front.[36]

As Ogino Fujio has argued, these kinds of platforms for Korean ex–thought criminals were one part of the larger imperialization (*kōminka*) campaigns in the colony. The mobilization of Korean tenkōsha has to be understood within the wider mobilization of Korean society at the time, parallel with the formation of youth groups, patriotic writers associations, and such, when the imperialization policy was emphasized in the colony.[37] By 1940, the All-Korean Emergency Patriotic Thought League had grown to almost 3,300 members.[38]

However, despite such developments, officials continued to question the significance and authenticity of ideological conversion in the colonial context into the late 1930s, rearticulating the aporias of imperial ideology explored earlier into the new discourse of tenkō in the colonies.

Considering Rehabilitation and Ideological Conversion in Colonial Korea

As explored in previous chapters, officials confronted certain interpretive and institutional challenges when implementing the Peace Preservation Law in colonial Korea, beginning with how to interpret the category of kokutai to prosecute anticolonial activists in Korea (thus contemplating the extension of imperial sovereignty to the colonies), and then the continuing repressive application of the Peace Preservation Law in the colony even as reform policies emerged in metropolitan Japan in the early 1930s. Later, when the Justice Ministry codified ideological conversion as the central policy of the Thought Criminal Protection and Supervision Law, officials began to question more closely what exactly conversion entailed in the colony. In this way, the new tenkō policy crystallized the ideological aporia that were articulated in earlier stages of the Peace Preservation Law's application in the colony.

Unlike developments in the metropole following the mass tenkō of 1933–1934, conversion protocols did not naturally emerge from the individual cases of conversion in the colony in the early 1930s. Rather, conversion protocols were institutionalized in Korea only after the passage of the Thought Criminal Protection and Supervision Law in 1936. To be sure, the Charges Withheld policy was implemented in colonial Korea early in the 1930s, and out of the over sixteen thousand suspects arrested under the Peace Preservation Law between 1928 and 1936, 6,383 individuals had served their prison sentences, were paroled, or were placed within one of the suspension programs (Charges Withheld or Suspended Sentence).[39] There were also cases of conversion in colonial Korea—over two thousand by 1935. However, as Hong Jong-wook has noted, it was not until after the establishment of the Thought Criminal Protection and Supervision system in early 1937 that tenkō became an institutionalized phenomenon in colonial Korea.[40] Hong argues that following the China Incident, many Korean activists reevaluated the prospects for national liberation in the new geopolitical conditions in East Asia. It was in the context of increasing cases of conversion in Korea that officials in Tokyo began to consider more closely the differences between tenkō in the metropole and colony.

What emerged from this research was an awareness of the disparities in the number of cases of indictment in colonial Korea compared to the metropole, as well as the higher rate of ideological recidivism. For example, in his 1938 study of recidivism in Peace Preservation Law cases introduced earlier, Tokuoka Kazuo explains these disparities by contrasting the purportedly two different ways in which activists were initially politicized. In the metropole, Japanese thought criminals were first exposed to Marxism, engaged in theoretical research, and then joined the movement. Korean activists, on the other hand, were concerned first and foremost with national liberation and joined the movement based on this motive; only later did they adopt Marxism, and only because it provided an explanation of the unstable socioeconomic conditions in the colony. Therefore, Tokuoka says, "the national question is central, and the communist movement is taken up as a means to attain this objective."[41] This, Tokuoka notes, has important consequences for implementing the new ideological conversion policy in the colonies. For us, such questions reveal the particular forms of imperial nationalism that informed the policing of political crime in the colony.

As Naoki Sakai has explained, a doctrine circulated in Japan in the late 1930s and early 1940s "which claimed that neither scientific racism nor ethnic nationalism was licit in the polity of the Japanese Empire and that the nation-state of Japan was explicitly created against the principle of ethnic nationalism (*minzokushugi*)."[42] Rather, officials posited that imperial Japan was a multiethnic nation-state, an ostensibly integrative and integrating polity, what Takashi Fujitani has called an "integrative form" of racism in Japan's total-war regime.[43] We see these distinctions and combinations—between ethnicity and nationalism, between exclusion and inclusion—coming into tension as officials contemplated the ideological conversion policy in colonial Korea.

For example, Tokuoka laments that while colonial thought criminals are able to discard the ideology of Marxism and break with the communist movement, this does nothing to affect their original inspiration, namely, national liberation. Tokuoka begins by recognizing that "of course it is not possible to make them grasp and master the Japanese spirit." However, implicitly touching on the distinction between ethnicity and nationality, Tokuoka sees hope in that, "because [Korean thought criminals] are without a doubt Japanese," it is possible for them "to awaken to national self-consciousness and to Japanese national consciousness." When this is accomplished, Korean tenkōsha understand "the true figure of Korea's national position within international circumstances, and come to recognize that Korea's greatest well-being is to have faith in Japan, and, with their fellow countrymen, [work to] realize the grand ideals of the Japanese nation and the Japanese spirit."[44] As we see here, colonial officials did not envision colonial conversion as recuperating an innate internal spirit, but as the recognition of the might and benevolence of an external power: that is, the Japanese imperial state.

These types of conceptual tensions can be found in other reports that analyzed the disparities in conversion cases between metropole and colony. For instance, the disproportion in prosecuting thought crime cases between metropole and colony was addressed in a 1939 report published by the Criminal Affairs Department of the Justice Ministry.[45] The author, Tokyo procurator Yoshida Hajime, begins his report by discussing the different modes of prosecuting, and degrees of punishing, thought criminals in colonial Korea in the 1930s, including a case where eighteen Korean communists were sentenced to death.[46] Similarly, Yoshida notes the relatively low number of suspended sentences given to thought criminals in Korea compared to the metropole, and the relatively higher degree and duration of incarceration.[47] Yoshida provided three interrelated reasons for this disparity: the particular uniqueness (*tokushusei*), complexity (*fukuzatsusei*), and seriousness (*jūdaisei*) of "Korean thought crime."[48] On the first quality, Yoshida repeats almost verbatim the Keijō High Court decisions that were introduced in chapter 2, when he writes that Korean thought crime was unique in that it combined communism's rejection of the private property system with the anticolonial movement's "national consciousness." Communists in Korea were thus fighting to "secede Chōsen from the bonds of the Empire" (*chōsen o teikoku no kihan yori ridatsu*) and establish a communist society. Yoshida called this blend nationalist communism (*kokuminteki kyōsanshugi*) and argued that the number of genuine communists (*junsei kyōsanshugisha*)— that is, communists who were not nationalist—in the colony was relatively low. Consequently, Yoshida reasoned that more thought criminals were sentenced and imprisoned in Korea since their nationalism obstructed efforts for them to renounce the movement and repent before trial.[49]

In regard to the complexity and seriousness of Korean thought crime, Yoshida explained that in the Japanese metropole the vast majority of thought criminals were arrested under the Peace Preservation Law for supporting organizations that aimed to "alter the kokutai." However, in colonial Korea, thought crime cases often included offenses such as arson and armed robbery, offenses that were covered by other criminal ordinances.[50] This, Yoshida explained, was another reason why indictments and prosecution rates were higher in the colony than in Japan. Last, Yoshida contrasted the criminal indictments under the Peace Preservation Law in Korea, noting that most criminals in Japan were not charged for forming or joining the JCP, but charged with "carrying out the objectives of the party" (*tō no mokuteki suikō kōi*), an infringement that was added in the 1928 revision, as discussed in chapter 2. However, in Korea thought criminals were arrested for the act of forming or joining an illegal organization, and therefore were more often indicted.[51]

This brought Yoshida to consider why there were relatively fewer cases of ideological conversion in Korea than in the Japanese metropole. He notes that, as with the metropole, Korea also entered a "period of conversion" in 1933 (the year Sano Manabu and Nabeyama Sadachika publicly critiqued the Comintern), with a parallel increase in the ratio of conversion cases.[52] However, Yoshida qualifies this development by noting that there was a "qualitative difference" in conversions between metropole and colony. It is worth citing Yoshida's explanation in full, for it reveals how the aporias of imperial ideology in the colony were rearticulated in the new discourse of conversion:

> In the metropole [*naichi*], where people innately have the Japanese spirit, converts awaken to the *kokutai* and their nationality [*kokuminsei*], abandon their dangerous revolutionary thought, and come in some way to serve the state. In contrast, many of the Korean thought criminals convert out of awe [*ifuku*] for our country's national strength and international standing, thus recognizing the impossibility of rebelling against Japan, and recognize that the movement for national liberation will not bring happiness to the Korean people. Consequently, [Korean thought criminals] convert based on sycophantic ideas that lacks faith [*shinnen naki jidaishugi shisō*].[53]

Conceiving it as a strategic-practical decision that lacked faith, Yoshida questions the authenticity of Korean tenkō, asking, "Among Korean tenkōsha, how many are true, complete tenkōsha, who truly recognize our kokutai and grasp the Japanese spirit? . . . Should we not be satisfied if Korean tenkōsha awaken to Japanese consciousness and have self-awareness as Japanese? Therefore, we should say that, compared to conversion in the metropole, Korean tenkō is inferior in its essential content and degree and has a much more mutable quality [*fudōsei*]."[54]

For officials like Yoshida, this problem crystallized in the higher number of cases of ideological recidivism and reverse tenkō (*gyaku-tenkō*) in colonial Korea. Yoshida laments that out of the 2,137 tenkōsha who converted between 1930 and 1935, 220, or around 10 percent, had returned to crimes outlawed by the Peace Preservation Law.[55]

Although the policy and practice of ideological conversion was predicated on an ideology of the Japanese spirit and its ability to subsume all particularities into a multiethnic empire, there was clearly an internal threshold for colonial peoples, as Tokuoka and Yoshida touched upon. Against its own claims of multiethnicity, integration, and the adoptability (*hōyōsei*) of the Japanese spirit, we see how imperial state ideology was, in the last instance, anchored to ethnicity (*minzokusei*)—Japanese ethnicity—which belied the inherent exclusions constitutive of this ideology. This was coded in Yoshida's terms, such as the essential (*honrai*), innate (*honsei*), and natural (*honnōteki*) Japanese spirit that purportedly resided in all ethnic Japanese. This required a different logic for colonial conversion: whereas thought criminals in the metropole were expected to turn inward to cultivate an inherent spirit in order to become reformed imperial subjects, thought criminals in Korea were expected to look outward and subjectively recognize the righteousness and might of an *external* power—that is, the sovereign power of the Japanese Empire and its position within the world.

Therefore, Yoshida's study implied that the colonial state was exercising a different configuration of power through the Peace Preservation Law compared to the metropole: where conversion in Japan was a result of reform policies and institutions mandated to train converts to govern themselves, in the colony conversion was still largely produced by confirming the power and might of the Japanese imperial state, both externally in East Asia and in its ability to domestically suppress any threats to imperial sovereignty.[56] In other words, repression was more explicitly connected to the operations of conversion in the colony than it was earlier in the metropole. Indeed, as a Chōsen Special Higher Police journal explained, "Tenkō in Korea is fundamentally different in that its outcome is a feeling of awe in our nation's righteousness and might in the world [*waga kuni no kokusaiteki seigi to iryoku ni ifuku*]."[57] Undoubtedly, the Chōsen Special Higher Police understood tenkō in relation to their mandate to suppress political crime, thereby expressing the "righteousness and might" of the imperial state.

To be sure, there were cases of colonial tenkōsha actively campaigning in support of Japan's military efforts in China, as mentioned earlier. Such cases were celebrated by officials as expressing the purported benevolence that Japan exercised in the colony, as well as the righteousness of Japan's colonial policy in contrast to the brutality of Western imperialism. Yoshida concludes his 1939 study by citing one Korean convert who declared that, in the name of "world peace" and the "stability of East Asia," converts such as himself would, although lacking the Japanese spirit themselves, "illuminate" and "make this spirit concrete [*gutaika*]" through their daily practices. Noting the present emergency, this convert argued that "as those of the Korean peninsula, we will strengthen the spirit of the unification of Japan and Korea, and illuminate the kokutai concept" in order to respond to the present crisis.[58] Such examples were meant to alleviate concerns that ideological conversion—and by extension, the ideology underwriting Japan's colonial enterprise—was not taking root in Japan's colony.

Consequently, similar to how the spiritual mobilization campaigns in Japan provided a way for tenkōsha to demonstrate their conversions, colonial mobilization and assimilation campaigns in the late 1930s provided the means for Korean thought criminals to demonstrate their own unique criminal reform. As Matsuda Toshihiko and others have revealed, there was an active contingent of colonial converts who mobilized in support of Japan's war in China and its effort to construct a New East Asian Order (Tōa shinchitsujo) and later the Greater East Asian Coprosperity Sphere (Daitōa kyōeiken).[59] By 1941, the various chapters of the All-Korean Emergency Patriotic Thought League became independent affiliates of a new, incorporated association called the Yamato Society (Yamato-juku).[60] The formation of the Yamato Society was an example of Korean tenkōsha declaring their independence within the wider conversion movement, not only organizationally but also in their declaration that they were moving beyond the theoretical debates of groups in the metropole, and truly practicing the essence of tenkō as colonial subjects in their everyday lives.[61] This competition among converts thereby further yoked the meaning and practice of conversion to imperial ideology, even as this ideology was articulated differently between metropole and colony.

Conversion as Ideology: Reformulating Tenkō for War Mobilization

Following Japan's invasion of China in July 1937, justice officials and converts connected ideological conversion to the war effort, portraying tenkō as an important tactic in Japan's larger mission to fortify the Japanese spirit and defend East Asia from foreign powers. This was a natural outgrowth of the increasing ideologization of criminal reform that took place in the mid-1930s. In fact, many departments within the imperial state now portrayed Japan's military struggle in China as, at its core, an existential battle between the Japanese spirit and foreign ideologies that had infiltrated East Asia since the nineteenth century. This notion was encapsulated in the term "thought war" (shisōsen), which referred to an ostensible ideological struggle that had crystallized in the present moment in the Spanish Civil War and the China Incident.[62] A newly formed interministerial body, the Cabinet Information Division (Naikaku jōhōbu), propagated the idea of thought war as it worked to streamline information between government agencies and explain the importance of the China Incident to the wider public.[63] Justice officials contributed to these Cabinet Information Division endeavors, introducing their policy of tenkō as a model for "national thought defense" in the global thought war.

HIRATA ISAO: TENKŌ AND NATIONAL THOUGHT DEFENSE

In early 1938, the Cabinet Information Division held a closed-door Thought War Symposium (Shisōsen kōshūkai) at the prime minister's residence in Tokyo with over one hundred bureaucrats, military officers, media executives, and intellectuals in attendance.[64] While the ostensible purpose of the symposium was to discuss information and propaganda following Japan's invasion of China in July 1937, the presentations had very little to do with the practical coordination of propaganda. Rather, the participants represented the China Incident as the East Asian front line of an extended global thought war against communism, equal in importance to the Spanish Civil War in Europe. The symposium participants argued that although Japan had escaped formal colonization by the West in the nineteenth century, it had been colonized by Western culture and thought. For participants, the China Incident provided the opportunity for the Japanese Empire to restore its cultural-spiritual essence, and expunge communism, liberalism, and individualism from the rest of East Asia. It was in this context that justice officials represented tenkō to their colleagues as a model for the spiritual cleansing of Japan and the cultural revitalization of Asia.

At the closed-door symposium, representatives from the Home and Justice ministries discussed thought war in relation to their decades-long efforts to suppress the domestic communist movement. In their contributions to the 1938 symposium, Justice and Home Ministry representatives retroactively narrated their fight against anarchism, communism, and other foreign political ideologies as the domestic front line within the protracted thought war. Home Ministry officials emphasized the continuing threat posed by domestic communism and the necessary measures to suppress it, while Justice Ministry officials emphasized rehabilitation, self-reflection, and thought guidance. Representatives from both ministries argued that Japan had been under assault from Western thought since the nineteenth century—what had been referred to for decades as the thought problem (shisō mondai)—and that to clarify the imperial kokutai would simultaneously resolve the domestic thought problem as well as the China Incident abroad.[65]

The Justice Ministry was represented at the 1938 symposium by none other than Hirata Isao, who linked his work at the Tokyo Protection and Supervision Center with the thought war. Hirata began his lecture, "Overcoming Marxism" ("Marukishizumu no kokufuku"), by reporting to his colleagues that the vast majority of suspects arrested under the Peace Preservation Law since 1928 were progressing through the process of ideological conversion.[66] To "overcome Marxism," Hirata explained, was not merely to discard Marxism, but rather required a convert to identify as an imperial subject. Consequently, Hirata repeated his claim that the Protection and Supervision Center network was the institutional expression of imperial benevolence, the embodiment of the unique "Japanese spirit within the Justice Ministry system."[67] In these centers, officials guided thought criminals toward a "self-awakening" (*jikaku*) as "true Japanese" (*hontō no nihonjin*), ultimately returning them to "being true human beings."[68]

Hirata confessed that at the beginning he had no clear idea what thought guidance entailed. Rather, he learned about ideological conversion from the tenkōsha that he was advising. In one anecdote, Hirata told the story of a Tokyo Imperial University law student and ex-communist who told Hirata that tenkō begins when one distinguishes between Japan's unique essence and the individualistic liberalism of the West. Paraphrasing the student, Hirata noted that it was impossible for Japanese "to be separated as individuals from the Japanese nation" and that only "as Japanese, [acting] through the Japanese nation, can we serve East Asia and world culture."[69] In this conceptualization, Hirata's advisee understood the source of Japan's national crisis not as the rise of a domestic communist movement, but rather the earlier inheritance of liberalism introduced during the Meiji period (1868–1912). Hirata reported that the law student explained his arrival at communism as the product of his liberal education: "In school, all we were taught was this thing called the world, about the human race [*jinrui*], about man [*ningen*], about humanity [*jindō*]. But, we were taught very little about the Japan that was under our very own feet every day. We were taught very little about the Japanese nation, the Japanese spirit, or the Japanese people. And this was expressed in our direct approval of the [JCP] slogan 'abolish the monarchy' and our direct support of its antiwar propaganda."[70]

The student implied that it was within his own generation's support for communism and its rejection of the Japanese kokutai that the "individualist, liberalist, utilitarian and internationalist ideology" of Hirata's earlier generation came to fruition. Hirata learned from this student that it is only after the cleansing of "individualistic-liberalist thought" that "has clouded," "soiled and stained" the essential Japanese spirit that Marxism can be overcome and the "true Japan can emerge."[71]

Such a cleansing was, of course, already taking place in the Protection and Supervision Centers, which Hirata reframed in terms of the military struggle in China. As analyzed in the introduction, Hirata portrayed the China Incident as a "war of love" (*ai no sensō*), an expression "of the love of the Japanese nation for the Chinese nation" as a "fellow Asian country."[72] He likened the valor displayed in the sweeping military victories of the Imperial Army in China to the swift justice executed against domestic communists, while the "loving care" (*aibu*) expressed by the army toward the Chinese civilian population was replicated in the Protection and Supervision Centers toward reforming communists. Hirata equated his work at the centers with the "pacification units" (*senbunhan*) that operated in occupied areas of China. For Hirata, the connection between the pacification of communists on the home front and the pacification of civilians in occupied China was another example of Japan's benevolent combination of "combat and pacification" in the global thought war.[73]

Hirata concluded his lecture by arguing that the "people who should effect tenkō are not only those defendants from the Communist Party, that is, the thought criminals, but we—this may be rude to say—we, from here forward, must [also] carry out a grand tenkō [*ōkii tenkō*]."[74] Hirata's lecture serves as a clear example of how, in the months following Japan's invasion of China, justice officials working on thought crime were connecting their policy of ideological conversion to thought war discourse, turning tenkō into a principle to be applied to the whole population.

THE RADIANT FIGURE OF REFORM: NAKAMURA YOSHIRŌ'S THEORY OF TENKŌ

Hirata was not alone in presenting ideological conversion as a necessary imperative for all imperial subjects to practice during wartime. His colleague from the Tokyo Thought Criminal Protection and Supervision Center, the procurator and guidance counselor (*hodōsha*) Nakamura Yoshirō, was also calling for all Japanese to ideologically convert. In a series of articles, Nakamura linked his work in the Tokyo Center to Japan's mission in East Asia, imagining a renovated empire after Japan wins the war in China.

In one 1938 pamphlet titled "Thought Policy in the Present Moment" ("Genka ni okeru shisō taisaku"), Nakamura begins by asking, "What happens after the war, what will we have to do then?"—an issue that, Nakamura argues, "the nation [will have to] face together collectively."[75] Nakamura's strategy was to present the Protection and Supervision Centers as providing a model for a renovated Japanese society after the resolution of the China Incident.[76] Here, Nakamura argued that the centers were "stations [*yakusho*] where the future Japanese spirit would be born and nurtured."[77] He explained that this spirit was cultivated through community involvement: the centers drew upon welfare, medical, and other services in order to rehabilitate political criminals, while upon their parole, reformed ex-communists would "purify society" (*shakai no junka*), serving as models for their communities.[78]

In the current crisis, Nakamura argued that by eradicating communism and popular-front thought, Japan was being "cleansed of liberalism, utilitarianism [*kōrishugi*], and profitism." Through such efforts, Japan would eventually stop "following European culture" (*saiō bunka ni taisuru tsuizui*) by "liquidating European remnants."[79] In this larger endeavor, Nakamura envisioned the Protection and Supervision Centers "at the forefront of thought guidance" and working to "awaken . . . the nation's spiritual consciousness."[80] All activities in the centers were facilitated so as to produce a collective spirit, wherein the tenkōsha would "emerge as peaceful Japanese" who had "mastered the Japanese spirit and come into consciousness of the kokutai."[81] Through self-reflection, a new imperial subject was formed, what Nakamura called the "radiant figure of reform" (*kagayakashii kōsei no sugata*).[82] This "radiant figure" was unique to the "Japanese people," a people charged with the task of winning "Eastern liberation" and establishing "an eternal Eastern peace."[83] As the model for this necessary self-reflection, Nakamura figured tenkōsha as "the vanguard of an unyielding national thought defense" (*kyōko na shisō kokubō no zenei to shite*), echoing Hirata's portrayal of tenkō in Japan's campaign for national thought defense reviewed earlier.

In another essay titled "It Is Not Solely Those Involved in Thought Incidents That Are Required to Convert" published in the December 1938 issue of *Kakushin* (*Renovation*), Nakamura invoked a skeptical interlocutor in order to explain conversion and praise the tenkōsha.[84] Rather than constituting a threat to the kokutai, Nakamura argued that these tenkōsha were pioneers (*senkaku*) of an emerging national movement: "the tenkō issue does not end with the so-called tenkō problem for tenkōsha; rather, does it not reflect the totality of issues facing all Japanese? Is it not said that today's generation exists within a critical period of historical change?"[85] In such a historical turning point, wherein "domestic problems are international problems, and international problems are domestic," Nakamura exclaimed that there would "not be one person who will not completely tenkō," and thus the "conversions of the tenkōsha are . . . one step ahead of a general tenkō of the nation."[86] Indeed, as we saw earlier in Kobayashi Morito's writings as well as in Hirata's more recent lectures, Nakamura represented tenkōsha as the vanguard of a spiritual renovation beginning to take place in the Japanese Empire. The first step in such a transformation was for all imperial subjects to grasp the crises that were afflicting Japan and follow the model of the tenkōsha by purifying their thoughts.[87]

Nakamura grounds the logic of ideological conversion in Japan's unique kokutai, which leads Nakamura's fictive interlocutor to ask about Taiwanese and Korean thought criminals: although they—as colonial subjects—are also Japanese (nihonjin), they are of different ethnic origins, thus perhaps are unable to truly convert. Nakamura counters that Japanese communist converts provide a model for their colonial comrades to follow, and points to the recent formation of tenkōsha groups such as the All-Korean Emergency Patriotic Thought League (Jikyoku taiō zenchō shisō hōkoku renmei) as an example of how tenkō is spreading in the colony.[88] However, as explored earlier in this chapter, Nakamura suggests that colonial conversion is a process of recognizing that Korea's destiny is to integrate further into imperial Japan. He celebrates the hundreds of converts in Korea who have "awakened to the pride of being subjects of the empire" (kōkoku kyomin to shite no kyōji ni mezame) and are engaging in patriotic activism in order to "strengthen the unity between Japan and Korea" (naisen ittai no kyōka), the unique telos of colonial conversion.[89]

Nakamura's essay culminates in a section titled "What Is the Essence of Tenkō?" to which he responds that, although not a scholar nor theorist, after considering all the different motivations for conversion, the essence of tenkō is when a thought criminal simply "recognizes 'I am Japanese.'"[90] Tellingly, Nakamura attributes this to the unique "state apparatus" (kokka kikan) that manifests "Japan's beautiful custom of the family system." Consequently, as detainees pass through the stages of prosecution, trial, incarceration, and rehabilitation, they recognize their camaraderie with prison officials which inspires them to reflect on the love of their parents. According to Nakamura, this series of recognitions produces "an awakening to the particularity of our national family-state," once again exemplifying the important function of the family ISA (Althusser) in the theorization and practice of tenkō discussed in chapter 3.[91] Nakamura explains that this transformative process underwrites all the different paths of tenkō, including religious as well as political conversions.

Nakamura concludes by arguing that the collective efforts of tenkōsha—both in the metropole and now also in colonial Korea—provide "a plan for the active establishment of a new Japanese culture" across the empire.

Similar to Hirata, he ends his article by exclaiming, "It is only when the entire nation undergoes a complete tenkō . . . [and] only when the true Japanese consciousness is reached, that the goals of the China Incident can be attained and the establishment of a foundation of eternal peace in the East can occur."[92] For both Hirata and Nakamura, tenkō was no longer simply a criminal justice policy to apply to communists; here all subjects of the emperor were obligated to clarify the kokutai and manifest the Japanese spirit in their daily lives. Nakamura's articles and Hirata's lecture are but a few examples of how officials were formulating the ideology of conversion in 1938 and linking tenkō to the purported thought war taking place around the world.

EXHIBITING CONVERSION: THE 1938 THOUGHT WAR EXHIBITION

Simultaneous with the closed-door Thought War Symposium that Hirata Isao attended in early 1938, the Cabinet Information Division also held a public Thought War Exhibition (Shisōsen tenrankai) in Takashimaya Department Store in downtown Tokyo.[93] The Cabinet Information Division hoped, as a 1937 planning report stated, to reveal through this exhibition "the importance of the thought war to the nation," particularly "in light of the gravity of the current situation."[94] Taking center stage in the exhibition were materials related to the state's thought crime policies, including an original copy of the Sano-Nabeyama letter that was advertised as one of the exciting spectacles to come see (figure 5.1).

The Takashimaya Department Store event was hugely successful, with attendance reportedly totaling 1.3 million visitors over the exhibition's eighteen-day run.[95] Encouraged by these numbers, the Cabinet Information Division sent the exhibition on a tour of department stores throughout Japan, including Marubutsu in Kyoto, Tamaya in Fukuoka, and Imai in Sapporo, as well as Mitsukoshi in Keijō Korea.[96]

The Thought War Exhibition re-presented the global political-economic crises of the 1930s as a conflict between spatialized thought regimes. For example, as attendees entered the exhibition hall on the eighth floor of Takashimaya Department Store, they would see a wall-sized illuminated map created by the store that detailed the threat of international communism.[97] The map, titled *Thought Tendencies of the Contemporary World as Seen from the Anti-Comintern Pact* (*Bōkyōkyōtei yori mitaru gendai sekai shisō no dōkō*), represented the coordinated efforts of the signatories of the Anti-Comintern Pact to contain communism within the borders of the Soviet Union. Japan, Germany, and Italy, represented by photographs of Konoe, Hitler, and Mussolini, formed a vector of ideological containment, overlaying the extension

Figure 5.1. A brief mention in the *Yomiuri Shimbun* advertises the Sano-Nabeyama tenkō declaration as one of the attractions to see in the Thought War Exhibition. "The Cabinet Information Division Provides a Glimpse of the Sano/Nabeyama Tenkō Statement: The Exhibition of the Thought War, Enveloping the World," *Yomiuri Shimbun*, February 2, 1938, morning edition.

of communism into Europe and Asia from the Soviet Union (signified by a picture of Stalin). The map depicted communism's western drive with an illuminated red tube that extended from the Soviet Union through the Popular Front government of Camille Chautemps in France to the border of Spain. To the east, another red tube extended downward into central China (bypassing the puppet state of Manchukuo, established in 1932 by Japan), positing the China Incident as the eastern front in the global thought war.

Another illuminated map, titled *Various Forces of World Thought That Are Assailing East Asia* (*Tōa o osou sekai shisō no shoseiryoku*), transfigured the competing colonialisms in China and East Asia into blocs of thought.[98] This map portrayed China as being enveloped by foreign thought: the Soviet Union stretched over Manchukuo into the northern tip of Sakhalin, with the Mongolian People's Republic to the west, and possessions of the US (Philippines) and France (French Indochina) to the south. Shanghai was shown as being split into French, English, and US intellectual concessions. Japan and its colonial possessions (Korea and Taiwan), the puppet state of Manchukuo, and the Japanese-occupied territories of northeastern China were not shaded on the map as the other areas were; rather, they were clear white. Indeed, in this map's cartographic representation, these Japanese-controlled areas were depicted as virtually free of ideology (if not thought itself). The implication was that the two polarities of the thought war in East Asia were (foreign) ideology versus the Japanese spirit.

Thought war was not only mapped as an external cartography of the world, but was also presented as the conflicting intellectual influences inside the mind of each Japanese imperial subject. Here, the contemporary political movements including the socialist, communist, and anticolonial movements inside the empire were portrayed as the result of dangerous foreign ideologies, linking the battlefront in China and the home front in one ideological field of struggle.[99] This is where the didactic message of the exhibition can be located, for middle-class Takashimaya shoppers were urged to reflect on their own thoughts and purify them of any harmful intellectual influences in order to become loyal imperial subjects. As the head of the Cabinet Information Division, Yokomizo Mitsuteru, explained in the commemorative guidebook to the exhibition, the recent China Incident inaugurated a new stage in the thought war as well as a turning point in world history. This demanded that "each and every Japanese, even those not on the field of military battle, must be active as a soldier of the thought war, so that we can confront the extended war as a unified empire."[100] This is where the Justice Ministry presented their tenkō policy as a model for all Japanese to follow.

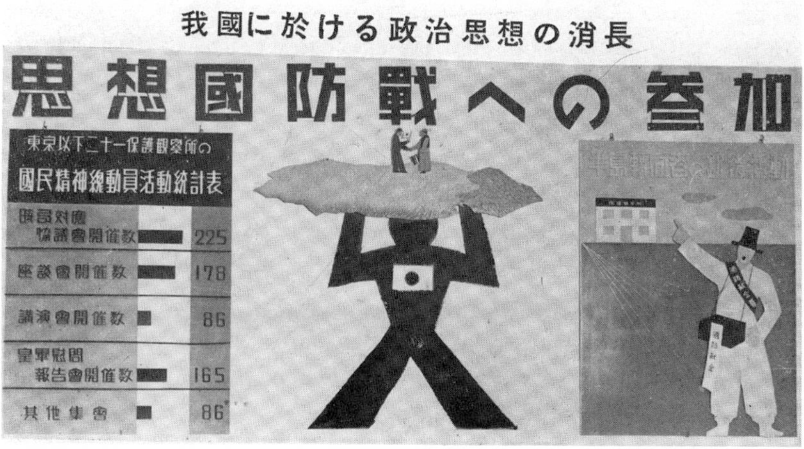

Figure 5.2. "The Vicissitudes of Political Thought in Our Nation: Joining the War for National Thought Defense," in *Shisōsen tenrankai kiroku zukan*, ed. Naikaku Jōhōbu (Tokyo: Naikaku Jōhōbu, 1938), 31.

The Justice Ministry put its new Protection and Supervision Center network and its tenkō policy on full display to the Takashimaya Department Store shopper. For example, in one area of the exhibition organized under the theme, *The Vicissitudes of Political Thought in Our Nation: Joining the War for National Thought Defense* (*Waga kuni ni okeru seiji shisō no shōchō: Shisō kokubōsen e no sanka*), the Justice Ministry's Protection and Supervision Centers were depicted as a bulwark against foreign ideologies (figure 5.2).

To represent this message, a silhouette of a Japanese soldier in the corner of the display carried the caption "The critical situation domestically and abroad demands the introspective self-reflection of the entire nation, thus inaugurating a crucial turning point in the nation's thought."[101] Similar to arguments made by Hirata and Nakamura, the exhibition presented ideological conversion as an imperative for each and every subject of the Japanese Empire, including, apparently, the middle-class Takashimaya Department Store shopper.

Furthermore, national thought defense was a responsibility of Japan's colonial subjects as well. For instance, a poster *The Vicissitudes of Political Thought in Our Nation* presented an image of a reformed resident Korean agitating in support of Japan's military efforts in China. Captioned "Activities on the Home Front by Ideological Converts from the Peninsula" (Hantō tenkōsha no jūgo katsudō), this image showed a colonial subject collecting war donations. In the center of the poster was an image of a Japanese and a representative of the provisional government of occupied China shaking hands, apparently cooperating for the ideological defense of East Asia. In this representation, ideological conversion was given as the basis for realizing the colonial policy of "Japan and Korea as one" (*naisen ittai*).

As advertised, the Justice Ministry displayed an original copy of Sano Manabu and Nabeyama Sadachika's coauthored official report (*jōshinsho*) as well as their 1933 declaration of ideological conversion.[102] Posters reported statistics about the number of incarcerated thought criminals who had performed tenkō as well as the supposed motivations for converting (figure 5.3).[103] Whereas in 1932 only 70 percent of parolees had begun the tenkō process, by 1936, 184 out of 200 parolees, or 90 percent, had reportedly started the conversion process. A pie chart broke down the motivations for effecting tenkō, including family reasons (37.5 percent), a return to national self-awareness (25 percent), a theoretical rejection of Marxism (13.9 percent), and arriving at some newfound (religious) faith (10.4 percent). Such displays celebrated the success of the tenkō policy and urged its expansion into a general mandate for all imperial subjects.

Another installation piece, titled *In Accordance with Imperial Benevolence: The Birth of the Protection and Supervision System, Unlike Any in the World* (*Ōmikokoro o honshite, sekai ni hirui naki, hogokansatsusho seido ikiru*), featured a map explaining the mandate of the Thought Criminal Protection and Supervision Centers, including photographs of the centers' activities and a flowchart that explained the rehabilitation process (figure 5.4).

The flowchart delineated the steps in the rehabilitation process, beginning with the indictment of the thought criminal (*shisōhannin*). It explained how the criminals were then assigned to a Protection and Supervision Center and how, through "securing livelihood" (*seikatsu no kakuritsu*) and "thought guidance" (*shisō no hodō*), they learned to "grasp the Japanese spirit" (*nihon seishin no haaku*).[104]

Posters created by tenkōsha parolees depicted how the thought war was being fought in villages, factories, and schools—sites that became spaces of ideological rehabilitation and national renewal. For example, one diorama, titled *A Reawakened Communized Village* (*Yomigaetta sekka mura*), described the political reform of a village after communist agitators were arrested and imprisoned. In atonement, the village set out to renovate the countryside by increasing agricultural output and opening new land for cultivation.[105] In a poster created by student converts, students were depicted agitating at their school, manipulated like puppets by a political organizer dressed in black as their parents looked on from a distant rice field.

治安維持法違反者中より 轉向者續出す			
年次	出獄者數	內轉向者	出獄者に對する轉向の比率
昭和7年	97	68	7割強
昭和8年	105	72	7割強
昭和9年	289	247	8割強
昭和10年	321	285	8割強
昭和11年	200	184	9割強

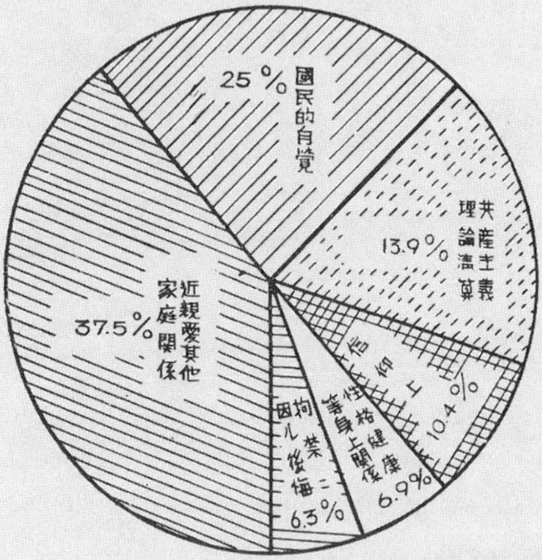

Figure 5.3. Table, "The Number of Tenkōsha among Peace Preservation Law Offenders," through 1937 and pie chart explaining motivations for tenkō. Naikaku Jōhōbu, ed., *Shisōsen tenrankai kiroku zukan* (Tokyo: Naikaku Jōhōbu, 1938), 31.

They are then portrayed as black angels with school caps, flying through the Protection and Supervision Centers and eventually emerging as pure white students.[106] Yet another poster described the industrial skills training program at the Imperial Renovation Society in Tokyo. Here the exhibition attendee learned that many tenkōsha laborers were reskilled for industrial production, thus gaining new confidence and embodying "skills for the nation" (*gijutsu hōkoku*).[107] Tellingly, each narrative of ideological conversion exhibited in this section concluded with the convert manifesting the imperial spirit by increasing production for the nation, whether farmer, student, or laborer.

Similar to Hirata and Nakamura's representations of tenkōsha discussed earlier, the 1938 Thought War Exhibition presented a radically new image of

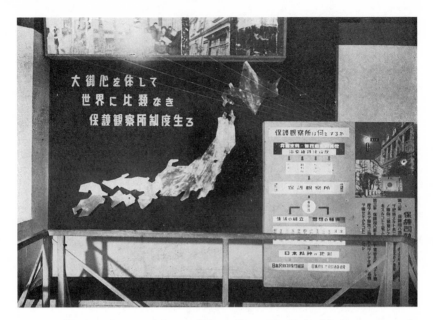

Figure 5.4. "In Accordance with Imperial Benevolence: The Birth of the Protection and Supervision System, Unlike Any in the World," in *Shisōsen tenrankai kiroku zukan*, ed. Naikaku Jōhōbu (Tokyo: Naikaku Jōhōbu, 1938), 34.

tenkōsha to the public: no longer did ex-communists embody the infiltration of foreign ideology into Japan's national polity (kokutai) as they once had; now they were transfigured into the vanguard of Japan's intellectual purification and spiritual awakening. Tenkōsha became exemplars of the potential for intellectual reflection and mobilization. Simultaneously, the Thought Crime Protection and Supervision Centers transformed the image of the imperial state as an apparatus staunchly defending against dangerous foreign thought into a benevolent guide for recuperating one's imperial subjectivity.

Preventative Detention and the 1941 Peace Preservation Law Revision

As the war in China dragged on into 1939, government officials and the public began to realize that the China Incident had become a military quagmire, depleting resources and driving mobilization campaigns relentlessly further into everyday life. In this context, there were renewed calls to revise the Peace Preservation Law in 1940 to prevent any new possible ideological threats in this unstable time of crisis. Specifically, officials hoped to instate the Preventative Detention system for the handful of recalcitrant communists who, nearing completion of their original prison sentences from the 1931–1932 trials, had refused to reject their dangerous ideas and ideologically convert. Recall that preventative detention was proposed in the 1934 Peace Preservation revision bill that failed to pass.[108] Now, with the Imperial Army in China and war raging in Europe, proponents of preventative detention declared that officials were standing at "the front line of national thought defense" in a particularly critical time.[109] Although Protection and Supervision Centers were overseeing thought criminals who had been paroled or placed in one of the suspension programs, and while the Preventative Detention system was to complement Protection and Supervision, this revision would once again emphasize the repressive function of the Peace Preservation Law apparatus. By this time, however, the elements of thought purification and spiritual resolve that had defined the conversion policy targeting political criminals had been translated into the wider National Spirit Mobilization Movement for the general populace, as we saw in the last section.

The logic behind this push to revise the Peace Preservation Law was outlined in a May 1940 meeting of justice officials working on thought crime cases.[110] Three reasons were given. First, the Peace Preservation Law in its 1925 and 1928 versions was designed to explicitly suppress communism, anarchism, and anticolonial nationalism. However, officials argued that new ideological threats had emerged in the latter half of the 1930s, including antifascist Popular Front groups, which officials saw as front organizations for reorganizing the JCP.[111] There were also "dangerous religious ideas" such as those espoused by new, unorthodox religions including Tenri honmichi.[112] Earlier, when the new religion Ōmotokyō was suppressed in 1935, there were debates about whether to apply the Peace Preservation Law or the Criminal Code (Article 74) to the group. Proponents argued that, under the new wartime conditions, it was necessary to revise the Peace Preservation Law so that its applicability to unorthodox religious groups was clear and straightforward.

Second, it was argued that procurators needed expanded powers to detain and investigate individuals arrested under the Peace Preservation Law. And, in this same spirit, the third argument for revision was to instate preventative detention, a policy that many politicians had rejected in the proposed 1934 revision to the Peace Preservation Law. Now, with the state mobilizing the empire for war, justice officials argued that preventative detention was necessary for recalcitrant communists who had fully served their prison sentences but still held dangerous ideas.[113] Taken together, justice officials wished to expand both the coverage of the Peace Preservation Law and the powers of procurators to oversee thought crime cases.[114]

Justice officials worked on this revision for the next half year. The resulting bill was presented by Vice Justice Minister Miyake Masatarō to the Seventy-Sixth Imperial Diet in February 1941.[115] Miyake argued that the revision was necessary so that the state could confront the increasing complexity of ideological threats, including those posed by the Comintern's Popular Front strategy, new religions, and nationalist movements in the colonies. Miyake explained that the parameters of the Peace Preservation Law needed to be widened so as to suppress (*torishimari*) those who joined or supported communist front groups (*gaibu dantai*) or other groups that intended to "alter the kokutai."[116] Similarly, Miyake argued that procurators required more discretion during criminal procedures for thought crime cases. And finally, Miyake argued for the necessity of the Preventative Detention system so that procurators had more time to uncover and eradicate the dangerous thought of a detainee, prevent ideological recidivism upon parole, and ultimately prevent that which "endangered state security" (*kokka chian ni kansuru kiken*).[117] Although preventative detention was critiqued in the 1934 revision debates analyzed in chapter 4, under the increasing strains of the war in China, members of the Diet were receptive to the argument that preventative detention was a necessary wartime policy.[118]

The revision passed the Diet on March 10, 1941, and ordinances were issued on May 14 in the Japanese metropole and colonies announcing the new law.[119] As many historians have noted, this was an entirely new law, growing to sixty-five articles, inspiring Okudaira and other scholars to refer to it as the New Peace Preservation Law (Shin-chianijihō).[120] The law stipulated that anyone who "organizes an association with the objective of altering the kokutai, or a person who has performed the duties of an official or leader of such a group" (*kessha no yakunin sono hoka shidōsha taru ninmu ni jūji shitaru mono*) would be sentenced to death, imprisonment for life, or not less than seven years. Additionally, anyone who was found guilty of forming or joining a group "with the objective of aiding an association" with the above objectives (i.e., altering the kokutai or rejecting the private property system) could also be condemned to death or life imprisonment. Tellingly, the crime of "rejecting the private property system" was moved down to Article 10 of the new law, further demonstrating that the kokutai remained the primary object to be protected. On the same day the new law was issued (May 14), the government issued orders to establish Preventative Detention Centers, including in Taiwan and Kwantung Leased Territory.[121] As legal historian Uchida Hirofumi has demonstrated, the New Peace Preservation Law was an important component within the larger construction of what Uchida calls the "wartime security legal system" (*senji chian hōsei*).[122]

The new law was also issued by the government of Manchukuo later that year, on December 27, 1941. As mentioned in chapter 2, security measures were passed at the time the new quasi-sovereign state of Manchukuo was established in 1932, including Manchukuo's own Public Peace Police Law. Soon thereafter, these laws were complemented by further security laws as Japanese advisers in Manchukuo became increasingly concerned about communist groups and Korean guerilla fighters operating inside Manchukuo.[123] Following Japan's invasion in 1937 and Manchuria's strategic location between northern China, the Soviet Union, and the Korean peninsula, officials believed it was necessary to implement the New Peace Preservation Law there.[124] As Nakazawa notes, the offense of altering the kokutai was interpreted as including groups threatening not only the Manchu (Qing) monarch but also the Japanese imperial household.[125] Although it is difficult to confirm exact numbers, Nakazawa reports that around 110,000 people were arrested in Manchukuo under the law between 1941 and 1945. Furthermore, with fears of ideological recidivism, it is reported that the Protection and Supervision as well as Preventative Detention systems were implemented at the end of 1943.[126]

Preventative Detention Centers had already been established in colonial Korea one month before the New Peace Preservation Law, on February 13, 1941 (Ordinance No. 8).[127] Ogino Fujio has noted how, in the context of the China Incident, colonial officials worried that the Protection and Supervision system was insufficient to deal with recalcitrant thought criminals in the colony.[128] Thus, in late 1940, the Korean Government-General started to prepare an outline for a Preventative Detention system particular to Korea's thought crime conditions, modeled on the proposal from the failed Peace Preservation Law revision bill of 1934.[129] This Preventative Detention system was implemented in colonial Korea in February, and was operative until it was replaced on May 1 when the New Peace Preservation Law went into effect. However, the Korean Preventative Detention system retained particular policies unique to the colonial situation, including an emphasis on isolating (*kakuri*) detainees so that, through education (*kyōka*), they would "grasp ideas that clarify the kokutai" and have "a resolute faith in the way of the imperial nation" instilled in them.[130]

Over the next few years, the New Peace Preservation Law was used by the Special Higher Police and other agencies to uncover a number of purported communist plots, as exemplified in infamous wartime incidents such as the roundup of ex-tenkōsha in the Mantetsu Research Bureau Incident (Mantetsu chōsabu jiken) in 1942–1943, and the Yokohama Incident (Yokohama jiken) in which Special Higher Police arrested dozens of intellectuals and journalists in 1943–1945, torturing many of the suspects.[131] Although relatively fewer compared to the early 1930s, arrests peaked in the metropole the year the Peace Preservation Law was revised, with annual totals of 1,212 in 1941, 698 in 1942, 600 in 1943, 501 in 1944, and 109 in the first half of 1945.[132] In colonial Korea, although statistics exist only for the early 1940s, 1,386 individuals were arrested in 1941, and 955 in 1942.[133] By December 1944, the Korean Government-General reported that fifty-nine individuals remained in Preventative Detention, including twenty recalcitrant nonconverts (hitenkōsha), twenty-five individuals who had advanced beyond partial conversion (juntenkō), and fourteen who were advancing toward partial tenkō.[134]

Heading up the new Tokyo Preventative Detention Center (Kōkinsho) was none other than Nakamura Yoshirō, who, as the detainee Matsumoto Kazumi recounted later, "managed the center with absolute faith in the universal truth of the Japanese spirit and emperorism."[135] Matsumoto reports that the Tokyo Preventative Detention Center was housed in the oldest building in the Toyotama Prison complex in the Nakano District.[136] Around sixty-five persons passed through the Tokyo Preventative Detention Center in the 1940s: fifty-three people allegedly connected to the JCP, Marxist cultural groups, the Popular Front movement, or radical labor unions; six resident Korean activists related to either the Korean labor or national liberation movement, and a handful of individuals from religious groups, including various Tenri sects and Christians. Within the first category, the Marxist theoretician Fukumoto Kazuo was one of the inmates at the Tokyo center, but was released after four months.[137]

Matsumoto recalls that Nakamura told detainees at the center that "compared to the detention centers in Hitler's Germany, the Preventative Detention Center is heaven, a result of the Emperor's benevolence and the glory of Japan's kokutai."[138] Indeed, officials used the esoteric *Fundamental Principles of the Kokutai* (*Kokutai no hongi*, 1937) as a textbook to guide detainees toward grasping the imperial kokutai.[139] In addition to studying *Kokutai no hongi*, Matsumoto recalls that prisoners were granted access only to books that "espoused the glory of the emperor system."[140] Additionally, philosophers, Buddhists, and Shinto priests as well as various justice officials would come to give lectures on the imperial kokutai. Only three detainees of the Tokyo Preventative Detention Center were reported to have been released early, and even then they were required to register at a Protection and Supervision Center (as was protocol). As a graduation present they were given their own copy of *Kokutai no hongi*.

The addition of Preventative Detention to the Peace Preservation Law apparatus required that officials implement a new definition of tenkō in order to assess which program a thought criminal who had served his or her prison sentence should be assigned to—Protection and Supervision, Preventative Detention, or parole. Here we find the most ideological definition for tenkō, defined as when a thought criminal "breaks with previous thought and practices the way of an imperial subject in everyday life" (*nichijō seikatsu ri ni shimindō o kyūko shi*).[141] Since anything less than "practicing the way of an imperial subject in everyday life" constituted a partial tenkō, this meant that partial conversion or juntenkō extended to the vast majority of thought criminals who had already discarded so-called dangerous thought. However, considering that Preventative Detention was to oversee nonconverts, and that the main elements of conversion had been translated into national mobilization policy, this new definition of tenkō functioned as a foil to legitimate the continued detention of thought criminals deemed too dangerous to be released from the Preventative Detention Centers, thus restoring the original repressive function of the Peace Preservation Law analyzed in chapter 2. By this point, of course, disciplinary power and governmental techniques were diffused throughout society to mobilize the general population for war.

Conclusion: Conversion in Japan's Holy War

As explored in this chapter, in the early years of the China Incident tenkōsha were expected to demonstrate their rehabilitation by proactively supporting the war effort in China, while at the same time they were celebrated as the vanguard of the spiritual purification and renovation of the Japanese Empire. In articles and speeches as well as public exhibitions, justice officials reformulated conversion as an ideological trope, what I have called the ideology of conversion. In this reformulation, tenkō was presented as the key to mobilizing the spiritual resolve of the entire Japanese Empire, solving the China Incident, and cleansing Japan and East Asia of harmful ideological influences.

However, as the war dragged on, the mobilization of converts lost its renovationist significance, and in this context conversion became a foil in the Peace Preservation Law to justify the prolonged detention of recalcitrant thought criminals. It is for this reason that my analysis concludes in the early 1940s, for although the Peace Preservation Law apparatus continued to operate until October 1945, its conversion policy had been abstracted from the Protection and Supervision Centers in 1937–1940 and translated into a wartime policy for the mobilization of the general population as exemplified by the National Spirit Mobilization Movement. The demotion of criminal rehabilitation during the war was symbolized by the government's decision to close the Justice Ministry's Bureau of Protection (Hogo-kyoku) in November 1943.[142] Additionally, the number of personnel working in the field of criminal reform declined dramatically.[143] And although the Cabinet Information Division held two more Thought War Exhibitions in 1939 and 1940, the optimism about conversion displayed in the initial 1938 exhibition was much more muted, as tenkō became connected to Japan's "holy war" (seisen) for the soul of East Asia.[144]

This increasing pessimism surrounding conversion can be found in Kobayashi Morito's wartime experiences. Recall that, as explored in earlier chapters, Kobayashi provided an early formulation of the practice of defection from Marxism as a religious experience (shūkyōteki na taiken) in the early 1930s, and then implemented and refined the definition of tenkō after 1934 as the head of the Imperial Renovation Society's Thought Section. Part of this effort involved retraining converted laborers in industrial production. Toward this end, the Imperial Renovation Society set up the Metalworks Vocational Center (Kinzokubu jusanjō) in 1937, as well as a factory in 1938 called the Reformed Workers Production Factory (Kōshinsha seisakusho) in the Kamata district of Tokyo.[145] Under intensifying wartime conditions, this factory was expanded in 1939, wherein tenkōsha laborers manufactured machinery parts up until the spring of 1945, when the location was firebombed in Allied bombing raids. Then, as Japan was preparing for the final defense of the homeland, Kobayashi collaborated with other reform officials and tenkōsha to create a private factory called Pacific Precision Instruments Inc. (Taiyō seiki kabushiki gaisha). This was the tragic conclusion of Kobayashi's conversion story: initiated with his religious conversion, sustained through his selfless efforts to assist hundreds of his comrades to convert and reintegrate into the imperial polity, to now mobilizing his fellow tenkōsha in a wartime factory. Whatever benevolent or spiritual value Kobayashi had invested in tenkō earlier in the 1930s was now overshadowed by the imperatives of Japan's holy war.

The Legacies of the Thought Rehabilitation
System in Postwar Japan

In this volume, we have explored how the Peace Preservation Law (Chianijihō) configured a modern security apparatus that, by the mid-1930s, combined various modes of power—including sovereign, disciplinary, and governmental techniques—to first suppress and then rehabilitate political criminals who were said to be threatening the imperial state. Moreover, in the 1930s this apparatus increasingly drew upon the tenets of imperial ideology to define criminal rehabilitation and the practice of ideological conversion (tenkō), thereby becoming one of the most important Ideological State Apparatuses (Althusser) of the interwar emperor system (tennōsei). This apparatus was not confined to the Japanese metropole but applied in Japan's colonies as well, most notably against the active anticolonial movement in Korea. As we have reviewed, the functional complexity of the apparatus and its constitutive modes of power combined differently in response to the different and changing political conditions in the metropole and colonies.

In addition to providing an archive for understanding how tennōsei ideology was articulated, transformed, and disseminated in the interwar Japanese Empire, the Peace Preservation Law can also serve as a site from which to consider how prewar institutions and practices influenced the postwar democratic order in Japan. Here I would like to conclude by pointing to three general legacies of the Peace Preservation Law's thought reform policies in the postwar period in order to suggest new areas for research: the political, intellectual-historical, and institutional transwar legacies.

First and most immediately, in regard to political legacies, the Allied Occupation arrived with the mandate to demilitarize and democratize Japan. In this spirit, on October 4, 1945, the General Headquarters (GHQ) issued the Removal of Restrictions on Political, Civil, and Religious Liberties directive (SCAPIN-93)—what is known as the Human Rights Directive.[1] This directive ordered the Japanese government to disband any organs that restricted, censored, or oversaw religious belief, thought, speech, published materials, and so on, including the Special Higher Police (Tokubetsu kōtō keisatsu) as well as the centers overseeing thought criminals including the Protection and Supervision and Preventative Detention Centers. On October 15, the Peace Preservation Law as well as the Thought Criminal Protection and Supervision Law were repealed.[2] Soon thereafter, detainees were released from Preventative Detention Centers (Yobō kōkin sho) in the Japanese metropole, including communists such as JCP leader Tokuda Kyūichi. The few remaining nonconverts (hi-tenkōsha) affiliated with the JCP were celebrated for remaining defiant against militarism and fascism while incarcerated throughout the war.[3] In addition to those emerging from the Preventative Detention Centers, over two thousand parolees in the metropole were released from Protection and Supervision status.[4]

However, at the same time as these directives were being carried out in the name of democratization and demilitarization, Japanese officials warned of growing political turbulence amid Japan's defeat and occupation. On October 18, just three days after the Peace Preservation Law was abolished, the Japanese government issued "On the Control of Mass Movements" ("Taishū undō no torishimari ni kansuru ken"), which expressed the Japanese state's concern with political threats arising from the unstable socioeconomic situation in the wake of defeat.[5] Soon thereafter, various ministries created offices that would control mass movements, which, unsurprisingly, were staffed by personnel from the prewar thought crime system.

For example, two months after the Special Higher Police were dissolved, the Home Ministry's Police Affairs Bureau (Keiho-kyoku) created a new Public Security Section (Kōan-ka) in December 1945, an office that was then established in local police departments across Japan in July 1946.[6] Despite the Home Ministry being disbanded in 1947, these local Security Sections continued to operate.[7] It should come as no surprise that many of the officials that staffed the Security Police (Kōan keisatsu) were previous Special Higher Police personnel. And, with the passage of the new Police Law in 1954, the Security Police were expanded and strengthened, exemplifying one of the clearest institutional continuities between the prewar and postwar police system at the local level.[8]

Turning to the Justice Ministry, in October the Justice Ministry started to voluntarily dissolve particular bureaus that dealt with thought crime, which continued up through an internal purge of twenty-five justice officials including prior thought procurators in July 1946.[9] Although a few high-profile procurators such as Ikeda Katsu were dismissed in the purges, many top officials in the Justice Ministry during the occupation period had in fact worked as thought procurators before the war.[10] With increasing labor agitation during the shortages and lockouts of 1946, the Justice Ministry joined with other ministries to collaborate to "preserve social order" (*shakai chitsujo hoji*) against new political and social threats. Toward this end, the Justice Ministry envisioned a new branch of prosecutors functioning as Security Prosecutors (Kōan kensatsu) as well as labor procurators (Rōdō gakari kenji) to complement the Home Ministry's Security Police mentioned above. In this way, the function of prewar thought procurators was translated into the new political conditions of the Occupation.[11]

To provide a legal mandate for the Security Police and Security Prosecutors upon the end of the Occupation, the newly sovereign Japanese government passed the Subversive Activities Prevention Law (No. 240, Hakai katsudō bōshihō) in 1952. Although this law was couched in terms of postwar freedoms such as protecting "thought, belief, assembly, organizing, expression, and academic freedom," its objective was "to secure the public safety" (*kōkyō no anzen no kakuho no tame*) against subversive political groups. Many critics at the time worried that this law was a version of the prewar Peace Preservation Law masquerading behind the rhetoric of postwar liberal democracy.[12] Therefore, when considering the political legacies in postwar Japan, while the transwar careers of high-profile politicians such as the Class A war criminal suspect and future prime minister Kishi Nobusuke (a.k.a. the "Phantom of Shōwa" or Shōwa no yōkai) clearly connect the wartime and postwar governments, it is also important to recognize that lower-level police and justice officials affiliated with the prewar Peace Preservation Law apparatus continued to police political threats into the postwar period and were armed with new political crime laws.

Second, the intellectual-historical legacies of the prewar thought reform system are perhaps the best known, for it was in the early postwar period that tenkō was reformulated as a question unique to Japan's modern intellectual history. Indeed, the prewar tenkō phenomenon became a historical foil against which a variety of thinkers, including Maruyama Masao, Tsurumi

Shunsuke, Yoshimoto Takaaki, and others, considered critical possibility and political praxis in the early postwar, reaching its most rigorous formulation in the subjectivity debates (*shutaisei ronsō*) of the late 1940s and 1950s.[13] Through the question of prewar tenkō, the political-intellectual positions of the postwar left were defined—most notably since many prewar tenkōsha returned to the JCP in the postwar, a phenomenon that their critics labeled an act of reverse tenkō (*gyaku-tenkō*).[14] Similarly, a new generation of leftist writers reconsidered the legacy of the prewar proletarian writers, analyzing prewar tenkō literature (*tenkō bungaku*) in order to define new critical possibilities for writers in the postwar.[15] As I discussed in chapter 3, the tenkō phenomenon inspired postwar intellectuals to consider a new framework for Japan's modern intellectual trajectory, wherein tenkō was generalized beyond the specific history of the interwar thought crime phenomenon to signify anytime a major shift occurred in modern Japanese intellectual history.[16] In this way, the ghosts that animated the Peace Preservation Law apparatus and the imperial polity in the 1930s continued to haunt the postwar in a different register, now as the search for a form of subjectivity adequate to (postwar) modernity.

It is important to note, however, that this problematic had less to do with understanding the complex ideological and institutional context that produced the interwar tenkō phenomenon and more to do with establishing the intellectual and political parameters of the postwar period. Indeed, Adam Bronson has called the late 1950s the "age of conversion," in which tenkō was reoriented to speak to new political conditions, largely of postwar intellectual questions.[17] As I have argued here, we cannot abstract the question of tenkō from the 1930s without first understanding the material apparatuses that generated the phenomenon and the ritualized forms that defined its practice. This is especially important, for at the same exact time that tenkō became the animating question for postwar writers and intellectuals, the criminal apparatuses in which tenkō was first formulated were reestablished by the Justice Ministry, although its explicitly political function was more muted than before. This is the third and final legacy I would like to briefly discuss.

The least studied area of transwar Japanese history in English-language scholarship is the institutional legacies of the prewar criminal rehabilitation system.[18] Very early in the Occupation, the Justice Ministry started to rebuild a protection and supervision system, beginning with reestablishing juvenile protection services in 1946, then passing a new Juvenile Law in July 1948 (Shōnenhō, No. 168, which took effect January 1, 1949). The Justice Ministry then expanded protection and reform to adult parolees and suspects in either the Suspended Indictment or Suspended Sentence programs, thereby replicating the prewar process in which juvenile reform was extended to adult suspects in the 1920s and 1930s.[19] These latter efforts were formalized through a series of laws in the late 1940s and early 1950s, including the Offenders Prevention and Rehabilitation Act (Hanzaisha yobō kōsei hō, No. 142) and the Suspended Sentence Protection and Supervision Law (Shikkō yūyosha hogokansatsu hō, No. 58), both passed in 1949, and then the extensive Judicial Protection Law (Hogo shihō, No. 204) in 1950, which established institutional and financial support for criminal rehabilitation.[20]

If the penal and legal institutions of criminal rehabilitation were being reestablished in the early postwar period, what of the ghosts that had animated the reform apparatuses in the 1930s, that is, the ideology of the imperial sovereign and his loyal subjects? Early in the Occupation, Emperor Hirohito had renounced his divinity in his so-called Declaration of Humanity (Ningen sengen) on New Year's Day 1946.[21] Soon thereafter, a new postwar constitution went into effect in May 1947 which declared that the emperor was no longer sovereign, but "the symbol of the State and of the unity of the people, deriving his position from the will of the people with whom resides sovereign power."[22] However, paradoxically, it was exactly in this new symbolic capacity that the imperial family started to make appearances at annual gatherings of criminal and youth reform officials. For example, Emperor Hirohito, whose image in the 1930s served as the divine inspiration for a criminal to reform as a loyal imperial subject, attended national gatherings commemorating the establishment of the postwar rehabilitation system.[23] Crown Prince Akihito and Princess Michiko and Prince and Princess Takamatsu would also attend national criminal reform gatherings throughout the postwar period. This custom continues up to the present.[24] In this way, at the same time that prewar criminal reform institutions were being reestablished in the name of postwar democracy, the emperor and the imperial family continued to provide symbolic value to the practice of criminal rehabilitation. Criminal reform continued to be measured by productive labor upon parole and the ability to reintegrate into society; however, if in the prewar this was guided by the ideology of the divine emperor and reintegration into the imperial kokutai, now in the postwar, criminal reform was measured through productive citizenship in the Japanese nation symbolized by the emperor.

Therefore, although there were important differences in their conceptualization and application, I contend that, similar to Jonathan Abel's suggestion that we reconsider the transwar history of the institutions and practices of censorship, we should situate the reestablishment of criminal reform in the 1940s and 1950s within a transwar continuum of efforts to institutionalize criminal rehabilitation, starting with experiments with juvenile protection in the 1920s, the pioneering 1936 Thought Criminal Protection and Supervision Law, its expansion in the 1939 Judicial Protection Services Law (Shihō hogo jigyō hō) through the early postwar criminal reform measures which culminated in the extensive Judicial Protection Law of 1950.[25]

This is especially important since official histories of the postwar criminal reform system tend to de-emphasize this prewar legacy, starting their historical timeline in the late 1940s in order to represent reform and rehabilitation as part of Japan's postwar democratization.[26] When these official histories do narrate the development of parole and protective services in twentieth-century Japan, they often do not mention the first time protection was codified and legally applied to adult detainees: that is, the 1936 Thought Criminal Protection and Supervision Law.[27] Yet the postwar reform system was clearly built upon the protocols established in the 1930s and was overseen by a cadre of justice officials who had worked in the prewar criminal reform system, including the offices that specialized in so-called thought crime.

Furthermore, when official histories do refer to the thought crime apparatus as a chapter in the prehistory (zenshi) of postwar rehabilitation efforts, there is no mention of the important colonial components of the prewar system, effectively confining this legacy to Japan's national history. If, as Umemori Naoyuki has argued, Japan's modern police and penitentiary system was modeled on the colonial police systems of Western imperial powers in the late nineteenth century, what Umemori calls a process of "colonial mediation," then I would suggest that we consider the postimperial mediations of Japan's colonial empire in the postwar police and rehabilitation system.[28] More research on the transwar legacies of the criminal rehabilitation apparatus are necessary so we can reflect on the significance that criminal reform policies developed during the consolidation of fascism and militarism in the 1930s were so easily adapted to the postwar liberal democratic order, functioning to discipline the population for rapid economic growth during the Cold War. This is especially important in light of the current political-legal transformations taking place in Japan in the name of national defense and the war on terror, which many Japanese legal scholars see as paralleling developments in the 1930s.[29]

Preface

1. For an overview of these cases, see Laura Yuen, Mukhtar Ibrahim, and Sasha Aslanian, "Called to Fight: Minnesota's ISIS Recruits," *Minnesota Public Radio News*, March 25, 2015, http://www.mprnews.org/story/2015/03/25/minnesota-isis#ayusuf.

2. Giorgio Agamben, *State of Exception*, trans. Kevin Attell (Chicago: Chicago University Press, 2005).

3. On the concept of radicalization, see Arun Kudnani, "Radicalisation: The Journey of a Concept," *Race and Class* 54, no. 2 (September 2012): 3–25.

4. Uchida Hirofumi, for example, has argued that current legal developments reflect the changes to the legal system in the 1920s and 1930s that prepared Japan for total war. See Uchida Hirofumi, *Keihō to sensō: Senji chian hōsei no tsukurikata* (Tokyo: Misuzu shobō, 2015). In particular, Uchida and others have pointed to the Peace Preservation Law when critiquing the inclusion of "criminal conspiracy" (*kyōbōzai*) in the revised 2017 Organized Crime Law (Soshikiteki hanzai shobatsu hō) that proponents argue is necessary for investigating and prosecuting supposed terrorism cases. See Uchida Hirofumi, *Chianijihō to kyōbōzai* (Tokyo: Iwanami, 2017); and Hōgaku Seminaa Henshūbu, ed., *Kyōbōzai hihyō: Kaisei soshikiteki hanzai shobatsu hō no kentō* (Tokyo: Nihon hyōronsha, 2017). On the passage of this controversial "conspiracy law" see: Colin Jones, "Will Japan's New Conspiracy Law Lead to 'Thought Crime'?" *The Diplomat*, July 17, 2017, https://thediplomat.com/2017/07/will-japans-new-conspiracy-law-lead-to-thought-crime/.

5. Brendan I. Koerner, "Can You Turn a Terrorist Back into a Citizen? A Controversial New Program Aims to Reform Homegrown ISIS Recruits Back into Normal Americans," *Wired*, January 24, 2017, https://www.wired.com/2017/01/can-you-turn-terrorist-back-into-citizen/.

6. See Mukhtar Ibrahim and Laura Yuen, "Judge Orders Study of Terror Defendants before Sentencing," *Minnesota Public Radio News*, March 2, 2016, https://www.mprnews.org/story/2016/03/02/judge-outlines-steps-to-divert-mn-terror-defendants-islamic-state-isis-recruitment. See also Stephen Montemayor, "Terror Suspects Will Test Deradicalization Program," *Minneapolis Star Tribune*, March 2, 2016, http://www.startribune.com/judge-orders-de-radicalization-study-for-4-terror-defendants/370806141. See also the announcement on the GIRDS website: "GIRDS Contracted to Design New Deradicalization Program in the United States," GIRDS, April 3, 2016,

http://girds.org/news/girds-contracted-to-design-new-deradicalization-program-in
-the-united-states.

7. Montemayor, "Terror Suspects Will Test Deradicalization Program." I thank Stephen Montemayor for meeting with me to discuss these cases in November 2016.

8. Daniel Koehler, cited in Stephen Montemayor, "Deradicalization Expert Concludes Testimony in Minnesota ISIL Case Evaluations," *Minneapolis Star Tribune*, September 21, 2016, http://www.startribune.com/deradicalization-expert-concludes
-testimony-in-minnesota-isil-case-evaluations/394354591/.

9. Koehler also met with chief probation officer Kevin Lowery and ten of his officers, training them "for counseling extremists." See Koerner, "Can You Turn a Terrorist Back into a Citizen?"

10. Kevin Lowry, cited in Montemayor, "Deradicalization Expert Concludes Testimony."

11. Ikeda Katsu, *Chianijihō*, in *Shinhōgaku zenshū* (Nihon Hyōronsha, 1939), vol. 19, 24. English translation (amended) from Patricia G. Steinhoff, "Tenkō and Thought Control," in *Japan and the World: Essays on Japanese History and Politics in Honour of Ishida Takeshi*, ed. Gail Lee Bernstein and Haruhiro Fukui (New York: St. Martin's, 1988), 79.

12. Montemayor, "Deradicalization Expert Concludes Testimony."

13. Mila Koumpilova, "Minnesota Officials Envision Probation Program for People Facing Terror Charges," *Minneapolis Star Tribune*, January 9, 2016, http://www
.startribune.com/minnesota-officials-envision-a-probation-program-for-people-facing
-terror-charges/364754521/.

14. Koerner, "Can You Turn a Terrorist Back into a Citizen?"

15. Koumpilova, "Minnesota Officials Envision Probation Program." See also Montemayor, "Terror Suspects Will Test Deradicalization Program."

16. Judge Davis was influenced by Koehler's pessimistic assessments of the defendants' varying potential for deradicalization. See Koerner, "Can You Turn a Terrorist Back into a Citizen?"

17. Stephen Montemayor and Faiza Mahamud, "Decades in Prison for Final 3 Sentenced in Minnesota ISIL Conspiracy Case," *Minneapolis Star Tribune*, November 16, 2016, http://www.startribune.com/final-3-of-minnesota-s-isil-defendants-appear-for
-sentencing/401501085/. See also Laura Yuen and Doualy Xaykaothao, "Third ISIS Sentence of the Day: 10 Years," *Minnesota Public Radio News*, November 15, 2016, https://
www.mprnews.org/story/2016/11/15/day-2-of-isis-trial.

18. Stephen Montemayor, "All Eyes on Minnesota Federal Judge before Sentencing in Nation's Biggest ISIL Recruitment Case," *Minneapolis Star Tribune*, November 12, 2016, http://m.startribune.com/all-eyes-on-minnesota-federal-judge-before-sentencing-in
-nation-s-biggest-isil-recruitment-case/400955075/.

19. The US Department of Homeland Security CVE website has since been revised. US Department of Homeland Security, "Terrorism Prevention Partnerships," accessed April 17, 2018, https://www.dhs.gov/terrorism-prevention-partnerships.

20. See Brennan Center for Justice, "Countering Violent Extremism (CVE): A Resource Page," November 2015, https://www.brennancenter.org/analysis/cve-programs
-resource-page.

21. See Mukhtar Ibrahim, "Community Response to Feds' MN Anti-terror Recruiting Efforts," *Minnesota Public Radio News*, February 23, 2016, https://www.mprnews.org /story/2016/02/23/somali-community-response-anti-terror-recruiting.

22. For one example, see "Full Text: Donald Trump's Speech on Fighting Terrorism," *Politico*, August 15, 2016, http://www.politico.com/story/2016/08/donald-trump -terrorism-speech-227025.

23. See Jennifer Hansler, "DHS Shifts Focus of Funding to Counter Violent Extremism," CNN, July 4, 2017, http://edition.cnn.com/2017/07/01/politics/cve-funding -changes/index.html.

24. See Adam Taylor, "The U.S. Keeps Killing Americans in Drone Strikes, Mostly by Accident," *Washington Post*, April 23, 2015, https://www.washingtonpost.com /news/worldviews/wp/2015/04/23/the-u-s-keeps-killing-americans-in-drone-strikes -mostly-by-accident/?utm_term=.9f197c6e3949. A secret Justice Department memo from 2011 outlined the justification for killing American-born jihadists, specifically arguing that such killings do not violate the citizen's right to due process as stated in the Fourth Amendment. On this memo, see Greg Miller, "Legal Memo Backing Drone Strike That Killed American Anwar al-Awlaki Is Released," *Washington Post*, June 23, 2014, https://www.washingtonpost.com/world/national-security/legal-memo -backing-drone-strike-is-released/2014/06/23/1f48dd16-faec-11e3-8176-f2c941cf35f1 _story.html?tid=a_inl&utm_term=.31c20c5dca38. Since taking office, President Trump has loosened the rules governing drone strikes. See Ken Dilanian, Hans Nichols, and Courtney Kube, "Trump Admin Ups Drone Strikes, Tolerates More Civilian Deaths: U.S. Officials," NBC *News*, March 14, 2017, http://www.nbcnews.com/news /us-news/trump-admin-ups-drone-strikes-tolerates-more-civilian-deaths-n733336; Eric Schmitt and Matthew Rosenberg, "C.I.A. Wants Authority to Conduct Drone Strikes in Afghanistan for the First Time," *New York Times*, September 15, 2017, https:// www.nytimes.com/2017/09/15/us/politics/cia-drone-strike-authority-afghanistan .html.

25. See Peter Baker, "Trump Abandons Idea of Sending Terror Suspect to Guantánamo," *New York Times*, November 2, 2017, https://www.nytimes.com/2017/11/02/us /politics/trump-new-york-terror-attack.html; Rebecca Ruiz, Adam Goldman, and Matt Apuzzo, "Terror Suspect Brought to U.S. for Trial, Breaking from Trump Rhetoric," *New York Times*, July 21, 2017, https://www.nytimes.com/2017/07/21/world/europe/al -qaeda-suspect-court-trump-sessions-guantanamo.html.

26. In each case, the underlying ideologies informing these programs were thrown into sharp relief when each state confronted acts of nationalist violence: for example, the Japanese imperial state struggled to apply its thought crime policy to rightist terrorists who killed industrialists and politicians in the name of the emperor in the 1930s, whereas the Trump administration is currently (summer 2017) hesitant to call the violence carried out by white supremacists and neo-Nazis acts of terrorism so as not to alienate some of its most vocal supporters. See Liam Stack, "Charlottesville Violence and Trump's Reaction Draw Criticism Abroad," *New York Times*, August 17, 2017, https://www.nytimes.com/2017/08/17/world/charlottesville-trump-world-reaction .html.

Introduction

1. These events are discussed in more detail in chapters 1 and 2. Hirata Isao oversaw the jailed communist Mizuno Shigeo, who, with others, critiqued the JCP from jail, and upon being paroled, formed a breakaway communist group that recognized the emperor. See Itō Akira, "Tenkō mondai no ikkōsatsu: Nihonkyōsantō rōdōshaha to Hirata Isao," *Chiba kōgyō daigaku kenkyū hōkoku*, no. 31 (February 1994): 29–41.

2. The 1927 Theses used the term "kunshusei" (literally, monarchical system). It was not until the 1932 Theses that the JCP and Comintern started using the specific term "emperor system" or tennōsei. For an English translation of the 1927 Theses and 1932 Theses, see George M. Beckmann and Genji Okubo, *The Japanese Communist Party, 1922–1945* (Stanford, CA: Stanford University Press, 1969), 295–308, 332–351, respectively.

3. Hirata Isao, "Marukishizumu no kokufuku," in *Shisōsen kōshūkai kōgi sokki*, vol. 3, ed. Naikaku Jōhōbu (Tokyo: Naikaku Jōhōbu, 1938), 205–236, 228.

4. Hirata, "Marukishizumu no kokufuku," 236.

5. Following Carl Schmitt's political-ontological distinction of friend/enemy, Michael Dutton analyzes the policing of politics in China and notes that the identification of a threat ultimately functions to define political subjectivity: "Enemies . . . take precedence for they are what defines us. Just as a legal trial has meaning only as a result of a breach in the law, or criminal law begins not with a deed but with a criminal misdeed, so too are we defined by our opposite." Michael Dutton, *Policing Chinese Politics: A History* (Durham, NC: Duke University Press, 2005), 6. Dutton's analysis of the policing of politics in the twentieth century is at the same time an attempt to bring Hannah Arendt's political ontology into conversation with Schmitt's. See Dutton, *Policing Chinese Politics*, 9–11.

6. On the National Spirit Mobilization Movement, see Thomas R. H. Havens, *Valley of Darkness: The Japanese People and World War Two* (New York: Norton, 1978), 11–33, 36–37.

7. Although Japanese scholars still find analytical and theoretical purchase in the term "tennōsei," "emperor-system" is rarely used in recent English language scholarship on Japan. Sheldon Garon has questioned the analytical value of the term "emperor system," noting that in the conventional scholarship it has been used in an ahistorical manner without any institutional or historical dynamism, and that it incorrectly suggests that all suppression stemmed from the omnipotent imperial state. Garon argues that scholars who have used the term overlook how social groups proactively collaborated with the state to manage other sectors of society. See Sheldon Garon, *Molding Japanese Minds: The State in Everyday Life* (Princeton, NJ: Princeton University Press, 1995), 61–63. My objective is to restore the institutional, practical, and ideological complexity of the emperor system by showing how its political security apparatus combined various modes of power over time, how its ideological underpinning changed, and how it drew upon volunteers in the community to police as well as reform political criminals.

8. For the canonical study of the Peace Preservation Law, see the updated edition of Okudaira Yasuhiro, *Chianijihō shōshi* (Tokyo: Iwanami Shoten, 2006).

9. An analysis conducted by the Ōhara Institute for Social Research reports 75,681 people were arrested under the law. See Ōhara Shakai Mondai Kenkyūsho, ed., *Taiheiyō sensōka no rōdō undō* (Tokyo: Rōdō Junpōsha, 1965), 131. Richard Mitchell cites a 1943 Justice Ministry Criminal Bureau report that lists 65,921 persons arrested between 1928 and 1941. See Richard H. Mitchell, *Thought Control in Prewar Japan* (Ithaca, NY: Cornell University Press, 1976), 142. No complete record exists for arrests in colonial Korea, particularly in the 1940s. However, both Hong Jong-wook and Mizuno Naoki have shown that already by 1933, over 15,000 arrests had been made. See Hong Jong-wook, *Senjiki chōsen no tenkōsha-tachi: Teikoku / shokuminchi no tōgō to kiretsu* (Tokyo: Yūshisha, 2011), 47; Mizuno Naoki, "Chianijihō to Chōsen: Oboegaki," *Chōsen kenkyū* 188, no. 4 (1979): 46.

10. Exemplary of this approach is Matsuo Hiroshi, *Chianijihō: Danatsu to teikō no rekishi* (Tokyo: Shinnihon Shūppansha, 1971); Matsuo Hiroshi, *Chianijihō to tokkō keisatsu* (Tokyo: Kyōikusha, 1979).

11. Indeed, Herbert Bix has suggested that the "various state organs" of the Peace Preservation Law "became entangled with the trend towards bureaucratically controlled mass-mobilization" specifically because state officials "lack[ed] . . . confidence in the intellectual efficacy of State Shinto as the sole support for emperor worship, but also, more importantly, from fear that, even in the absence of self-professed revolutionary forces, the domestic situation in a time of exceedingly rapid economic change remained highly volatile and fraught with contradictions." Herbert Bix, "Rethinking 'Emperor-System Fascism': Ruptures and Continuities in Modern Japanese History," *Bulletin of Concerned Asian Scholars* 14, no. 2 (June 1982): 8.

12. Richard H. Mitchell, *Janus-Faced Justice: Political Criminals in Imperial Japan* (Honolulu: University of Hawaii Press, 1992); Mitchell, *Thought Control in Prewar Japan*; Okudaira Yasuhiro, *Chianijihō shōshi*, new ed. (Tokyo: Iwanami Shoten, 2006). I engage with this literature more extensively in chapters 1 and 2.

13. Okudaira Yasuhiro, "Shiryō kaisetsu," in *Gendaishi shiryō 45: Chianijihō*, ed. Okudaira Yasuhiro (Tokyo: Misuzu Shobō, 1973), xx; Okudaira, *Chianijihō shōshi*, 104. For another example, see Richard H. Mitchell, "Japan's Peace Preservation Law of 1925: Its Origins and Significance," *Monumenta Nipponica* 28, no. 3 (autumn 1973): 317–345. More recently, Uchida Hirofumi has analyzed the Peace Preservation Law from a legal standpoint, emphasizing that the law undermined legal protections and was used to suppress movements for legal rights. See Uchida Hirofumi, *Chianijihō no kyōkun: Kenri undō no seigen to kenpō kaisei* (Tokyo: Misuzu Shobō, 2016).

14. For a narrative example of this combination/confrontation, see Richard H. Mitchell, "Legacies," in Mitchell, *Janus-Faced Justice*, 1–35.

15. For example, Richard Mitchell argues, "by [the] inclusion of '*kokutai*' the government was telegraphing to all subjects its intention to preserve the Japanese way of life in the face of rapid change. Therefore, the new peace law should be viewed as a strong effort toward integration." Mitchell, "Japan's Peace Preservation Law of 1925," 343.

16. Garon argues that "moral suasion" was "influenced by traditional forms of statecraft." Garon, *Molding Japanese Minds*, xiv.

17. Indeed, Herbert Bix goes so far as to call Richard Mitchell's study of the Peace Preservation Law an "apologia" for the prewar state's repression. See Herbert Bix,

"Kawakami Hajime and the Organic Law of Japanese Fascism," *Japan Interpreter* 12, no. 1 (winter 1978): 130.

18. In this regard, *Thought Crime* is inspired by Andre Schmid's call to move beyond national histories and consider the prewar Japanese Empire as one imperial unit. See Andre Schmid, "Colonialism and the 'Korea Problem' in the Historiography of Modern Japan: A Review," *Journal of Asian Studies* 59, no. 4 (November 2000): 951–976. One of the earliest studies of the Peace Preservation Law in colonial Korea was Park Kyong-sik, "Chianijihō ni yoru chōsenjin danatsu" (1976), in *Tennōsei kokka to zainichi chōsenjin* (Tokyo: Shakai Hyōronsha, 1986), 87–130.

19. Mizuno Naoki, "Nihon no chōsen shihai to chianijihō," in *Chōsen no kindaishi to nihon*, ed. Hatada Takeshi (Tokyo: Yamato Shobō, 1987), 127–140; Mizuno Naoki, "Shokuminchi dokuritsu undō ni taisuru chianijihō no tekiyō," in *Shokuminchi teikoku nihon no hōteki kōzō*, ed. Asano Toyomi and Matsuda Toshihiko (Tokyo: Shinzansha Shuppan, 2004), 417–459; Suzuki Keifu, *Chōsen shokuminchi tōchihō no kenkyū: Chianhō ka no kōminka kyōiku* (Sapporo: Hokkaidō Daigaku Tosho Kankōkai, 1989); Hong Jong-wook, *Senjiki chōsen no tenkōsha-tachi: Teikoku / shokuminchi no tōgō to kiretsu* (Tokyo: Yūshisha, 2011); Keongil Kim, "Japanese Assimilation Policy and Thought Conversion in Colonial Korea," in *Colonial Rule and Social Change in Korea, 1910–1945*, ed. Hon Yung Lee, Yong Chool Ha, and Clark W. Sorensen (Seattle: Center for Korean Studies, University of Washington Press, 2013), 206–233.

20. On Jameson's conceptual distinction between contradiction, which could be dialectically resolved (i.e., *Aufheben*) through praxis, and aporia, which necessarily "generates a whole more properly narrative apparatus," see Fredric Jameson, *The Political Unconscious: Narrative as a Socially Symbolic Act* (Ithaca, NY: Cornell University Press, 1981), 50, 82–83.

21. Maruyama Masao, "Theory and Psychology of Ultra-nationalism" (1946), in *Thought and Behaviour in Modern Japanese Politics*, ed. Ivan Morris (London: Oxford University Press, 1963), 1, 8–10. For an insightful critique of Maruyama's influential thesis, see the introduction to Reto Hofmann, *The Fascist Effect: Japan and Italy, 1915–1952* (Ithaca, NY: Cornell University Press, 2016). Fujita Shōzō, "Tennōsei" (1954), reprinted in Fujita Shōzō, *Tennōsei kokka no shihai genri* (Tokyo: Miraisha, 1966), 161–169. Fujita began by arguing that the various and wide usage of the term "tennōsei" was not one of categorical ambiguity, but in fact represented the "complexity" of the emperor system itself. He distinguished three basic usages of the term: first, that the emperor existed as sovereign; second, that tennōsei referred to the "regime" that became "the political structure of modern Japan" in which bureaucrats exercised authority in the name of the imperial sovereign independent of the Diet. Finally, Fujita noted "a kind of metaphorical usage" of the term "tennōsei" as a "particular social phenomenon" that signified the unique "forms" through which the tennōsei governed society. Fujita, "Tennōsei," 161–162. See also Fujita Shōzō, "Tennōsei kokka no shihai genri" (1956), reprinted in Fujita, *Tennōsei kokka no shihai genri*, 6–115. See Takeda Kiyoko, *Tennōkan no sōkoku: 1945nen zengo* (Tokyo: Iwanami Shoten, 1978). English translation: Kiyoko Takeda, *The Dual-Image of the Japanese Emperor*, trans. Ian Nash (New York: New York University Press, 1988). Walter Skya argues that Shintō ideology was inscribed in the

Meiji Constitution and was continually reconceptualized in constitutional and political theory in the 1910s, 1920s, and 1930s. See Walter A. Skya, *Japan's Holy War: The Ideology of Radical Shintō Ultranationalism* (Durham, NC: Duke University Press, 2009).

22. See Carol Gluck, *Japan's Modern Myths: Ideology in the Late Meiji Period* (Princeton, NJ: Princeton University Press, 1987); T. Fujitani, *Splendid Monarchy: Power and Pageantry in Modern Japan* (Berkeley: University of California Press, 1996); Yoshimi Yoshiaki, *Grassroots Fascism: The War Experience of the Japanese People*, trans. Ethan Mark (New York: Columbia University Press, 2015); Garon, *Molding Japanese Minds*. See also: Barak Kushner, *The Thought War: Japanese Imperial Propaganda* (Honolulu: University of Hawai'i Press, 2006).

23. Umemori Naoyuki, "Modernization through Colonial Mediations: The Establishment of the Police and Prison System in Meiji Japan" (PhD diss., University of Chicago, 2002); Daniel V. Botsman, *Punishment and Power in the Making of Modern Japan* (Princeton, NJ: Princeton University Press, 2007). In many ways, *Thought Crime* is an attempt to extend Umemori and Botsman's respective studies of power in modern Japan into the 1920s and 1930s.

24. My focus on the transforming ideological nature of the Peace Preservation Law is informed by the recent work of Ogino Fujio and Itō Akira, who, in their own ways, have considered the complexities of the Peace Preservation Law in relation to the ideology of the prewar emperor system. See Ogino Fujio, *Shōwa tennō to chian taisei* (Tokyo: Shinnihon Shuppansha, 1993); Itō Akira, *Tenkō to tennōsei: Nihon kyōsanshugi undō no 1930nendai* (Tokyo: Keisō Shobō, 1995).

25. Gilbert Ryle, *The Concept of Mind* (London: Penguin, 2000), 21. Ryle argued that Cartesian dualism—what he called the "Official Doctrine"—posits that "every human being is both body and mind," where although the body is situated in the space of an external world and thus governed by mechanical laws and observable, minds do not exist in space but are rather "invisible, inaudible" and have "no size or weight," rendering them unknowable to others (14). And yet, in this dualism, minds are still categorized as "things, but different sorts of things from bodies"; "mental processes are causes and effects, but different sorts of causes and effects from bodily movements" (20). Ryle believed this to be a "category mistake" in which "the facts of mental life" are represented "as if they belonged to one logical type or category" applicable to the facts of physical life "when they actually belonged to another" (17).

26. As is well known, *Leviathan* begins with the section "Of Man," in which Hobbes formulated a theory of the mind in relation to the world of bodies; only afterward does Hobbes extrapolate from this a theory of the commonwealth and sovereignty. See Thomas Hobbes, *Leviathan* (New York: Penguin Classics, 1982).

27. One could say that Itō's 1889 *Commentaries* on the Meiji constitution was an attempt to work through the paradox that although the collective minds of Itō's constitutional committee drafted the Meiji Constitution, the document was presented as an expression of the timeless and unbroken reign of emperors.

28. Ryle, *The Concept of Mind*, 24, 17.

29. A. J. Ayer, "An Honest Ghost?," in *Ryle, A Collection of Critical Essays*, ed. Oscar P. Wood and George Pitcher (Garden City, NY: Doubleday, 1970), 73. Cited in Daniel C.

Dennett, "Introduction: Re-introducing *The Concept of Mind*," in Ryle, *The Concept of Mind*, xiii.

30. Arthur Koestler, *The Ghost in the Machine* (London: Penguin, 1989), 202. Consequently, Koestler followed Ryle insofar as rejecting the assumption that the mind is some ghostly, nonmaterial entity inhabiting the material body, but implicitly retained Cartesian dualism by locating the ghost in the neurophysiological evolution of the human brain. See his chapter "The Three Brains," 267–296.

31. David Easton, "The Political System Besieged by the State," *Political Theory* 9, no. 3 (August 1981): 316. Importantly, Easton was targeting Nicos Poulantzas's state theory and the influence it enjoyed in European and North American political science circles in the 1970s.

32. Easton, "The Political System Besieged by the State," 305–306.

33. See Timothy Mitchell, "The Limits of the State: Beyond Statist Approaches and Their Critics," *American Political Science Review* 85, no. 1 (March 1991): 77–96; Timothy Mitchell, "Society, Economy, and the State Effect," in *State/Culture: State-Formation after the Cultural Turn*, ed. George Steinmetz (Ithaca, NY: Cornell University Press, 1999), 76–97. In regard to extending this critique to Ryle, Daniel C. Dennett has implied such an interpretation when, pursuing a different question, he argued that the underlying questions of Ryle's *The Concept of Mind* "are about *what people do*," and not about "*how brains make it possible* for people to do what they do" (italics in original). I would argue that this emphasis opens into questions related to social practice (i.e., doing) and how such practices appear as if there is a spectral mind that makes people "do what they do." See Dennett, "Introduction," xiii.

34. Mitchell, "Society, Economy, and the State Effect," 85.

35. Mitchell's criticism can be extended to one of the theoretical inspirations for *Thought Crime*, Michel Foucault. Foucault famously argued that scholars have yet "to cut off the King's head" when studying forms of power, by which he meant that we remain trapped by theories of "sovereignty" and state repression, thus overlooking other modes of power operating beyond the parameters of the sovereign state. Michel Foucault, "Truth and Power," in *Power/Knowledge: Selected Interviews and Other Writings, 1972–1977*, ed. Colin Gordon (New York: Vintage, 1980), 121. Similar to Timothy Mitchell's critique of David Easton, however, Mitchell Dean has argued that in Foucault's attempt to move beyond state theories of sovereignty, "the problem remains of how is it that this headless body often behaves *as if* it indeed had a head." Mitchell Dean, *Critical and Effective Histories: Foucault's Methods and Historical Sociology* (London: Routledge, 1994), 156. For more on this critique of Foucault, see also Thomas Lemke, *Foucault, Governmentality, and Critique* (Boulder, CO: Paradigm, 2012), 12. Indeed, Nicos Poulantzas was moving toward exploring this paradox in his last book, which, tellingly, Easton does not include in his critique mentioned above. See Nicos Poulantzas, *State, Power, Socialism*, trans. Patrick Camiller (London: Verso, 2014). In this last work, Poulantzas noted the curious resonance between Foucault's aversion to the state and North American political scientists like Easton. See Poulantzas, *State, Power, Socialism*, 44. As I elaborate in more detail below, this is why it is important to pair Foucault's analysis of the "microphysics" of power dispersed throughout society with Louis Althusser's theory of ISAs,

so that we can account for how the operations of power that Foucault finds dispersed throughout society do in fact circulate through and congeal in certain institutions and juridical-penal practices to produce what Timothy Mitchell has called "the state-effect," whether or not such institutions or practices are juridically defined as belonging to the state. Here I follow Bob Jessop and Thomas Lemke, who each in their own way understand particular operations of power in society as within the strategic field of the state. Bob Jessop, *State Power: A Strategic-Relational Approach* (Cambridge: Polity, 2008); and Lemke, *Foucault, Governmentality, and Critique.*

36. I seek to counter the well-known "god that failed" thesis of communist disillusion and defection, for, beyond the strategic errors of the Communist International that Poulantzas and others have analyzed, if the god of communism failed, it was partly because other gods were at work against communism: in this case, quite literally the purportedly divine emperor and the Japanese spirit (*nihon seishin*). The metaphor of the god that failed comes from a collection by the same name: Richard Crossman, ed., *The God That Failed* (New York: Bantam, 1950). It should be noted that among the contributors to this volume is Arthur Koestler of "ghost in the machine" fame. For the strategic failures of the Comintern policies to combat the rise of fascism, see Nicos Poulantzas, *Fascism and Dictatorship: The Third International and the Problem of Fascism,* trans. Judith White (London: Verso, 1979).

37. Nihon Keisatsusha, ed., *Shisō keisatsu tsūron,* rev. ed. (Tokyo: Nihon Keisatsusha, 1940), 1.

38. For a history of the term "kokutai" in modern Japan, see Konno Nobuyuki, *Kindai nihon no kokutairon* (Tokyo: Perikansha, 2008).

39. See Louis Althusser, "Ideology and Ideological State Apparatuses (Notes Towards an Investigation)," in *Lenin and Philosophy and Other Essays,* trans. Ben Brewster (New York: Monthly Review Press, 2001), 85–126; and Louis Althusser, *On the Reproduction of Capitalism: Ideology and Ideological State Apparatuses,* trans. G. M. Goshgarian (London: Verso, 2014); Michel Foucault, *Discipline and Punish: The Birth of the Prison,* trans. Alan Sheridan (New York: Vintage, 1995); Michel Foucault, *The Punitive Society: Lectures at the Collège de France, 1972–1973,* trans. Graham Burchell (London: Palgrave Macmillan, 2015); Michel Foucault, *"Society Must Be Defended": Lectures at the Collège de France, 1975–1976,* trans. David Macey (New York: Picador, 2003); Poulantzas, *State, Power, Socialism.*

40. See Warren Montag, "'The Soul Is the Prison of the Body': Althusser and Foucault, 1970–1975," *Yale French Studies,* no. 88 (1995): 53–77; Warren Montag, "Althusser and Foucault: Apparatuses of Subjection," in *Althusser and His Contemporaries: Philosophy's Perpetual War* (Durham, NC: Duke University Press, 2013). My analysis has also been influenced by Jason Read, *The Micro-Politics of Capital: Marx and the Prehistory of the Present* (Albany: State University of New York Press, 2003); and Jan Rehmann, *Theories of Ideology: The Powers of Alienation and Subjection* (Chicago: Haymarket, 2013).

41. Jessop, *State Power.* As Stuart Hall reminds us, however, Poulantzas's attempt to craft a new theory of the state by bringing together Althusser's structuralist Marxism and Foucault's poststructural theory of power produces its own unique (and for Hall, insurmountable) problems. See: Stuart Hall, "Nicos Poulantzas: State, Power, Socialism" in Poulantzas, *State, Power, Socialism,* vii–xvii.

42. Michel Foucault, "Body/Power" in *Power/Knowledge: Selected Interviews and Other Writings, 1972–1977*, 58. Indeed, as I discuss in chapter 3, this assumption has informed conventional explanations of the ideological conversion phenomenon in interwar Japan, in which it was explained that the state's ability to successfully coerce activists to change their ideas indicated the weakness of liberal subjectivity (*shutaisei*) in prewar Japan.

43. Montag, "'The Soul Is the Prison of the Body,'" 59.

44. See Althusser, "Ideology and Ideological State Apparatuses," 114. Althusser calls theories of ideology that rest upon idealist dualities of mind and body, ideas and reality, the "ideology of ideology." He points to how these kinds of dualisms lead to a theory of ideology as the mystification of the mind that distorts or inverts an objective, external reality. In eighteenth-century Enlightenment theories of ideology, this mystification was attributed to despots; in the nineteenth century, Althusser tells us, Ludwig Feuerbach and the early writings of Karl Marx attributed this mystification to the particular forms of social existence. Althusser, "Ideology and Ideological State Apparatuses," 110–111.

45. Harry Harootunian, "Hirohito Redux," *Critical Asian Studies* 33, no. 4 (2001): 609. I consider this point further in chapter 3.

46. Althusser, "Ideology and Ideological State Apparatuses," 123. Italics in the original.

47. Althusser, "Ideology and Ideological State Apparatuses," 123.

48. I thank Tak Fujitani for his insightful suggestions regarding Foucault's threefold schema of power in relation to my research.

49. On governmentality, see Michel Foucault, "Governmentality," in *The Foucault Effect: Studies in Governmentality*, edited by Graham Burchell, Colin Gordon, and Peter Miller (Chicago: University of Chicago Press, 1991), 87–104. My reading of Foucault's tripartite theory of power has been influenced by Lemke, *Foucault, Governmentality, and Critique.*

50. Foucault, "Governmentality," 102. Here, I am influenced by Takashi Fujitani who, in his first book, *Splendid Monarchy* (1996), argued that, in contrast to Foucault's historical narrative in *Discipline and Punish*, monarchical and disciplinary power converged in Meiji Japan: that is, the monarch was the visible sovereign of the new polity, as well as the observer who disciplined society through his panoptic gaze. See Fujitani, *Splendid Monarchy*, 141–145. Fujitani's more recent work finds Foucault's theory of governmentality manifest in the colonial governance of Korea in the 1930s, particularly after 1937, when "colonial power began to constitute Koreans as a population that in the aggregate should be healthy, reproductive, and long lived." Takashi Fujitani, "Right to Kill, Right to Make Live: Koreans as Japanese and Japanese as Americans during WWII," *Representations* 99, no. 1 (summer 2007): 16.

51. Althusser, "Ideology and Ideological State Apparatuses," 96, 97, 100.

52. Poulantzas, *State, Power, Socialism*, 33.

53. On "bad subjects," see Althusser, "Ideology and Ideological State Apparatuses," 123. I pursue this theoretical question further in a forthcoming article, Max Ward, "Cinema of 'Bad Subjects:' The Limits of the Kafkaesque Subject in Ōshima Nagisa's *Death by Hanging* (1968)" forthcoming in *CineEast: Journal of East Asian Cinemas.*

54. Poulantzas, *State, Power, Socialism*, 37. On Poulantzas's theory of the "strategic field" of the state, see Jessop, *State Power*, 123–126. Interestingly, when Poulantzas turns his attention to Althusser, he seems to replicate Foucault's general critique of theories that reduce the operation of state power to repression alone. For example, Poulantzas argues that Althusser's thesis "rests on the idea of a State that acts and functions through repression and ideological inculcation, and *nothing else*. It assumes that the State's efficacy somehow lies in what it forbids, rules out, and prevents; or in its capacity to deceive, lie, obscure, hide, and lead people to believe what is false." Revealing Foucault's influence, Poulantzas counters, "the State also acts in a positive fashion, *creating, transforming and making* reality." Poulantzas, *State, Power, Socialism*, 30. However, as I argue, Althusser's ISA theory allows for such productive aspects of power.

55. On Althusser's distinction between secondary and primary ideologies, see Althusser, *On the Reproduction of Capitalism*, 83–84.

56. I thank Katsuya Hirano for suggesting that I make this theoretical distinction more explicit. As many critics have argued, Althusser failed to adequately theorize interpellation as well as the connection between the practical operations of the ISAs and the always already interpellated subject. However, my objective in *Thought Crime* is to understand how the various institutions within the Peace Preservation Law apparatus functioned to rehabilitate political criminals, and how we might read the ideological forms and practices inscribed in these apparatuses as indexing the transformation of imperial ideology in the 1930s. Therefore, I will disregard Althusser's psychoanalytical theory of interpellation and focus on his theory of ISAs. For critiques of Althusser's theory of interpellation, see Judith Butler, "Conscience Doth Make Subjects of Us All: Althusser's Subjection," in *The Psychic Life of Power: Theories in Subjection* (Stanford, CA: Stanford University Press, 1997), 106–131; Slavoj Žižek, *The Sublime Object of Ideology* (London: Verso, 2008), 42–43. For a recent counter-argument which I believe provides a more persuasive and productive reading of Althusser's theory of ISAs and ideology, see Matthew Lampert, "Resisting Ideology: On Butler's Critique of Althusser" in *Diacritics* Vol. 43, No. 2 (2015), 124–147.

57. Althusser, "Ideology and Ideological State Apparatuses," 112.

58. Althusser, "Ideology and Ideological State Apparatuses," 114. Montag contends that this is not a linear or causal sequence in which a preexisting ideology creates these apparatuses and their constitutive ritualized practices, but rather that "ideology is immanent in its apparatuses and their practices, it has no existence apart from these apparatuses and is entirely coincident with them." Montag, "'The Soul Is the Prison of the Body,'" 63.

59. Mitchell, *Janus-Faced Justice*.

60. Althusser, "Ideology and Ideological State Apparatuses," 123.

61. Foucault, "Governmentality," 87–104.

62. Foucault, "Governmentality," 103.

63. I believe that my critical-theoretical analysis of the official documents does not reproduce the errors that Herbert Bix faults Richard Mitchell for committing: namely that by only using official sources, Mitchell has written a history of the Peace Preservation Law from a "ruling class perspective." See Bix, "Kawakami Hajime and the Organic Law of Japanese Fascism," 131.

CHAPTER 1. Kokutai and the Aporias of Imperial Sovereignty

1. For studies of the Peace Preservation Law, see Matsuo Hiroshi, *Chianijihō: Danatsu to teikō no rekishi* (Tokyo: Shinnihon Shuppansha, 1971) and Matsuo Hiroshi, *Chianijihō to tokkō keisatsu* (Tokyo: Kyōikusha, 1979); Ushiomi Toshitaka, *Chianijihō* (Tokyo: Iwanami Shoten, 1977); Okudaira Yasuhiro, *Chianijihō shōshi*, new ed. (Tokyo: Iwanami Shoten, 2006); Richard H. Mitchell, "Japan's Peace Preservation Law of 1925: Its Origins and Significance," *Monumenta Nipponica* 28, no. 3 (autumn 1973), 317–345; Richard H. Mitchell, *Thought Control in Prewar Japan* (Ithaca, NY: Cornell University Press, 1976); and Ogino Fujio, *Shōwa tennō to chian taisei* (Tokyo: Shinnihon Shuppansha, 1993). For the relationship between political parties and the Peace Preservation Law, see Nakazawa Shunsuke, *Chianijihō: Naze seitō seiji ha "akuhō" o unda ka* (Tokyo: Chūōkō Shinsho, 2012). For a legal analysis of the Peace Preservation Law, see Uchida Hirofumi, *Chianijihō no kyōkun: Kenri undō to kenpō kaisei* (Tokyo: Misuzu Shobō, 2016). On the application of the Peace Preservation Law in colonial Korea, see Mizuno Naoki, "Nihon no chōsen shihai to chianijihō," in *Chōsen no kindaishi to nihon*, ed. Hatada Takeshi (Tokyo: Yamato Shobō, 1987), 127–140; Mizuno Naoki, "Shokuminchi dokuritsu undō ni taisuru chianijihō no tekiyō," in *Shokuminchi teikoku nihon no hōteki kōzō*, ed. Asano Toyomi and Matsuda Toshihiko (Tokyo: Shinzansha Shuppan, 2004), 417–459; Suzuki Keifu, *Chōsen shokuminchi tōchihō no kenkyū: Chianhō ka no kōminka kyōiku* (Sapporo: Hokkaidō Daigaku Tosho Kankōkai, 1989); Hong Jong-wook, *Senjiki chōsen no tenkōsha-tachi* (Tokyo: Yūshisha, 2011).

2. Okudaira Yasuhiro argues that the only previous appearance of kokutai in a law was in the 1873 Newspaper Ordinance (Shimbunshi hakkōjōme), signifying something akin to national prestige (*kokui*). See Okudaira, *Chianijihō shōshi*, 60.

3. For a complete English translation of the Meiji Constitution, see Appendix X in George M. Beckmann, *The Making of the Meiji Constitution: The Oligarchs and the Constitutional Development of Japan, 1868–1891* (Westport, CT: Greenwood, 1957; reprint, 1975), 150–156.

4. On an earlier process of refiguring neo-Confucian categories to speak to new geopolitical circumstances, see Bob Tadashi Wakabayashi, *Anti-foreignism and Western Learning in Early Modern Japan: The New Theses of 1825*, Harvard East Asian Monographs 126 (Cambridge, MA: Harvard University Press, 1992).

5. For the full English translation of the Rescript, see Wm. Theodore de Bary, Carol Gluck, and Arthur E. Tiedemann, eds., *Sources of Japanese Tradition*, vol. 2: *1600–2000*, Part Two, *1868–2000* (New York: Columbia University Press), 108–109. For the early debates over interpreting the Rescript, see Sharon Nolte, "National Morality and Universal Ethics: Onishi Hajime and the Imperial Rescript on Education," *Monumenta Nipponica* 38, no. 3 (autumn 1983): 283–294.

6. On these debates, see Walter A. Skya, *Japan's Holy War: The Ideology of Radical Shintō Ultranationalism* (Durham, NC: Duke University Press, 2009).

7. For an overview of theories of kokutai in modern Japan, see Konno Nobuyuki, *Kindai nihon no kokutairon* (Tokyo: Perikansha, 2008).

8. Okudaira Yasuhiro, "Shiryō kaisetsu," in *Gendaishi shiryō 45: Chianijihō*, ed. Okudaira Yasuhiro (Tokyo: Misuzu Shobō, 1973), xx, cited here after as GSS45. Okudaira

points to *kokutai*'s usage in early modern Kokugaku writings as signifying "national customs" (*kuniburi*) and its appearance in the Imperial Rescript on Education and State Shinto education. See also Okudaira Yasuhiro, "Some Preparatory Notes for the Study of the Peace Preservation Law in Pre-war Japan," *Annals of the Institute of Social Science* 14 (1973): 49–69; and Okudaira, *Chianijihō shōshi*, 56–65.

9. Okudaira, "Shiryō kaisetsu," xv. See also Okudaira, *Chianijihō shōshi*, 104.

10. Mitchell, "Japan's Peace Preservation Law of 1925," 343. Drawing upon Durkheim's sociological understanding of law as a means of social integration, Patricia Steinhoff argues that kokutai signified both "the legal and constitutional structure of the nation and its spiritual and cultural structure centering around the emperor system and the family system." Thus, by defining a crime as "changing [or altering] the *kokutai*," the law was meant to defend "the political system, traditional social relationships, and the central symbols of the nation." Patricia Steinhoff, *Tenkō: Ideology and Societal Integration in Prewar Japan* (New York: Garland, 1991), 33.

11. For examples of how this assumption has informed analyses of the law in the colonies, see Chulwoo Lee, "Modernity, Legality, and Power in Korea under Japanese Rule," in *Colonial Modernity in Korea*, ed. Gi-Wook Shin and Michael Robinson (Cambridge, MA: Harvard University Press, 1999), 21–51, especially Lee's discussion of kokutai, 45–46.

12. For an example of this distinction in the area studies paradigm, see Richard H. Minear, *Japanese Tradition and Western Law: Emperor, State, and Law in the Thought of Hozumi Yatsuka* (Cambridge, MA: Harvard University Press, 1970).

13. Ogino, *Shōwa tennō to chian taisei*, 14. Ogino's use of *maryoku* recalls Tsurumi Shunsuke's earlier thesis of the "amuletic use of words" during the interwar period, in which kokutai served as one of Tsurumi's prime examples. For Tsurumi, this meant that these terms were invoked without a clear sense of what they meant and allowed the masses to be misled by the state. Tsurumi's thesis was premised upon a faith that words could be concretely understood, which would undermine their ideological uses. See Tsurumi Shunsuke, "Kotoba no omamoriteki shiyōhō ni tsuite," *Shisō no kagaku* 1 (May 1946); English translation, F. J. Daniels, "Mr. Tsurumi-Syunsuke on the 'Amuletic' Use of Words: A Translation, with Commentary," *Bulletin of the School of Oriental and African Studies, University of London* 18, no. 3 (1956): 514–533.

14. Ogino, *Shōwa tennō to chian taisei*, 30, 31, 34, and 4–5.

15. For instance, see William Scheuerman's analysis of Locke's argument for a liberal "rule of law." William Scheuerman, *Between the Norm and the Exception: The Frankfurt School and the Rule of Law* (Cambridge, MA: MIT Press, 1994), 68–70.

16. Robert H. Jackson, *Sovereignty: Evolution of an Idea* (Cambridge: Polity, 2007), ix.

17. Hans Kelmo and Quentin Skinner, "Introduction: A Concept in Fragments," in *Sovereignty in Fragments: The Past, Present and Future of a Contested Concept*, ed. Hans Kelmo and Quentin Skinner (Cambridge: Cambridge University Press, 2010), 3–4.

18. Jens Bartelson, *Sovereignty as Symbolic Form* (London: Routledge, 2014), 4.

19. Jens Bartelson, *A Genealogy of Sovereignty* (Cambridge: Cambridge University Press, 1995), 51.

20. Bartelson's primary concern is with the epistemological conditions for conceptualizing sovereignty in political theory. However, his observations can also apply to

political practices that invoke sovereignty as their condition of possibility. This kind of inquiry has been pursued along a different theoretical trajectory by Guillaume Sibertin-Blanc, and his reconsideration of Gilles Deleuze and Félix Guattari in relation to Marxist theories of the state. See Guillaume Sibertin-Blanc, *State and Politics: Deleuze and Guattari on Marx*, trans. Ames Hodges (Los Angeles: Semiotext(e), 2016), in particular chapter 2, "Capture: For a Concept of Primitive Accumulation of State Power," 45–83.

21. This paradox of sovereignty as a "composite of inside and outside" of the nation-state can, when shorn of its Kantian basis, perhaps be considered along with Gavin Walker's theory of the paradox of primitive or original capitalist accumulation, in which capital reproduces and redemarcates an outside internal to itself as the condition for its own reproduction. This returns Bartelson and others' discursive analyses to the socio-historical—in other words, the material—practices and social relationships constitutive of capitalist modernity. See Gavin Walker, *The Sublime Perversion of Capital: Marxist Theory and the Politics of History in Modern Japan* (Durham, NC: Duke University Press, 2016).

22. As is well known, Schmitt argued that the constitutional norm is grounded upon a constituent power that is not completely prescribed by constitutional norms. In contrast to legal positivism, which assumed a pure realm of juridical rationality, Schmitt posited the primacy of the political state and the sovereign, which, in a decision to suspend the constitution during a crisis, exposes the ontological ground of legal rationality, what Schmitt called "concrete life." It was not the substantive qualities of the sovereign decision conjured during the exception that interested Schmitt, but rather the notion of the decision itself and how it revealed the political ontology of a constitutional order. Carl Schmitt, *Political Theology: Four Chapters on the Concept of Sovereignty*, trans. George Schwab (Chicago: University of Chicago Press, 1985). On recent theorists, see Giorgio Agamben, *Homo Sacer: Sovereign Power and Bare Life*, trans. Daniel Heller-Roazen (Stanford, CA: Stanford University Press, 1998); Giorgio Agamben, *State of Exception*, trans. Kevin Attell (Chicago: University of Chicago Press, 2005); David Dyzenhaus, "The Politics of the Question of Constituent Power," in *The Paradox of Constitutionalism: Constituent Power and Constitutional Form*, ed. Martin Loughlin and Neil Walker (Oxford: Oxford University Press, 2007).

23. For a provocative reading of Schmitt with Marx, see Gavin Walker, "Primitive Accumulation and the Formation of Difference: On Marx and Schmitt," *Rethinking Marxism* 23, no. 3 (2011): 384–404.

24. In other words, it is a perpetual "event" inscribed in the constitutional order, which is assumed as its origin. See the editors' introduction to Martin Loughlin and Neil Walker, eds., *The Paradox of Constitutionalism: Constituent Power and Constitutional Form* (Oxford: Oxford University Press, 2007), 2.

25. William E. Connolly, "The Complexities of Sovereignty," in *Giorgio Agamben: Sovereignty and Life*, ed. Matthew Calarco and Steven DeCaroli (Stanford, CA: Stanford University Press, 2007), 24.

26. Appendix X in Beckmann, *The Making of the Meiji Constitution*, 150.

27. Jean-Jacques Rousseau, cited in Connolly, "The Complexities of Sovereignty," 24.

28. Itō Hirobumi, *Commentaries on the Constitution of the Empire of Japan*, 2nd ed., trans. Miyoji Ito (Tokyo: Chūō Daigaku, 1906), 2–3.

29. On this point of the presuppositions of the sovereign state, see Guillaume Sibertin-Blanc, "Aporia in the Origin of the State: Impossible Genesis and Untraceable Beginning," and "The Movement of Self-Presupposition of the *Urstaat*: Antinomic History of the State-Form," in Sibertin-Blanc, *State and Politics*, 24–31, and 31–38.

30. See Takashi Fujitani, "The Constitution's Promulgation," in *Splendid Monarchy: Power and Pageantry in Modern Japan* (Berkeley: University of California Press, 1996), 107–111.

31. Agamben, *Homo Sacer*, 26.

32. See Schmitt, *Political Theology*, 6–7; the editors' introduction to Loughlin and Walker, *The Paradox of Constitutionalism*, 2–4; Agamben, *State of Exception*, particularly chapter 1.

33. Addressing a different problematic, Poulantzas argues, "The activity of the State always overflows the banks of law, since it can, within certain limits, modify its own law. The State is not the simple representation of some eternal law, be it a universal prohibition or a law of nature. If such were the case—and this needs to be made clear—law would have *de jure* primacy over the State." Nicos Poulantzas, *State, Power, Socialism*, trans. Patrick Camiller (London: Verso, 2014), 85. In another direction, Guillaume Sibertin-Blanc has explored this through Deleuze and Guattari's idea of the *Urstaat*, a state form that presents itself as its own its condition of possibility. See Sibertin-Blanc, *State and Politics*, 22.

34. Mizuno Naoki, "Chianijihō to Chōsen: Oboegaki," *Chōsen kenkyū* 188, no. 4 (1979): 46. For an overview of the different legal systems in Japan's empire, see Edward I-te Chen, "The Attempt to Integrate the Empire: Legal Perspectives," in *The Japanese Colonial Empire, 1895–1945*, ed. Ramon H. Myers and Mark R. Peattie (Princeton, NJ: Princeton University Press, 1984), 240–274.

35. For an overview of the Morito Incident, see Miyachi Masato, "Morito Tatsuo jiken: Gakumon no jiyū no hatsu no shiren," in *Nihon seiji saiban shiroku 3: Taishō*, ed. Wagatsuma Sakae (Tokyo: Daiichi Hōki Shuppan, 1969), 228–272; Richard Mitchell, *Censorship in Imperial Japan* (Princeton, NJ: Princeton University Press, 1983), 182–189. Article 42 of the Newspaper Law stated that the author, editor, or publisher of any printed material that "profanes the majesty of the imperial household" (*kōshitsu no songen o bōtoku*), calls to "change the state form" (*seitai no henkai*), or "subverts the laws of the state" (*chōken o binran*) can be imprisoned for up to two years. See Miyachi, "Morito Tatsuo Jiken," 239. Article 23 of this 1909 law also defined an infringement as publishing material that "disturbs the public peace" (*annei chitsujo o midashi*) or "damages customs" (*fūzoku o gai suru*).

36. The decision, along with the various appeals, is reprinted in Miyachi, "Morito Tatsuo Jiken," 253–271.

37. On the Rice Riots, see Michael Lewis, *Rioters and Citizens: Mass Protest in Imperial Japan* (Berkeley: University of California Press, 1990); on the Rice Riots in relation to security laws, see Matsuo, *Chianijihō*, 80–82. On the March First Movement, see Frank Baldwin, "Participatory Anti-imperialism: The 1919 Independence Movement,"

Journal of Korean Studies 1 (1979): 123–162. For the Japanese Government-General's response to the March First movement, see Mark E. Caprio, *Japanese Assimilation Policies in Colonial Korea, 1910–1945* (Seattle: University of Washington Press, 2009), chapters 3 and 4.

38. Naimushō keihokyoku, "Kagekishugi torishimarihō (amerika, furansu, doitsu, berugii, roshia, burajiru, igirisu, itaria)," September 1921, reprinted in Ogino Fujio, ed., *Chianijihō kankei shiryōshū*, vol. 1 (Tokyo: Shinnihon Shuppansha, 1996), 56–73.

39. Existing laws such as the 1909 Newspaper Law (Shimbunshihō) used to prosecute Morito and Ōuchi criminalized the publication and distribution of any print material that "disrupts the public peace" (*annei chitsujo binran*) or "subverted the laws of the state" (*chōken o binran*), among other offenses. Another existing law, the 1900 Public Peace Police Law, established a registration system for political groups, thus restricting the formation and assembly of any groups that were not first cleared with the police. This 1900 law also granted the police powers to interrupt speeches or assemblies that were interpreted as threatening the public peace (*annei chitsujo*) and allowed the Home Ministry to pursue suspected secret political organizations. The 1922 Antiradical Bill inherited some of the language of these laws, as well as their emphasis on distributing or propagating subversive materials. Because of this, many legislators questioned why a new law was necessary if these other laws already covered similar crimes.

40. On this 1922 bill, see Matsuo Takayoshi, "Kageki shakaishugi undō torishimari hōan ni tsuite: 1922nen dai45gikai ni okeru," *Jinbun Gakuhō* 20 (October 1964): 247–267.

41. Naimushō, "Kageki shakai undō torishimari hōritsuan keika" (January 1923), in Ogino, *Chianijihō kankei shiryōshū*, vol. 1, 23.

42. For an overview of these three security measures in colonial Korea, see Mizuno Naoki, "Chianijihō no seitei to shokuminchi Chōsen," *Jinbun Gakuhō* 83 (March 2000): 99–100, 101–105, and 105–107, respectively. See also Lee, "Modernity, Legality, and Power in Korea under Japanese Rule," 42–43.

43. Mizuno, "Chianijihō no seitei to shokuminchi Chōsen," 105; Lee, "Modernity, Legality, and Power in Korea under Japanese Rule," 43.

44. This variety of public peace ordinances in colonial Korea would later produce a significant amount of debate concerning when to apply the Peace Preservation Law over other ordinances. For an overview of these ordinances in relation to the Peace Preservation Law, see the May 1939 Justice Ministry report by Yoshida Hajime, "Chōsen ni okeru shisōhan no kakei narabini ruihan jōkyō," Shisō jōsei shisatsu hōkokushū (Sono 6), in *Shisō kenkyū shiryō: Tokushū dai 69 gō*, ed. Shihōshō keijikyoku, reprinted in *Shakai mondai shiryō sōsho: Dai 1 shū* (Tokyo: Tōyō Bunkasha, 1971), 1–2.

45. The bill was delivered by Justice Minister Ōki Enkichi and Home Minister Tokonami Takejirō. The preliminary drafts of the bill are reproduced in Ogino, *Chianijihō kankei shiryōshū*, vol. 1, 25–38.

46. Cited in GSS45, 6. The Chian keisatsu hō is reproduced in Ogino, *Chianijihō kankei shiryōshū*, vol. 1, 17–19.

47. Article 6 of the bill extended coverage to the activities of Japanese nationals outside of the country. See GSS45, 4; and Mitchell, "Japan's Peace Preservation Law of 1925," 331.

48. GSS45, 7.

49. GSS45, 7.

50. English translation in Mitchell, "Japan's Peace Preservation Law of 1925," 331. Translation amended. Original Japanese can be found in GSS45, 3–4. Also in Shihōshō keijikyoku shisōbu, ed., *Dai45kai teikoku gikai: Kageki shakai undō torishimari hōan giji sokkiroku narabini iinkai giji sokkiroku*. Shisō kenkyū shiryō, Tokushū dai 10 gō (Shihōshō keijikyoku, 1934), republished by Shakai mondai shiryō kenkyūkai, vol. 1, no. 8 (Tokyo: Tōyōbunkasha, 1972), 1–2. Hereafter this collection cited as SMSKK, vol. 1, no. 8.

51. Mitchell, "Japan's Peace Preservation Law of 1925," 331. Translation amended. Article 2 applied to anyone who formed a society or meeting in order to carry out the propaganda activities listed in Article 1. Article 4 criminalized anyone who gave financial support to such activities; Article 5 stipulated leniency to those who cooperated; and Article 6 stated that the above crimes applied to Japanese subjects who engaged in such activities abroad.

52. GSS45, 6.

53. SMSKK, vol. 1, no. 8, 46–47. In response to a question concerning the meaning of *chōken binran*, Hayashi pointed to earlier uses of the term and argued that it meant "to illegally destroy the fundamental laws of the state." SMSKK, vol. 1, no. 8, 34–35.

54. On kokutai in Hozumi Yatsuka's early constitutional interpretations, see Skya, *Japan's Holy War*, 63–64. On the constitutional debate between Uesugi Shinkichi and Minobe Tatsukichi over the term "kokutai," see Skya, *Japan's Holy War*, 158; Minear, *Japanese Tradition and Western Law*, 64–71; and Frank O. Miller, *Minobe Tatsukichi: Interpreter of Constitutionalism in Japan* (Berkeley: University of California Press, 1965), 60–72.

55. Historians disagree about which bill was more ambiguous. Richard Mitchell argues that the term "chōken" used in the 1922 Antiradical Bill was a much clearer category than kokutai and could have averted the "legal Hydra" that was created when kokutai was used in the 1925 bill. See Mitchell, *Thought Control in Prewar Japan*, 67. In contrast, Elise Tipton argues that "the phrases 'attempt to change the *kokutai*' and 'denial of the private property system' [in the later Peace Preservation Law] represented Home Ministry officials' attempts to limit and clarify the scope of the law, for they replaced traditionally used but vague phrases, such as 'subvert the Constitution and laws of the state' and 'public peace and order.'" Elise Tipton, *The Japanese Police State: The Tokkō in Interwar Japan* (Sydney: Allen and Unwin, 1990), 112.

56. SMSKK, vol. 1, no. 8, 63.

57. SMSKK, vol. 1, no. 8, 63.

58. The edited bill is reprinted in SMSKK, vol. 1, no. 8, 198–199.

59. SMSKK, vol. 1, no. 8, 49. However, the Home Ministry had already defined these terms in a report before the bill was presented to the Diet in February 1922. In this document, drafted by Police Bureau commissioner Kawamura Teishirō, it is explained that anarchism "is an ideology that rejects state authority" and "does not recognize the existence of the state." In regard to communism, Kawamura explained that it is "an ideology that calls for abolishing the system of private property—the basis of our current economic organization—and that property . . . be socialized [*shakai no kyōyū*]."

Naimushō, "Kageki shakai undō torishimari hō shakugi" written by Kawamura Teishirō, February 1922, reprinted in Ogino, *Chianijihō kankei shiryōshū*, vol. 1, 46, 46–47. Kawamura extended the potential application of this law to other political movements as well, noting that Article 1 would apply to anarchism, syndicalism, Bolshevism, and republicanism; Articles 1 and 3 would apply to communism, syndicalism, and guild socialism; and Article 3 would apply to state socialism. See Ogino, *Chianijihō kankei shiryōshū*, vol. 1, 46.

60. Ogino Fujio has shown that even though "anarchism" and "communism" were deleted from the bill, these remained the intended targets that threatened "the laws of state" and "fundamental structure of society" respectively. See Ogino, *Shōwa tennō to chian taisei*, 17–18. This would also inform the targets of the Peace Preservation Bill, in which kokutai was said to target anarchism, and "private property system" would apply to communism (32).

61. See Nijō Atsumoto's summary of the changes to the law by the time it reached the Lower House: SMSKK, vol. 1, no. 8, 199–207.

62. The revised bill deliberated in the House of Peers is reproduced in SMSKK, vol. 1, no. 8, 320–321. See the subsequent explanation by Tokonami Takejirō about these revisions: SMSKK, vol. 1, no. 8, 326–327, 328–330.

63. Translation of Article 1 from Mitchell, *Thought Control in Prewar Japan*, 48, translation amended.

64. This is in reference to the activities of Kondō Eizō, who went to Shanghai in May 1921 to meet with Comintern agents. He returned to Japan with a large amount of money and was subsequently detained by the police in Shimonoseki. Lacking evidence, the police released Kondō and upon his arrival in Tokyo he formed a communist group among radicals from the Enlightened People's Society (Gyōminkai). The police arrested members distributing leaflets in October 1921, rounding up the rest of the members in November. This came to be known as the Enlightened People's Communist Party Incident (Gyōmin kyōsantō jiken). See George M. Beckmann and Genji Okubo, *The Japanese Communist Party, 1922–1945* (Stanford, CA: Stanford University Press, 1969), 32–35.

65. On law in the formation of the Japanese Empire, see the essays collected in Asano Toyomi and Matsuda Toshihiko, eds., *Shokuminchi teikoku nihon no hōteki tenkai* (Tokyo: Shinzansha, 2004).

66. Chen, "The Attempt to Integrate the Empire," 241–242.

67. Naimushō, "Kageki shakai undō torishimari hō shakugi," 47. It should be noted that early Home Ministry drafts of what became the Antiradical Bill explicitly contained terms that Kawamura had used to explain the phrase "to subvert the laws of state." For instance, see the ordinance draft (*chokureian*) of August 20, 1922, in which Article 1 reads in part, "individuals who engage in activities in order to subvert the laws of state such as to overthrow the government or seizing part of the realm [*seifu o tenpuku shi mata ha hōdo o sensetsu*] shall be sentenced to up to ten years in prison." Reprinted in Ogino, *Chianijihō kankei shiryōshū*, vol. 1, 31.

68. Mizuno, "Shokuminchi dokuritsu undō ni taisuru chianijihō no tekiyō," 420. The only hint of this kind of interpretation appeared in passing, when, in a House of

Peers committee meeting on March 14, Home Minister Tokonami Takejirō declared, "Recently in our country socialists have contacted the communist party of Russia and are spreading extremism. They have received funds directly from the worker-farmer government of Russia in order to establish a Bolshevik movement [*sekka undō*]. Furthermore, Koreans have served as go-between, and are using the Bolshevik movement for the objective of Korean independence." However, Tokonami was emphasizing the political context in which the bill was drafted, and did not specifically make the connection between "subverting the laws of the state" and calling for Korean independence. Tokonami Takejirō, in the fifth committee meeting of the House of Peers on March 14, 1922, reprinted in SMSKK, vol. 1, no. 8, 119. See also Mizuno, "Chianijihō no seitei to shokuminchi Chōsen," 111; Matsuo, "Kageki shakaishugi undō torishimari hōan ni tsuite," 248–249.

69. Naimushō, "Kageki shakai undō torishimari hō shakugi," 52. Cited in Mizuno, "Chianijihō no seitei to shokuminchi Chōsen," 111–112.

70. Itō Sukehiro and Miyagi Chōgorō's exchange is reprinted in SMSKK, vol. 1, no. 8, 110. Also cited in Mizuno, "Chianijihō no seitei to shokuminchi Chōsen," 112.

71. Mitchell, "Japan's Peace Preservation Law of 1925," 332.

72. Mitchell summarized the February 21 Tokyo edition of an *Asahi Shimbun* editorial. See Mitchell, "Japan's Peace Preservation Law of 1925," 332.

73. For example, see Yuasa Kurahei's continuing criticism of the ambiguity of this bill in the House of Peers on March 23, in SMSKK, vol. 1, no. 8, 332–339.

74. On the first formation of the JCP, its suppression and self-dissolution, see Beckmann and Okubo, *The Japanese Communist Party*, 48–78; Odanaka Toshiki, "Dai ichi kyōsantō jiken: Nihon kyōsantō sōritsu to chianijihō jidai zenya no saiban," in Wagatsuma, *Nihon seiji saiban shiroku 3*, 339–378; Richard H. Mitchell, *Janus-Faced Justice: Political Criminals in Imperial Japan* (Honolulu: University of Hawaii Press, 1992), 36–40.

75. On the Peace Preservation Law in the context of establishing diplomatic relations with the Soviet Union, see Kobayashi Yukio, "Nisso kihon jōyaku daigojō to chianijihō" (1959), in *Nisso seiji gaikōshi: Roshia kakumei to Chianijihō* (Tokyo, Yūhikaku, 1985), 309–352.

76. On the Universal Male Suffrage Bill and the later 1928 general election, see Thomas Havens, "Japan's Enigmatic Election of 1928," *Modern Asian Studies* 11, no. 4 (1977): 543–555. It is often argued that since universal male suffrage and the Peace Preservation Law were passed within months of each other, they serve as a kind of carrot-and-stick (*ame to muchi*) approach used by the state in dealing with reform movements. However, Okudaira, Nakazawa, and Mizuno have all critiqued this explanation since the two laws originated independently from each other and developed through their own ministerial and legislative processes. See Okudaira, *Chianijihō shōshi*, 49–56; Nakazawa, *Chianijihō*, 44–46; Mizuno, "Nihon no chōsen shihai to chianijihō," 128–129.

77. See Mizuno, "Chianijihō no seitei to shokuminchi Chōsen," 109.

78. On the earthquake, see J. Charles Schencking, *The Great Kanto Earthquake and the Chimera of National Reconstruction in Japan* (New York: Columbia University Press, 2013).

79. See Nimura Kazuo, "Kantō daishinsai to kameido jiken," *Rekishi Hyōron* 281 (October 1973): 39–69; Mitchell, *Janus-Faced Justice*, 41–43.

80. See Mitchell, *Janus-Faced Justice*, 45–49; Tamiya Hiroshi, "Amakasu jiken: Kenpei ni gyakusatsu sareta museifushugisha Ōsugi Sakae," in Wagatsuma, *Nihon seiji saiban shiroku 3*, 412–438.

81. On these pogroms, see J. Michael Allen, "The Price of Identity: The 1923 Kantō Earthquake and Its Aftermath," *Korean Studies* 20 (1996): 64–96.

82. See Sonia Ryang, "The Great Kantō Earthquake and the Massacre of Koreans in 1923: Notes on Japan's Modern National Sovereignty," *Anthropological Quarterly* 76, no. 4 (Autumn 2003): 731–748; Takashi Fujitani, "Right to Kill, Right to Make Live: Koreans as Japanese and Japanese as Americans during WWII," *Representations* 99, no. 1 (summer 2007): 13–39.

83. See Okudaira, *Chianijihō shōshi*, 55–56. The ordinances and the subsequent debate to extend the ordinances are reprinted in Ogino, *Chianijihō kankei shiryōshū*, vol. 1, 82–85, 85–132.

84. On the Toranomon Incident and trial of Nanba Daisuke, see Tanaka Tokihiko, "Toranomon jiken: Kōtaishi o sogeki shita Nanba Daisuke," in Wagatsuma, *Nihon seiji saiban shiroku 3*, 439–483; Mitchell, *Janus-Faced Justice*, 49–51.

85. See: Nakazawa, *Chianijihō*, 33–46.

86. For instance, compare the flowcharts that Ogino has outlined concerning the process of drafting the Antiradical and Peace Preservation bills: Ogino Fujio, "Kaisetsu: Chianijihō seiritsu • 'kaisei' shi," in Ogino, *Chianijihō kankei shiryōshū*, vol. 4, 526 and 547, respectively.

87. See Okudaira, "Some Preparatory Notes," 62.

88. Ogino, *Shōwa tennō to chian taisei*, 20–22; see the various Justice Ministry drafts collected in Ogino, *Chianijihō kankei shiryōshū*, vol. 1, 151–154.

89. Naimushō, "Chianijihō shingi zairyō" (1924), reprinted in Ogino, *Chianijihō kankei shiryōshū*, vol. 1, 172–173; 172. For a discussion of this document, see Nakazawa, *Chianijihō*, 203.

90. None of the original documents remain of this draft ordinance, but Mizuno Naoki has culled from newspaper reports the basic motivation for and outline of the ordinance. He speculates that this work was in response to increasing labor activism and the formation of groups influenced by communism in 1924. See Mizuno, "Chianijihō no seitei to shokuminchi Chōsen," 108–110.

91. Naimushō, "Chianijihōan narabini shōan" (1924), reprinted in Ogino, *Chianijihō kankei shiryōshū*, vol 1., 154–155.

92. The only exception was a January 24, 1925, proposed revision put forth by the Cabinet Legislation Bureau. See Ogino, *Shōwa tennō to chian taisei*, 22–27.

93. Mizuno, "Shokuminchi dokuritsu undō ni taisuru chianijihō no tekiyō," 421.

94. Historians generally agree that this new bill was better written and its advocates were better prepared to field questions during committee and Diet deliberations. Additionally, as indicated above, there had been more preparatory communication and collaboration between ministries. Okudaira, *Chianijihō shōshi*, 45–47; Tipton, *The Japanese Police State*, 22.

95. The first version of the bill presented to the Fiftieth Imperial Diet is reprinted in GSS45, 51.

96. These two concepts appear in the constitutional interpretations of Hozumi Yatsuka, Minobe Tatsukichi, and Uesugi Shinkichi. See Miller, *Minobe Tatsukichi*, 27–38, 65–67; Minear, *Japanese Tradition and Western Law*, 64–71; Skya, *Japan's Holy War*, 62–64, 158. For an interesting reconsideration of kokutai as a mode of modern subjectivization, see Satofumi Kawamura, "The National Polity and the Formation of the Modern National Subject in Japan," *Japan Forum* 26, no. 1 (2014): 25–45. Kawamura's reconsideration of kokutai resonates with my analysis in later chapters of how the Peace Preservation Law became an apparatus for the rehabilitation of political criminals as loyal imperial subjects.

97. See Naimushō, "Chianijihōan ryakkai" (February 1925), reprinted in Ogino, *Chianijihō kankei shiryōshū*, 179–182; 180.

98. See Naimushō, "Chianijihō seitei no riyū oyobi kaishaku gaiyō" (February 1925), reprinted in Ogino, *Chianijihō kankei shiryōshū*, 182–183; 182. The German terms Staatsform and Regierungsform are rendered in roman characters in the text and can be roughly translated as "national polity" and "state form" respectively.

99. Shihōshō, "Kokutai, Seitai, Shiyūzaisan seido ni kansuru mondō" (February 1925), reprinted in Ogino, *Chianijihō kankei shiryōshū*, 183–185; 183–184.

100. Naimushō, "Chianijihō seitei no riyū oyobi kaishaku gaiyō," 183.

101. See Okudaira, "Some Preparatory Notes," 62.

102. *GSS45*, 52. As mentioned above, diplomatic relations were established with the Soviet Union in February. In addition to materials on the relationship between the Peace Preservation Law and diplomatic relations with the Soviet Union referenced above, see Kobayashi Yukio, *Nisso seiji gaikōshi: Roshia kakumei to Chianijihō* (Tokyo: Yūhikaku, 1985).

103. *GSS45*, 52.

104. *GSS45*, 53.

105. *GSS45*, 54–55.

106. This includes the debates over "the system of private property" (*shiyūzaisan seido*) phrase as well. For instance, Hoshijima asked whether public works funded by the government, such as public utilities or the national rail system, constituted a repudiation of the private property system. See *GSS45*, 55.

107. *GSS45*, 64.

108. *GSS45*, 56.

109. *GSS45*, 57.

110. *GSS45*, 57.

111. *GSS45*, 57.

112. See Maeda Yonezō's explanation of the revisions in *GSS45*, 92–99.

113. See Maeda's explanation (*GSS45*) and the arguments presented by Yokoyama Kintarō, Nakamura Keijirō, and Yamazaki Tatsunosuke to the March 6 committee in favor of deleting "seitai" from the bill. See *GSS45*, 88–91.

114. The debates from March 7 are reprinted in Kōtō Hōin Kenjikyoku, ed., *Chianijihō teian tōgi: Teikoku gikai ni okeru shitsugi ōtō giji* (Tokyo: Kōtō Hōin Kenjikyoku Shisōbu Hensan, 1928), 57. This collection cited as *CTT* hereafter.

115. *CTT*, 65–66.

116. *CTT*, 66–67, 72.

117. Kikuchi Kenjirō's questions are reprinted in *CTT*, 69–71.

118. *CTT*, 72

119. *CTT*, 72.

120. Sawayanagi's comments are reprinted in *CTT*, 138–143.

121. *CTT*, 138.

122. *CTT*, 139.

123. *CTT*, 144.

124. See for instance the exchange between Baron Den Kenjirō and Yamaoka Man-nosuke from the Justice Ministry in the Fourth Committee Meeting of the House of Peers on March 17. Reprinted in Shakai mondai shiryō kenkyūkai, ed., *Chianijihōan giji sokkiroku narabi ni iin kaigi roku: Dai 50 kai teikoku gikai* (Tokyo: Tōyō Bunkasha, 1972), 698–699. For a concise discussion of the geographic application of the law, see Mizuno, "Chianijihō to Chōsen," 49–50.

125. See Mizuno, "Shokuminchi dokuritsu ni taisuru chianijihō no tekiyō," 421. See also Nakazawa, *Chianijihō*, 203.

126. These imperial decrees are reprinted in Ogino, *Chianijihō kankei shiryōshū*, vol. 1, 167–168. It should be noted that in addition to Japan's formal colonies, the law was used to arrest Japanese radicals in Shanghai as well. See the reports drafted by the Japanese Consulate General in Shanghai covering the period 1927–1937, reprinted in Ogino, *Chianijihō kankei shiryōshū*, vol. 1, 566–574.

127. English translation from Mitchell, "Japan's Peace Preservation Law of 1925," 339–340; and Mitchell, *Thought Control in Imperial Japan*, 63–64. Translation amended. For the final version that became law, see *GSS45*, 51.

128. This pamphlet was a transcript of an instructional lecture that Furuta gave to a police training group in 1925. See Furuta Masatake, *Keisatsu kyōyō shiryō. Dai ippen: Chianijihō* (Tokyo: Keisatsu Kōshū Jogaku Yūkai, 1925).

129. Furuta, *Keisatsu kyōyō shiryō*, 8–9.

130. Furuta, *Keisatsu kyōyō shiryō*, 9.

131. Furuta, *Keisatsu kyōyō shiryō*, 10.

132. See the four editorials from the *Tokyo Asahi Shimbun* collected in *GSS45*, 100–104.

133. Kiyose's essay "Chianijihō o ronzu" (1926) is reprinted in *GSS45*, 104–112.

134. See *GSS45*, 110–112.

135. Mizuno, "Chianijihō to Chōsen," 52–53.

CHAPTER 2. Transcriptions of Power

1. On Althusser's distinction between the Repressive State Apparatus and Ideological State Apparatuses, see Louis Althusser, "Ideology and Ideological State Apparatuses (Notes Towards an Investigation)," in *Lenin and Philosophy and other Essays*, trans. Ben Brewster (New York: Monthly Review Press, 2001), 85–126. I will discuss this distinction in detail in chapter 3.

2. On arrests in the metropole, see Odanaka Toshiki, "San • ichigo, yon • ichiroku jiken: Chianijihō saiban to hōtei tōsō," in *Nihon seiji saiban shiroku*, vol. 4: *Shōwa • zen*,

ed. Wagatsuma Sakae (Tokyo: Daiichi Hōki Shuppan, 1968–1970), 148. Okudaira tallies a total of 14,622 arrests for 1933. See Okudaira Yasuhiro, "Chianijihō ihan jiken nendo betsu shori jinin hyō," in *Gendaishi shiryō 45: Chianijihō*, ed Okudiara Yasuhiro (Tokyo: Misuzu Shobō, 1973), 646–649, hereafter cited as GSS45. See also Nakazawa Shunsuke, *Chianijihō: Naze seitō seiji ha "akuhō" o unda ka* (Tokyo: Chūōkō Shinsho, 2012), 131. On the expansion of the law beyond the JCP, see Okudaira Yasuhiro, *Chianijihō shōshi*, new ed. (Tokyo: Iwanami Shoten, 2006), 138–147, 147–154, 192–239; Nakazawa, *Chianijihō*, 130–133; Matsuo Hiroshi, *Chianijihō: Danatsu to teikō no rekishi* (Tokyo: Shinnihon Shuppansha, 1971), 156–163.

3. On Kobayashi Takiji and the proletarian literature movement, see Donald Keene, "Japanese Literature and Politics in the 1930s," *Journal of Japanese studies 2*, no. 2 (summer 1976): 225–248; Heather Bowen-Struyk, "Rethinking Japanese Proletarian Literature" (PhD diss., Department of Comparative Literature, University of Michigan, 2001).

4. For a discussion about the relatively high rate of indictment in the colony, see Nakazawa, *Chianijihō*, 204–207.

5. There are debates on whether any executions were carried out under the Peace Preservation Law. There were executions of Korean activists, but as Okudaira, Mizuno, and Mitchell note, these sentences drew upon other laws in addition to the Peace Preservation Law. On this debate, see Richard H. Mitchell, *Janus-Faced Justice: Political Criminals in Imperial Japan* (Honolulu: University of Hawaii Press, 1992), 162–164.

6. Performing investigative and prosecutorial functions similar to district attorneys, procurators were assigned to district courts by the Justice Ministry. For brief histories of the procuracy in modern Japan, see Atsushi Nagashima, "The Accused and Society: The Administration of Criminal Justice in Japan" (excerpt), in *The Japanese Legal System: Introductory Cases and Materials*, ed. Hideo Tanaka (Tokyo: University of Tokyo Press, 1976), 541–547; Meryll Dean, *Japanese Legal System: Text, Cases and Materials*, 2nd ed. (London: Cavendish, 2002), 114–115.

7. Procurators were responsible for producing the Decision of the Preliminary Hearing (Yoshin shūketsu kettei sho), which was sent to the trial judge and served as the state's case against a suspect. On this process, see Patricia Steinhoff, *Tenkō: Ideology and Societal Integration in Prewar Japan* (New York: Garland, 1991), 37.

8. On thought procurators, see Ogino Fujio, *Shisō kenji* (Tokyo: Iwanami Shoten, 2000). On the specific responsibilities and practices of thought procurators, see Tozawa Shigeo, "Shisō hanzai no kensatsu jitsumu ni tsuite" (1933), reprinted in *Gendaishi Shiryō 16: Shakaishugi undō 3*, ed. Yamabe Kintarō (Tokyo: Misuzu Shobō, 1963), 15–36. On Japanese thought procurators in wartime colonial Korea, see Mizuno Naoki, "Shisō kenji-tachi no 'senchū' to 'sengo': Shokuminchi shihai to shisō kenji," in *Nihon no Chōsen • Taiwan shihai to shokuminchi kanryō*, ed. Matsuda Toshihiko and Yamada Atsushi (Kyoto: Shibunkaku Shuppan, 2009), 472–493.

9. The only study to focus on the role of Hirata Isao is Itō Akira, "Tenkō mondai no Ikkōsatsu: Nihonkyōsantō rōdōshaha to Hirata Isao," *Chiba kōgyō daigaku kenkyū hōkoku*, no. 31 (February 1994): 29–41. In regard to the English literature, Hirata Isao receives passing mention in Richard Mitchell's pioneering studies (referred to as "Hirata

Susumu"). See Richard H. Mitchell, *Thought Control in Prewar Japan* (Ithaca, NY: Cornell University Press, 1976), 171–172; and Mitchell, *Janus-Faced Justice*, 73–74, 77–78.

10. See Matsuo, *Chianijihō*.

11. For instance, Matsuo does not mention the tenkō policy in his history of the Peace Preservation Law. See Matsuo, *Chianijihō*.

12. By the 1930s, however, the Justice Ministry also implemented the law largely through administrative measures rather than judicial proceedings. For instance, Okudaira argues that because procurators and judges relied on the police to investigate and apprehend thought criminals, over time "the Ministry of Justice itself was inclined more to administrative regulations rather than to judicial ones." Okudaira Yasuhiro, "Some Preparatory Notes for the Study of the Peace Preservation Law in Pre-war Japan," *Annals of the Institute of Social Science* 14 (1973): 58.

13. On the Special Higher Police, see Elise Tipton, *The Japanese Police State: The Tokkō in Interwar Japan* (Sydney: Allen and Unwin, 1990).

14. For example, Elise Tipton argues that the practices of the Special Higher Police in the 1930s reflected "rule by law" in which "there is a formal commitment to administration under the law but a lack of legal limitation on policy formation." Tipton notes that even rule by law was not fully implemented, leaving the police "substantially outside the control of justiciable law." Tipton, *The Japanese Police State*, 53.

15. Mitchell, *Janus-Faced Justice*, 156–157. See also Patricia Steinhoff's 1969 dissertation, reprinted as a book in 1991, in which tenkō is portrayed as an expression of "cultural patterns" of Japanese society. Steinhoff, *Tenkō*, 6.

16. Mitchell argues that while police from the Home Ministry often brutalized detainees illegally, continuing a long tradition dating back to the Meiji period, judges and procurators from the Justice Ministry defended the "procedural rights" of detainees and thus respected the "rule of law." Mitchell, *Janus-Faced Justice*, xii, 70.

17. See Michel Foucault, *The Punitive Society: Lectures at the Collège de France, 1972–1973*, trans. Graham Burchell (London: Palgrave Macmillan, 2015); Michel Foucault, *Discipline and Punish: The Birth of the Prison*, trans. Alan Sheridan (New York: Vintage, 1977). Foucault allows us to ask different questions in contrast to conventional studies of the Peace Preservation Law, including the legal-administrative approach (e.g., Mitchell, Okudaira) as well as the integrative-functionalist approach (e.g., Steinhoff, Hoston).

18. See Foucault, *Discipline and Punish*, 194. See also Michel Foucault, *"Society Must Be Defended": Lectures at the Collège de France*, trans. David Macey (New York: Picador, 2003), lecture on January 14, 1976, 23–41. As I will argue in chapter 3, the path for Foucault's intervention had already been cleared by Louis Althusser's famous 1969–1970 article on ideology and ideological state apparatuses. See Althusser, "Ideology and Ideological State Apparatuses," 85–126.

19. See for example the section "The Control of Activity" in Foucault, *Discipline and Punish*, 149–156.

20. Recently, scholars have argued that Foucault's theory of disciplinary power reveals important aspects of how power operates in capitalist society. See Jason Read, *The Micro-politics of Capital: Marx and the Prehistory of the Present* (Albany: State University of New York Press, 2003), in particular 83–90.

21. This is derived from Jason Read's concise summary of Foucault. See Read, *The Micro-politics of Capital*, 85.

22. I refer to the English translations of these works: Foucault, *Discipline and Punish*; and Michel Foucault, *History of Sexuality*, vol. 1: *An Introduction*, trans. Robert Hurley (New York: Vintage, 1978).

23. Foucault, *The History of Sexuality*, vol. 1, 144. For secondary studies on Foucault's theory of law, see Alan Hunt and Gary Wickman, *Foucault and Law: Towards a Sociology of Law as Governance* (London: Pluto, 1994); Carole Smith, "The Sovereign State v Foucault: Law and Disciplinary Power," *Sociological Review* 48 (2000): 283–306.

24. Nicos Poulantzas, *State, Power, Socialism* (London: Verso, 2014), 77. Poulantzas continues that Foucault "fails to understand the function of the repressive apparatuses (army, police, judicial system, etc.) as means of exercising physical violence that are located at the heart of the modern State. They are treated instead as mere parts of the disciplinary machine which patterns the internalization of repression by means of normalization" (77).

25. My objective is not to correct the reading of Foucault, but rather to emphasize specific points at which his more nuanced contemplations in his lectures generate new ways to consider the relationship between juridical and disciplinary power. Here I draw upon readings that have attempted to rethink the relationship between juridical and disciplinary modes of power in Foucault's work. See, for instance, Ben Golder and Peter Fitzpatrick, *Foucault's Law* (New York: Routledge, 2009). Jan Goldstein contends that Foucault "was never fully in control of his views on this issue and never arrived at a completely consistent formulation" of the relationship between law and discipline. Jan Goldstein, "Framing Discipline with Law: Problems and Promises of the Liberal State," *American Historical Review* 98, no. 2 (April 1993): 369.

26. See Foucault, *The Punitive Society*, 107, 110, 140.

27. See Goldstein, "Framing Discipline with Law."

28. Foucault, "Society Must Be Defended," 37.

29. Foucault, *The Punitive Society*, 178. Following his genealogical method, Foucault contends that criminology emerges from this transcription: that is, as a discourse that "assures the juridico-medical transcription" of the criminal—the target of juridical power—as, at the same time, the "delinquent" that requires disciplinary examination and rehabilitation (178).

30. Summarizing Foucault's distinction, Jason Read has noted that "one can always fall short of a norm—thus there is the possibility for an infinite intervention, continual surveillance, and improvement." Read, *The Micro-politics of Capital*, 85.

31. Foucault, *The Punitive Society*, 34, 131.

32. On the transition from repression to reform, I have in mind Serizawa Kazuya's early work, in which he suggests that in the debates over law, sovereignty, and democracy in the 1920s, state power was effectively "freed" from the discourse of law and constitutionality, allowing for more authoritarian theories to emerge in the 1930s. See Serizawa Kazuya, *"Hō" kara kaihō sareru kenryoku: Hanzai, kyōki, hinkon soshite taishō demokurashii* (Tokyo: Shinyōsha, 2001).

33. Gakuren members were also involved in the earlier Enlightened People's Communist Party Incident (Gyōmin kyōsantō jiken) of 1923, which involved many lecturers, graduates, and students from Waseda University. See George M. Beckmann and Genji Okubo, *The Japanese Communist Party, 1922–1945* (Stanford, CA: Stanford University Press, 1969), 32–35.

34. On Gakuren, see Henry Smith, *Japan's First Student Radicals* (Cambridge, MA: Harvard University Press, 1972), chapter 4.

35. Matsuo Kōya, "Kyōto gakuren jiken: Hatsudō sareta chianijihō," in *Nihon seiji saiban shiroku*, vol. 4: *Shōwa • zen*, ed. Wagatsuma Sakae (Tokyo: Daiichi Hōki Shuppan, 1968–1970), 74.

36. On this incident, see Matsuo, "Kyōto gakuren jiken," 64–96; Okudaira, *Chianijihō shōshi*, 74–92; Mitchell, *Thought Control in Prewar Japan*, 70–77; Steinhoff, *Tenkō*, 38–40.

37. Okudaira, *Chianijihō shōshi*, 84. Another case in which the private property clause was applied in metropolitan Japan was in November 1927: the so-called Hokkaidō Collectivist Party Incident (Hokkaidō shūsantō jiken). See Okudaira, *Chianijihō shōshi*, 72–74.

38. This claim comes from Matsuo, "Kyōto gakuren jiken," 64. For a comparative consideration of these first two applications of the Peace Preservation Law, see Ogino Fujio, "Kaisetsu: Chianijihō seiritsu • 'kaisei' shi," in *Chianijihō kankei shiryōshū*, vol. 4, ed. Ogino Fujio (Tokyo: Shinnihon Shuppansha, 1996), 570–574.

39. For instance, Mizuno has shown how in a case brought against members of the Shinkankai (a socialist national liberation group formed in 1927), charges ranged from violations of the publication law, Ordinance No. 7 (discussed in chapter 1), to a high court decision in 1930 arguing for the application of the Peace Preservation Law. See Mizuno Naoki, "Shokuminchi dokuritsu undō ni taisuru chianijihō no unyō," in *Shokuminchi teikoku nihon no hōteki kōzō*, ed. Asano Toyomi and Matsuda Toshihiko (Tokyo: Shinzansha Shuppan, 2004), 431–434.

40. Kōtōhōin Kenjichō, "Chianijihō no tekiyō ni kansuru ken" (June 1925), cited in Mizuno, "Shokuminchi dokuritsu undō ni taisuru chianijihō no unyō," 423. The discretion when to use this law rather than earlier ordinances such as Ordinance No. 7 was left to procurators. See chapter 1 for an overview of the security ordinances in effect in colonial Korea at the time the Peace Preservation Law was enacted.

41. For a discussion of how officials consider the application of the kokutai clause in the colony, see Ogino Fujio, *Shōwa tennō to chian taisei* (Tokyo: Shinnihon Shuppansha, 1993), 72–74. Mizuno Naoki has analyzed how procurators in Japan continued to debate how to apply the Peace Preservation Law against Korean nationalists agitating in the metropole. See Mizuno, "Shokuminchi dokuritsu undō ni taisuru chianijihō no unyō," 437–451. For the application of this clause to noncommunist nationalist groups, see Mizuno, "Shokuminchi dokuritsu undō ni taisuru chianijihō no unyō," 424–425. For a general overview of the various independence groups in Korea during the 1920s, see Michael Robinson, "Ideological Schism in the Korean Nationalist Movement, 1920–1930: Cultural Nationalism and the Radical Critique," *Journal of Korean Studies* 4 (1982–1983): 241–268.

42. For information on the early arrests and prosecutions under the Peace Preservation Law in colonial Korea, see the 1929 report written by the Procuracy of the Chōsen Supreme Court: Chōsen kōtōhōin kenjikyoku, "Chōsen chianijihō ihan chōsa: 1," reprinted in Ogino, *Chianijihō kankei shiryōshū*, vol. 1, 258–266.

43. The Keijō District Court decision in the Korean Communist Party Incident case, February 13, 1928, cited in Mizuno, "Shokuminchi dokuritsu undō ni taisuru chianijihō no unyō," 428.

44. The Keijō District Court decision in the Kantōshū Communist Party Incident, December 27, 1928, cited in Mizuno, "Shokuminchi dokuritsu undō ni taisuru chianijihō no unyō," 428. We can interpret this explicit declaration of capitalist property relations in colonial Korea as a kind of implicit recognition of the primacy of territory, extraction, and capitalist social relations to Japan's colonial enterprise.

45. For an overview of cases brought to trial in colonial Korea in the late 1920s, see the report issued by the procuracy of the Chōsen High Court: Chōsen kōtō hōin kenjikyoku, "Chōsen chianijihō ihan chōsa: 1," 258–266. In this report, the procuracy identified four illegal ideologies in Chōsen at that time: anarchism, communism, nationalism, and the combination of communism and nationalism (260).

46. The 1927 Theses called for a two-stage revolution, explaining, "The bourgeois-democratic revolution of Japan will rapidly grow into a socialist revolution precisely because the contemporary Japanese state, with all its feudal attributes and relics, is the most concentrated expression of Japanese capitalism, embodying a whole series of its most vital nerves; to strike at the state is to strike at the capitalist system of Japan as a whole." English translation from Beckmann and Okubo, *The Japanese Communist Party*, 298. See also Germaine A. Hoston, *Marxism and the Crisis of Development in Prewar Japan* (Princeton, NJ: Princeton University Press, 1986), chapter 3; Matsuo, *Chianijihō to tokkō keisatsu*, 119–122. For an analysis of the emperor system in JCP and prewar Comintern theses, see Fukunaga Misao, *Kyōsantōin no tenkō to tennōsei* (Tokyo: Sanichi Shobō, 1978), chapter 4.

47. On these arrests and the subsequent prosecutions that followed, see Odanaka, "San • ichigo, yon • ichiroku jiken," 123–257. For information on these arrests in relation to the Peace Preservation Law, see Ushiomi Toshitaka, *Chianijihō* (Tokyo: Iwanami Shoten, 1977), 42–43; Mitchell, *Janus-Faced Justice*, 53–56; Okudaira, *Chianijihō shōshi*, chapter 4; Matsuo, *Chianijihō to tokkō keisatsu*, 117–129.

48. Ogino, *Shisō kenji*, 31–32.

49. In April, the Home Ministry banned the Labor-Farmer Party (Rōdōnōmintō), the All-Japan Proletarian Youth League (Zen nihon musan seinen dōmei), and the Japan Labor Union Council (Nihon rōdō kumiai hyōgikai). Nakazawa, *Chianijihō*, 97.

50. For summaries of this expansion, see Mitchell, *Thought Control in Prewar Japan*, 88–94; Tipton, *The Japanese Police State*, 23–25; Matsuo, *Chianijihō to tokkō keisatsu*, 129–131.

51. Ogino, *Shisō kenji*, 8.

52. See Steinhoff's summary of a May 1928 directive sent to thought procurators. Steinhoff, *Tenkō*, 40–42.

53. For the government's explanation of the necessity for this revision, see GSS45, 179–180. Preliminary reports reveal that officials believed the revision was necessary in light of information gathered from the March 15 arrests; in particular, that the JCP was agitating under the slogan "abolish the monarchy" as outlined in the Comintern's 1927 Theses. See Shihōshō keijikyoku, "Chianijihō chū kaisei hōritsuan riyū" (April 26, 1928), reprinted in Ogino, *Chianijihō kankei shiryōshū*, vol. 1, 270–271. See also the Justice Ministry's explanation after the revision that "our flawless kokutai" (*kinō muketsu no waga kokutai*) was threatened by a "foreign ideological threat" (*shisōteki gaikanzai*). "Chianijihō chū kaisei chokureian riyū setsumeisho," reprinted in Ogino, *Chianijihō kankei shiryōshū*, vol. 1, 308–309. For an overview of the March arrests and the revision, see Ogino, "Kaisetsu," 579–584.

54. The revision is reprinted in GSS45, 114. On the role of Suzuki Kisaburō (Home Minister up until May 1928) and Justice Minister Hara Yoshimichi in preparing the 1928 revision, see Nakazawa, *Chianijihō*, 99–100.

55. On the format of passing the revision as an emergency imperial ordinance, see Ogino, "Kaisetsu," 584–592.

56. For deliberations in the Privy Council in 1928 and the following Imperial Diet in 1929, see GSS45, 115–146 and 146–178 respectively.

57. See the graph in Ogino, *Shisō kenji*, 59. See also Ogino, "Kaisetsu," 579.

58. On this addition, see Steinhoff, *Tenkō*, 46. Anyone convicted of joining an organization with the objective of altering the kokutai or anyone who was not a member but still "acted in order to further its aims" (*kessha no mokuteki kōi no tame ni suru kōi o tame shitaru*) would receive a minimum of two years in prison. Similarly, for anyone to not only form or join an organization with the objective of "rejecting the private property system" but also to "act in order to further its aims" was now punishable with a sentence of up to ten years. The revised law is reprinted in GSS45, 114. On the importance of this emphasis on "furthering the aims" in the revision, see Nakazawa, *Chianijihō*, 95–96.

59. See Tanaka's statements to the Privy Council in GSS45, 120, 121. See also Tanaka's public statements on the 3.15 Incident arrests, translated in Beckmann and Okubo, *The Japanese Communist Party*, 156.

60. GSS45, 121. Note that Mochizuki's phrase "the glory of our kokutai" was a reference to the 1890 Imperial Rescript on Education (see chapter 1).

61. GSS45, 121.

62. Other platforms of the 1927 Comintern Theses were establishing a people's republic, eliminating parliament, repealing antilabor and antifarmer laws, the confiscation of all lands held by the imperial household, to defend Soviet Russia, a noninterference policy in the Chinese revolution, and independence for all colonial people. For a translation of the 1927 Theses, see Appendix D in Beckmann and Okubo, *The Japanese Communist Party*, 295–308. For a discussion of the often-fraught relationship between the JCP and the Comintern, see Hoston, *Marxism and the Crisis of Development in Prewar Japan*, 57–98.

63. As with the initial passage of the law in 1925, the Justice Ministry's Criminal Affairs Bureau conducted comparative research on the revision (as an emergency imperial ordinance) in February 1929 in preparation for Diet deliberation. See Shihōshō keiji-

kyoku, "Chianiji rippō rei hikaku" (February 15, 1929), reprinted in Ogino, *Chianijihō kankei shiryōshū*, vol. 1, 320–329.

64. Cited in GSS45, 147.

65. GSS45, 147.

66. A common form of critique was to press Justice Minister Hara and other advocates to clearly distinguish between this emergency ordinance and the Civil Disturbance Ordinance (Nairanzai) of the Criminal Code. See, for instance, Saitō Takao's comments (GSS45, 162–165) and Taketomi Wataru's comments (GSS45, 148–150).

67. Okudaira, "Some Preparatory Notes," 67–68.

68. On the various responses to the revision by the political parties, see Nakazawa, *Chianijihō*, 95–118.

69. On the JCP during these years of mass arrests, see chapters 6 and 7 of Beckmann and Okubo, *The Japanese Communist Party*, 138–196.

70. For number of arrests per year in Japan under the Peace Preservation Law, see Okudaira, *Chianijihō shōshi*, 132–135. For colonial Korea, see the graphs in Hong Jong-wook, *Senjiki chōsen no tenkōsha-tachi: Teikoku / shokuminchi no tōgō to kiretsu* (Tokyo: Yūshisha, 2011), 47 and 63.

71. For an overview of Peace Preservation Law arrests in Korea between 1925 and 1930, see Park Kyong-sik, "Chianijihō ni yoru chōsenjin danatsu" (1976), in *Tennōsei kokka to zainichi chōsenjin* (Tokyo: Shakai Hyōronsha, 1986), 100–102.

72. The 1929 Sapporo Appellate Court and the 1931 Tokyo Appellate Court decisions are reprinted in GSS45, 577–581 and 581–583 respectively. See also Ogino, *Shōwa tennō to chiantaisei*, 52–60, 66.

73. See Mizuno, "Shokuminchi dokuritsu undō ni taisuru chianijihō no unyō," 431–436.

74. Chōsen High Court ruling, July 21, 1930, cited in Mizuno, "Shokuminchi dokuritsu undō ni taisuru chianijihō no unyō," 433.

75. Decision in the Chōsen Student Vanguard League Incident (Chōsen gakusei zenei dōmei jiken) case, June 25, 1931, cited in Mizuno, "Shokuminchi dokuritsu undō ni taisuru chianijihō no unyō," 435.

76. Recall that there was a legal distinction between naichi—referring to the territory of Japan at the time of the promulgation of the Meiji Constitution in 1889—and gaichi, or outer territories, which referred to its subsequent colonial acquisitions. On this, see Edward I-te Chen, "The Attempt to Integrate the Empire: Legal Perspectives," in *The Japanese Colonial Empire, 1895–1945*, ed. Ramon H. Myers and Mark R. Peattie (Princeton, NJ: Princeton University Press, 1984), 241–242.

77. Mizuno, "Shokuminchi dokuritsu undō ni taisuru chianijihō no unyō," 436.

78. See GSS45, appendix 1, 646–647. See also Ogino Fujio, *Tokkō keisatsu* (Tokyo: Iwanami Shoten, 2012), 66.

79. Nakazawa, *Chianijihō*, 130–131.

80. See Hong, *Senjiki chōsen no tenkōsha-tachi*, 47. For comparative statistics on the changing application of ordinances in colonial Korea in the 1920s, see Suzuki Keifu, *Chōsen shokuminchi tōchihō no kenkyū: Chianhō ka no kōminka kyōiku* (Sapporo: Hokkaidō Daigaku Tosho Kankōkai, 1989), 182.

81. Additionally, Ogino notes that 15,111 were arrested in Korea by 1934 under the law. For these figures, see Ogino, "Kaisetsu," 606. For a short summary of the law's application in Taiwan and Kantōshū, see Nakazawa, *Chianijihō*, 207–208.

82. See Erik Esselstrom, *Crossing Empire's Edge: Foreign Ministry Police and Japanese Expansionism in Northeast Asia* (Honolulu: University of Hawai'i Press, 2009), chapters 4 and 5, especially 108–115.

83. Louise Young, *Japan's Total Empire: Manchuria and the Culture of Wartime Imperialism* (Berkeley: University of California Press, 1998), 143–144.

84. Thomas Dubois has called Manchukuo a "quasi-sovereign" or "inauthentic" sovereign state. See Thomas David Dubois, "Inauthentic Sovereignty: Law and Legal Institutions in Manchukuo," *Journal of Asian Studies* 69, no. 3 (August 2010): 749–770.

85. See Manshūkoku seifu, Ordinances No. 80 and 81 (September 10, 1932), reprinted in Ogino, *Chianijihō kankei shiryōshū*, vol. 4, 427–429. Also see Manshūkoku seifu, "Chian keisatsu hō" (September 12, 1932), in Ogino, *Chianijihō kankei shiryōshū*, vol. 4, 429–431. See also Nakazawa, *Chianijihō*, 209.

86. For a helpful summary of the various security laws and police organizations that advised and/or operated in Manchukuo in the 1930s, see Ogino, "Kaisatsu," 748–764.

87. On the establishment of the Thought Division (Shisōbu) in the Procuracy, see Ogino, *Shisō kenji*, 29–33.

88. Sano Manabu was captured by the consular police in Shanghai on June 16. See Esselstrom, *Crossing Empire's Edge*, 109–111. See also Yamamoto Katsunosuke, *Nihon kyōsanshugi undōshi* (Tokyo: Seki Shobō, 1950), 189–191. For a dramatic account of how Sano and others were captured, see Suzuki Takeshi, *Sano manabu ichimi o hōtei ni okuru made* (Tokyo: Keiyūsha, 1931). For the prosecution's case against Sano Manabu, see Shihōshō keijikyoku shisōbu, "Nihon kyōsantō chūōbu kankei hikokunin ni taisuru tōkyō chihō saibansho hanketsu," in *Shisō kenkyū shiryō* Tokushū No. 2, ed. Shihōshō Keijikyoku (Tokyo: Shihōshō Keijikyoku, 1932), 294–299.

89. The official record of these prosecutions is: Shihōshō keijikyoku shisōbu, "Nihon kyōsantō chūōbu kankei hikokunin ni taisuru tōkyō chihō saibansho hanketsu." On these trials, see Odanaka, "San • ichigo, yon • ichiroku jiken," 145–220; Ueda Seikichi, *Shōwa saibanshi ron: Chianijihō to hōritsukatachi* (Tokyo: Ōtsuki Shoten, 1983), 1–84; Beckmann and Okubo, *The Japanese Communist Party*, 215–221; Mitchell, *Thought Control in Prewar Japan*, 104–109.

90. Odanaka, "San • ichigo, yon • ichiroku jiken," 218–220.

91. Ogino, *Shisō kenji*, 36–38, 43.

92. Ogino cites an article by the Tokyo procurator Ikeda Katsu, who notes that beginning in 1931, "moral suasion" (*kyōka*) started to be an important topic discussed by officials administering thought crime cases. See Ogino, "Kaisetsu," 615–617.

93. Kawai distributed a letter titled "Boku ga nihon kyōsantō yori dattō o ketsuishi jihaku suru ni itaru katei" in March 1929; Mizuno published a letter titled "Nihon kyōsantō dattō ni saishi tōin shokun ni" in May. See Shimane Kiyoshi, "Nihon kyōsantō rōdōsha-ha: Mizuno shigeo," in *Kyōdō kenkyū: Tenkō*, vol. 1, ed. Shisō no kagaku kenkyūkai (Tokyo: Heibonsha, 1959), 154 and 152–157. On Kawai, Mizuno, and the later Labor Faction, see Beckmann and Okubo, *The Japanese Communist Party*, 183–187.

94. The following summary of Mizuno's critique is derived from Fukunaga Misao, *Kyōsantōin no tenkō to tennōsei* (Tokyo: Sanichi Shobō, 1978), 19–27.

95. Cited in Shimane, "Nihon kyōsantō rōdōsha ha," 152.

96. Itō Akira has argued that Mizuno's critique was an expression of a general "sense of defeat." See Itō Akira, "Tenkō mondai no Ikkōsatsu: Nihonkyōsantō rōdōshaha to Hirata Isao," *Chiba kōgyō daigaku kenkyū hōkoku*, no. 31 (February 1994): 30.

97. On the role of procurators in drafting and disseminating these critiques, see the reflections of the ex–Labor Faction member Asano Akira: Asano Akira and Kageyama Masaharu, *Tenkō-Nihon e no kaiki: Nihon kyōsantō kaitōha shuchō* (Tokyo: Akatsuki Shobō, 1983), 219–232.

98. Although Kawai was critiqued as part of the Dissolutionist Faction, he did not follow Mizuno in forming the Labor Faction. He continued to be politically active until a second arrest in 1934. See the biographical entry for Kawai in Kobayashi Morito, *"Tenkōki" no hitobito: Chianijihōka no katsudōka gunzō* (Tokyo: Shinjidaisha, 1987), 305.

99. Nihon Kyōsantō Chūōiinkai, "Shakai fashisuto kaitōha o funsai seyo!," *Mushin Panfuretto*, no. 10 (September 1931), collected by the Kyōdo Minyō Kenkyūkai, Tokyo. See also Germaine A. Hoston, "Emperor, Nation and the Transformation of Marxism to National Socialism in Prewar Japan: The Case of Sano Manabu," *Studies in Comparative Communism* 18, no. 1 (spring 1985): 25–47. On the failure of the Communist International's social-fascism line, see Nicos Poulantzas, *Fascism and Dictatorship: The Third International and the Problem of Fascism*, trans. Judith White (London: Verso, 1979).

100. For instance, see Germaine A. Hoston, *The State, Identity, and the National Question in China and Japan* (Princeton, NJ: Princeton University Press, 1994), 327–360. I briefly address how the national question has been explained in area studies in Max Ward, "Historical Difference and the Question of East Asian Marxism(s)," in *East Asian Marxisms and Their Trajectories*, ed. Joyce Liu and Viren Murthy, Interventions Series (London: Routledge, 2017), 88–91. For more nuanced analyses of the national question in Japanese Marxism, see Itō Akira, *Tennōsei to shakaishugi* (Tokyo: Keisō Shobō, 1988); Gavin Walker, *The Sublime Perversion of Capital: Marxist Theory and the Politics of History in Modern Japan* (Durham, NC: Duke University Press, 2016); Katsuhiko Endo, "The Science of Capital: The Uses and Abuses of Social Science in Interwar Japan" (PhD diss., New York University, 2004).

101. See Asano's reflections in Asano and Kageyama, *Tenkō-Nihon e no kaiki*, 230.

102. On the national question in Marxist theory and communist political strategy, see Walker Connor, *The National Question in Marxist-Leninist Theory and Strategy* (Princeton, NJ: Princeton University Press, 1984).

103. For a reflection on Mizuno's defection and its impact in the 1930s, see Nabeyama Sadachika, "Mizuno shigeoron ni shokuhatsu sareta," *Ronsō* 4:10, no. 19 (November 1962): 215–221. For a biography of Mizuno's work after the war, including his tenure as president of Japan Broadcasting Company (NHK), see Ōya Shōichi, "Mizuno shigeoron," *Bungei shunju* 33, no. 22 (December 1955): 124–135.

104. Itō Akira, *Tenkō to tennōsei: Nihon kyōsanshugi undō no 1930nendai* (Tokyo: Keisō Shobō, 1995), 25–28; Asano and Kageyama, *Tenkō-Nihon e no kaiki*, 220–223.

105. Itō Akira contends that while Mizuno and Hirata probably had a heated theoretical debate, the point for Hirata was not "the total rejection of Marxian thought, [but rather] pressing the single point of the kokutai." Itō, *Tenkō to tennōsei*, 27.

106. Asano and Kageyama, *Tenkō-Nihon e no kaiki*, 225–226.

107. Asano Akira quoted in Itō, *Tenkō to tennōsei*, 25.

108. Asano and Kageyama, *Tenkō-Nihon e no kaiki*, 226. Asano argues that Hirata was "95%" responsible for the defections that occurred at this time (223).

109. Itō, *Tenkō to tennōsei*, 26, 21, 40; see also Itō, "Tenkō mondai no Ikkōsatsu," 30.

110. Hirata Isao, cited in Itō, *Tenkō to tennōsei*, 29.

111. See Kobayashi Morito's biographical account of his conversion, written under the pen name Ono Yōichi, *Kyōsantō o dassuru made* (Tokyo: Daidōsha, 1932). This text is analyzed in chapter 3.

112. Mitchell, *Thought Control in Prewar Japan*, 141.

113. For early youth reformatories, see David Ambaras, *Bad Youth: Juvenile Delinquency and the Politics of Everyday Life in Modern Japan* (Berkeley: University of California Press, 2006), 44–65 and 104–105. See also Moriya Katsuhiko, *Shōnen no hikō to kyōiku: Shōnen hōsei no rekishi to genjō* (Tokyo: Keisōshobō, 1977), chapter 3. For early parolee "protection" services, see Uchida Hirofumi, *Kōsei hogo no tenkai to kadai* (Kyoto: Hōritsu Bunkasha, 2015), 1–8 and 9–26. On this early history of reform, see also Kōsei Hogo Gojūnen Shi Henshū Iinkai, ed., *Kōsei hogo gojūnen shi: Chiiki shakai to tomo ni ayumu kōsei hogo* (Tokyo: Zenkoku Hogoshi Renmei, 2000), vol. 1: 3–7.

114. On the new Juvenile Law of 1922, see Moriya, *Shōnen no hikō to kyōiku*, chapter 4; Ambaras, *Bad Youth*, chapter 4.

115. This law is reprinted in Uchida, *Kōsei hogo no tenkai to kadai*, 10–16. For the legal debates over this law, see 17–19.

116. Uchida, *Kōsei hogo no tenkai to kadai*, 20.

117. Ambaras, *Bad Youth*, 107–108.

118. For an early explanation of reform related to these new suspension policies, see "Kiso yūyosha shikkō yūyosha no hogo ni tsuite," *Hōsei kaihō* 10, no. 3 (June 1926): 4–11. On the rise of hogoshugi in regard to youth crime in prewar Japan, see Moriya, *Shōnen no hikō to kyōiku*, 61–151.

119. On criminal rehabilitation in general in prewar Japan, see Suzuki Kazuhisa, "Waga kuni no kōsei hogo jigyō no hatten to kokusaiteki hanzaisha shogū no dōkō," in *Kōsei hogo no kadai to tenbō: Kōsei hogo seido shikō 50shūnen kinen ronbunshū* (Tokyo: Nihon Kōsei Hogo Kyōkai, 1999), 131–160.

120. Miyake Masatarō, *An Outline of the Japanese Judiciary*, 2nd ed., rev. (Tokyo: Japan Times and Mail), 25.

121. Okudaira, *Chianijihō shōshi*, 158. However, the number of Suspended Indictments remained relatively low during this period; for instance, only sixteen cases in 1928 and twenty-seven in 1929. It was not until 1930 that procurators started to use this more (292 cases in 1930), and subsequently, with the establishment of Charges Withheld in 1931. See the graph in Mitchell, *Thought Control in Prewar Japan*, 142.

122. An excerpt of Directive No. 270 is reprinted in Ogino, *Chianijihō kankei shiryōshū*, vol. 1, 539–540.

123. For a brief summary of these policies in the early 1930s, see Nakazawa, *Chianijihō*, 137–141.

124. Ogino, *Shisō kenji*, 60–61.

125. This procedure was formalized in Directives No. 1527 (1928), No. 1637 (1928), and No. 1637 (1929). See Shihōshō Keijikyoku Shisōbu, ed., "Shisō jimu ni kansuru kunrei tsūchoshū," in *Shisō kenkyū shiryō*, Tokushū 1 gō (September 1932): 15–19.

126. See Shihōshō keijikyoku shisōbu ed., "Shisō jimu ni kansuru kunrei tsūchoshū," 19–35.

127. Regulation No. 2006, "Shisōhannin taisuru ryūho shobun toriatsukai kitei" (December 26, 1932), reprinted in Ogino, *Chianijihō kankei shiryōshū*, vol. 1, 541–542. See also: Ogino *Shisō kenji*, 60–61.

128. This protocol is reviewed in Ogino, *Shisō kenji*, 61; Okudaira, *Chianijihō shōshi*, 160.

129. "Shisōhannin taisuru ryūho shobun toriatsukai kitei," 541.

130. Okudaira reports that over 80 percent of guarantors were family members of the suspect. Okudaira, *Chianijihō shōshi*, 160.

131. An observation made by Poulantzas is suggestive here: "The massive accumulation of paper in the modern state organization is not merely a picturesque detail but a material feature essential to its existence and functioning." Poulantzas attributes this function of the accumulation of paper to the "intellectuals-functionaries," which we could apply to thought procurators (shisō kenji) like Hirata Isao. See Poulantzas, *State, Power, Socialism*, 59.

132. Hong, *Senjiki chōsen no tenkōsha-tachi*, 47.

133. This percentage is derived from the graph in Mitchell, *Thought Control in Prewar Japan*, 142.

134. On reform efforts targeting Koreans who committed conventional crime, see Kim Songon, "Chōsenjin no shihō hogo ni tsuite," *Hogo Jihō* 14, no. 12 (December 1934): 32–37. The disparity between metropolitan and colonial implementations of the Peace Preservation Law is also noted in Chulwoo Lee, "Modernity, Legality and Power in Korea under Japanese Rule," in *Colonial Modernity in Korea*, ed. Gi-Wook Shin and Michael Robinson (Cambridge, MA: Harvard University Press, 1999), 48.

135. Yoshida Hajime, "Chōsen ni okeru shisōhan no kakei narabini ruihan jōkyō," Shisō jōsei shisatsu hōkokushū (Sono 6), in *Shisō kenkyū shiryō: Tokushū dai 69 gō*, ed. Shihōshō keijikyoku, reprinted in *Shakai mondai shiryō sōsho: Dai 1 shū* (Tokyo: Tōyō Bunkasha, 1971), 9.

136. Mizuno, "Chianijihō to chōsen • Oboegaki," 50–51.

137. Foucault, *Discipline and Punish*, 251.

138. Foucault, *Discipline and Punish*, 251.

139. Recall Poulantzas's qualification of Louis Althusser's distinction between Repressive State Apparatuses and Ideological State Apparatuses in the introduction, wherein he argues that specific apparatuses can "slide" between repressive and ideological functions. Poulantzas, *State, Power, Socialism*, 33.

140. See "Chianijihō ihan jiken nendo betsu shori jinin hyō," in GSS45, 647. Although there are some minor differences in the exact numbers, see also Mitchell, *Thought Control in Prewar Japan*, 142; Steinhoff, *Tenkō*, 47; Nakazawa, *Chianijihō*, 130–131. According

to a Special Higher Police (Tokkō) report, over the Peace Preservation Law's twenty-year history, while 67,431 persons were arrested under the law in the home islands, only 5,595 (8.3 percent) individuals were prosecuted. See Yūgami Kōichi, "Jidai haikei ni tsuite," in Kobayashi, *"Tenkōki" no hitobito*, 270.

CHAPTER 3. Apparatuses of Subjection

1. The title of this chapter derives from Warren Montag, "Althusser and Foucault: Apparatuses of Subjection," in *Althusser and His Contemporaries: Philosophy's Perpetual War* (Durham, NC: Duke University Press, 2013).

2. Louis Althusser, "Ideology and Ideological State Apparatuses (Notes Towards an Investigation)," in *Lenin and Philosophy and Other Essays*, trans. Ben Brewster (New York: Monthly Review Press, 2001), 85–126. A few scholars have suggested the theoretical purchase of Althusser's theory of the ISAs to understand the emperor system in modern Japan. For example, Harry Harootunian has drawn upon Althusser's theory and argued that the imperial institution has functioned to interpellate Japanese "as subjects (not primarily imperial subjects—shinmin—even though this was obviously included in the formulation, but as subjects—shutai or shukan)" in both the pre- and postwar periods. Harry Harootunian, "Hirohito Redux," *Critical Asian Studies* 33, no. 4 (2001): 609. Ultimately, Harootunian critiques Althusser's assumption that there is a nonideological outside from which science can illuminate the operations of ideology. For this reason, he turns to Slavoj Žižek's qualification of Althusser's theory of interpellation (609–611). For Žižek's theory of ideology, see Slavoj Žižek, *The Sublime Object of Ideology* (London: Verso, 2008); Slavoj Žižek, "The Spectre of Ideology," in *Mapping Ideology*, ed. Slavoj Žižek (New York: Verso, 1994), 1–33. In regard to the 1930s in particular, James Dorsey has suggested in passing that the ideological conversions of the 1930s "were prompted by a combination of what Althusser has called 'Ideological State Apparatuses and Repressive State Apparatuses.'" James Dorsey, "From Ideological Literature to a Literary Ideology: 'Conversion' in Wartime Japan," in *Converting Cultures: Religion, Ideology and Transformations of Modernity*, ed. Dennis Washburn and A. Kevin Reinhart (Leiden: Brill, 2007), 466. Following these suggestions, my objective in this chapter is to more fully elaborate the operations of imperial state ideology through the lens of Althusser's theory of ISAs.

3. The canonical text on tenkō in English is Patricia Steinhoff's 1969 PhD dissertation, later published as: *Tenkō: Ideology and Societal Integration in Prewar Japan* (New York: Garland, 1991). Similar to Richard Mitchell's early studies of the Peace Preservation Law, Steinhoff explains tenkō as addressing the need for social integration during a particularly turbulent period of Japanese modernization.

4. For examples of tenkō as an intellectual phenomenon, see Yamaryō Kenji, *Tenkō no jidai to chishikijin* (Tokyo: Sanichi Shobō, 1978); Andrew Barshay, *State and Intellectual in Imperial Japan: The Public Man in Crisis* (Berkeley: University of California Press, 1988). In the case of colonial Korea, see Matsuda Toshihiko, "Shokuminchi makki chōsen ni okeru tenkōsha no undō: Kang Yŏng-sŏk to nihon kokutai gaku • tōa renmei undō," *Jinbun Gakuhō* 79 (March 1997): 131–161. Two exceptions to this intellectual

approach are Patricia Steinhoff's early sociological analysis of tenkō as state policy and Itō Akira's study of tenkō in the social history of the prewar communist movement. See Steinhoff, *Tenkō*; Itō Akira, *Tenkō to tennōsei: Nihon kyōsanshugi undō no 1930nendai* (Tokyo: Keisō Shobō, 1995).

5. For a thought-provoking attempt to understand the historical and political connections between Taishō democracy and Shōwa fascism, see Andrew Gordon, *Labor and Imperial Democracy in Prewar Japan* (Berkeley: University of California Press, 1992).

6. For instance, see Yamaryō, *Tenkō no jidai to chishikijin*. Andrew Barshay and Carl Friere have pointed out how, in the early postwar period, tenkō "served both narrowly as a moral litmus test in evaluating the careers of intellectuals active before and after the war and more broadly as a metaphor for the collective experience of an entire generation of Japanese." Andrew Barshay and Carl Friere, "The Tenkō Phenomenon," in *Sources of Japanese Tradition*, 2nd ed., vol. 2: *1600 to 2000*, ed. Wm. Theodore de Bary, Carol Gluck, and Arthur E. Tiedemann (New York: Columbia University Press, 2005), 940.

7. Sano Manabu and Nabeyama Sadachika, "Kyōdō hikoku dōshi ni tsuguru sho" (1933), in *Sano Manabu chosakushū*, vol. 1, by Sano Manabu (Tokyo: Sano Manabu chosakushū kankōkai 1959), 3–20. For an English translation, see Sano Manabu and Nabeyama Sadachika, "A Letter to Our Fellow Defendants," trans. Andrew Barshay and Carl Freire, in *Sources of Japanese Tradition*, 2nd ed., vol. 2, ed. Wm. Theodore de Bary, Carol Gluck, and Arthur E Tiedman (New York: Columbia University Press, 2005), 940–947. For the JCP's reaction to the Sano-Nabeyama statement, see *Sekki* (*Red Flag*), June 16, July 1, and July 11, 1933. Fukunaga Misao argues that the distinguishing feature in the Sano-Nabeyama letter compared to Mizuno Shigeo's earlier critique of the JCP was their claim that the party had taken on a petit bourgeois character following the mass arrests of 1928–1929. See Fukunaga Misao, *Kyōsantōin no tenkō to tennōsei* (Tokyo: Sanichi Shobō, 1978), 29–30.

8. The first newspaper reports on Sano and Nabeyama's change in direction were in the morning editions on June 10. The letter was first published in its entirety in the July 1933 issue of the journal *Kaizō* and again in August in *Chūōkōron*. See Itō, *Tenkō to tennōsei*, 139–140. For a biographical recollection about how the letter was distributed in jail by procurators, see Hayashida Shigeo, "Tenkō būmu," in *Gokuchū no shōwashi: Toyotama keimusho*, ed. Kazahaya Yasoji (Tokyo: Aoki Shoten, 1986), 102–106.

9. According to an article in the *Asahi Shimbun*, authorities distributed the letter to six hundred detained JCP members on June 13. Then on June 15 procurator Hirata Isao and chief procurator Miyagi Chōgorō met with Sano and Nabeyama at Ichigaya Prison in order to assess the situation among JCP members ("Tenkō dōi no kiun, jochō ni noridasu," *Asahi Shimbun*, June 15, 1933, evening ed., 2). Similarly, Chaplain Fujii Eshō published a series of articles in the June 14, 15, and 17 editions of the morning *Yomiuri Shimbun* explaining "How Did Sano Manabu and the Others Convert?" ("Ika ni shite Sano Manabu-shi ra ha tenkō shita ka") (see figure 3.3).

10. Patricia Steinhoff calculates that by the end of July, 548 other detained communists— 133 convicted JCP members and 415 of those awaiting trial—had formally defected from the party, 31 percent (548) of the 1,762 communists in custody. Steinhoff, *Tenkō*,

6. Okudaira confirms this number: Okudaira Yasuhiro, *Chianijihō shōshi*, new ed. (Tokyo: Iwanami Shoten, 2006), 155. Ushiomi Toshitaka cites a 1936 report stating that 73 percent of those indicted under the Peace Preservation Law had committed tenkō by 1936. Ushiomi Toshitaka, *Chianijihō* (Tokyo: Iwanami Shoten, 1977), 100.

11. Itō, *Tenkō to tennōsei*, chapter 5; Nakazawa Shunsuke, *Chianijihō: Naze seitō seiji ha "akuhō" o unda ka* (Tokyo: Chūōkō Shinsho, 2012), 141–144.

12. George Beckmann and Okubo Genji date the organizational death of the JCP to arrests that occurred in fall 1932. See George M. Beckmann and Genji Okubo, *The Japanese Communist Party, 1922–1945* (Stanford, CA: Stanford University Press, 1969), 237–238, 239–253.

13. As I will explain later in this chapter, Sano and Nabeyama did use the term "*tenkō*" in a subsequent addendum to the letter, but in a negative, pejorative, sense.

14. For example, see the original letter published in *Kaizō*, July 1933, 191–199.

15. For example, a headline in the June 10, 1933, morning edition of *Yomiuri Shimbun* declared that Sano and Nabeyama had "discarded communism and converted to fascism" (*fassho ni tenkō*). See figure 3.1.

16. See Regulation No. 2006, "Shisōhannin taisuru ryūho shobun toriatsukai kitei," December 26, 1932, in Ogino Fujio, ed., *Chianijihō kankei shiryōshū* (Tokyo: Shinnihon Shuppansha, 1996), vol. 1, 541–542. See also Ogino Fujio, *Shisō kenji* (Tokyo: Iwanami Shoten, 2000), 60–61.

17. On the increased reform efforts made by the Justice Ministry, see Ogino, *Shisō kenji*, 72–76.

18. Sano Manabu and Nabeyama Sadachika, "Kinpaku seru naigai jōsei to nihon minzoku oyobi sono rōdōsha kaikyū sensō oyobi naibu kaikaku no sekkin o mae ni shite komintaan oyobi nihon kyōsantō o jiko hihan suru," *Shisō shiryō*, May 1933. This extremely rare hand-copied document was circulated to prisons throughout Japan as "Useful Materials for Thought Guidance," or "Shisō kyōka no kōzairyō." This document contains both Sano and Nabeyama's longer explanation of their critique (1–118) as well as the letter to their fellow defendants (119–132).

19. There are debates over to what degree the authorities influenced the wording of this document. For a description of how Sano and Nabeyama came to draft this letter, see Nakano Sumio, "Sano, Nabeyama tenkō no shinsō," *Kaizō*, July 1933, 200–204. Elsewhere, Yoshimoto Takaaki disagrees with Honda Shūgo's argument that Sano and Nabeyama's letter bears the mark of state pressure, and rather argues that he believes "the intellectual content of the statement to be independent of the process that created it." Yoshimoto Takaaki, "On Tenkō, or Ideological Conversion" (1958), trans. Hisaaki Wake, in *Translation in Modern Japan*, ed. Indra Levy (London: Routledge, 2011), 103.

20. For example, the entry for tenkō in the authoritative *Kodansha Encyclopedia of Japan* tells us that the "term was coined in 1933 by Sano Manabu and Nabeyama Sadachika" when they "announced from prison that they had made a political 'change of direction' and were breaking their ties with the Communist Party." Entry for "tenkō" in Kodansha, ed., *Kodansha Encyclopedia of Japan*, vol. 8 (Tokyo: Kodansha, 1983), 6–7.

21. For instance, see Tokuoka Kazuo, *Chianijihō ihan jiken no saihan ni kansuru kenkyū* (Tokyo: Shihōshō Keijikyoku, 1938).

22. For instance, see Shimane Kiyoshi, *Tenkō: Meiji ishin to bakushin* (Tokyo: Sanichi Shobō, 1969); Takeuchi Yoshimi, "What Is Modernity? (The Case of Japan and China)" (1948), in *What Is Modernity? Writings of Takeuchi Yoshimi*, by Takeuchi Yoshimi, trans. Richard F. Calichman (New York: Columbia University Press, 2005), 53–81, esp. 74–76. This tendency to see tenkō as a constitutive principle in Japanese modernity continues today. For instance, in his attempt to distinguish between what he calls the "Taishō-thing" and "Shōwa-thing" (Taishōteki na mono, Shōwateki na mono), Karatani Kōjin finds multiple conversions (tenkō) occurring in the prewar period, which he theorizes as when writers and intellectuals posit an other/otherness (*tasha/tashasei*) to be internalized and/or overcome, including God in mid-Meiji Christianity (e.g., Uchimura Kanzō), through naturalism, to the otherness of the masses (*taishū*) informing proletarian literature, and finally the West in the discourses of "returning to Japan" (*nihon kaiki*) and "overcoming modernity" (*kindai no chōkoku*). See Karatani's essay: "Kindai nihon no hihyō: Shōwa senki," in *Kindai nihon no hihyō*, 1, ed. Karatani Kōjin (Tokyo: Iwanami Shoten, 1997), 13–44, in particular, 39–41.

23. For instance, see two collections of essays: Saotome Yūgorō, ed., *Tenkōsha no shuki* (Tokyo: Daidōsha, 1933); and Kobayashi Morito, ed., *Tenkōsha no shisō to seikatsu* (Tokyo: Daidōsha, 1935). I will analyze these two works later in this chapter and in chapter 4. For the officially recognized motivations for tenkō, see the reports summarized in Nakazawa, *Chianijihō*, 143; also Steinhoff, *Tenkō*, 99–127.

24. For instance, see Hirata Isao, "Kyōsantōin no tenkō ni tsuite," mimeograph of lecture, February 8, 1934, archived at the Ōhara Institute for Social Research, Hōsei University, Tokyo.

25. Itō, *Tenkō to tennōsei*, 135.

26. For an overview of these debates, see Victor J. Koschmann, *Revolution and Subjectivity in Postwar Japan* (Chicago: University of Chicago Press, 1996).

27. On Science of Thought, see Adam Bronson, *One Hundred Million Philosophers: Science of Thought and the Culture of Democracy in Postwar Japan* (Honolulu: University of Hawai'i Press, 2016).

28. Tsurumi Shunsuke, "Tenkō no kyōdō kenkyū ni tsuite," in *Kyōdō kenkyū: Tenkō*, vol. 1, ed. Shisō no Kagaku Kenkyūkai (Tokyo: Heibonsha, 1959), 6. See also Tsurumi Shunsuke, *An Intellectual History of Wartime Japan, 1931–1945* (London: KPI Limited, 1986), 12–13.

29. Tsurumi, *An Intellectual History of Wartime Japan*, 12. See also Tsurumi, "Tenkō no kyōdō kenkyū ni tsuite," 5–7.

30. For just a few examples of the continuing influence of Tsurumi's definition, see Patricia G. Steinhoff, "Tenkō and Thought Control," in *Japan and the World: Essays on Japanese History and Politics in Honour of Ishida Takeshi*, ed. Gail Lee Bernstein and Haruhiro Fukui (New York: St. Martin's, 1988), 78–94; and, extended to the case of colonial Korea, Hong Jong-wook, *Senjiki chōsen no tenkōsha-tachi: Teikoku / shokuminchi no tōgō to kiretsu* (Tokyo: Yūshisha, 2011), 2–6.

31. Okudaira Yasuhiro, "Some Preparatory Notes for the Study of the Peace Preservation Law in Pre-War Japan," *Annals of the Institute of Social Science*, no. 14 (1973): 53. Okudaira went on to write the foundational studies on the Peace Preservation Law.

However, by approaching tenkō solely as an administrative policy in the prewar Japanese justice system, Okudaira and others necessarily set aside questions of ideology, power, and subjection and did not analyze the myriad ways individuals practiced and experienced tenkō under the guidance of the state. When tenkō is mentioned in these institutional studies, it is often explained as a uniquely Japanese mode for dealing with political crime. For instance, Richard Mitchell argues that the tenkō policy "was a humane method of handling communist political criminals" that "fit in so snugly with traditional values." See Richard H. Mitchell, *Janus-Faced Justice: Political Criminals in Imperial Japan* (Honolulu: University of Hawai'i Press, 1992), 156–157.

32. Nabeyama Sadachika, "Tenkō o megutte," in *Kataritsugu shōwashi*, vol. 1, ed. Itō Takashi (Tokyo: Asahi Bunko, 1990), 215. It could be argued that Nabeyama was trying to justify his defection by emphasizing internal spontaneity. However, we can find this emphasis in other theories of tenkō as well. For instance, in his 1958 essay "On Tenkō," Yoshimoto Takaaki argues that the Sano-Nabeyama statement contains positions written from "internal conviction" and thus rejects the argument that "compulsory force and oppression by the authorities were the most significant elements among the external conditions of Japanese ideological conversion." However, even though he grants Sano and Nabeyama "internal conviction," Yoshimoto argues that they were, ultimately, "backwater intellectuals" (*inaka interi*) who failed to confront the dual social structure of modern Japan, which consisted of both modern elements and feudal remnants. Consequently, Yoshimoto argues that, having abandoned the modern social theory of Marxism, their conversion represented an "unconditional surrender to the dominant elements of Japanese feudalism." Yoshimoto Takaaki, "Tenkōron" (1958), in *Yoshimoto Takaaki Zenhūsen*, vol. 3: *Seiji shisō* (Tokyo: Daiwa Shobō, 1986), 15, 19. English translation: Yoshimoto Takaaki, "On Tenkō, or Ideological Conversion" (1958), trans. Hisaaki Wake, in *Translation in Modern Japan*, ed. Indra Levy (London: Routledge, 2011), 106, 109.

33. See Nabeyama, "Tenkō o megutte," 236–240, 227–230. In the 1990s, Tsurumi published an essay in which he recognized that Shisō no kagaku kenkyūkai's study failed to take into consideration the particular circumstances of the JCP in the 1930s. See Tsurumi Shunsuke, "Kokumin to iu katamari ni umekomarete," in *Tenkō sairon*, by Tsurumi Shunsuke, Suzuki Tadashi, and Iida Momo (Tokyo: Heibonsha, 2001), 7–30.

34. See Althusser, "Ideology and Ideological State Apparatuses," 114.

35. For an outline of ideology in Althusser's theoretical trajectory leading up to the ISAS article, see Gregor McLennan, Victor Molina, and Roy Peters, "Althusser's Theory of Ideology," in *On Ideology*, ed. Center for Contemporary Cultural Studies (London: Hutchinson University Library, 1978), 77–105. The *La Pensée* article combined portions of draft notes that Althusser had written in 1969 and 1970, in which he was starting to elaborate a theory of the determinations of law, ideology, and the state in the reproduction of capitalism. These notes were published posthumously as Louis Althusser, *On the Reproduction of Capitalism: Ideology and Ideological State Apparatuses* (London: Verso, 2014). Balibar has called these notes a "partial montage" of a more systematic theory that was, by its very nature, "unfinishable." Étienne Balibar, "Althusser and the 'Ideological State Apparatuses,'" in Althusser, *On the Reproduction of Capitalism*, ix. See also

Warren Montag, *Althusser and His Contemporaries: Philosophy's Perpetual War* (Durham, NC: Duke University Press, 2013), 142.

36. As I noted in the introduction, I am purposely disregarding Althusser's problematic theory of interpellation, which he develops from Lacan, and rather will focus on his theory of ISAs in order to analyze the policies and practices developed in criminal reform groups like the Imperial Renovation Society.

37. Some have critiqued Althusser for extending the state beyond its conventional parameters. For instance, see Perry Anderson, "The Antinomies of Antonio Gramsci," *New Left Review*, no. 100 (November–December 1976): 35–36.

38. In an interview, Foucault explained a dispositif as "a thoroughly heterogeneous ensemble consisting of discourses, institutions, architectural forms, regulatory decisions, laws, administrative measures, scientific statements, philosophical, moral, and philanthropic propositions—in short, the said as much as the unsaid. Such are the elements of the apparatus [*dispositif*]. The apparatus itself is the system of relations that can be established between these elements." Michel Foucault, "Confession of the Flesh" (interview with *Ornicar?*, July 10, 1977), in *Power/Knowledge: Selected Interviews and Other Writings, 1972–1977*, ed. Colin Gordon (New York: Pantheon, 1980), 194. Foucault elaborated that a dispositif is a "formation which has as its major function at a given historical moment that of responding to an *urgent need*. The apparatus thus has a dominant strategic function" (195). Foucault theorizes a dispositif as animated by two strategic tendencies: first, the apparatus is functionally overdetermined as its effects resonate throughout its other elements, and second, Foucault notes, "there is a perpetual process of *strategic elaboration*" that alters the strategic direction of the apparatus (195). On Foucault's theory of dispositif, see Giorgio Agamben, *What Is an Apparatus? And Other Essays*, trans. David Kishik and Stefan Pedatella (Stanford, CA: Stanford University Press, 2009).

39. In a 1970 postscript to the ISA essay, Althusser attempted to distinguish between the function of ideology in reproduction and the constitutive exploitation of capitalist social relations more generally. See Althusser, "Ideology and Ideological State Apparatuses," 124.

40. Althusser, "Ideology and Ideological State Apparatuses," 96, 97. In his draft notes on ISAs, Althusser succinctly explained, "An Ideological State Apparatus is a system of defined institutions, organizations, and the corresponding practices. Realized in these institutions, organizations, and practices of this system is all or part (generally speaking, a typical combination of certain elements) of the State Ideology. The ideology realized in an ISA ensures its systemic unity on the basis of an 'anchoring' in material functions specific to each ISA; these functions are not reducible to that ideology, but serve it as a 'support.'" Althusser, *On the Reproduction of Capitalism*, 77.

41. Althusser, "Ideology and Ideological State Apparatuses," 101.

42. Althusser, *On the Reproduction of Capitalism*, 70.

43. Althusser, "Ideology and Ideological State Apparatuses," 114.

44. Althusser, "Ideology and Ideological State Apparatuses," 115. Warren Montag points out that Pascal's "hypothetical libertine . . . poses more complicated problems" since the libertine desires to believe in God but only encounters emptiness. Montag

argues that while Pascal is presenting a "theory of the conditioning of the mind through the body that makes the soul a mere reflection of the body without substance or material form," Althusser "has set for himself the directly opposite objective: to demonstrate the material existence of ideas, beliefs, and consciousness." Montag, *Althusser and His Contemporaries*, 153–154.

45. Althusser, "Ideology and Ideological State Apparatuses," 116–117. On this point, see Judith Butler, "Conscience Doth Make Subjects of Us All: Althusser's Subjection," in *The Psychic Life of Power: Theories in Subjection* (Stanford, CA: Stanford University Press, 1997), 112. For an incisive critique of Butler's reading of Althusser, see Matthew Lampert, "Resisting Ideology: On Butler's Critique of Althusser" in *Diacritics* 43, no. 2 (2015): 124–147.

46. Althusser likens interpellation to a police officer's hail on the street corner— "Hey, you there!"—which we naturally respond to since we recognize that, of course, the hail was meant for us. Hailing is not an empirical sequence but rather an internal logic of ideology; it does not happen out there but is simultaneous and constitutive of ideology. Althusser recognizes the impossibility of the "temporal succession" constitutive of his theory of interpellation, noting that "in reality these things happen without any succession. The existence of ideology and the hailing or interpellation of individuals as subjects are one and the same thing." Althusser, "Ideology and Ideological State Apparatuses," 118. Furthermore, as many theorists have noted, Althusser's theory rests upon a subtle but necessary theoretical impossibility: that is, the notion of a presubjected "concrete individual" (118). Judith Butler notes, "If there is no subject except as a consequence of this subjection, the narrative that would explain this requires that the temporality not be true, for the grammar of that narrative presupposes that there is no subjection without a subject who undergoes it." See Butler, "Conscience Doth Make Subjects of Us All," 117, 111–112. In addition to Lampert's critique of Butler mentioned earlier, see also: Pierre Macherey, "Judith Butler and the Althusserian Theory of Subjection," trans. Stephanie Bundy, *Décalages* 1, no. 2 (2013): 1–22.

47. Althusser, "Ideology and Ideological State Apparatuses," 115, 123.

48. Althusser, "Ideology and Ideological State Apparatuses," 123.

49. On this question, see Butler, "Conscience Doth Make Subjects of Us All," 106–131.

50. Critiquing Poulantzas, Laclau argues that the multiple and overdetermined nature of ideological interpellations renders the process in which a fully interpellated class subject is formed "never . . . complete: it will always have an ambiguity." From this, Laclau asks "how are ideologies transformed?" to which he answers, "through class struggle, which is carried out through the production of subjects and the articulation/disarticulation of discourses." Ernesto Laclau, "Fascism and Ideology," in *Capitalism, Fascism, Populism: Politics and Ideology in Marxist Theory* (London: Verso, 1977), 109. For Poulantzas's passing mention of disarticulation, see Nicos Poulantzas, "Internationalization of Capitalist Relations and the Nation-State," in *The Poulantzas Reader: Marxism, Law and the State*, ed. James Martin (London: Verso, 2008), 253, 258.

51. See Hong, *Senjiki chōsen no tenkōsha-tachi*. Also Keongil Kim, "Japanese Assimilation Policy and Thought Conversion in Colonial Korea," in *Colonial Rule and Social Change in Korea, 1910–1945*, ed. Hon Yung Lee, Yong Chool Ha, and Clark W. Sorensen (Seattle: Center for Korean Studies, University of Washington Press, 2013), 206–233.

52. If anything, this decision would constitute an act of what Jean-Paul Sartre had called "bad faith," in which consciousness negates both the freedom and the decision upon which someone chooses from a given range of options. On "bad faith," see Jean-Paul Sartre, *Being and Nothingness: A Phenomenological Essay on Ontology*, trans. Hazel E. Barnes (New York: Washington Square, 1953), 47–70.

53. On so-called *gisō-tenkō*, see Steinhoff, *Tenkō*, 195–196.

54. Itō Akira makes this argument. See Itō, "'Hyōmen no ito' no tsuikyū to tenkō no yarinaoshi," in *Tenkō to tennōsei*, 274–287.

55. Foucault was not willing to reduce power to a function of capitalist exploitation, what he later critiqued as the "economism" in liberal and Marxian theories of power. See Michel Foucault, "Two Lectures," in *Power/Knowledge*, 88–89. However, Althusser directly argued, "Everything that happens in a capitalist social formation, including the forms of state repression that accompany it . . . is rooted in the material base of capitalist relations of production, which are relations of capitalist exploitation, and in a system of production in which production is itself subordinated to exploitation and thus to the production of capital on an extended scale." Althusser, *On the Reproduction of Capitalism*, 33, italics in original.

56. On tenkō literature, see: Yukiko Shigeto, "The Politics of Writing: Tenkō and the Crisis of Representation" (PhD diss., University of Washington, 2009); George Sipos, "The Literature of Political Conversion (Tenkō) of Japan" (PhD diss., University of Chicago, 2013). The Rōdō undōshi kenkyūkai (Labor Movement History Research Group) is one of the few groups to have noted Kobayashi's important role in the tenkō phenomenon. Kobayashi delivered a series of closed lectures to this research group in the mid-1970s. Drafts of these lectures were distributed within the Rōdō undōshi kenkyūkai under the title "Nihon shakai undōshi hishi." Chapters 4 through 7 are archived at Ohara shakai mondai kenkyūsho at Hosei University, Tokyo. Portions of these lectures were published as "Waga hansei no kaisō" in *Rōdō undōshi kenkyū*, no. 9 (1972). Later these lectures were revised and published as Kobayashi Morito, *"Tenkōki" no hitobito: Chianijihōka no katsudōka gunzō* (Tokyo: Shinjidaisha, 1987). For secondary research on Kobayashi Morito conducted by members of the Rōdō undōshi kenkyūkai, see Itō, *Tenkō to Tennōsei*; Ishidō Kiyotomo, "Kobayashi Morito no tadotta michi," in Kobayashi, *"Tenkōki" no hitobito*, 253–267.

57. A short biographical summary of Kobayashi Morito's life can be found in Tsunazawa, *Nō no shisō to nihon kindai* (Nagoya: Fubaisha, 2004), 10–13. For Kobayashi's reflections on his life trajectory, see Kobayashi, *"Tenkōki" no hitobito*, 12–27.

58. For information on the 1928 general elections, see Thomas Havens, "Japan's Enigmatic Election of 1928," *Modern Asian Studies* 11, no. 4 (1977): 543–555.

59. Kobayashi Morito (Ono Yōichi, pseud.), *Kyōsantō o dassuru made* (Tokyo: Daidōsha, 1932), 1.

60. Kobayashi, *"Tenkōki" no hitobito*, 20.

61. Kobayashi, *"Tenkōki" no hitobito*, 21. This use of tenkō is anachronistic for the period Kobayashi is recounting; it would be a few more years before tenkō came to signify an act of defection or apostasy.

62. For the prosecution's case against Kobayashi Morito and twelve other suspects, see "Kobayashi Morito hoka jūnimei chianijihō ihan hikoku jiken yoshin shūketsu

kettei sho," in *Shakaishugi undō*, vol. 3: *Gendaishi shiryō 16*, ed. Yamabe Kentarō (Tokyo: Misuzu Shobō, 1965), 540–546.

63. For a short biography on Miyagi, see Ko Miyagi Moto Shihō Daijin Kenpi Jikkōiin Jimusho, ed., *Miyagi Chōgorō shōden* (Tokyo: Ko Miyagi Moto Shihō Daijin Kenpi Jikkōiin Jimusho, 1950). For Fujii, see Yamashita Zongyō, "Fujii Eshō," in *Nihon keiji seisakushi jō no hitobito kenkyūkai*, ed. Nihon Keiji Seisaku Kenkyūkai (Tokyo: Nihon Kajo Shuppan, 1989).

64. In an interview with Patricia Steinhoff in December 1967, a tenkōsha named Kawasaki Tateo reports that while the leadership of the JCP were held in Ichigaya Prison, many rank-and-file members were held in Toyotama Prison. See Steinhoff, *Tenkō*, 149. For documents and reflections written by activists held in Toyotama Prison, see the first part: "Gokuchū no ki," in Kazahaya, *Gokuchū no shōwashi*, 5–107.

65. Tellingly, in the postwar Kobayashi narrates his experiences in prison and at the Imperial Renovation Society as a series of encounters with fate (*innen*) and destiny (*shukuen*), particularly meeting Chaplain Fujii and Chief Procurator Miyagi while serving his prison sentence in Tokyo. See Kobayashi, *"Tenkōki" no hitobito*, 24–26.

66. In a 1933 publication, Kobayashi is listed as an "Imperial Renovation Society Rehabilitation Counselor" (Teikoku kōshinkai hogo iin). See Kobayashi Morito, "Shisōhan no hogo o ika ni subeki ya: Teikoku kōshinkai ni okeru jiken ni motozuite," *Hogo Jihō 17*, no. 6 (June 1933): 16–24, reprinted in Ogino Fujio, ed., *Chianijihō kankei shiryōshū*, vol. 3 (Tokyo: Shinnihon Shuppansha, 1996), 13–18. Ogino lists this essay as published in the May issue. Despite this, the pagination I reference comes from the Ogino collection.

67. Other rehabilitation groups at the time focused on parolees (*karishakuhō*) or those who had finished their full prison sentences. For a discussion of the Imperial Renovation Society in comparison to other *hogo dantai*, see Ko Miyagi Moto Shihō Daijin Kenpi Jikkōiin Jimusho ed., *Miyagi Chōgorō shōden*, 153–160.

68. Miyagi was an early proponent of *hogoshugi* within the Justice Ministry, and spent his entire life advocating for the importance of rehabilitation, particularly in relation to juvenile delinquents. See Akira Morito, "Taishō shōnenhō no shikō to 'shihō hogo' no gainen," *Hanzai Shakai Kenkyū 20* (1997): 64–86; Kasagi Nihaya, "Miyagi Chōgorō no shōnenhō shisō," *Takada Hōgaku*, no. 4 (March 2005): 1–16; Ko Miyagi Moto Shihō Daijin Kenpi Jikkōiin Jimusho ed., *Miyagi Chōgorō shōden*; Yamada Kenji, "Miyagi Chōgorō," *Tsumi to batsu 34*, no. 1 (1996): 47–53. For Miyagi's writings on the relationship between thought crime and hogo, see Miyagi Chōgorō, *Hōritsuzen to hōritsuaku* (Tokyo: Dokusho Shinpōsha Shuppanbu, 1941), part 5.

69. See Kobayashi, "Shisōhan no hogo o ika ni subeki ya," 17; Kobayashi, *"Tenkōki" no hitobito*, 120.

70. On these funding sources, see Ko Miyagi Moto Shihō Daijin Kenpi Jikkōiin Jimusho ed., *Miyagi Chōgorō shōden*, 155–156.

71. Based on a report from 1935, Itō Akira provides the following numbers of thought criminals under supervision at the center: 1931–1932, 8 people; 1932–1933, 43 people; 1933–1934, 143 people; and 1934–1935, 178 people. Itō, *Tenkō to tennōsei*, 228. Kobayashi reports that on any given day, upwards of fourteen or fifteen people would be looking for employment counseling. Kobayashi, *"Tenkōki" no hitobito*, 225.

72. Kobayashi, *Kyōsantō o dassuru made*.

73. Looking back on the importance of this text, Kobayashi's advisee and colleague Chaplain Fujii Eshō recounts that after this book was published, the Imperial Renovation Society soon found itself assisting over two hundred paroled thought criminals. See Fujii Eshō, "Shisōhan shakuhōsha no hogo hōhō," *Hogo Jihō* 19, no. 1 (January 1935): 16.

74. Kobayashi, *Kyōsantō o dassuru made*, 75, 172, 161, 150, and 159 respectively. These are just a few of the terms that Kobayashi uses to signify his conversion process throughout the text.

75. Consider for instance the title of the work—*Up until Leaving the Communist Party*. On one level, this suggests a temporal logic of narrative closure. That is, it is not whether Kobayashi discarded communism, but rather an explanation—and thus an instructional aid—for how one abandons radical politics. At the same time, this also reflects Althusser's theory of the retroactive temporality at work in ideological subjection discussed earlier.

76. Chapters 1 through 5 are titled as follows: "The 3.15 Incident," "The Sprouts [*mebae*] of Marxism," "The Leveller's Movement," "A Friend to the Small Cultivators," and "Marxist Vanguard."

77. Kobayashi, *Kyōsantō o dassuru made*, 56.

78. On the idea of the vanishing mediator, see Fredric Jameson, "The Vanishing Mediator: Narrative Structure in Max Weber," *New German Critique*, no. 1 (winter 1973): 52–89.

79. Kobayashi, *Kyōsantō o dassuru made*, 66. In an insightful interpretation, Tsunazawa understands the function of mountains, rivers, and rice fields in Kobayashi's writing as symbolizing the space of the village as a site of healing: "Even in the world of the village, replete more so than anywhere else with poverty and contradiction, [the village] performs a sufficient function as a space where wounds are mended." Tsunazawa, *Nō no shisō to nihon kindai*, 21.

80. See Kobayashi, *Kyōsantō o dassuru made*, 74–76.

81. Kobayashi, *Kyōsantō o dassuru made*, 81.

82. Kobayashi, *Kyōsantō o dassuru made*, 88.

83. Kobayashi, *Kyōsantō o dassuru made*, 122.

84. Kobayashi reports that he was influenced by a book by Kobayashi Sanzaburō to explore the connection between mind and body, spiritual and physical health. See Kobayashi Sanzaburō, *Seimei no shinpi: Ikiru chikara to ijutsu no gacchi* (Kyoto: Seizasha, 1922).

85. This sequence of Kobayashi's reunification of mind and body unfolds through a series of chapters titled "Injury of Flesh" ("Ketsuniku e no nayami"), "The First Step in the Change in Direction," "Madness? Death?," "The Mystery of Life," "The Body's Rehabilitation" ("Nikutai no fukkatsu"), and finally, "The Erasure of Marxism."

86. This notion of unification (gacchi) will be a continuing ideological trope in Kobayashi's later writings. It is predicated on Kobayashi's claim that unlike Western materialism, Japanese thought conceives of mind and body, ideas and matter, as inseparably connected, what he understands through the Buddhist principle "busshin

ichinyo" (roughly: "matter and mind are one"). See Kobayashi's later writing: *Tenkōsha no shisō to seikatsu*, 10.

87. Kobayashi, *Kyōsantō o dassuru made*, 52. This is a common trope in tenkō biographies; we will see how another convert, Kojima Yuki, explained the appeal of the JCP in this way later in this chapter.

88. Kobayashi, *Kyōsantō o dassuru made*, 150–151.

89. Kobayashi, *Kyōsantō o dassuru made*, 176–180. On the use of "self" (*jiga, jibun, jiko*) in conversion biographies, see Steinhoff, *Tenkō*, 132.

90. Kobayashi, *Kyōsantō o dassuru made*, 181.

91. Kobayashi, *Kyōsantō o dassuru made*, 180.

92. In this schema, society was no longer understood as constituted by class conflict, but had become a multiplicity of wills that were sublimated at a higher plane. Kobayashi argued that without these multiple wills and their sublimation, "this world would perish into mere scientific existence" (*Kyōsantō o dassuru made*, 153). These wills provided the drive for self-betterment, but required their mediation at a higher plane through what he sees as a transcendental "blind will" (*mōmokuteki ishi*)—that is, the domain of Buddha's mercy. Here Kobayashi argued that "Buddhist faith is the fusion [*yūgō*] of our egos [*wareware no shōga*]; it is here that our world has formed" (153).

93. In the preface to the text, Kobayashi writes, "Unable to discover personal solace in Marxism, in the end I have arrived at religion," again emphasizing socialist activism as a search for individual peace. Kobayashi, *Kyōsantō o dassuru made*, 4.

94. Kobayashi, *Kyōsantō o dassuru made*, 169.

95. Kobayashi, *Kyōsantō o dassuru made*, 169.

96. Chapter 7 is titled "The First Step toward a Change in Direction" ("Hōkōtenkan e no dai-ippo").

97. Kobayashi, *Kyōsantō o dassuru made*, 75, 162.

98. Kobayashi, *Kyōsantō o dassuru made*, 75. We can read Kobayashi's critique as indirectly related to the problems of Comintern policies in the 1920s concerning the different conditions and political situations in each country. This proved catastrophic with the rise of fascism and the belated shift to a popular front strategy. See Nicos Poulantzas, *Fascism and Dictatorship: The Third International and the Problem of Fascism*, trans. Judith White (London: Verso, 1979).

99. Kobayashi, *Kyōsantō o dassuru made*, 162–163.

100. Kobayashi, *Kyōsantō o dassuru made*, 162–163.

101. Kobayashi, *Kyōsantō o dassuru made*, 163.

102. In the postwar, Maruyama Masao would explain tenkō as signifying "an escape from the tensions of self-regulation imposed according to a theory (or formula); like the release of a tightly coiled spring, *tenkō* brought about an instantaneous return to a 'natural' world of 'inclusivity.'" Maruyama Masao, *Nihon no shisō* (Tokyo: Iwanami Shinsho, 1961), 15. English translation from James Dorsey, "From Ideological Literature to a Literary Ideology: 'Conversion' in Wartime Japan," in *Converting Cultures: Religion, Ideology and Transformations of Modernity*, edited by Dennis Washburn and A. Kevin Reinhart (Leiden: Brill, 2007), 472.

103. Kobayashi, *Kyōsantō o dassuru made*, 163.

104. Kobayashi, *Kyōsantō o dassuru made*, 163. See Tsunazawa's analysis of this aspect of Kobayashi's thought in Tsunazawa, *Nō no shisō to nihon kindai*, 22–23.

105. Kobayashi, *Kyōsantō o dassuru made*, 164. For an analysis of the debates over this passage from the Communist Manifesto, see Roman Rosdolsky, "The Workers and the Fatherland: A Note on a Passage in the 'Communist Manifesto,'" *Science and Society* 29, no. 3 (1965): 330–337.

106. Steinhoff refers to a report delivered by Kōji Konaka in a thought administrators' conference in 1938, where Kōji refers to three types of tenkō categorized by the Imperial Renovation Society: political (*seijiteki*), citizen (*shiminteki*), and religious (*shūkyōteki*). See Steinhoff, *Tenkō*, 129. It is important to recognize that not only did the state's categories change over time, but also that such conceptual developments are implicated in the phenomenon we seek to analyze; namely, the transformations in emperor system ideology in the 1930s.

107. Kobayashi, *Kyōsantō o dassuru made*, 257.

108. Kobayashi, *Kyōsantō o dassuru made*, 258.

109. The editors of *Hogo Jihō* translated its title into English as *Aid and Guidance: The Bulletin of the Central Ex-Prisoners' Aid Association of Japan*.

110. The publication *Hoseikai Kaihō* was in print from 1917 to 1929. Representing the dominant discourse of hogo (protection) in justice circles in the mid-1920s, the bulletin changed its name to *Hogo Jihō* in 1929. Similarly, the bulletin's demise in 1939 signals how resources were directed to the war effort following Japan's invasion of China in 1937, and the parallel eclipse of rehabilitation by total-war mobilization measures. I discuss this transformation in criminal reform measures in the late 1930s in chapter 5.

111. Before 1933, a few articles had been published intermittently in *Hogo Jihō* addressing thought crime and reforming thought criminals. But it was not until 1933 that this became a dominant topic in the bulletin. Kobayashi's first essay in *Hogo Jihō* was published in September 1932, on his experience with what he called "indirect rehabilitation" (*kansetsu hogo*) at the Imperial Renovation Society. See Kobayashi Morito, "Kansetsu hogo taiken o kataru," *Hogo Jihō* 16, no. 9 (September 1932): 43–47.

112. Kobayashi, "Shisōhan no hogo o ika ni subeki ya."

113. In addition to this article, a March 3, 1933, *Tokyo Asahi Shimbun* article in the evening edition reports that a "Rare Suspended Sentence is Given to a Converted Party Member" ("Tenkō tōin ni shikkō yūyo: mezurashii sokketsu," 2).

114. See "Tenkō shisōhannin ni hogo gakari shinsetsu: Shihōkan kaigi ni tōshin," *Yomiuri Shimbun*, evening ed., May 23, 1933, 2.

115. Kobayashi, "Shisōhan no hogo o ika ni subeki ya," 14.

116. Here Kobayashi admitted that while rehabilitation groups should not too strongly reject a convert's political commitments or activities, they must "guard against the dangers" (*kikensei o yobō*) that this continued activity presented. Kobayashi, "Shisōhan no hogo o ika ni subeki ya," 14.

117. Kobayashi, "Shisōhan no hogo o ika ni subeki ya," 14–15.

118. Kobayashi, "Shisōhan no hogo o ika ni subeki ya," 15. Kyōka is translated in English variously as "influence," "indoctrination," or "moral suasion." On kyōka in the

formation of the modern Japanese nation-state, see Carol Gluck, *Japan's Modern Myths: Ideology in the Late Meiji Period* (Princeton, NJ: Princeton University Press, 1987), 12, 103, 279; Sheldon Garon, *Molding Japanese Minds: The State in Everyday Life* (Princeton, NJ: Princeton University Press, 1997), xiv, 7.

119. Kobayashi, "Shisōhan no hogo o ika ni subeki ya," 16.

120. In chapter 4, we will see how this concern for moral guidance will develop into what Michel Foucault has theorized as a distinct mode of power, which he calls governmentality.

121. Kobayashi, "Shisōhan no hogo o ika ni subeki ya," 21.

122. Here Kobayashi distinguished between the various employment opportunities for the different classes of tenkōsha, including, for intellectuals, finding work as reporters, in publishing, and in libraries; for laborers, recognizing the difficulties they faced by finding industrial work after being jailed; and many others, who, unable to find employment, were attempting to establish small shops or find other sources of income. See Kobayashi, "Shisōhan no hogo o ika ni subeki ya," 16–17. Kobayashi notes the important role of the Japan Red Support Group (Nihon Sekishoku Kyūenkai), a political prisoner support group started in 1927 and which continued in different formations into the postwar period. Kobayashi was envisioning another kind of group that would counter such socialist-inspired groups by publishing anti-Marxist or religious materials in order to urge a prisoner to convert (17). On the Japan Red Support Group, see Takizawa Ichirō, *Nihon sekishoku kyūenkai shi* (Tokyo: Nihon Hyōronsha, 1993).

123. Hirata Isao in *Hōritsu Shimbun*, August 20, 1933, cited in Ogino, *Shisō kenji*, 66.

124. The record for this event is published as "Shisōhan ni kansuru hogo jigyō kōshūkai," *Hogo Jihō* 17, no. 7 (July 1933): 51–65. Sano and Nabeyama appropriated the name of Stalin's "socialism in one country" and called their new national socialism *ikkoku shakaishugi*. See Sano Manabu and Nabeyama Sadachika, eds., *Nihonkyōsantō oyobi komintaan hihan: Ikkoku shakaishugi ni tsuite* (Tokyo: Musansha, 1934). Also, Germaine A. Hoston, "Emperor, Nation and the Transformation of Marxism to National Socialism in Prewar Japan: The Case of Sano Manabu," *Studies in Comparative Communism* 18, no. 1 (spring 1985): 25–47, and Germaine A. Hoston, "Ikkoku shakai-shugi: Sano Manabu and the Limits of Marxism as Cultural Criticism," in *Culture and Identity: Japanese Intellectuals during the Interwar Years*, ed. J. Thomas Rimer (Princeton, NJ: Princeton University Press, 1990), 168–186.

125. Around this time, other endeavors were taking place that addressed dangerous thought. For instance, in April 1933, two months before the Sano-Nabeyama defection, it was announced that a cabinet-level committee would be formed, staffed with officials from the Home, Justice, and Education Ministries as well as prison wardens, military officials, and others, in order to develop a national thought policy (*shisō taisaku*). This committee met between July and October 1933, issuing policy proposals such as "Education and Religion," "Correcting Thought," "Regulating Thought," and "Social Policy." As its mandate stated, such a broad thought policy required, first, the further "clarification and spread [*fukyū tettei*] of the Japanese spirit that is the guiding principle of the state" and second, the "investigation of unhealthy thought and a plan for its correction [*zesei*]." On the formation of this committee, see Monbushō shisōkyoku, ed.,

Shisōkyoku yōkō, November 1934. Itō cites this report and provides a general summary of the committee meeting. See Itō, *Tenkō to tennōsei*, 156.

126. For a list of the lectures, including individual synopses, see "Shisōhan ni kansuru hogo jigyō kōshūkai," 52, 58–63.

127. See the synopsis of Akamatsu Katsumaro's lecture "Nihon seishin to gendai shakai undō," in "Shisōhan ni kansuru hogo jigyō kōshūkai," 59–60. For an analysis of Akamatsu's political transformations in the 1930s see: Stephen Large, "Buddhism and Political Renovation in Prewar Japan: The Case of Akamatsu Katsumaro," *The Journal of Japanese Studies* 9, no. 1 (Winter, 1983): 33–66.

128. See the itemized list: "Shisōhan ni kansuru hogo jigyō kōshūkai," 63–64.

129. Saotome, *Tenkōsha no shuki*.

130. At the time of writing this piece in October 1933, Shiono Suehiko (1880–1949) was head of the Corrections Division in the Justice Ministry (Shihōshō gyōkeikyokuchō). For a short biographical sketch of Shiono, see Ogino, *Shisō kenji*, iv.

131. Shiono Suehiko, "Jo," in Saotome, *Tenkōsha no shuki*, 1–2; Preface 1.

132. Shiono, "Jo," Preface 1.

133. Shiono, "Jo," Preface 2.

134. Saotome, "Hensha no kotoba," in Saotome, *Tenkōsha no shuki*, 1.

135. Saotome, "Hensha no kotoba," 1.

136. Saotome, "Hensha no kotoba," 2.

137. See Saotome's concluding remarks: Saotome, "Hensha no kotoba," 2.

138. Additionally, many of the contributors found lower or midtier employment upon being released, including driving a taxi, working on the family farm, running a used bookstore, and one contributor becoming a housewife. See the biographical sketches in Saotome, *Tenkōsha no shuki*, 4–6.

139. These names are most likely pseudonyms in order to protect the identity of the parolees.

140. For instance, the industrial laborer Uchimura Shigeru joined the military in 1932, whereas the intellectual Murai Hisashirō was employed by a major newspaper.

141. A biographical sketch of Kojima notes that she joined the movement as a student, and was arrested and sent to Ichigaya Prison. Upon converting, her sentence was suspended and she was released from prison. She married and was living in Akita Prefecture at the time. See Saotome, *Tenkō no shuki*, 4.

142. Kojima Yuki, "Daihi no ote ni sugaru made," in Saotome, *Tenkō no shuki*, 43–73. On the ideology of ryōsai kenbo in twentieth-century Japan, see Kathleen Uno, "The Death of 'Good Wife, Wise Mother'?," in *Postwar Japan as History*, ed. Andrew Gordon (Berkeley: University of California Press, 1993), 293–322.

143. Kojima, "Daihi no ote ni sugaru made," 51.

144. Kojima, "Daihi no ote ni sugaru made," 52. Her full explanation is as follows: "My power as one person was small. But this small power, through its connection with this large group [*idai shūdan*], would become great, or, by integrating with this grand power, my own power would become grand. And through my own power, I could carry out important work. . . . Here, in one stroke [*ikkyoshuittōsoku*] was the influence of the Japanese Communist Party." Kojima, "Daihi no ote ni sugaru made," 52.

145. Kojima, "Daihi no ote ni sugaru made," 55–56.

146. Itō Akira argues that such concerns cited to explain one's defection (such as love for one's family) did not just suddenly emerge at the moment of imprisonment but were felt by activists as they participated in the communist movement. It was only after the mass arrests and the increasing sense of defeat that struck the communist movement that the family became an excuse for defection. See Itō, *Tenkō to tennōsei*, 141–144.

147. Kojima, "Daihi no ote ni sugaru made," 63.

148. For another essay in *Tenkōsha Memoirs* that links filial love and Buddhist compassion, see Murai Hisashirō, "Fubo ha saijō no kami nari," in Saotome, *Tenkōsha no shuki*, 74–94.

149. Kojima, "Daihi no ote ni sugaru made," 73.

150. Kobayashi Morito (Ono Yōichi, pseud.), "Marukisuto ha gokuchū ika ni shūkyō o taiken shita ka," in Saotome, *Tenkō no shuki*, 240. As with his earlier biography, Kobayashi starts with a review of the Marxist critique of religion as the negation of reality, moving through a reassessment of religion while in jail, and ultimately his religious experience (*shūkyōteki na taiken*), which caused him to have total faith (*zettaiteki na shinkō*) in Buddhism. He concluded, "It is not when we theoretically demonstrate religion, but only when we enter into a life of faith [*shinkō no seikatsu*] that religion becomes our flesh and blood" (233, 240). Kobayashi outlined three principles that underlay a religious conversion, which we can interpret as principles that guided Kobayashi's efforts in the Imperial Renovation Society. First, he began by drawing upon a central tenet of True Pure Land Buddhism by arguing that "the possibility of establishing true faith begins from faith in Other-Power" (*tariki no shinkō*) (241). This rendered tenkō not an act of one's own will, but the very negation of this will in the Other-Power of Buddhist grace. This also conveniently provided an explanation for the counseling Kobayashi received from Chaplain Fujii as well as his own efforts advising ex-communists in the Imperial Renovation Society. From this principle derived the second: the "notion of reciprocal compassion" (*kanjō hōon no nen*), which, Kobayashi explained, constituted all human relations, whether interpersonal, familial, or social. A social praxis that denied this spirit, such as materialism, could not capture this "feeling of compassion" and thus lacked an ethos to justify social engagement (242). The third and last principle was that "total salvation [*issai no kyūsai*] emerges from the fundamental principle of benefiting oneself by benefiting others [*jiri rita*]" (243). Collectively, these three principles infused his efforts to rehabilitate political criminals at the Imperial Renovation Society with Buddhist ethics of compassion and selfless dedication toward others.

151. This essay collected a three-part series of articles that Kobayashi had written for *Hogo Jihō* under the same title, "Tenkōsha ha doko ni iku." See the September 1933, January 1934, and April 1934 issues of *Hogo Jihō*. Kobayashi Morito, "Tenkōsha ha doko ni iku," in Saotome, *Tenkōsha no shuki*, 245–260. The main portion of Kobayashi's essay reports his recent visit to a small collective farm in Gunma Prefecture started by Yamaguchi Hayato. Yamaguchi was a religious tenkōsha whom Kobayashi had mentored through the auspices of the Imperial Renovation Society. After being released from jail, Yamaguchi returned to Gunma and organized the cooperative farm under the Zen Buddhist Baizhang Huaihai's (720–814) slogan "Those who don't work, don't eat" (*ichinichi*

nasazareba, ichinichi kurawazu, 一日不作一日不食). See Kobayashi, "Tenkōsha ha doko ni iku," 247. Although Yamaguchi's rural collective retained private property, it communally managed labor and consumption. At this time in 1933, there were roughly twenty members in the cooperative, with Yamaguchi acting as director. To Kobayashi, Yamaguchi's collective farm provided an example of how tenkōsha could continue to be committed to social reform (here, rural revitalization), while also continuing to reform themselves as patriotic subjects—a theme that he would continue to emphasize in later writings. See Yamaguchi's contribution to *Tenkōsha Memoirs*: Yamaguchi Hayato, "Kyōsanshugi yori shūkyō e," in Saotome, *Tenkōsha no shuki*, 1–42. See also Itō, *Tenkō to tennōsei*, 222–223.

152. Kobayashi, "Tenkōsha ha doko ni iku," 259.

153. For some contributors like Kojima, the conversion narrative concluded with her religious awakening and a return to a quiet life as a housewife. Other contributors like Yamaguchi Hayato and Kobayashi Morito concluded their essays by describing a continued commitment to social reform. One essay by Murai Hisashirō concluded with a more explicit expression of imperial ideology, with Murai arguing, "If the various Western states are based on Hegelian philosophy and its 'ideal ethical state,' then, we can begin to grasp our Japanese Empire as 'an ideal religious state' [*shūkyōteki risō kokka*], based on the Japanese kokutai that the left rejects." Murai, "Fubo ha saijō no kami nari," 94.

154. As noted in chapter 2, the tenkō phenomenon appeared at the same time that arrests peaked under the Peace Preservation Law. For instance, in 1933 alone, 14,622 individuals were arrested. See Okudaira, *Chianijihō shōshi*, 133. For a procurator's consideration of tenkō in relation to the continuing arrests, see Tozawa Shigeo, "Shisō hanzai no kensatsu jimu ni tsuite" (1933), in *Gendaishi shiryō 16: Shakaishugi undō*, vol. 3, ed. Yamabe Kentarō (Tokyo: Misuzu Shobō, 1965), 15–36.

155. Itō Akira cites a 1935 report that gives the following statistics on tenkō: out of the 650 JCP members in jail, 505 had or were in the process of declaring tenkō; only 145 prisoners were reported to not have declared tenkō. Itō, *Tenkō to tennōsei*, 133.

156. Itō cites a 1936 report by procurator Ikeda Katsu: Itō, *Tenkō to tennōsei*, 142.

157. See Itō, *Tenkō to tennōsei*, 87–88. On the relationship between *zainichi* Koreans and the JCP, see Mun Gyong Su, "Nihon kyōsantō to zainichi chōsenjin," in *Zainichi chōsenjin mondai no kigen* (Musashino: Kurein, 2007), 132–136. Also Nishikawa Hiroshi, "Zainichi chōsenjin kyōsantōin・dōchō no jittai: Keihokyoku shiryō ni yoru 1930nendai zenhanki no tōkeiteki bunseki," *Jinbun Gakuhō* 50 (March 1981): 31–53. In regard to conversion in colonial Korea, the Charges Withheld policy was extended to colonial Korea around the same time, although, as Keongil Kim suggests, officials were reluctant to apply the policy. Kim, "Japanese Assimilation Policy and Thought Conversion in Colonial Korea," 213. To support this claim, Kim refers to a 1996 master's thesis written by Chi Sŭngjun. See n. 33, 230.

158. Writing in 1935, Kobayashi mentions that the Imperial Renovation Society had recently taken on forty Korean converts seeking assistance. See Kobayashi Morito, "Nihon kokumin to shite no jikaku ni tatte," in *Tenkōsha no shisō to seikatsu*, ed. Kobayashi Morito (Tokyo: Daidōsha, 1935), 76–79.

159. One report lists 955 parolees receiving some kind of assistance from the Imperial Renovation Society in mid-1934. *Shakai undō tsūshin*, May 9, 1935, cited in Itō, *Tenkō to tennōsei*, 228.

160. Kobayashi, *"Tenkōki" no hitobito*, 28–30; Kobayashi Morito, "Shōwa jūichinen ni okeru wareware no kibō," *Tensei*, February 1936, 10–11, cited in Itō, *Tenkō to tennōsei*, 229.

161. Kobayashi, "Nihon kokumin to shite no jikaku ni tatte," 66.

CHAPTER 4. Nurturing the Ideological Avowal

1. On arrest statistics, see Okudaira Yasuhiro, "Chianijihō ihan jiken nendo betsu shori jinin hyō," in *Gendaishi shiryō 45: Chianijihō*, ed. Okudaira Yasuhiro (Tokyo: Misuzu Shobō, 1973), 646–649. Hereafter cited as GSS45.

2. Nakazawa Shunsuke, *Chianijihō: Naze seitō seiji ha 'akuhō' o unda ka* (Tokyo: Chūōkō Shinsho, 2012), 147. Richard H. Mitchell has argued that, at this time, the Peace Preservation Law "had the gait of a peglegged sailor. Investigation, interrogation, and prosecution—the strong leg—were going well; but the other leg—conversion and rehabilitation—was weak." Richard H. Mitchell, *Thought Control in Prewar Japan* (Ithaca, NY: Cornell University Press, 1976), 121. However, as I argue in chapter 2, conversion and rehabilitation were proposed in response to the very success of the "strong leg" in producing a large population of detainees. Even if momentarily out of balance, we need to account for the functional relationship between the two modes of power.

3. On the establishment of the Thought Criminal Protection and Supervision system, see Uchida Hirofumi, *Kōsei hogo no tenkai to kadai* (Kyoto: Hōritsu Bunkasha, 2015), chapter 3, "Shisōhan hogo katsu hō no seitei to hogokansatsu seido," 27–48.

4. On Althusser's distinction between secondary and primary ideologies, see Louis Althusser, *On the Reproduction of Capitalism: Ideology and Ideological State Apparatuses*, trans. G. M. Goshgarian (London: Verso, 2014), 83–84.

5. Later, Althusser calls the primary ideology "State Ideology." See Althusser, *On the Reproduction of Capitalism*, 77, 81.

6. Althusser, *On the Reproduction of Capitalism*, 77. As I mentioned in chapter 3, I have reservations about Althusser's theory of interpellation and therefore am not arguing that interpellation was successful or a seamless process in the Peace Preservation Law apparatus. Rather, I am interested in how this apparatus functioned on the logic of interpellation.

7. Michel Foucault, "Governmentality," in *The Foucault Effect: Studies in Governmentality*, ed. Graham Burchell, Colon Gordon, and Peter Miller (Chicago: University of Chicago Press, 1991), 102.

8. Foucault, "Governmentality," 102.

9. Michel Foucault, "Technologies of the Self" (1982), in *Essential Works of Foucault 1954–1984*, vol. 1: *Ethics*, ed. Paul Rabinow (New York: Penguin, 1997), 249, 242. We might think of Buddhism's emphasis on self-negation as what Foucault called elsewhere the "renunciation of the self."

10. Foucault, "Governmentality," 100.

11. Foucault, "Governmentality."

12. Foucault, "Governmentality," 103. Foucault explains that, rather than a new mode of power initiated and disseminated from the state, governmentality "is at once internal and external to the state, since it is the tactics of government which make possible the continual definition and redefinition of what is within the competence of the state and what is not" (103). The process by which reform was formalized in the 1930s brought such tactics under the purview of the state, thus redefining what was within its sovereign sphere.

13. See Max Ward, "Crisis Ideology and the Articulation of Fascism in Interwar Japan: The 1938 Thought-War Symposium," *Japan Forum* 26, no. 4 (2014): 462–485. Indeed, before Japan's invasion of China, it was common for justice officials to discuss the Peace Preservation Law functioning, as what one procurator claimed in 1934, as the "preparatory construction for general state mobilization" (*kokka sōdōin no junbi kōsaku*). See the comments by Tokyo Procurator Ikeda Katsu (1934), cited in Ogino Fujio, *Shisō kenji* (Tokyo: Iwanami Shoten, 2000), 79.

14. See Althusser, *On the Reproduction of Capitalism*, 83–84. In regards to the title for this section, it is possible to find various officials noting a shift from conversion to rehabilitation taking place in 1935. This particular iteration (*tenkō jidai yori hogo jidai e*) comes from Honjō Tetsuzō, "Tenkō to hogo ni kansuru kōsai," *Hogo Jihō* 19, no. 1 (January 1935): 29.

15. On the Taikōjuku kenkyūsho, see Kobayashi Morito, *"Tenkōki" no hitobito: Chianijihōka no katsudōka gunzō* (Tokyo: Shinjidaisha, 1987), 115–116.

16. On the Kokumin shisō kenkyūsho and its journal, *Kokumin Shisō*, see Kobayashi, *"Tenkōki" no hitobito*, 116–119, 126–131; Itō Akira, *Tenkō to tennōsei: Nihonkyōsanshugiundō no 1930nendai* (Tokyo: Keisō Shobō, 1995), 209–211. Kobayashi reports that he was responsible for assisting with both centers. Kobayashi, *"Tenkōki" no hitobito*, 118.

17. For example, the inaugural issue of *Tensei* contained articles titled "Renovating One's View of Life and Awakening to the Nation," "The Errors of Marx's Theory of Value," "World Thought and the Divine Way," and "The Hope of World Thought," as well as more personal essays recounting experiences with prison and conversion. The table of contents from the inaugural issue of *Tensei* from August 1935 is reprinted in Kobayashi, *"Tenkōki" no hitobito*, 127–129.

18. For example, see the September 1934 roundtable discussion with Ikeda Katsu, Miyagi Chōgorō, Tozawa Shigeo, and many other officials: "Shisōhan tenkōsha o ika ni suru ka," *Hogo Jihō* 18, no. 10 (October 1934): 23–30.

19. Fujii Eshō, "Shisōhan shakuhōsha no hogo hōhō," *Hogo Jihō* 19, no. 1 (January 1935): 13–28.

20. Fujii, "Shisōhan shakuhōsha no hogo hōhō," 15. Fujii notes that 449 thought criminals had been paroled between January 1930 and June 1934. These statistics are limited to metropolitan Japan.

21. Fujii, "Shisōhan shakuhōsha no hogo hōhō," 27.

22. Fujii, "Shisōhan shakuhōsha no hogo hōhō," 16–17.

23. Fujii, "Shisōhan shakuhōsha no hogo hōhō," 17.

24. Fujii, "Shisōhan shakuhōsha no hogo hōhō," 18.

25. Fujii, "Shisōhan shakuhōsha no hogo hōhō," 19, 20.

26. Fujii, "Shisōhan shakuhōsha no hogo hōhō," 19.

27. Fujii, "Shisōhan shakuhōsha no hogo hōhō," 22–23.

28. Fujii also provided examples of how the Imperial Renovation Society responded to the particular needs of female and student converts: In regard to the former, the society had recently formed a Women's Section (Fujinbu) in order to restore the morals of those women who, by joining the JCP, had "lost the traditional Japanese ideal of chastity" (*nihon korai no teisō kannen o torisatta*). In regard to student converts, Fujii argues that, having spent many years in jail, these thought criminals were unable to return to school to finish their degrees, but at the same time, were unwilling to be reeducated to become "engineers or laborers." This was posing particular challenges for the Imperial Renovation Society. See Fujii, "Shisōhan shakuhōsha no hogo hōhō," 25–26.

29. Michel Foucault, *Wrong-Doing, Truth-Telling: The Function of Avowal in Justice*, trans. Stephen W. Sawyer (Chicago: University of Chicago Press, 2014), 24.

30. Foucault, *Wrong-Doing, Truth-Telling*, 17.

31. Kobayashi Morito, ed., *Tenkōsha no shisō to seikatsu* (Tokyo: Daidōsha, 1935). This second volume of tenkōsha biographies was advertised in daily newspapers, which may indicate a stronger effort to publicize the volume to the general public. See for instance the advert for *Tenkōsha no shisō to seikatsu* and the new magazine *Tensei* on the front page of the morning edition of *Yomiuri Shimbun*, December 1, 1935.

32. Kobayashi Morito, "Nihon kokumin to shite no jikaku ni tatte," in Kobayashi, *Tenkōsha no shisō to seikatsu*, 3–98.

33. Kobayashi, "Nihon kokumin to shite no jikaku ni tatte," 5.

34. Kobayashi, "Nihon kokumin to shite no jikaku ni tatte," 8. Recall that, along with the educational apparatus, Louis Althusser identifies the family as the primary ISA in the modern era. See Louis Althusser, "Ideology and Ideological State Apparatuses (Notes towards an Investigation)," in *Lenin and Philosophy and Other Essays*, trans. Ben Brewster (New York: Monthly Review Press, 2001), 104.

35. Kobayashi, "Nihon kokumin to shite no jikaku ni tatte," 16, 15. Kobayashi claimed that "the Japanese nation emerged and developed from the family, becoming its form today" (8).

36. Kobayashi, "Nihon kokumin to shite no jikaku ni tatte," 19–20.

37. Kobayashi, "Nihon kokumin to shite no jikaku ni tatte," 7.

38. Kobayashi, "Nihon kokumin to shite no jikaku ni tatte," 8.

39. Kobayashi, "Nihon kokumin to shite no jikaku ni tatte," 12.

40. Kobayashi, "Nihon kokumin to shite no jikaku ni tatte," 89.

41. Kobayashi, "Nihon kokumin to shite no jikaku ni tatte," 40. Here Kobayashi is implicitly critiquing theorists, such as Minobe Tatsukichi, who would delimit imperial sovereignty within a constitutional framework. I discuss Minobe's so-called organ theory (*kikan setsu ron*) of the state and the Minobe Incident later in the chapter.

42. Sano Manabu and Nabeyama Sadachika, eds., *Nihonkyōsantō oyobi komintaan hihan: Ikkoku shakaishugi ni tsuite* (Tokyo: Musansha, 1934).

43. For Kobayashi's close reading and critique of Sano and Nabeyama, see Kobayashi, "Nihon kokumin to shite no jikaku ni tatte," 20–36. Although Kobayashi remained

critical of the revolutionary politics espoused by both the Labor Faction (also known as the Kaitō-ha, analyzed in chapter 2) and Sano and Nabeyama, he argued that when the Labor Faction presented their critique in 1930–1931, such a stance was extremely difficult to make. This was an attempt to take the bravado out of Sano and Nabeyama's decision to defect in 1933 (11).

44. Kobayashi, "Nihon kokumin to shite no jikaku ni tatte," 31–32.

45. Kobayashi, "Nihon kokumin to shite no jikaku ni tatte," 35.

46. Kobayashi, "Nihon kokumin to shite no jikaku ni tatte," 38.

47. Kobayashi, "Nihon kokumin to shite no jikaku ni tatte," 39.

48. Kobayashi, "Nihon kokumin to shite no jikaku ni tatte," 39.

49. This point recalls a similar move in area studies and in some forms of postcolonial studies to identify the source of contradiction outside of Europe, not in capitalist exploitation and unevenness, but in a purported disjuncture between (Western) capitalism and non-Western culture. On this point, see Max Ward, "Historical Difference and the Question of East Asian Marxism(s)," in East Asian Marxisms and Their Trajectories, ed. Joyce Liu and Viren Murthy, Interventions Series (London: Routledge, 2017), 87–102.

50. Kobayashi, "Nihon kokumin to shite no jikaku ni tatte," 40. Through this cultural prism, Kobayashi was forgetting that the Peace Preservation Law also protected the "system of private property"—code for the legal forms that expressed and mediated capitalist social relations. Recall that earlier in the decade the procurator Hirata Isao was willing to accept the defections of the Labor Faction even though they still called for the overthrow of capitalism.

51. Kobayashi, "Nihon kokumin to shite no jikaku ni tatte," 40, 41. In a later section titled "Concerning Concrete Issues" ("Gutaiteki mondai ni tsuite"), Kobayashi struggled to negotiate between the exacerbated social contradictions of the mid-1930s and his elevation of the Japanese spirit as an integrating force: "We have said that in the true Japanese spirit there is no class-consciousness. This is true. But in reality, in certain aspects [bubunteki ni], we cannot deny that various contradictions exist. We must try as hard as possible to integrate [tōitsu] these contradictions" (52).

52. Kobayashi, "Nihon kokumin to shite no jikaku ni tatte," 41.

53. Kobayashi, "Nihon kokumin to shite no jikaku ni tatte," 42. Kobayashi discusses the various social stations that tenkōsha were now returning to (38–44).

54. Kobayashi, "Nihon kokumin to shite no jikaku ni tatte," 53. Kobayashi believed that national education could guide national integration by expunging received Western forms such as liberalism and Marxism from curriculum and emphasizing the Japanese essence (44).

55. Kobayashi, "Nihon kokumin to shite no jikaku ni tatte," 44.

56. Kobayashi summarized six principles of this new standpoint: (1) the unity of emperor and subject that constitutes Japan's unique family-nation-state structure; (2) the historical singularity of the imperial kokutai; (3) Japan's "ability to embrace" (hōyōsei) and assimilate foreign elements; (4) the rejection of class divisions based on Japan's unique family structure; (5) the unique fusion of spirit and matter (busshin ichinyo) in Japanese thought; and (6) the "realization of Japan's new mission" (nihon kokumin no

shin-shimei no jikaku). These principles are outlined in Kobayashi, "Nihon kokumin to shite no jikaku ni tatte," 46–49.

57. On Koreans active in the interwar Japanese communist movement, see Mun Gyong Su, "Nihon kyōsantō to zainichi chōsenjin," in *Zainichi chōsenjin mondai no kigen* (Musashino: Kurein, 2007), 131–150, in particular 132–136. Also Nishikawa Hiroshi, "Zainichi chōsenjin kyōsantōin • dōchō no jittai: Keihokyoku shiryō ni yoru 1930nendai zenhanki no tōkeiteki bunseki," *Jinbun Gakuhō* 50 (March 1981): 31–53.

58. For example, see "Chōsenjin saishō no tenkōsha arawareru," *Tokyo Asahi Shimbun*, September 10, 1933, evening edition, 11. (Figure 4.1)

59. See Sim Kil-bok (沈吉福), "Chōsen ni okeru shisōhan hogo jigyō no kensetsu no tame ni," in Kobayashi, *Tenkōsha no shisō to seikatsu*, 396–406. Interestingly, Sim Kil-bok discusses the necessity for tenkō in the colony through the logic of territorial sovereignty that was discussed in chapters 1 and 2. For instance, he argues that the importance of thought reform policies in Korea was because Korea occupied "an important space between Manchukuo and Japan [*naichi*]." In other words, Sim understood the significance of Korean tenkō in strategic, geopolitical terms (402).

60. Kobayashi, "Nihon kokumin to shite no jikaku ni tatte," 78.

61. Kobayashi, "Nihon kokumin to shite no jikaku ni tatte," 49.

62. In a later section, Kobayashi somewhat qualified his call to discard the terms "Japanese" and "Korean," urging his readers not to overlook important differences in circumstances: "along with recognizing that . . . there is increasing assimilation and an increasingly closer relationship between Japanese and Korean culture, we must also fully recognize the particular circumstances [*tokushu jijō*] of the domestic Koreans." Kobayashi, "Nihon kokumin to shite no jikaku ni tatte," 78.

63. Kobayashi, "Nihon kokumin to shite no jikaku ni tatte," 50.

64. Kobayashi, "Nihon kokumin to shite no jikaku ni tatte," 50.

65. Kobayashi, "Nihon kokumin to shite no jikaku ni tatte," 49.

66. This theme is reiterated by the Korean contributor to *Thought and Lives of Tenkōsha*, Sim Kil-bok. See Sim, "Chōsen ni okeru shisōhan hogo jigyō no kensetsu no tame ni," 396–406.

67. Kobayashi, "Nihon kokumin to shite no jikaku ni tatte," 76–78.

68. Kobayashi, "Nihon kokumin to shite no jikaku ni tatte," 76.

69. On these policies in colonial Korea, see Michael Robinson, "Forced Assimilation, Mobilization, and War," in *Korea Old and New: A History*, ed. Carter J. Eckert, Ki-baik Lee, Young Ick Lew, Michael Robinson, and Edward W. Wagner (Cambridge, MA: Harvard University Press, 1990), 305–326; Mark Caprio, *Japanese Assimilation Policies in Colonial Korea, 1910–1945* (Seattle: University of Washington Press, 2009). In relation to assimilation policies in Taiwan, see Leo T. S. Ching, *Becoming Japanese: Colonial Taiwan and the Politics of Identity* (Berkeley: University of California Press, 2001).

70. Kobayashi, "Nihon kokumin to shite no jikaku ni tatte," 67–75. Kobayashi notes the society's collaboration with various employment agencies in Tokyo, including the Employment Division of the Tokyo City Social Office (Tōkyōshi shakaikyoku

shokugyōka tōkyōku) and the Tokyo Government Employment Offices (Tōkyōfu shōkaisho) (69).

71. The term *onshi* designates an imperial donation. For information on this farm, see Kobayashi, "Nihon kokumin to shite no jikaku ni tatte," 83–84; Kobayashi, *"Tenkōki" no hitobito*, 121–122; Miyagi, *Miyagi chōgorō shōden*, 156–172.

72. Elsewhere, Director Miyagi Chōgorō wrote in a Justice Ministry report that the "farm is the hospital for the soul and body—one must not be forced into [labor] and overworked. One must have the opportunity to appreciate flowers, to pat a cow, to commune with nature." Miyagi quoted in Yamada Kenji, "Miyagi Chōgorō," *Tsumi to batsu* 34, no. 1 (1996): 51.

73. Kobayashi provided an extensive list of the private groups that were working to support tenkōsha: Kobayashi, "Nihon kokumin to shite no jikaku ni tatte," 62–63. For one of the few analyses of this network, see Itō, *Tenkō to tennōsei*, 200–217. Regarding the Wind of Light Society, see Kobayashi, "Nihon kokumin to shite no jikaku ni tatte," 77–78. Here Kobayashi reports that while the Special Higher Police held roundtable discussions to address the issue of supporting and reforming Korean thought criminals, groups like the Wind of Light Society would carry out such work with more care and instruction. This reaffirms how the repression of the Special Higher Police would complement the moral guidance being cultivated in smaller support groups. See Kobayashi, "Nihon kokumin to shite no jikaku ni tatte," 78.

74. Kobayashi, "Nihon kokumin to shite no jikaku ni tatte," 64–65.

75. Kobayashi, "Nihon kokumin to shite no jikaku ni tatte," 66.

76. Ikeda Katsu, "Shisō hannin kyōka no keiken hihan," *Keisatsu Kenkyū*, November 1936, cited in Ogino, *Shisō kenji*, 82. Elsewhere, I proposed the tripartite schema of protection/prevention/production for understanding the changing operations of the Peace Preservation Law apparatus into the late 1930s: i.e., from protecting the kokutai in the 1920s, through the prevention of recidivism in the early 1930s, to finally the production of imperial subjects in the late 1930s. See Max Ward, "The Problem of 'Thought': Crisis, National Essence and the Interwar Japanese State" (PhD diss., New York University, 2011).

77. See Ogino Fujio, "Kaisetsu: Chianijihō seiritsu・'kaisei' shi," in *Chianijihō kankei shiryōshū*, vol. 4, ed. Ogino Fujio (Tokyo: Shinnihon Shuppansha, 1996), 611–613.

78. See the table consisting of figures from a January 1943 Justice Ministry report in Ogino, *Shisō kenji*, 73.

79. Ogino cites an earlier 1930 Tokyo Procuracy Thought Section report that emphasized prevention of thought crime (not recidivism) as a central objective. Ogino, *Shisō kenji*, 44–45. On the prevention of recidivism (*saihan bōshi*) in the early 1930s, see Okudaira Yasuhiro, *Chianijihō shōshi*, new ed. (Tokyo: Iwanami Shoten, 2006), 158. For an extensive review of the question of ideological recidivism, see Tokuoka Kazuo, *Chianijihō ihanjiken no saihan ni kansuru kenkyū* (Tokyo: Shihōshō Keijikyoku, 1938). I analyze Tokuoka's study in chapter 5. For official discussions of how to identify, administer, and secure tenkō, see the proceedings of the Shisō jimukai: "Tenkō ni kansuru jikō" (May 1934), in Shakai mondai shiryō kenkyūkai, ed., *Shisō jimukai dō gijiroku* (Tokyo: Tōyō Bunkasha, 1976), 128–139.

80. For example, see Ogino's summaries of Justice Ministry reports from this time: Ogino, *Shisō kenji*, 74–76.

81. These reports are collected in Ogino Fujio, ed., *Chianijihō kankei shiryōshū*, vol. 2 (Tokyo: Shinnihon Shuppansha, 1996), 13–30. For an overview of these reports and the subsequent Diet deliberations on the revision proposals, see Nakazawa, *Chianijihō*, 145–152.

82. See the first draft proposal developed by the Justice Ministry's Criminal Division: Shihōshō keijikyoku, "Chianijihō kaisei hōritsuan" (December 13, 1933), in Ogino, *Chianijihō kankei shiryōshū*, vol. 2, 30–33. In addition to proposals developed by the bureaucracy, thought policy proposals were also issued by political parties. See, for instance, the proposals drafted by the Minseitō (July 1933) and Seiyūkai (December 1933) in GSS45, 198–199 and 201–203 respectively.

83. For the government's accepted revision proposal from February 1934 and the subsequent revisions made in the Lower House and House of Peers in March 1934, see Seifu, "Chianijihō [Kaisei hōritsuan]," and Shūgiin, "Chianijihō kaisei hōritsuan," in Ogino, *Chianijihō kankei shiryōshū*, vol. 2, 33–36 and 41–45 respectively. In regard to the 1934 bill presented in committee of the Sixty-Fifth Imperial Diet and the resulting debates: "Chianijihō kaisei hōritsuan giji soku kiroku narabi ni iinkai giroku," in GSS45, 204–250. For Justice Ministry reference materials that attended this revision proposal, see Shihōshō, "Chianijihōan sankō shiryō" and "Shisō gyōkei sankō shiryō" (both February 1934), in Ogino, *Chianijihō kankei shiryōshū*, vol. 2, 77–95 and 95–99 respectively.

84. On the topic of retroactive application, see Suzuki Keifu, *Chōsen shokuminchi tōchihō no kenkyū: Chianhō ka no kōminka kyōiku* (Sapporo: Hokkaidō Daigaku Tosho Kankōkai, 1989), 180–181. As we will see, retroactive application was included in the 1936 Thought Criminal Protection and Supervision Law. For a concise overview of the 1934 revision proposal, see Nakazawa, *Chianijihō*, 146. For a summary of the attempts to revise the Peace Preservation Law in both 1934 and 1935, see Okudaira, *Chianijihō shōshi*, 178–182. On preventative detention in the 1934 revision proposal, see Okudaira Yasuhiro, "Chianijihō ni okeru yobō kōkin," in *Fashizumuki no kokka to shakai 4: Senji nihon no hōtaisei*, ed. Tokyo Daigaku Shakai Kagaku Kenkyūsho (Tokyo: Tokyo Daigaku Shuppansha, 1979), 173–191.

85. See Koyama's explanation of the revision bill, in "Chianijihō kaisei hōritsuan giji soku kiroku narabi ni iinkai giroku," in GSS45, 207–210.

86. I refer to portions of these deliberations collected in GSS45 and Ogino, *Chianijihō kankei shiryōshū*, vol. 2. A full record of the 1934 Diet deliberations is collected in Shakai mondai shiryō kenkyūkai, ed., *Chianijihō ni kansuru giji sokkiroku narabi ni innkai giroku: Dai65kai teikoku gikai*, 3 vols. (Tokyo: Tōyō Bunkasha, 1975).

87. Concerning the constitutionality of preventative detention, see for example Mikami Hideo's question during a February 16 Lower House deliberation: "Chianijihō kaisei hōritsuan giji soku kiroku narabi ni iinkai giroku," in GSS45, 210–212. On the clarification of tenkō, see "Tenkō mondai," in Ogino, *Chianijihō kankei shiryōshū*, vol. 2, 48–50. On the debates over preventative detention in the revision proposal, see Okudaira, "Chianijihō ni okeru yobō kōkin," 180–191.

88. On these incidents, see Stephen Large, "Nationalist Extremism in Early Shōwa Japan: Inoue Nisshō and the 'Blood-Pledge Corps Incident,' 1932," *Modern Asian Studies* 35, no. 3 (2001): 533–564. Justice officials had been addressing the issue of the right-wing thought movement in earlier ministerial and committee meetings. For example, see the section "Uyoku shisō jiken ni kansuru jikō," in the November 7, 1934, proceedings of the Shisō jimukai, in Shakai mondai shiryō kenkyūkai, ed., *Shisō jimukai dō gijiroku* (Tokyo: Tōyō Bunkasha, 1976), 104–108.

89. To meet these nationalist threats, some in the Diet advocated for inserting the phrase "altering the state form" (*seitai henkaku*). Recall that "seitai" was stricken from the original 1925 Peace Preservation Bill. See the Home Ministry's official response to such a proposal: Naimushō, "Chianijihōchū ni 'seitai henkaku' ni kansuru kitei o mōbeku shi to suru an ni taisuru hantai riyū" (1934), in Ogino, *Chianijihō kankei shiryōshū*, vol. 2, 41. See also Ogino, *Shisō kenji*, 76–78.

90. See Nakazawa, *Chianijihō*, 147–151. For Soeda Kenichirō's question on March 16, see "Chianijihō kaisei hōritsuan giji soku kiroku narabi ni iinkai giroku," in GSS45, 226–229.

91. John Person, "Between Patriotism and Terrorism: The Policing of Nationalist Movements in 1930s Japan," *Journal of Japanese Studies* 43, no. 2 (summer 2017): 289–318. A similar debate over the application of the law to rightists occurred in a May 1934 meeting of thought procurators between Hirata Isao and Moriyama Takeichirō. See Ogino, *Shisō kenji*, 77–78.

92. Recall that Althusser posited that two ISAs are central to the capitalist social formation: the educational ISA and the family ISA. Although he elaborated on the former, Althusser does not discuss the family apart from a few passing observations. See Althusser, "Ideology and Ideological State Apparatuses," 96, fn8.

93. Iwata Chūzō speaking in the House of Peers, March 17, 1934: "Chianijihō kaisei hōritsuan giji soku kiroku narabi ni iinkai giroku," in GSS45, 230.

94. Iwata was citing a newspaper article about a rightist "imperial reverence communist group" (*sonnō kyōsanshugi dantai*), which was apparently composed of tenkōsha. He cited their platform, which called for the eradication of the class privileges protected by corrupt political parties, "liberation from world capitalism and the establishment of a socialist state." GSS45, 231.

95. In a later Upper House deliberation, Uzawa Fusaaki posed a similar question in relation to the construction of a socialist state on the rejection of individual property rights, which assumedly would indicate a major transformation of the kokutai. See GSS45, 236–237.

96. GSS45, 235. Koyama recalled that although there had been talk about adding a clause about rightists at the time that the revision was drafted, this was ultimately rejected. He reminded the Diet that "the Peace Preservation Law was first issued in order to suppress so-called leftists," but as far as right-wing groups were concerned, "the government is still researching this issue." In light of the recent right-wing actions, he tried to calm fears by reminding Diet members that when rightists acted through violent means, the regular Civil Code could be applied to suppress them. As John Person has argued, underneath such technical issues was the more fundamental problem that

radical rightist groups were carrying out assassinations in the name of the very thing that the Peace Preservation Law was supposed to protect: the imperial kokutai. See Person, "Between Patriotism and Terrorism."

97. See Justice Ministry notes as well as the official version of the bill issued on March 4, 1935: "Shihōshō no kisō sakugyō" and "Chianijihō (kaisei hōritsuan)," in Ogino, *Chianijihō kankei shiryōshū*, vol. 2, 222–224 and 224–226 respectively. For Justice Ministry reference materials that attended the 1935 revision proposal, see Shihōshō keijikyoku, "Chianijihō kaiseian sankō shiryō" (March 8, 1935) and "Chianijihō kaisei iinkai yōkyū shohyō" (March 9, 1935), in Ogino, *Chianijihō kankei shiryōshū*, vol. 2, 228–237 and 238–251 respectively.

98. Nakazawa, *Chianijihō*, 151–152. For the separate bill pertaining to current right-wing incidents, see Seifu, "Fuhō danketsu nado shobatsu ni kansuru hōritsuan," in Ogino, *Chianijihō kankei shiryōshū*, vol. 2, 226–227. Nakazawa notes that the Home Ministry did not agree with this separate bill: Nakazawa, *Chianijihō*, 152. For the Justice Ministry's explanation for erasing preventative detention from the 1935 revision bill, see Shihōshō, "Kaisei chii hōan kara yobō kōkinsei o sakujo" (September 1934) and "Chianijihō kaisei an: Gikai teishutsu ni kettei, 'Yobō kōkin' ha sakujo" (January 1935), in Ogino, *Chianijihō kankei shiryōshū*, vol. 2, 222, 222–223 respectively.

99. Suzuki, *Chōsen shokuminchi tōchihō no kenkyū*, 181.

100. As Ogino has noted, these reports were made possible by the increased funding in the Justice Ministry of measures to "prevent thought crime" (*shisō hanzai bōatsu*). See Ogino, *Shisō kenji*, 72–76. These 1935 reference materials also included two surveys of thought crime in colonial Korea and one on Taiwan. For the Korean surveys, see Takumushō Kanrikyoku, "Chōsen ni okeru shisō hanzai chōsa shiryō" (two parts, both issued March 1935), in Ogino, *Chianijihō kankei shiryōshū*, vol. 2, 257–285 and 286–317. For the Taiwan survey, see Takumushō Kanrikyoku, "Taiwan ni okeru shisō undō chōsa shiryō" (March 1935), in Ogino, *Chianijihō kankei shiryōshū*, vol. 2, 317–323.

101. The following references to Diet deliberations are derived from "Chianijihō kaisei • fuhō danketsu nado shobatsu ni kansuru hōritsuan giji sokkiroku narabi ni iinkai giroku" in GSS45, 250–267.

102. On the Minobe Incident, see Miyazawa Toshiyoshi, *Tennō kikansetsu jiken: Shiryō ha kataru*, 2 vols. (Tokyo: Yūhikaku, 1997); and Walter A. Skya, *Japan's Holy War: The Ideology of Radical Shintō Ultranationalism* (Durham, NC: Duke University Press, 2009), chapter 3. For discussions concerning the 1935 revision's failure in relation to the Minobe Incident, see Nakazawa, *Chianijihō*, 152–154; Ushiomi Toshitaka, *Chianijihō* (Tokyo: Iwanami Shoten, 1977), 106; Matsuo Hiroshi, *Chianijihō to tokkō keisatsu* (Tokyo: Kyōikusha, 1979), 169. On the influence of the Minobe Incident in Justice Ministry thought crime policies, see Ogino, *Shisō kenji*, 81. John Person has a forthcoming article on Minoda Muneki's role in creating this incident.

103. Retired Imperial Army General Kikuchi Takeo critiqued Minobe's theory in the House of Peers on February 15, 1935. Kikuchi believed Minobe's theory rejected Japan's kokutai and called for the government to ban his work. Minobe was called to the House of Peers to explain his theory on February 25. With rightist criticism continuing, Minobe stepped down from the House of Peers in September; Nakazawa, *Chianijihō*, 153.

104. See Monbushō, ed., *Kokutai no Hongi* (Tokyo: Monbushō, 1937), translated as *Kokutai no Hongi: The Cardinal Principles of the National Entity of Japan*, trans. John Owen Gauntlett (Cambridge, MA: Harvard University Press, 1949). Alan Tansman has argued that the "interest of the . . . [*Kokutai no hongi*] lies less in its content than in its formal qualities as an example of a fascist aesthetic that shared similar sensibility with other, more nuanced, works of the period. . . . Its prestige would seem to have grown out of its very abstruseness, its ability to persuade readers that they could 'get' the essence of its 'venerable' words and phrases without discerning their precise meanings. It was, in essence, a performative document." Alan Tansman, *The Aesthetics of Japanese Fascism* (Berkeley: University of California Press, 2008), 152.

105. I refer to portions of these deliberations collected in GSS45 and Ogino, *Chianijihō kankei shiryōshū*, vol. 2. A full record of the 1935 Diet deliberations is collected in Shakai mondai shiryō kenkyūkai, ed., *Shisōhan hogo kansatsu hō ni kansuru sokkiroku: Dai69kai teikoku gikai* (Tokyo: Tōyō Bunkasha, 1973).

106. Here, Makino cites Minobe as arguing that "kokutai is a concept that expresses the historical fact that [there has been] unbroken imperial rule from the founding of the empire, as well as the ethical fact that the national people are incomparably loyal and revere the emperor. [However] this is not indicated in the current constitutional system. The reason for [positing] kokutai in the current constitutional system, is to emphasize the universality [*bannō*] of imperial sovereignty, which is a complete misunderstanding of the spirit of the Constitution." Minobe Tatsukichi, quoted by Makino on March 20, 1935, in Lower House session: "Chianijihō kaisei • fuhō danketsu nado shobatsu ni kansuru hōritsuan giji sokkiroku narabi ni iinkai giroku," in GSS45, 253.

107. Minobe, quoted by Makino, in GSS45, 253. Makino's citation of Minobe continues: "Monarchy or republic are clearly legal concepts that are connected to currently applied [theories] of constitutional orders. In other words, they are terms that refer to contemporary constitutional systems. Moreover, the meaning [of such terms] does not refer to a past history, nor any sense of the nation's ethical sentiments [*rinriteki kanjō*]. Although a country may be called a monarchy [*kunshusei*], this is nothing to do with that country's history, nor the feelings of the people toward the monarch. This is a completely separate issue" (254).

108. See Ohara's inquiry: GSS45, 254.

109. Interestingly, Nakatani became the president of Japan Motion Pictures (Nikkatsu) in 1934 and oversaw a major restructuring of the company at the time. Jasper Sharp, *Historical Dictionary of Japanese Cinema* (Lanham, MD: Scarecrow, 2011), 181.

110. Exchange between Matsuda Genji and Nakatani Sadayori on March 22 in the Lower House: "Chianijihō kaisei • fuhō danketsu-ra shobatsu ni kansuru hōritsuan giji sokkiroku narabi ni iinkai giroku," in GSS45, 259.

111. GSS45, 259.

112. GSS45, 259.

113. See Nakazawa, *Chianijihō*, 152.

114. At the same time, officials had to answer concerns that they had been too lenient on ex-communists. For instance, in 1934 Diet committee deliberations over the 1934 revision bill, some officials expressed doubts that tenkō was merely camouflage for

dangerous political activists, as well as concern over Sano Manabu and Nabeyama Sadachika's new politics of socialism in one country. See "Tenkō mondai," in Ogino, *Chianijihō kankei shiryōshū*, vol. 2, 48–50. Also, while the Home Ministry collaborated with the Justice Ministry on the 1934 and 1935 revision bill drafts, they did not support the Justice Ministry's proposal for the 1936 Thought Criminal Protection and Supervision bill. See Nakazawa, *Chianijihō*, 157.

115. A 1935 Justice Ministry Criminal Division report gives the following statistics between 1928 and 1934: out of 10,353 individuals not released after their initial interrogation, 4,059 were indicted, 3,869 received Suspended Indictments, and 2,425 were placed in Charges Withheld (a policy formalized in 1931). See Shihōshō keijikyoku, "Chianijihō kaiseian sankō shiryō" (March 8, 1935), in Ogino, *Chianijihō kankei shiryōshū*, vol. 2, 229.

116. Ogino interprets the application of the law beyond suspected communist groups as signaling that the law was no longer "targeting just social movements that harmed the peace [*chian o gai suru*], but now was directed toward anyone that harmed the social order and public tranquility [*shakai chitsujo naishi shakai no seihitsu*]." Ogino, *Shōwa tennō to chian taisei*, 75. On the suppression of Ōmotokyō in the 1930s and more generally, see Ogino, *Shōwa tennō to chian taisei*, 75–79; Garon, *Molding Japanese Minds*, 60–87; Okudaira, *Chianijihō shōshi*, 222–234. For excerpts from police summaries on the 1935 Ōmotokyō Incident, see Keihokyoku, "Ōmotokyō chianijihō ihan narabini fukei jiken gaiyō" (November 1935) and Keihokyoku, "Ōmotokyō higisha chōshusho sakusei yōkō" (May 14, 1936), in Ogino, *Chianijihō kankei shiryōshū*, vol. 2, 403–406 and 406–410 respectively. On the trial of Ōmotokyō, see Miyachi Masato, "Dai ni ji Ōmotokyō jiken: Senjika shūkyō danatsu no kiten," in *Nihon seiji saiban shiroku 5: Shōwa • go*, ed. Wagatsuma Sakae (Tokyo: Daiichi Hōki Shuppan, 1969), 95–140. On the extension of the Peace Preservation Law to Popular Front groups including the Rōnō-ha, see Okudaira, *Chianijihō shōshi*, 203–222. For a police summary of the suppression of Popular Front groups, see Keihokyoku, "Jinmin sensen undō no hontai" (January–February 1938), in Ogino, *Chianijihō kankei shiryōshū*, vol. 2, 410–417. On the trials of Popular Front groups, see Odanaka Toshiki, "Jinmin sensen jiken: Hansen • hanfashizumu seiryoku e no danatsu," in Wagatsuma, *Nihon seiji saiban shiroku 5*, 273–328.

117. Yoshida Hajime, "Chōsen ni okeru shisōhan no kakei narabini ruihan jōkyō," in *Shisō jōsei shisatsu hōkokushū* (Sono 6), in *Shisō kenkyū shiryō: Tokushū dai 69 gō*, ed. Shihōshō keijikyoku, reprinted in *Shakai mondai shiryō sōsho: Dai 1 shū* (Tokyo: Tōyō Bunkasha, 1971), 1–47. Hong Jong-wook cites this source in *Senjiki chōsen no tenkōshatachi: Teikoku/shokuminchi no tōgō to kiretsu* (Tokyo: Yūshisha, 2011), 52.

118. Keongil Kim, "Japanese Assimilation Policy and Thought Conversion in Colonial Korea," in *Colonial Rule and Social Change in Korea, 1910–1945*, ed. Hon Yung Lee, Yong Chool Ha, and Clark W. Sorensen (Seattle: Center for Korean Studies, University of Washington Press, 2013), 213, and 230, fn34.

119. Suzuki, *Chōsen shokuminchi tōchihō no kenkyū*, 182. Suzuki demonstrates how by 1930 the Peace Preservation Law had overshadowed the application of other security laws when prosecuting independence activists in the late 1920s (e.g., the 1907 Public Peace Law and 1919 Ordinance No. 7) (140).

120. See for example the two-part series by a procurator in Osaka: Adachi Katsukiyo, "Shisōhansha no hogo taisaku," *Hogo Jihō* 19, no. 6 (June 1935): 4–12; and *Hogo Jihō* 19, no. 7 (July 1935): 9–18. In such discussions, officials advocated for the passage of the Peace Preservation Law revision bills under deliberation in the Diet at the time or, later, the Thought Criminal Protection and Supervision Law, which was developed after the other revision failed. See, for example, Yamagata Nirō, "Nanzan no shisōhan hogo kansatsu hōan," *Hogo Jihō* 20, no. 2 (February 1936): 9–18.

121. For instance, Fujii Eshō, Hirata Isao, and Kobayashi Morito held a discussion for female tenkōsha in Tokyo to describe their experiences and hardships: "Tenkō fujin no nayami o kiku kai," *Hogo Jihō* 18, no. 10 (October 1934): 11–18.

122. Itō, *Tenkō to tennōsei*, 253. On the limits of these early groups and the challenges tenkōsha were experiencing, see Mitchell, *Thought Control in Prewar Japan*, 129–134. These challenges are reflected in the increasing number of paroled thought criminals seeking membership in the Imperial Renovation Society: whereas only eight ex-communists became members of the society in 1931, 278 were admitted in 1934. These numbers come from Fujii Eshō, "Shisōhan hogo jigyō no tenbō: Hogo kansatsu no jicchi o hikaete," *Hogo Jihō* 20, no. 2 (February 1936): 11–15. Fujii reports that in 1932 and 1933, 43 and 143 thought criminals were admitted, respectively. These statistics do not include those paroled ex-communists who came to the society for temporary assistance.

123. The Shōtokukai was an incorporated foundation (*zaidan hōjin*). See Shōtokukai, "Zaidan hōjin shōtokukai gaiyō" (August 1936), in Ogino Fujio, ed., *Chianijihō kankei shiryōshū*, vol. 3 (Tokyo: Shinnihon Shuppansha, 1996), 31. Also see Ogino, *Shisō kenji*, 68.

124. A later Justice Ministry report in support of passing this law replicated the arguments that Moriyama presented in this meeting. See Shihōshō, "Shisōhan hogokansatsu seido no hitsuyō" (April 15, 1936), in Ogino, *Chianijihō kankei shiryōshū*, vol. 3, 44–46.

125. Uchida, *Kōsei hogo no tenkai to kadai*, 30.

126. Foucault, "Governmentality," 103.

127. Moriyama Takeichirō, "'Shisō hogo kansatsu seido' ni tsuite" (November 1935), in Ogino, *Chianijihō kankei shiryōshū*, vol. 3, 38–39.

128. Moriyama explained that this new law would apply to four dispositions related to the Peace Preservation Law—Suspended Indictment, Suspended Sentence, parolees, and those who had fully served their sentences. Similar to the juvenile rehabilitation policies, a reformee would be placed under the supervision of a guidance officer (*hogoshi*). Moriyama, "'Shisō hogo kansatsu seido' ni tsuite," 39. Notice that Moriyama does not make reference to Charges Withheld. This was because with the passage of this proposed bill, the conventional Suspended Indictment of the Japanese Criminal Code would replace Charges Withheld administered specifically for thought criminal cases since 1931. We can assume that the widely applied Charges Withheld disposition was included in Moriyama's reference to Suspended Indictment.

129. Moriyama, "'Shisō hogo kansatsu seido' ni tsuite," 39.

130. See Shihōshō, "Shisōhan hogo kansatsu hōan yōkō" (January 8, 1936), in Ogino, *Chianijihō kankei shiryōshū*, vol. 3, 40. For the Justice Ministry's official summary of the

bill, see Shihōshō, "Shisōhan hogo kansatsu hōan riyūsho," submitted with "Shisōhan hogo kansatsu hōan" (April 1936), in Ogino, *Chianijihō kankei shiryōshū*, vol. 3, 42. For a history of the passage of this bill, see Kikuta Kōichi, "Shisōhan hogo kansatsu hō no rekishiteki bunseki," parts I and II, *Hōritsu Ronsō* 44, nos. 5–6 (October 1971): 95–132, and *Hōritsu Ronsō* 45, no. 1 (January 1972): 85–126, respectively.

131. Hayashi Raizaburō, "Shisōhan hogo kansatsu hōteian riyū setsumei," in GSS45, 273.

132. On the retroactive application of this law, see Kikuta, "Shisōhan hogo kansatsu hō no rekishiteki bunseki, II," 89.

133. Hayashi Raizaburō, "Shisōhan hogo kansatsu hōteian riyū setsumei," in GSS45, 273.

134. GSS45, 273.

135. See Seifu, "Shisōhan hogo kansatsu hō shikō kijitsu no ken" (Ordinance 400), "Shisōhan hogo kansatsu hō shikō rei" (Ordinance 401), "Hogo kansatsu sho kansei" (Ordinance 403), and "Hogo kansatsu shinsakai kansei" (Ordinance 405), all issued on November 14, 1936, in Ogino, *Chianijihō kankei shiryōshū*, vol. 3, 47–51. For a detailed collection of all materials related to the establishment of the law, including its relation to other civil codes, see Kido Yoshio, *Shisōhan hogokansatsuhōki shū* (Tokyo: Gansuidō Shoten, 1937).

136. For colonial Korea, see Seifu, "Chōsen sōtokufu hogo kansatsu rei," "Chōsen sōtokufu hogo kansatsu sho kansei," and "Chōsen sōtokufu hogo kansatsu shinsa kaikansei" (all issued December 12, 1936), in Ogino, *Chianijihō kankei shiryōshū*, vol. 3, 52–53. For analysis of the application of this law in colonial Korea, see Suzuki, *Chōsen shokuminchi tōchihō no kenkyū*, 181–183. For the implementation of this law in colonial Korea and the Kwantung Leased Territory, see Ogino Fujio, "Kaisetsu: Chianijihō seiritsu • 'kaisei' shi," in *Chianijihō kankei shiryōshū*, vol. 4, ed. Ogino Fujio (Tokyo: Shinnihon Shuppansha, 1996), 686–690.

137. For the ordinances related to the Kwantung Leased Territory, including establishing a Protection and Supervision Center in Dalian, see Seifu, "Kantōshū shisō hogo kansatsu rei" (No. 793), "Kantōshū hogo kansatsusho kansei" (No. 794), and "Kantōshū hogo kansatsu shinsakai kansei" (No. 795), in Ogino, *Chianijihō kankei shiryōshū*, vol. 3, 53–55. The law was not issued in Taiwan, Karafuto, or the South Sea Islands.

138. See Ogino, "Kaisetsu: Chianijihō seiritsu • 'kaisei' shi," 686–687. See also Ogino, *Shisō kenji*, 92. For a record of location and staff of the Protection and Supervision Centers in colonial Korea, see Chōsen Sōtokufu, "Hogo kansatsu sho shokuin haichi hyō" (December 1936), in Ogino, *Chianijihō kankei shiryōshū*, vol. 3, 510–511. Hong reports that the 1,160 cases overseen by the Keijō Protection and Supervision Center were distinguished as follows: 328 Suspended Indictments, 198 Suspended Sentences, 608 individuals who had served their full sentences, and 26 who were paroled. Hong Jong-wook, "Senjiki chōsen ni okeru shisōhan tōsei to Yamato-juku," *Kankoku chōsen bunka kenkyū*, no. 16 (March 2017): 44.

139. Hong, *Senjiki chōsen no tenkōsha-tachi*, 50.

140. Masunaga Shōichi (January 1937), cited in Ogino, "Kaisetsu: Chianijihō seiritsu • 'kaisei' shi," 687.

141. Ushiomi Toshitaka notes that the Thought Criminal Protection and Supervision Law was a "revision of the Peace Preservation Law which changed its formal structure." Ushiomi Toshitaka, *Chianijihō* (Tokyo: Iwanami Shoten, 1977), 107.

142. For example, in the July 1936 issue of *Hogo Jihō* dedicated to this new law, Kobayashi Morito relayed the concerns he was hearing from other converts, including how the state was expecting to extract conversion from those who had, up to that point, refused to tenkō, and concern over whether the new law would increase police intervention into the daily lives of tenkōsha, which would cause unnecessary hardships that might in fact have a negative result in securing conversion. Kobayashi Morito, "Shisōhan hogo kansatsuhō ni taisuru jakkan no kōsatsu: Hitotsu tenkōsha to shite," *Hogo Jihō* 20, no. 7 (July 1936): 16–21, in Aomori hogo kansatsusho, ed., *Shisōhan hogo kansatsu hō* (1937), collected in Ogino, *Chianijihō kankei shiryōshū*, vol. 3, 73–76. Chaplain Fujii Eshō conveyed similar concerns surrounding the protocols outlined in the new law: Fujii Eshō, "Shisōhan hogo kansatsu hō ni tsuite: Jitsumuka no tachiba kara," *Hogo Jihō* 20, no. 7 (July 1936): 13–16, reprinted in Aomori hogo kansatsusho, ed., *Shisōhan hogo kansatsu hō* (1937), collected in Ogino, *Chianijihō kankei shiryōshū*, vol. 3, 76–78.

143. For example, at a 1936 roundtable attended by forty-three tenkōsha and thought reform officials, it was common for tenkōsha to describe the difficulties that police surveillance caused once they were paroled. See Hankan Gakuryō, ed., *Hankan Gakuryō shisōhan tenkōsha zadankai kiroku* (Tokyo: Hankan Gakuryō Tōkyō Jimusho, 1936).

144. See "Shisōhan hogokansatsu hō tekiyō mondai" and "Shisōhan hogokansatsu hō ni tsuite," *Chōsen Nippō*, June 11 and June 14, 1936, in Ogino, *Chianijihō kankei shiryōshū*, vol. 3, 86–88.

145. See Itō's discussion of concerns raised by the Osaka-based Dōyūkai: Itō, *Tenkō to tennōsei*, 259–260.

146. Mitchell, *Thought Control in Prewar Japan*, 139. Statistics on recidivism in colonial Korea exist up until 1935, averaging 10 percent, with most cases occurring early in the 1930s. See Hong, *Senjiki chōsen no tenkōsha-tachi*, 52.

147. Jan Goldstein reconsiders the logical relationship between sovereign law and disciplinary power in Foucault's theory and has called this the "framing of discipline by law." Jan Goldstein, "Framing Discipline with Law: Problems and Promises of the Liberal State," *American Historical Review* 98, no. 2 (April 1993): 364–375.

CHAPTER 5. The Ideology of Conversion

1. Hirata Isao, "Hogo kansatsu sho no shimei" (December 14, 1936), in *Shisōhan hogo kansatsu hō*, ed. Aomori Hogo Kansatsu Sho (1937), reprinted in Ogino Fujio, ed., *Chianijihō kankei shiryōshū*, vol. 3 (Tokyo: Shinnihon Shuppansha, 1996), 79–80.

2. Hirata explicated that the Japanese spirit was symbolized in the mythical three imperial regalia—the mirror, jewel, and sword—in which the sword represented justice and the jewel benevolence, and the mirror reflected and combined these two into one. In Hirata's ideological analogy, the Peace Preservation Law combined justice and benevolence: justice was exacted against dangerous threats against the imperial state,

and benevolence was expressed in the reform of thought criminals as loyal imperial subjects. Hirata, "Hogo kansatsu sho no shimei," 78–79.

3. Hirata, "Hogo kansatsu sho no shimei," 79–80.

4. On this 1939 law, see Uchida Hirofumi, *Kōsei hogo no tenkai to kadai* (Kyoto: Hōritsu Bunkasha, 2015), 67–69; Kōsei Hogo Gojūnen Shi Henshū Iinkai, ed., *Kōsei hogo gojūnen shi: Chiiki shakai to tomo ni ayumu kōsei hogo* (Tokyo: Zenkoku Hogoshi Renmei, 2000), vol. 1, 192–193. Distinguishing between protection (hogo) and supervision (kansatsu), Kato Michiko has argued that, despite the emphasis on protection in these two laws (1936 and 1939), in actuality, the power of supervision was extended and overshadowed the function of protection. See Kato Michiko, "Senzen kara sengo fukkōki ni okeru hogo kansatsu seido no dōnyū to hensen," *Ōyō shakaigaku kenkyū*, no. 55 (2013): 223–226. At this time the system for youth protection (*shōnen hogo kikō*) was also expanded. See Moriya Katsuhiko, *Shōnen no hikō to kyōiku: Shōnen hōsei no rekishi to genjō* (Tokyo: Keisōshobō, 1977), 132–151; David Ambaras, *Bad Youth: Juvenile Delinquency and the Politics of Everyday Life in Modern Japan* (Berkeley: University of California Press, 2006), 166–191.

5. Hirata, "Hogo kansatsu sho no shimei," 78, 80.

6. As was noted in chapter 4, centers were established in colonial Korea in December 1936.

7. For a detailed discussion concerning the meaning of tenkō in relation to these new centers, see the meeting of the newly appointed directors in Shihōshō, "Dai ikkai hogo kansatsu shochō kaidō gijiroku" (November 25–6, 1936), in Ogino, *Chianijihō kankei shiryōshū*, vol. 3, 89–169.

8. Moriyama Takechirō, *Shisōhan hogo kansatsu hō kaisetsu* (Tokyo: Shōkadō Shoten, 1937), 62–65. This famous definition of tenkō is cited in Nakazawa Shunsuke, *Chianijihō: Naze seitō seiji ha "akuhō" o unda ka* (Tokyo: Chūōkō Shinsho, 2012), 160; Ogino Fujio, *Shisō kenji* (Tokyo: Iwanami Shoten, 2000), 90; Ushiomi Toshitaka, *Chianijihō* (Tokyo: Iwanami Shoten, 1977), 96–97.

9. I thank Tak Fujitani for suggesting that I emphasize this relation between societal mobilization and penal repression during wartime.

10. In November 1941, there were eleven guidance officials (*hodōkan*) overseeing the network, assisted by forty-five rehabilitation officers and thirty-nine clerks. See Shihōshō, "Hogo kansatsu sho no kakujū," in Ogino, *Chianijihō kankei shiryōshū*, vol. 3, 353. For the list of the twenty-two centers, the basic structure of the system, see Appendix 2, Chart 2, "Justice Ministry Protection and Supervision System in 1936," in Richard H. Mitchell, *Thought Control in Prewar Japan* (Ithaca, NY: Cornell University Press, 1976), 198.

11. For Kwantung-related ordinances, see Seifu, "Kantōshū shisōhan hogo kansatsu rei" (December 18, 1938), which includes "Kantōshū hogo kansatsusho kansei" and "Kantōshū hogo kansatsu shinsakai kansei," in Ogino, *Chianijihō kankei shiryōshū*, vol. 3, 53–55.

12. See Seifu, "Shisōhan hogo kansatsu hō shikō kijitsu no ken" (Ordinance 400), "Shisōhan hogo kansatsu hō shikō rei" (Ordinance 401), "Hogo kansatsu sho kansei" (Ordinance 403), and "Hogo kansatsu shinsakai kansei" (Ordinance 405), all issued on November 14, 1936, in Ogino, *Chianijihō kankei shiryōshū*, vol. 3, 47–51. For a detailed

collection of all materials related to the establishment of the law, including its relation to other civil codes, see Kido Yoshio, *Shisōhan hogokansatsuhōki shū* (Tokyo: Gansuidō Shoten, 1937).

13. For an example and explanation of these reports, see Shihōshō, "Shisōhan hogo kansatsu hō shikō rei dai san jō ni okeru tsūchi yōshiki ni kansuru ken" (February 4, 1937), in Ogino, *Chianijihō kankei shiryōshū*, vol. 3, 60–61.

14. See Shihōshō, "Shisōhan hogo kansatsu hō shikō rei dai san jō ni okeru tsūchi yōshiki ni kansuru ken," 61. Nakazawa cites a late 1933 Prison Bureau report that distinguishes between (1) tenkōsha, identified as those who had "renounced revolutionary thought" and had either "broken with the social movement" or planned to participate in the "legal social movement"; (2) *juntenkōsha*, identified as those who were reconsidering "revolutionary thought" and moving toward "renunciation" or those who, while still holding "revolutionary ideas," had broken with the "social movement"; and (3) *hitenkōsha*. See summary: Nakazawa, *Chianijihō*, 142.

15. Moriyama Takeichirō, "Hogo kansatsu no yōhi kettei no hyōjun," in *Shisōhan hogo kansatsu hō*, ed. Aomori Hogo Kansatsusho (1937), in Ogino, *Chianijihō kankei shiryōshū*, vol. 3, 70–71.

16. Matsuo Hiroshi, *Chianijihō to tokkō keisatsu* (Tokyo: Kyōikusha, 1979), 170.

17. On the Virtuous Brilliance Society, see chapter 4. For example, a review of the Tokyo Protection and Supervision Center's activities reveals close coordination with the Imperial Renovation Society and its members. See Tokyo Hogo Kansatsu Sho, *Jimu seiseki hōkoku sho* (1937), in Ogino, *Chianijihō kankei shiryōshū*, vol. 3, 175–224. In addition to reporting on the center's activities, this report includes extensive information on groups affiliated with the center as well as its liaison with other centers throughout Japan.

18. Yamagata Jirō, "Shisōhan hogo kansatsu hō no unyō ni kansuru yōbō," in *Hogo Jihō* 21, no. 1 (January 1937): 34–36. He divided the target (*taishō*) of the Protection and Supervision Law into four categories: (1) those who had "completely converted and have a secure foundation in their daily lives"; (2) those who, although having converted, "have instability in their lives"; (3) those whose thoughts are "insecure" (*dōyō*) but who have stable lives; and finally (4) those who lack stability in both their thought and daily lives (35–36).

19. For the ordinances related to colonial Korea, see *Hogo Jihō* 21, no. 2 (February 1937): 48–51. For records of national meetings of reform officials, see *Hogo Jihō* 21, no. 2 (February 1937): 51–57.

20. Tokuoka Kazuo, *Chianijihō ihan jiken no saihan ni kansuru kenkyū* (Tokyo: Shihōshō Keijikyoku, 1938), 179.

21. Tokuoka, *Chianijihō ihan jiken no saihan ni kansuru kenkyū*, 179–180.

22. See *Hogo Jihō* 21, no. 10 (October 1937).

23. See the report: Kaku Hogo Kansatsusho Hoka, "Nicchū sensōka no shisōhan hogo kansatsu" (1937–1938), in Ogino, *Chianijihō kankei shiryōshū*, vol. 3, 342–352.

24. Richard Mitchell implies that the initiative to link tenkō to the war came from Prime Ministers Konoe Fumimaro (1937–39) and Hiranuma Kiichirō (1939). Richard H. Mitchell, *Thought Control in Prewar Japan* (Ithaca: Cornell University Press, 1976), 164–166. Patricia Steinhoff argues: "the use of *tenkōsha* for patriotic propaganda was but one small aspect of a full-scale nationalistic drive throughout the country."

Patricia G. Stienhoff, *Tenkō: Ideology and Societal Integration in Prewar Japan* (New York and London: Garland Publishing 1991), 209. It is important to recognize, however, that officials and tenkōsha were already representing conversion in terms of national thought defense well before July 1937, which I have outlined in earlier chapters. This demonstrates a much more organic relationship between thought criminal rehabilitation and later wartime mobilization.

25. For an early example of how criminal rehabilitation was being reconsidered in the context of the China Incident, see Hoseikai, ed., *Jihen ni yomigaeru hanzaisha* (Tokyo: Hoseikai, 1937). This pamphlet concludes with an article on the patriotic activities of tenkōsha, 57–59. See also the 1938 pamphlet by the head of the Hoseikai, Matsui Kazuyoshi: *Kokka sōryokusen to shihō hogo jigyō* (Tokyo: Hoseikai, 1938).

26. On Konoe Fumimaro, see Yoshitake Oka, *Konoe Fumimaro: A Political Biography* (Tokyo: University of Tokyo Press, 1983); and Kazuo Yagami, *Konoe Fumimaro and the Failure of Peace in Japan, 1937–1941* (Jefferson, NC: McFarland, 2006).

27. For instance, see the reports from 1937–1938 collected in the section "Nicchū sensōka no shisōhan hogo kansatsu sho" (342–353), in Ogino, *Chianijihō kankei shiryōshū*, vol. 3, 342–353.

28. Seimeikai, ed., *Shisō tenkōsha ha ika ni katsudō shite iru ka* (Osaka: Seimeikai, 1937). The pamphlet reports that the Seimeikai consisted of sixty out of the over one thousand tenkōsha under supervision by the Osaka Center (1).

29. Seimeikai, *Shisō tenkōsha ha ika ni katsudō shite iru ka*, 3.

30. Seimeikai, *Shisō tenkōsha ha ika ni katsudō shite iru ka*, 3.

31. See Seimeikai, *Shisō tenkōsha ha ika ni katsudō shite iru ka*, 10–14. As if the message was not clear enough, the pamphlet concluded with contact information for people at *Osaka Asahi Shimbun* and *Osaka Mainichi Shimbun* who were collecting donations.

32. See for instance this 1938 pamphlet: Ishii Toyoshichirō, *Shihō hogo sōsho dai 17 shū: Saiban to hogo* (Tokyo: Zen Nihon Shihō Hogo Jigyō Renmei, 1938), in particular 23–28.

33. Ishii, *Shihō hogo sōsho dai 17 shū*, 25.

34. Kokumin Seiji Keizai Kenkyūsho, ed., *"Kokunai bōkyō" Sensen no sankyotō: Shiono, Suetsugu, Araki* (Tokyo: Kokumin Seiji Keizai Kenkyūsho, 1938), 16–22.

35. Shihō Hogo Jigyō Renmei, ed., *Shihō hogo sōsho dai 19 shū: Kōa no soseki* (Tokyo: Zen Nihon Shihō Hogo Jigyō Renmei, 1939).

36. Jikyoku taiō zenchō shisō hōkoku renmei founding statement (July 1938), cited in Mizuno Naoki, "Nihon no chōsen shihai to Chianijihō," in *Chōsen no kindaishi to nihon*, ed. Hatada Takeshi (Tokyo: Yamato Shobō, 1987), 139. On the formation of the Jikyoku taiō zenchō shisō hōkoku renmei and its organizational structure, see Hong Jong-wook, "Senjiki chōsen ni okeru shisōhan tōsei to Yamato-juku," *Kankoku chōsen bunka kenkyū*, no. 16 (March 2017): 46–47 and 49.

37. Michael Robinson claims that by "the 1940s, every Korean was associated with at least one mass organization." Michael Robinson, "Ideological Schism in the Korean Nationalist Movement, 1920–1930: Cultural Nationalism and the Radical Critique," *Journal of Korean Studies* 4 (1982–1983): 316.

38. Ogino Fujio, "Kaisetsu: Chianijihō seiritsu · 'kaisei' shi," in Ogino, *Chianijihō kankei shiryōshū*, vol. 4, 689; Hong, "Senjiki chōsen ni okeru shisōhan tōsei to Yamato-

juku," 47. Hong also reports that there were efforts to make this league independent from its metropolitan counterparts in Japan (47).

39. Hong Jong-wook cites these numbers from a 1936 Justice Ministry report. See Hong, "Senjiki chōsen ni okeru shisōhan tōsei to Yamato-juku," 44.

40. Hong Jong-wook, *Senjiki chōsen no tenkōsha-tachi: Teikoku/shokuminchi no tōgō to kiretsu* (Tokyo: Yūshisha, 2011), 50, 46–64.

41. Tokuoka, *Chianijihō ihan jiken no saihan ni kansuru kenkyū*, 191. This recalls the decisions in which Korean courts rationalized the application of the Peace Preservation Law—initially envisioned as a law to be used against communists—to nationalist activists in the colonies (see chapter 2).

42. Naoki Sakai, "Ethnicity and Species: On the Philosophy of the Multiethnic State and Japanese Imperialism," in *Confronting Capital and Empire: Rethinking Kyoto School Philosophy*, ed. Viren Murthy, Fabian Schafer, and Max Ward (Leiden: Brill, 2017), 148. See also Mark Driscoll, "Conclusion: Postcolonialism in Reverse," in Yuasa Katsuei, *Kannani and Document in Flames: Two Japanese Colonial Novels*, trans. Mark Driscoll (Durham, NC: Duke University Press, 2005).

43. See: T. Fujitani, *Race for Empire: Koreans as Japanese and Japanese as Americans during World War II* (Berkeley: University of California Press, 2011), 7. Fujitani notes that this was a "strategic disavowal of racism" for war mobilization (12).

44. Tokuoka, *Chianijihō ihan jiken no saihan ni kansuru kenkyū*, 192. Mizuno Naoki analyzes Tokuoka's report along with other studies in order to consider the application of the Peace Preservation Law and its later tenkō policy in colonial Korea. See Mizuno, "Nihon no chōsen shihai to Chianijihō," 137–138.

45. Yoshida Hajime, "Chōsen ni okeru shisōhan no kakei narabini ruihan jōkyō," in Shisō jōsei shisatsu hōkokushū (Sono 6), in *Shisō kenkyū shiryō: Tokushū dai 69 gō*, ed. Shihōshō Keijikyoku, in *Shakai mondai shiryō sōsho: Dai 1 shū* (Tokyo: Tōyō Bunkasha, 1971), 1–47.

46. Yoshida, "Chōsen ni okeru shisōhan no kakei narabini ruihan jōkyō," 7. These suspects were arrested in the Fifth Kantō Communist Party Incident in 1930–1931. However, since the defendants were prosecuted with a variety of different laws, their execution was not sentenced under the Peace Preservation Law. On this, see Mizuno Naoki, "Chianijihō to chōsen • Oboegaki," *Chōsen Kenkyū* 188, no. 4 (1979): 50–51; Nakazawa, *Chianijihō*, 206. Richard H. Mitchell, *Janus-Faced Justice: Political Criminals in Imperial Japan* (Honolulu: University of Hawaii Press, 1992), 163–164.

47. Yoshida, "Chōsen ni okeru shisōhan no kakei narabini ruihan jōkyō," 7–8.

48. Yoshida, "Chōsen ni okeru shisōhan no kakei narabini ruihan jōkyō," 9–11. Indeed, it was common for reports of conventional crime in colonial Korea to include asides about the "particular nature" of crime in Korea due to Korean culture, customs, and feudal vestiges that distinguished it from the metropole. For example, see Terada Seiichi, "Chōsen ni okeru hanzai genshō no tokuchō," *Hōseikai kaihō* 4, no. 3 (May 1920): 1–36.

49. Yoshida, "Chōsen ni okeru shisōhan no kakei narabini ruihan jōkyō," 9. These concerns were also articulated by mobilized tenkōsha associations as well. See Hong, "Senjiki chōsen ni okeru shisōhan tōsei to Yamato-juku," 49.

50. Yoshida, "Chōsen ni okeru shisōhan no kakei narabini ruihan jōkyō," 9–10. On this point, see Mizuno, "Nihon no chōsen shihai to Chianijihō," 136.

51. Yoshida, "Chōsen ni okeru shisōhan no kakei narabini ruihan jōkyō," 10–12. Yoshida notes that, in the 655 indictments in 1937, over half of the cases involved forming or joining an illegal organization (153 and 249 cases respectively; see the table on page 11).

52. See Yoshida's review of tenkō statistics, "Chōsen ni okeru shisōhan no kakei narabini ruihan jōkyō," 12–13.

53. Yoshida, "Chōsen ni okeru shisōhan no kakei narabini ruihan jōkyō," 13.

54. See Yoshida's comparative reflections of tenkō, "Chōsen ni okeru shisōhan no kakei narabini ruihan jōkyō," 12–14.

55. Yoshida, "Chōsen ni okeru shisōhan no kakei narabini ruihan jōkyō," 14.

56. As mentioned above, Hong Jong-wook has argued that we must understand the vicissitudes of tenkō cases in colonial Korea in relation to the changing geopolitical context in regard to both Comintern policy as well as Japan's position in East Asia. Hong, *Senjiki chōsen no tenkōsha-tachi*, 46–64.

57. From *Tokkō keisatsuhō*, no. 3 (year unknown), cited in Mizuno, "Nihon no chōsen shihai to Chianijihō," 138.

58. See the extended citation in Yoshida, "Chōsen ni okeru shisōhan no kakei narabini ruihan jōkyō," 45–46.

59. See Matsuda Toshihiko, "Shokuminchi makki chōsen ni okeru tenkōsha no undō: Kang Yŏng-sŏk to nihon kokutai gaku • tōa renmei undō," *Jinbun Gakuhō* 79 (March 1997): 131–161; Matsuda Toshihiko, *Tōa renmei undō to chōsen • chōsenjin: Nicchū sensōki ni okeru shokuminchi teikoku nihon no danmen* (Tokyo: Yūshisha, 2015). For the mobilization of zainichi Koreans, see Park Kyong-sik, *Tennōsei kokka to zainichi chōsenjin* (Tokyo: Shakai Hyōronsha, 1986), 148–270.

60. On the Yamato-juku, see Hong, "Senjiki chōsen ni okeru shisōhan tōsei to Yamato-juku," 43–67.

61. A summary of a 1942 article, cited in Hong, *Senjiki chōsen no tenkōsha-tachi*, 50. Mizuno Naoki posits that the Yamato Society was at the center of the "purification of thought" (*shisō jōka*) in the colony during wartime. Mizuno Naoki, "Senjiki chōsen ni okeru chian seisaku: 'Shisō jōka kōsaku' to Yamato-juku o chūshin ni," *Rekishigaku Kenkyū*, no. 777 (2003): 1–11.

62. On the concept of thought war, see Barak Kushner, *The Thought War: Japanese Imperial Propaganda* (Honolulu: University of Hawai'i Press, 2006); and Max Ward, "Crisis Ideology and the Articulation of Fascism in Interwar Japan: The 1938 Thought War Symposium," *Japan Forum* 26, no. 4 (December 2014): 463–465.

63. On the Cabinet Information Division, see the study in two installments: Fukushima Jūrō, "Senji genron tōsei kikan no saikenshō 'jōhōkyoku' e no dōtei 1: Naikaku jōhō iinkai setsuritsu to sono haikei," *Janarizumu kenkyū* 23, no. 1 (1986): 98–109; and Fukushima Jūrō, "Senji genron tōsei kikan no saikenshō 'jōhōkyoku' e no dōtei 2: Naikaku jōhōbu no jidai," *Janarizumu kenkyū* 23, no. 2 (1986): 68–77. See also Uchikawa Yoshimi, "Naikaku jōhōkyoku no setsuritsu katei: Nihon fashizumu keiseiki no masu media soshikika seisaku," in *Masu mediahō seisakushi kenkyū* (Tokyo: Yuhikaku, 1989), 193–237. The Cabinet Information Division was staffed by so-called

renovationist bureaucrats (*kakushin kanryō*), a new breed of imperial officials who believed it was their duty to alleviate the dislocations endemic to capitalism, replace the inefficient political process, streamline colonial development, and completely remake the Japanese Empire through rational planning and bureaucratic intervention. On the renovationist bureaucrats, see Hashikawa Bunzō, "Kakushin kanryō," in *Kenryoku no shisō: Gendai nihon shisō taikei 10*, ed. Kamishima Jirō (Tokyo: Chikuma Shobō, 1965), 251–273.

64. This section is derived from Ward, "Crisis Ideology and the Articulation of Fascism in Interwar Japan." On this symposium, see Satō Takumi, "The System of Total War and the Discursive Space of the Thought War," in *Total War and "Modernization,"* ed. Yamanouchi Yasushi, J. Victor Koschmann, and Ryuichi Narita (Ithaca, NY: Cornell University East Asia Program, 1998), 289–313. There were two more annual symposia, held in 1939 and 1940.

65. See the lecture transcript of the Chief of the Police Bureau in the Home Ministry: Tomita Kenji, "Shisōsen to keisatsu," in *Shisōsen kōshūkai kōgi sokki*, ed. Naikaku Jōhōbu (Tokyo: Naikaku Jōhōbu, 1938), vol. 3, 113–136. On the history of the thought problem in interwar Japan, see Max Ward, "The Problem of 'Thought': Crisis, National Essence and the Interwar Japanese State" (PhD diss., New York University, 2011).

66. Hirata reported that roughly 10 percent of detainees still believed in Marxism, while another 10 percent had "truly overcome Marxism" by "grasping the Japanese spirit." The remaining 80 percent were thus at various stages of "completing tenkō." Hirata Isao, "Marukishizumu no kokufuku," in Shisōsen kōshūkai kōgi sokki, ed. Naikaku Jōhōbu (Tokyo: Naikaku Jōhōbu, 1938), vol. 3, 206.

67. Hirata, "Marukishizumu no kokufuku," 228. Hirata contrasted the Japanese centers to the German political concentration camps (Konzentrationslager) and the Kuomintang's repentance centers in China (what Hirata referred to as Hansei-in; literally, reflection centers; 227).

68. Hirata, "Marukishizumu no kokufuku," 228, 227.

69. Hirata, "Marukishizumu no kokufuku," 214.

70. Hirata, "Marukishizumu no kokufuku," 210–211.

71. Hirata, "Marukishizumu no kokufuku," 215.

72. Hirata, "Marukishizumu no kokufuku," 223.

73. Hirata, "Marukishizumu no kokufuku," 228.

74. Hirata, "Marukishizumu no kokufuku," 236.

75. Nakamura Yoshirō, "Genka ni okeru shisōtaisaku," *Kyōiku Panfuretto*, no. 323 (November 1938), 2.

76. Nakamura cites Hirata Isao's explanation of the centers as embodying Japan's unique familial structure. Hirata explained that, in the centers, political criminals were "collectively disciplined [*tōsei ni fuku suru*] based on the family principle" and were able to "grow under the guidance of familial affection." Hirata Isao, quoted by Nakamura, "Genka ni okeru shisōtaisaku," 4–5.

77. Nakamura, "Genka ni okeru shisōtaisaku," 5.

78. Nakamura, "Genka ni okeru shisōtaisaku," 14.

79. Nakamura, "Genka ni okeru shisōtaisaku," 19.

80. Nakamura, "Genka ni okeru shisōtaisaku," 19. In this context, guidance officials like Nakamura would carry out their duties with the "sentiment of a parent toward one's own child." Nakamura, "Genka ni okeru shisōtaisaku," 20.

81. Nakamura, "Genka ni okeru shisōtaisaku," 21.

82. Nakamura, "Genka ni okeru shisōtaisaku," 24.

83. Nakamura, "Genka ni okeru shisōtaisaku," 25.

84. Nakamura Yoshirō, "Tenkō o yōsei sarete iru mono ha shisō jiken kankeisha nomi de nai," *Kakushin*, December 1938, 171–180. For example, Nakamura writes that he was often asked if converts had truly converted, and if conversion was just "camouflage" for their continued dangerous activities (172). Later in the article he cites Moriyama Takeichirō's five stages of conversion analyzed above in order to explain the process of conversion (174–175).

85. Nakamura, "Tenkō o yōsei sarete iru mono ha shisō jiken kankeisha nomi de nai," 173.

86. Nakamura, "Tenkō o yōsei sarete iru mono ha shisō jiken kankeisha nomi de nai," 173, 172, 173–174.

87. For example, Nakamura uses the term "recognition of crisis" (*jikyoku ninshiki*) throughout this piece.

88. Nakamura, "Tenkō o yōsei sarete iru mono ha shisō jiken kankeisha nomi de nai," 173. On this group, see Mizuno Naoki, "Senjiki chōsen ni okeru chian seisaku: 'Shisō jōka kōsaku' to yamato-juku o chūshin ni," *Rekishigaku kenkyū*, no. 777 (July 2003): 8.

89. Nakamura, "Tenkō o yōsei sarete iru mono ha shisō jiken kankeisha nomi de nai," 173.

90. Nakamura, "Tenkō o yōsei sarete iru mono ha shisō jiken kankeisha nomi de nai," 175.

91. Nakamura, "Tenkō o yōsei sarete iru mono ha shisō jiken kankeisha nomi de nai," 175.

92. Nakamura, "Tenkō o yōsei sarete iru mono ha shisō jiken kankeisha nomi de nai," 178, 180.

93. I have analyzed this exhibition at length in Max Ward, "Displaying the Worldview of Japanese Fascism: The Tokyo Thought War Exhibition of 1938," *Critical Asian Studies* 47, no. 3 (2015): 414–439. Here I focus on how the Justice Ministry presented their tenkō policy and the Protection and Supervision Center network in the event.

94. Naikaku Jōhōbu, ed., *Shisōsen tenrankai kiroku zukan* (Tokyo: Naikaku Jōhōbu, 1938), 1.

95. Naikaku Jōhōbu, *Shisōsen tenrankai kiroku zukan*, 135. These numbers are most likely exaggerated.

96. The exhibition was held at the following department stores: Takashimaya, Tokyo; Takashimaya, Osaka; Marubutsu, Kyoto; Tamaya, Fukuoka; Tamaya, Sasebo; Tamaya, Saga-city; Sentoku, Fukumoto City; Tokiha, Ōita; Imai, Sapporo; and Mitsukoshi in Keijō. Prefectural and local municipal governments financially sponsored the event outside Tokyo, illustrating the coordination between the Cabinet Information Division, the Home Ministry, municipal offices, local business, and the Korean Government-General. See Naikaku Jōhōbu, *Shisōsen tenrankai kiroku zukan*, 135.

97. Naikaku Jōhōbu, *Shisōsen tenrankai kiroku zukan*, 25.

98. See Naikaku Jōhōbu, *Shisōsen tenrankai kiroku zukan*, 30 and 11.

99. On the economic crisis in interwar Japan, see Takafusa Nakamura, "Depression, Recovery and War, 1920–1945," in *Cambridge History of Japan*, vol. 6: *The Twentieth Century*, ed. Peter Duus (Cambridge: Cambridge University Press, 1988), 451–493.

100. Yokomizo Mitsuteru, "Shisōsen ni tsuite," in *Shisōsen tenrankai kiroku zukan*, ed. Naikaku jōhōbu (Tokyo: Naikaku Jōhōbu, 1938), 1–3.

101. Naikaku Jōhōbu, *Shisōsen tenrankai kiroku zukan*, 32.

102. Naikaku Jōhōbu, *Shisōsen tenrankai kiroku zukan*, 32.

103. Naikaku Jōhōbu, *Shisōsen tenrankai kiroku zukan*, 32.

104. Naikaku Jōhōbu, *Shisōsen tenrankai kiroku zukan*, 31.

105. Naikaku Jōhōbu, *Shisōsen tenrankai kiroku zukan*, 35.

106. This poster included statistics concerning students involved in "thought incidents": out of a total of 1,128 arrested, 148 students were indicted, 598 were given Suspended Indictments (Kiso yūyo), and 381 were placed in reserved indictments (Kiso ryūho). Naikaku Jōhōbu, *Shisōsen tenrankai kiroku zukan*, 36.

107. Naikaku Jōhōbu, *Shisōsen tenrankai kiroku zukan*, 36.

108. On the earlier proposals and later implementation of preventative detention, see: Okudaira Yasuhiro, "Chianijihō ni okeru yobō kōkin," in *Fashizumuki no kokka to shakai 4: Senji nihon no hōtaisei*, ed. Tokyo Daigaku Shakai Kagaku Kenkyūsho (Tokyo: Tokyo Daigaku Shuppansha, 1979), 165–229.

109. See for instance the proceedings from the May 1940 meeting of thought procurators: Shihōshō Keijikyoku, "Shisō jimuka kaidō gijiroku" (May 1940), in Ogino, *Chianijihō kankei shiryōshū*, vol. 4, 19.

110. The following is derived from Shihōshō Keijikyoku, "Shisō jimuka kaidō gijiroku" (May 1940), 19–63.

111. Officials pointed to the acceptance of the popular front strategy at the Seventh World Congress of the Communist International in August 1935 as proof of these organizations' communist intentions.

112. On the Peace Preservation Law and the suppression of new religions such as Ōmotokyō, see Okudaira Yasuhiro, *Chianijihō shōshi*, new ed. (Tokyo: Iwanami, 2006), 222–239. See also Sheldon Garon, "Defining Orthodoxy and Heterodoxy," in *Molding Japanese Minds: The State in Everyday Life* (Princeton, NJ: Princeton University Press, 1997), 60–87. On Tenrikyō and Tenri honmichi, see Robert Kisala, "Schisms in Japanese New Religious Movements," in *Sacred Schisms: How Religions Divide*, ed. James R. Lewis and Sarah M. Lewis (Cambridge: Cambridge University Press, 2009), 83–93.

113. Shihōshō Keijikyoku, "Shisō jimuka kaidō gijiroku" (May 1940), 20–22.

114. Other issues that emerged during the drafting of the revision bill were further separating the kokutai and private property system offenses since the kokutai was something absolute (*zettaisei*) while private property was not. See Hirata Isao's contribution to the May 1940 meeting: Shihōshō Keijikyoku, "Shisō jimuka kaidō gijiroku," 24.

115. The bill is reprinted in Okudaira Yasuhiro, ed., *Gendaishi shiryō 45: Chianijihō* (Tokyo: Misuzu Shobō, 1973), 277–284, hereafter cited as GSS45. For an overview of the 1941 bill and its discussion in the Diet, see Mitchell, *Thought Control in Prewar Japan*, 166–170.

116. See Miyake Masatarō's presentation to a committee of the Seventy-Sixth Imperial Diet on February 12, 1941, reprinted in GSS45, 284–289.

117. GSS45, 289.

118. For the political context within the Imperial Diet and state at the time, see Naka-zawa, Chianijihō, 175–177. For overviews of the system after 1941, see Matsuo, Chianijihō to tokkō keisatsu, 198–206; Okudaira, Chianijihō shōshi, 250–262.

119. For the final text of this law and its promulgation, see Seifu, "Shin chianijihō" (March 10, 1941), and Seifu, "Chian ijihō kaisei hōritsu shikō kijitsu no ken" (May 14, 1941), in Ogino, Chianijihō kankei shiryōshū, vol. 4, 69–75 and 105 respectively. Also GSS45, 523–533.

120. Translations amended from the abbreviated English translation of the 1941 law: appendix 4, "Peace Preservation Law, 1941, Articles 1–16," in Mitchell, Thought Control in Prewar Japan, 201–203. For an extensive analysis of the new crimes defined in the law, see Ogino, "Kaisetsu," 703–711. For an extensive legal analysis of the proposal, passage and application of the New Peace Preservation Law, see Uchida Hirofumi, Chianijihō no kyōkun: Kenri undō no seigen to kenpō kaisei (Tokyo: Misuzu Shobō, 2016), 450–497

121. Ogino, Chianijihō kankei shiryōshū, vol. 4, 105 and 106 respectively. The or-dinances establishing the Preventative Detention system are reprinted in Ogino, Chianijihō kankei shiryōshū, vol. 4, 109–110.

122. Uchida Hirofumi, Keihō to sensō: Senji chian hōsei no tsukurikata (Tokyo: Misuzu Shobō, 2015). Provocatively, Uchida argues that contemporary legal changes (2018) being carried out by the Abe Shinzō regime reflect developments that prepared Japan for total war in the 1930s.

123. I thank Louise Young for reminding me of these parallel developments in Man-chukuo. For an extensive overview of security laws and institutions in Manchukuo, see Ogino, "Kaisetsu," 748–764.

124. Nakazawa refers to an April 1941 report drafted by the Kwantung Military's Staff Section (Kantōgun sanbōbu) that cites concern about infiltration by Soviet and Chi-nese communists. See Nakazawa, Chianijihō, 210.

125. Nakazawa, Chianijihō, 210.

126. Nakazawa, Chianijihō, 210–211.

127. See Chōsen sōtoku, "Chōsen shisōhan yobō kōkin ryō" (February 12, 1941), in Ogino, Chianijihō kankei shiryōshū, vol. 4, 84–87. For the Government-General's expla-nation for implementing Preventative Detention in the colony, see Chōsen sōtokufu, "Riyū to setsumei" (November 1940), in Ogino, Chianijihō kankei shiryōshū, vol. 4, 87–89. On the Peace Preservation Law in wartime colonial Korea, see Mizuno Naoki, "Senjiki chōsen no chianji taisei," in Iwanami kōza: Ajia • Taiheiyō sensō 6: Shihai to bōryoku, ed. Kurosawa Aiko et al. (Tokyo: Iwanami Shoten, 2006), 95–122.

128. Ogino, "Kaisetsu," 700–701.

129. Ogino, "Kaisetsu," 701. See the draft proposal prepared by the Korean Government-General: Chōsen sōtokufu, "Chōsen shisōhan yobō kōkin ryō nado no sōan" (fall 1940), in Ogino, Chianijihō kankei shiryōshū, vol. 4, 76–84.

130. A Preventative Detention report cited in Ogino, "Kaisetsu," 723.

131. For an overview of recent research on the Mantetsu Research Bureau Incident, see Matsumura Takao, "Mantetsu chōsabu danatsu jiken (1942 • 43nen) sairon," Mita

gakkai zasshi 105, no. 4 (January 2013): 719–754. For a firsthand account of the Yoko-hama Incident, see Kuroda Hidetoshi, *Yokohama jiken* (Tokyo: Gakugei Shorin, 1975). See also Janice Matsumura, *More Than a Momentary Nightmare: The Yokohama Incident and Wartime Japan* (Ithaca, NY: Cornell University East Asia Program, 1998); Ogino Fujio, *Yokohama jiken to chianijihō* (Tokyo: Kinohanasha, 2006). For a general overview of the application of the New Peace Preservation Law between 1941 and 1945, see Naka-zawa, *Chianijihō*, 181–200; and Uchida, *Chianijihō no kyōkun*, 459–497.

132. These numbers are derived from the graph in Nakazawa, *Chianijihō*, 183. Different numbers are given in appendix 1, "Chianijihō ihan jiken nendo betsu shori jinin hyō," in GSS45, 646–649.

133. See the table "Chianijihō ihan jiken nendo betsu shori" in Hong Jong-wook, *Senjiki chōsen no tenkōsha-tachi* (Tokyo: Yūshisha, 2011), 63.

134. Chōsen sōtokufu, "Yobō kōkin shūyōsha no jōkyō" (December 1944), in Ogino, *Chianijihō kankei shiryōshū*, vol. 4, 325. Ogino notes that in August 1944, there were 2,897 thought criminals in Korea in the Protection and Supervision system. See Ogino, "Kaisetsu," 687.

135. Matsumoto Kazumi, "Tokyo yobō kōkinsho no kaisō," in *Gokuchū no shōwashi: Toyotama keimusho*, ed. Kazahaya Yasoji (Tokyo: Aoki Shoten, 1986), 167, cited in Ogino, "Kaisetsu," 723. For another account of life inside a Preventative Detention Center, see Tsuchiya Shukurō, *Yobō kōkin sho* (Tokyo: Banseisha, 1988).

136. In addition to Matsumoto, see Ogino, "Kaisetsu," 722.

137. Mitchell, *Janus-Faced Justice*, 142. Reports on Fukumoto's ideological develop-ment, as well as his own thought reports, are collected in Shihōshō keijikyoku, ed., *Shisō shiryō panfuretto tokushū 12: Tokuda Kyūichi, Shiga Yoshio, Fukumoto Kazuo ni kansuru yobōkōkin seikyū jiken kiroku* (Tokyo: Shihōshō Keijikyoku, December 1942).

138. Matsumoto, "Tokyo yobō kōkinsho no kaisō," 179. The following information comes from Matsumoto's recollections.

139. Monbushō, ed., *Kokutai no hongi* (Tokyo: Monbushō, 1937). On the use of *Kokutai no hongi* in the Tokyo Center, see Matsumoto, "Tokyo yobō kōkinsho no kaisō," 174–175. Matsumoto reports that a thought criminal who successfully demonstrated conversion and was released received a copy of the *Kokutai no hongi* as a gift (181).

140. Matsumoto, "Tokyo yobō kōkinsho no kaisō," 177.

141. See Shihōshō, "Chianijihō ihan shūyōsha no tenkō bunrui ni kansuru ken tsūchō" (November 13, 1941), in Ogino, *Chianijihō kankei shiryōshū*, vol. 4, 301. This definition applied to the Protection and Supervision System as well. See Moriyama Takeichirō, "Shihōshō hogo kyoku" (Order No. 16739, September 12, 1941), in Ogino, *Chianijihō kankei shiryōshū*, vol. 3, 357–358.

142. Ogino, "Kaisetsu," 685.

143. Interestingly, because of the later increase in tenkō cases in colonial Korea, Ogino reports that as late as 1944, there were 2,897 individuals under Protection and Supervision in Korea. Ogino, "Kaisetsu," 687.

144. The second exhibition was less of a production than the 1938 exhibit, with fewer advertisements, a tour that included only two other locations (Osaka and Nagoya), and a simpler commemorative book published in a smaller quantity. On the 1940 Thought War Exhibition, see Naikaku Jōhōbu, ed., *Shisōsenten: Dainimen* (Tokyo: Naikaku

Jōhōbu, 1940). On the idea of holy war, see Walter Edwards, "Forging Tradition for a Holy War: The 'Hakkō Ichiu' Tower in Miyazaki and Japanese Wartime Ideology," *Journal of Japanese Studies* 29, no. 2 (summer 2003): 289–324. Public advertisements presented the 1940 Thought War Exhibition in Tokyo in the following manner: "The assault of the thought war, which attempts to break the unity of our spirit [*kokoro no danketsu*], must be decisively crushed. To prepare the unshakable one million spirits is itself to serve as a soldier of the thought war." Conversion was represented as merely a tactic in Japan's intensifying holy war. See the advertisement on page 6 of the February 9, 1940, *Tokyo Asahi Shimbun*, morning edition.

145. On the Metalworks Vocational Center, see Kobayashi, *"Tenkōki" no hitobito*, 225–230; on the Reformed Workers Production Factory, 233–236. Kobayashi reports that the factory manufactured parts in conjunction with the larger Japan Shipbuilding Machines Incorporated (Nihon zōsen kikai kabushiki gaisha).

Epilogue

1. GHQ/SCAP, "Seijiteki, kōminteki oyobi shūkyōteki jiyū ni taisuru seigen jokyo no ken" (October 4, 1945), in *Chianijihō kankei shiryōshū*, vol. 4, ed. Ogino Fujio (Tokyo: Shinnihon Shuppansha, 1996), 368–371.

2. For the repeal of the Peace Preservation Law, among other institutions, see Seifu, Order Nos. 542 (October 13), 575 (October 15), and 638 (November 20), in Ogino, *Chianijihō kankei shiryōshū*, vol. 4, 371–372. The 1900 Public Peace Police Law (Chian keisatsu hō) was repealed on November 21.

3. John Dower, *Embracing Defeat: Japan in the Wake of World War II* (New York: Norton, 1999), 69, 236.

4. Ogino Fujio, *Shisō kenji* (Tokyo: Iwanami Shoten, 2000), 186.

5. Ogino, *Shisō kenji*, 192–193.

6. The Home Ministry was reorganized soon afterward but demonstrates how the prewar police continued into the immediate postwar and beyond. See Ogino Fujio, "Kaisetsu: Chianijihō seiritsu • 'kaisei' shi," in Ogino, *Chianijihō kankei shiryōshū*, vol. 4, 746. See also Ogino Fujio, *Tokkō keisatsu* (Tokyo: Iwanami Shoten, 2012), 222.

7. Ogino, *Tokkō keisatsu*, 224–225.

8. On the construction of the postwar security police, see Ogino Fujio, *Sengo kōan taisei no kakuritsu* (Tokyo: Iwanami Shoten, 1999).

9. Ogino, *Shisō kenji*, 185–191.

10. On the discrepancies between GHQ's dismantling of the Home and Justice Ministry bureaus dealing with political crime, see Ogino, *Shisō kenji*, 188. In total, twenty-five justice officials were dismissed, including the prominent procurator Ikeda Katsu, who was working in Nagoya at the time. However, after the Occupation ended in 1952, Ikeda was assigned to the Supreme Court in 1954 (iv–v, 189–192). On the return of justice officials that were dismissed earlier, see 200–201. On thought procurators, see 183.

11. See Ogino, *Shisō kenji*, 193–196.

12. On this law, see John M. Maki, "Japan's Subversive Activities Prevention Law," *Western Political Quarterly* 6, no. 3 (September 1953): 489–511; Cecil H. Uyehara, *The Subversive Activities Prevention Law: Its Creation, 1951–1952* (Leiden: Brill, 2010).

13. For an overview of the subjectivity debates, see Victor J. Koschmann, *Revolution and Subjectivity in Postwar Japan* (Chicago: University of Chicago Press, 1996).

14. The two most infamous JCP tenkōsha, Sano Manabu and Nabeyama Sadachika, remained staunch critics of the JCP after the war.

15. See Honda Shūgo, *Tenkō bungakuron* (Tokyo: Miraisha, 1957). Honda himself was arrested in 1933 for his association with the proletarian writers's movement. For a translated collection of early essays from this debate, see Atsuko Ueda, Michael Bourdaghs, Richi Sakakibara, and Hirokazu Toeda, eds., *The Politics and Literature Debate in Postwar Japanese Criticism, 1945–1952* (Lanham, MD: Lexington, 2017).

16. Shisō No Kagaku Kenkyūkai, ed., *Kyōdō kenkyū: Tenkō*, 3 vols. (Tokyo: Heibonsha, 1959–1962). See also Takeuchi Yoshimi, "What Is Modernity? (The Case of Japan and China)" (1948), in *What Is Modernity? Writings of Takeuchi Yoshimi*, trans. Richard F. Calichman (New York: Columbia University Press, 2005), 53–81.

17. Adam Bronson, *One Hundred Million Philosophers: Science of Thought and the Culture of Democracy in Postwar Japan* (Honolulu: University of Hawai'i Press, 2016), 161–195.

18. In Japanese scholarship, Ogino Fujio and others have suggested these legacies. See Ogino, *Sengo chian taisei no kakuritsu*; Uchida Hirofumi, *Chianijihō to kyōbōzai* (Tokyo: Iwanami Shoten, 2017), 95–187; and Uchida Hirofumi, *Keihō to sensō: Senji chian hōsei no tsukurikata* (Misuzu Shobō, 2015), 97–101.

19. For the new 1947 Juvenile Offenders Law, see Uchida Hirofumi, *Kōsei hogo no tenkai to kadai* (Kyoto: Hōritsu Bunkasha, 2015), 129–140; Moriya Katsuhiko, *Shōnen no hikō to kyōiku: Shōnen hōsei no rekishi to genjō* (Tokyo: Keisōshobō, 1977), 152–195. For an extensive overview of this history, see chapter 7, "Sengo kōsei hogo no seiseiki naishi junbiki," in Uchida, *Kōsei hogo no tenkai to kadai*, 99–239.

20. On these laws, see Kōsei Hogo Gojūnen Shi Henshū Iinkai, ed., *Kōsei hogo gojūnen shi: Chiiki shakai to tomo ni ayumu kōsei hogo* (Tokyo: Zenkoku Hogoshi Renmei, 2000), vol. 1, 8–9. For the original bill, explanation, and subsequent Diet debates over the Offenders Prevention and Rehabilitation Act, see Kōsei Hogo Gojūnen Shi Henshū Iinkai, *Kōsei hogo gojūnen shi*, vol. 2, 449–480. In the new postwar Judicial Protection system, probationary duties for both youths and adults were combined in 1952 into the office of probation officers (*hogoshi*). And with the prohibition of prostitution in 1958, the protection system came to oversee the reform of women arrested for prostitution as well.

21. On SCAP's involvement in the emperor's Declaration of Humanity, see Dower, *Embracing Defeat*, 308–314.

22. Glenn D. Hook and Gavan McCormack, *Japan's Contested Constitution: Documents and Analysis* (London: Routledge, 2001), 4.

23. See images of Emperor Hirohito attending the Tenth and Twentieth Anniversary Celebrations of the Criminal Reform System (Kōsei hogo seido) in October 1959 in Hibiya Park and October 1969 in Nippon Budōkan arena, in Kōsei Hogo Gojūnen Shi Henshū Iinkai, *Kōsei hogo gojūnen shi*, 250 and 282 respectively.

24. See the report of the Fiftieth Anniversary (1999) of the (postwar) Criminal Reform System in which Emperor Akihito and Empress Michiko attended, in Kōsei Hogo Gojūnen Shi Henshū Iinkai, *Kōsei hogo gojūnen shi*, frontmatter and 393–394.

25. Jonathon E. Abel, *Redacted: The Archives of Censorship in Transwar Japan* (Berkeley: University of California Press, 2012), 17–20.

26. For example, see the section "Kōsei hogo zenshi II," in Kōsei Hogo Gojūnen Shi Henshū Iinkai, *Kōsei hogo gojūnen shi*, vol. 1, 164–195.

27. For example, see Ministry of Japan Rehabilitation Bureau, *Non-institutional Treatment of Offenders in Japan* (Tokyo: Hōmushō Hogokyoku, 1974), 1–5.

28. See Umemori Naoyuki, "Modernization through Colonial Mediations: The Establishment of the Police and Prison System in Meiji Japan" (PhD diss., University of Chicago, 2002).

29. I touch on this briefly in the preface. For recent legal critiques of these developments, see Uchida, *Keihō to sensō*; Uchida, *Chianijihō to kyōbōzai*; Hōgaku Seminaa Henshūbu, ed., *Kyōbōzai hihyō: Kaisei soshikiteki hanzai shobatsu hō no kentō* (Tokyo: Nihon Hyōronsha, 2017); and Colin Jones, "Will Japan's New Conspiracy Law Lead to 'Thought Crime'?" *The Diplomat*, July 17, 2017, https://thediplomat.com/2017/07/will-japans-new-conspiracy-law-lead-to-thought-crime/.

Newspapers and Online Sources

Asahi Shimbun (1920–1945)

Brennan Center for Justice. "Countering Violent Extremism (CVE): A Resource Page." December 2017. https://www.brennancenter.org/analysis/cve-programs-resource-page.

Chūōkōron (1933)

CNN (2017)

Diplomat (2017)

Hogo Jihō (1929–1939)

Hōritsu Shimbun (1933)

Hōsei Kaihō (1917–1929)

Kaizō (1933)

Kakushin (1938)

Minneapolis Star Tribune (2015–2017)

Minnesota Public Radio News (2015–2017)

NBC News (2017)

New York Times (2017)

Politico (2016)

Sekki (1933)

The Telegraph (2014)

US Department of Homeland Security. "Countering Violent Extremism." https://www.dhs.gov/countering-violent-extremism (Accessed: November 1, 2016)

Washington Post (2014–2015)

Wired (2017)

Yomiuri Shimbun (1933–1945)

Articles, Books, and Reports

Abel, Jonathon E. *Redacted: The Archives of Censorship in Transwar Japan.* Berkeley: University of California Press, 2012.

Adachi Katsukiyo. "Shisōhansha no hogo taisaku" (1). *Hogo Jihō* 19, no. 6 (June 1935): 4–12.

Adachi Katsukiyo. "Shisōhansha no hogo taisaku" (2). *Hogo Jihō* 19, no. 7 (July 1935): 9–18.

Agamben, Giorgio. *Homo Sacer: Sovereign Power and Bare Life.* Translated by Daniel Heller-Roazen. Stanford, CA: Stanford University Press, 1998.

Agamben, Giorgio. *State of Exception.* Translated by Kevin Attell. Chicago: Chicago University Press, 2005.

Agamben, Giorgio. *What Is an Apparatus? And Other Essays.* Translated by David Kishik and Stefan Pedatella. Stanford, CA: Stanford University Press, 2009.

Akamatsu Katsumaro. "Nihon seishin to gendai shakai undō." In "Shisōhan ni kansuru hogo jigyō kōshūkai." *Hogo Jihō* 17, no. 7 (July 1933): 59–60.

Allen, J. Michael. "The Price of Identity: The 1923 Kantō Earthquake and Its Aftermath." *Korean Studies* 20 (1996): 64–96.

Althusser, Louis. "Ideology and Ideological State Apparatuses (Notes towards an Investigation)." In *Lenin and Philosophy*

and Other Essays, translated by Ben
Brewster, 85–126. New York: Monthly
Review Press, 2001.

Althusser, Louis. On the Reproduction of
Capitalism: Ideology and Ideological
State Apparatuses. Translated by G. M.
Goshgarian. London: Verso, 2014.

Ambaras, David. Bad Youth: Juvenile
Delinquency and the Politics of Everyday
Life in Modern Japan. Berkeley: Univer-
sity of California Press, 2006.

Anderson, Perry. "The Antinomies of
Antonio Gramsci." New Left Review,
no. 100 (November–December 1976):
5–78.

Aomori Hogo Kansatsusho, ed. Shisōhan
hogo kansatsu hō (1937). In Ogino,
Chianijihō kankei shiryōshū, vol. 3,
65–80.

Asano Akira and Kageyama Masahara.
Tenkō-Nihon e no kaiki: Nihonkyōsantō
kaitōha shuchō. Tokyo: Akatsuki Shobō,
1983.

Asano Toyomi and Matsuda Toshihiko,
eds. Shokuminchi teikoku nihon no
hōteki kōzō. Tokyo: Shinzansha Shuppan, 2004.

Ayer, A. J. "An Honest Ghost?" In Ryle:
A Collection of Critical Essays, edited
by Oscar P. Wood and George Pitcher.
Garden City, NY: Doubleday, 1970.

Baldwin, Frank. "Participatory Anti-
imperialism: The 1919 Independence
Movement." Journal of Korean Studies 1
(1979): 123–62.

Balibar, Étienne. "Althusser and the 'Ideological State Apparatuses.'" In On the
Reproduction of Capitalism, vii–xviii.

Barshay, Andrew. State and Intellectual in
Imperial Japan: The Public Man in Crisis.
Berkeley: University of California
Press, 1988.

Barshay, Andrew, and Carl Friere. "The
Tenkō Phenomenon." In de Bary,

Gluck, and Tiedemann, Sources of
Japanese Tradition, vol. 2, 1600 to 2000,
2nd ed.

Bartelson, Jens. A Genealogy of Sovereignty.
Cambridge: Cambridge University
Press, 1995.

Bartelson, Jens. Sovereignty as Symbolic
Form. London: Routledge, 2014.

Beckmann, George M. The Making of the
Meiji Constitution: The Oligarchs and
the Constitutional Development of Japan,
1868–1891. Westport, CT: Greenwood,
1957; reprint, 1975.

Beckmann, George M., and Genji Okubo.
The Japanese Communist Party, 1922–
1945. Stanford, CA: Stanford University
Press, 1969.

Bernstein, Gail Lee, and Haruhiro Fukui,
eds. Japan and the World: Essays on
Japanese History and Politics in Honour
of Ishida Takeshi. New York: St. Martin's, 1988.

Bix, Herbert. "Kawakami Hajime and
the Organic Law of Japanese Fascism."
Japan Interpreter 13, no. 1 (winter 1978):
118–133.

Bix, Herbert. "Rethinking 'Emperor-
System Fascism': Ruptures and Continuities in Modern Japanese History."
Bulletin of Concerned Asian Scholars 14,
no. 2 (June 1982): 2–19.

Bowen-Struyk, Heather. "Rethinking
Japanese Proletarian Literature." PhD
diss., Department of Comparative Literature, University of Michigan, 2001.

Bronson, Adam. One Hundred Million
Philosophers: Science of Thought and the
Culture of Democracy in Postwar Japan.
Honolulu: University of Hawai'i Press,
2016.

Burchell, Graham, Colin Gordon, and
Peter Miller, eds. The Foucault Effect:
Studies in Governmentality. Chicago:
University of Chicago Press, 1991.

Butler, Judith. *The Psychic Life of Power: Theories in Subjection.* Stanford, CA: Stanford University Press, 1997.

Calarco, Matthew, and Steven DeCaroli, eds. *Giorgio Agamben: Sovereignty and Life.* Stanford, CA: Stanford University Press, 2007.

Caprio, Mark E. *Japanese Assimilation Policies in Colonial Korea, 1910–1945.* Seattle: University of Washington Press, 2009.

Center for Contemporary Cultural Studies, ed. *On Ideology.* London: Hutchinson University Library, 1978.

Chen, Edward I-te. "The Attempt to Integrate the Empire: Legal Perspectives." In *The Japanese Colonial Empire, 1895–1945,* edited by Ramon H. Myers and Mark R. Peattie, 240–274. Princeton, NJ: Princeton University Press, 1984.

Ching, Leo T. S. *Becoming Japanese: Colonial Taiwan and the Politics of Identity.* Berkeley: University of California Press, 2001.

Clinton, Maggie. *Revolutionary Nativism: Fascism and Culture in China, 1925–1937.* Durham, NC: Duke University Press, 2017.

Connolly, William E. "The Complexities of Sovereignty." In *Giorgio Agamben: Sovereignty and Life,* edited by Matthew Calarco and Steven DeCaroli, 23–42. Stanford, CA: Stanford University Press, 2007.

Connor, Walker. *The National Question in Marxist-Leninist Theory and Strategy.* Princeton, NJ: Princeton University Press, 1984.

Daniels, F. J. "Mr. Tsurumi-Syunsuke on the 'Amuletic' Use of Words: A Translation, with Commentary." *Bulletin of the School of Oriental and African Studies, University of London* 18, no. 3 (1956): 514–533.

Dean, Meryll. *Japanese Legal System: Text, Cases and Materials,* 2nd ed. London: Cavendish, 2002.

Dean, Mitchell. *Critical and Effective Histories: Foucault's Methods and Historical Sociology.* London: Routledge, 1994.

de Bary, Wm. Theodore, Carol Gluck, and Arthur E. Tiedemann, eds. *Sources of Japanese Tradition,* vol. 2: *1600 to 2000: Part Two, 1868–2000,* 2nd ed. New York: Columbia University Press, 2005.

Dennett, Daniel C. "Introduction: Reintroducing *The Concept of Mind.*" In *The Concept of Mind,* by Gilbert Ryle. London: Penguin, 2000.

Dorsey, James. "From Ideological Literature to a Literary Ideology: 'Conversion' in Wartime Japan." in *Converting Cultures: Religion, Ideology and Transformations of Modernity,* edited by Dennis Washburn and A. Kevin Reinhart, 465–483. Leiden: Brill, 2007.

Dower, John. *Embracing Defeat: Japan in the Wake of World War II.* New York: Norton, 1999.

Driscoll, Mark. "Conclusion: Postcolonialism in Reverse," in Yuasa Katsuei, *Kannani and Document in Flames: Two Japanese Colonial Novels,* trans. Mark Driscoll. Durham, NC: Duke University Press, 2005.

Dubois, Thomas David. "Inauthentic Sovereignty: Law and Legal Institutions in Manchukuo." *Journal of Asian Studies* 69, no. 3 (August 2010): 749–770.

Dutton, Michael. *Policing Chinese Politics: A History.* Durham, NC: Duke University Press, 2005.

Duus, Peter, ed. *Cambridge History of Japan,* vol. 6: *The Twentieth Century.* Cambridge: Cambridge University Press, 1988.

Dyzenhaus, David. "The Politics of the Question of Constituent Power." In *The Paradox of Constitutionalism: Constituent Power and Constitutional Form*, edited by Martin Loughlin and Neil Walker. Oxford: Oxford University Press, 2007.

Easton, David. "The Political System Besieged by the State." *Political Theory* 9, no. 3 (August 1981): 303–325.

Edwards, Walter. "Forging Tradition for a Holy War: The 'Hakkō Ichiu' Tower in Miyazaki and Japanese Wartime Ideology." *Journal of Japanese Studies* 29, no. 2 (summer 2003): 289–324.

Endo, Katsuhiko. "The Science of Capital: The Uses and Abuses of Social Science in Interwar Japan." PhD diss., New York University, 2004.

Esselstrom, Erik. *Crossing Empire's Edge: Foreign Ministry Police and Japanese Expansionism in Northeast Asia*. Honolulu: University of Hawai'i Press, 2009.

Foucault, Michel. *Discipline and Punish: The Birth of the Prison*. Translated by Alan Sheridan. New York: Vintage, 1995.

Foucault, Michel. "Governmentality." In *The Foucault Effect: Studies in Governmentality*, edited by Graham Burchell, Colin Gordon and Peter Miller, 87–104. Chicago: University of Chicago Press, 1991.

Foucault, Michel. *History of Sexuality*, vol. 1: *An Introduction*. Translated by Robert Hurley. New York: Vintage, 1978.

Foucault, Michel. *Power/Knowledge: Selected Interviews and Other Writings, 1972–1977*. Edited by Colin Gordon. New York: Vintage, 1980.

Foucault, Michel. *The Punitive Society: Lectures at the Collège de France, 1972–1973*. Translated by Graham Burchell. London: Palgrave Macmillan, 2015.

Foucault, Michel. *"Society Must Be Defended": Lectures at the Collège de France, 1975–1976*. Translated by David Macey. New York: Picador, 2003.

Foucault, Michel. "Technologies of the Self" (1982). In *Essential Works of Foucault, 1954–1984*, vol. 1: *Ethics*, edited by Paul Rabinow, 223–251. New York, Penguin, 1997.

Foucault, Michel. *Wrong-Doing, Truth-Telling: The Function of Avowal in Justice*. Translated by Stephen W. Sawyer. Chicago: University of Chicago Press, 2014.

Fujii Eshō. "Shisōhan hogo jigyō no tenbō: Hogo kansatsu no jicchi o hikaete." *Hogo Jihō* 20, no. 2 (February 1936): 11–15.

Fujii Eshō. "Shisōhan hogo kansatsu hō ni tsuite: Jitsumuka no tachiba kara." *Hogo Jihō* 20, no. 7 (July 1936): 13–16.

Fujii Eshō. "Shisōhan shakuhōsha no hogo hōhō." *Hogo Jihō* 19, no. 1 (January 1935): 13–28.

Fujita Shōzō. "Shōwa Hachi-nen o Chūshin to suru Tenkō no Jōkyō." In *Tenkō*, vol. 1, edited by Shisō no Kagaku no Kenkyūkai, 32–63. Tokyo: Heibonsha, 1959.

Fujita Shōzō. *Tennōsei kokka no shihai genri*. Tokyo: Miraisha, 1966.

Fujitani, Takashi. *Splendid Monarchy: Power and Pageantry in Modern Japan*. Berkeley: University of California Press, 1996.

Fujitani, Takashi. "Right to Kill, Right to Make Live: Koreans as Japanese and Japanese as Americans during WWII." *Representations* 99, no. 1 (summer 2007): 13–39.

Fukunaga Misao. *Kyōsantōin no tenkō to tennōsei*. Tokyo: Sanichi Shobō, 1978.

Fukushima Jūrō. "Senji genron tōsei kikan no saikenshō 'jōhōkyoku' e no dōtei 1:

Naikaku jōhō iinkai setsuritsu to sono haikei." *Janarizumu Kenkyū* 23, no. 1 (1986): 98–109.

Fukushima Jūrō. "Senji genron tōsei kikan no saikenshō 'jōhōkyoku' e no dotei 2: Naikaku jōhōbu no jidai." *Janarizumu kenkyū* 23, no. 2 (1986): 68–77.

Furuta Masatake. *Keisatsu kyōyō shiryō. Dai ippen: Chianijihō.* Tokyo: Keisatsu Kōshū Jogaku Yūkai, 1925.

Garon, Sheldon. *Molding Japanese Minds: The State in Everyday Life.* Princeton, NJ: Princeton University Press, 1995.

GHQ/SCAP. "Seijiteki, kōminteki oyobi shūkyōteki jiyū ni taisuru seigen jōkyō no ken" (October 4, 1945). In Ogino, *Chianijihō kankei shiryōshū*, vol. 4, 368–371.

Gluck, Carol. *Japan's Modern Myths: Ideology in the Late Meiji Period.* Princeton, NJ: Princeton University Press, 1987.

Golder, Ben, and Peter Fitzpatrick. *Foucault's Law.* New York: Routledge, 2009.

Goldstein, Jan. "Framing Discipline with Law: Problems and Promises of the Liberal State." *American Historical Review* 98, no. 2 (April 1993): 364–375.

Gordon, Andrew. *Labor and Imperial Democracy in Prewar Japan.* Berkeley: University of California Press, 1992.

Hall, Stuart. "Nicos Poulantzas: State, Power, Socialism." In Nicos Poulantzas, *State, Power, Socialism*, translated by Patrick Camiller, vii–xvii. London: Verso, 2014.

Hankan Gakuryō, ed. *Hankan Gakuryō shisōhan tenkōsha zadankai kiroku.* Tokyo: Hankan Gakuryō Tōkyō Jimusho, 1936.

Harootunian, Harry. "Hirohito Redux." *Critical Asian Studies* 33, no. 4 (2001): 609–636.

Hashikawa Bunzō. "Kakushin kanryō." In *Kenryoku no shisō: Gendai nihon shisō taikei 10*, edited by Kamishima Jirō, 251–273. Tokyo: Chikuma Shobō, 1965.

Hatada Takeshi, ed. *Chōsen no kindaishi to nihon.* Tokyo: Yamato Shobō, 1987.

Havens, Thomas R. H. "Japan's Enigmatic Election of 1928." *Modern Asian Studies* 11, no. 4 (1977): 543–555.

Havens, Thomas R. H. *Valley of Darkness: The Japanese People and World War Two.* New York: Norton, 1978.

Hayashida Shigeo. "Tenkō būmu." In *Gokuchū no shōwashi: Toyotama keimusho*, edited by Kazahaya Yasoji, 102–106. Tokyo: Aoki Shoten, 1986.

Hirata Isao. "Hogo kansatsu sho no shimei" (December 14, 1936). In *Shisōhan hogo kansatsu hō*, edited by Aomori Hogo Kansatsu Sho, 1937. In Ogino, *Chianijihō kankei shiryōshū*, vol. 3, 65–80.

Hirata Isao. "Kyōsantōin no tenkō ni tsuite." Lecture, February 8, 1934. Archived at the Ōhara Institute for Social Research, Hōsei University, Japan.

Hirata Isao. "Marukishizumu no kokufuku." In *Shisōsen kōshūkai kōgi sokki,* Vol. 3, edited by Naikaku Jōhōbu, 205–236. Tokyo: Naikaku Jōhōbu, 1938).

Hobbes, Thomas. *Leviathan.* New York: Penguin Classics, 1982.

Hofmann, Reto. *The Fascist Effect: Japan and Italy, 1915–1952.* Ithaca, NY: Cornell University Press, 2016.

Hōgaku Seminaa Henshūbu, ed. *Kyōbōzai hihyō: Kaisei soshikiteki hanzai shobatsu hō no kentō.* Tokyo: Nihon Hyōronsha, 2017.

Hogo Jihō, ed. "Shisōhan ni kansuru hogo jigyō kōshūkai." *Hogo Jihō* 17, no. 7 (July 1933): 51–65.

Hogo Jihō, ed. "Tenkō fujin no nayami o kiku kai." *Hogo Jihō* 18, no. 10 (October 1934): 11–18.

Honda Shūgo. *Tenkō bungakuron.* Tokyo: Miraisha, 1957.

Hong Jong-wook. "Senjiki chōsen ni okeru shisōhan tōsei to Yamato-juku." *Kankoku Chōsen Bunka Kenkyū*, no. 16 (March 2017): 43–67.

Hong Jong-wook. *Senjiki chōsen no tenkōsha-tachi: Teikoku / shokuminchi no tōgō to kiretsu.* Tokyo: Yūshisha, 2011.

Honjō Tetsuzō. "Tenkō to hogo ni kansuru kōsai." *Hogo Jihō* 19, no. 1 (January 1935): 29–38.

Hon Yung Lee, Yong Chool Ha, and Clark W. Sorensen, eds. *Colonial Rule and Social Change in Korea, 1910–1945.* Seattle: Center for Korean Studies, University of Washington Press, 2013.

Hook, Glenn D. and Gavan McCormack. *Japan's Contested Constitution: Documents and Analysis.* London: Routledge, 2001.

Hoseikai, ed. *Jihen ni yomigaeru hanzaisha.* Tokyo: Hoseikai, 1937.

Hoston, Germaine A. "Emperor, Nation and the Transformation of Marxism to National Socialism in Prewar Japan: The Case of Sano Manabu." *Studies in Comparative Communism* 18, no. 1 (spring 1985): 25–47.

Hoston, Germaine A. "Ikkoku shakaishugi: Sano Manabu and the Limits of Marxism as Cultural Criticism." In *Culture and Identity: Japanese Intellectuals during the Interwar Years*, edited by J. Thomas Rimer, 168–186. Princeton, NJ: Princeton University Press, 1990.

Hoston, Germaine A. *Marxism and the Crisis of Development in Prewar Japan.* Princeton, NJ: Princeton University Press, 1986.

Hoston, Germaine A. *The State, Identity, and the National Question in China and Japan.* Princeton, NJ: Princeton University Press, 1994.

Hunt, Alan, and Gary Wickman. *Foucault and Law: Towards a Sociology of Law as Governance.* London: Pluto, 1994.

Ikeda Katsu. "Shisō hannin kyōka no keiken hihan." *Keisatsu Kenkyū*, November 1936.

Ikeda Katsu, Miyagi Chōgorō, Tozawa Shigeo, et al. "Shisōhan tenkōsha o ika ni suru ka." *Hogo Jihō* 18, no. 10 (October 1934): 23–30.

Ishidō Kiyotomo. "Kobayashi Morito no tadotta michi." In Kobayashi, *"Tenkōki" no hitobito*, 253–267.

Ishii Toyoshichirō. *Shihō hogo sōsho dai 17 shū: Saiban to hogo.* Tokyo: Zen Nihon Shihō Hogo Jigyō Renmei, 1938.

Itō Akira. "Tenkō mondai no ikkōsatsu: Nihon kyōsantō rōdōshaha to Hirata Isao." *Chiba kōgyō daigaku kenkyū hōkoku*, no. 31 (February 1994): 29–41.

Itō Akira. *Tenkō to tennōsei: Nihon kyōsanshugi undō no 1930nendai.* Tokyo: Keisō Shobō, 1995.

Itō Akira. *Tennōsei to shakaishugi.* Tokyo: Keisō Shobō, 1988.

Itō Hirobumi. *Commentaries on the Constitution of the Empire of Japan*, 2nd ed. Translated by Miyoji Ito. Tokyo: Chūō Daigaku, 1906.

Itō Takashi, et al., eds. *Kataritsugu shōwashi*, vol. 1. Tokyo: Asahi Bunko, 1990.

Jackson, Robert H. *Sovereignty: Evolution of an Idea.* Cambridge: Polity, 2007.

Jameson, Fredric. *The Political Unconscious: Narrative as a Socially Symbolic Act.* Ithaca, NY: Cornell University Press, 1981.

Jameson, Fredric. "The Vanishing Mediator: Narrative Structure in Max Weber."

New German Critique, no. 1 (winter 1973): 52–89.

Jessop, Bob. *State Power: A Strategic-Relational Approach*. Cambridge: Polity, 2008/.

Karatani Kōjin, ed. *Kindai nihon no hihyō*, 1. Tokyo: Iwanami Shoten, 1997.

Karatani Kōjin. "Kindai nihon no hihyō: Shōwa senki." In *Kindai nihon no hihyō*, 1, edited by Karatani Kōjin, 13–44. Tokyo: Iwanami Shoten, 1997.

Kasagi Nihaya. "Miyagi Chōgorō no shōnenhō shisō." *Takada Hōgaku*, no. 4 (March 2005): 1–16.

Kato Michiko. "Senzen kara sengo fukkōki ni okeru hogo kansatsu seido no dōnyū to hensen." *Ōyō shakaigaku kenkyū*, no. 55 (2013): 219–233.

Kawamura, Satofumi. "The National Polity and the Formation of the Modern National Subject in Japan." *Japan Forum* 26, no. 1 (2014): 25–45.

Kazahaya Yasoji, ed. *Gokuchū no shōwashi: Toyotama keimusho*. Tokyo: Aoki Shoten, 1986.

Keene, Donald. "Japanese Literature and Politics in the 1930s." *Journal of Japanese Studies* 2, no. 2 (summer 1976): 225–248.

Keihokyoku. "Jinmin sensen undō no hontai" (January–February 1938). In Ogino, *Chianijihō kankei shiryōshū*, vol. 2, 410–417.

Keihokyoku. "Ōmotokyō chianijihō ihan narabini fukei jiken gaiyō" (November 1935). In Ogino, *Chianijihō kankei shiryōshū*, vol. 2, 403–406.

Keihokyoku. "Ōmotokyō higisha chōshusho sakusei yōkō" (May 14, 1936). In Ogino, *Chianijihō kankei shiryōshū*, vol. 2, 406–410.

Kelmo, Hans, and Quentin Skinner, eds. *Sovereignty in Fragments: The Past, Present and Future of a Contested Concept*. Cambridge: Cambridge University Press, 2010.

Keongil Kim. "Japanese Assimilation Policy and Thought Conversion in Colonial Korea." In *Colonial Rule and Social Change in Korea, 1910–1945*, edited by Hong Yung Lee, Yong Chool Ha, and Clark W. Sorensen, 206–233. Seattle: Center for Korean Studies, University of Washington Press, 2013.

Kido Yoshio. *Shisōhan hogokansatsuhōki shū*. Tokyo: Gansuidō Shoten, 1937.

Kim Songon. "Chōsenjin no shihō hogo ni tsuite." *Hogo Jihō* 14, no. 12 (December 1934): 32–37.

Kisala, Robert. "Schisms in Japanese New Religious Movements." In *Sacred Schisms: How Religions Divide*, edited by James R. Lewis and Sarah M. Lewis, 83–105. Cambridge: Cambridge University Press, 2009.

Kobayashi Morito. "Kansetsu hogo taiken o kataru." *Hogo Jihō* 16, no. 9 (September 1932): 43–47.

Kobayashi Morito [Ono Yōichi, pseud.]. *Kyōsantō o dassuru made*. Tokyo: Daidōsha, 1932.

Kobayashi Morito [Ono Yōichi, pseud.]. "Marukisuto ha gokuchū ika ni shūkyō o taiken shita ka." In Saotome, *Tenkōsha no shuki*, 231–244.

Kobayashi Morito. "Nihon kokumin to shite no jikaku ni tatte." In *Tenkōsha no shisō to seikatsu*, edited by Kobayashi Morito, 3–98. Tokyo: Daidōsha, 1935.

Kobayashi Morito. "Shisōhan hogo kansatsuhō ni taisuru jakkan no kōsatsu: Hitotsu tenkōsha to shite." *Hogo Jihō* 20, no. 7 (July 1936): 16–21.

Kobayashi Morito. "Shisōhan no hogo o ika ni subeki ya: Teikoku kōshinkai ni okeru jiken ni motozuite." *Hogo Jihō* 17, no. 6 (June 1933): 16–24.

Kobayashi Morito. "Shōwa jūichinen ni okeru wareware no kibō." *Tensei*, February 1936, 10–11.

Kobayashi Morito. *"Tenkōki" no hitobito: Chianijihōka no katsudōka gunzō.* Tokyo: Shinjidaisha, 1987.

Kobayashi Morito. "Tenkōsha ha doko ni iku." In Saotome, *Tenkōsha no shuki*, 245–260.

Kobayashi Morito, ed. *Tenkōsha no shisō to seikatsu.* Tokyo: Daidōsha, 1935.

Kobayashi Sanzaburō. *Seimei no shinpi: Ikiru chikara to ijutsu no gacchi.* Kyoto: Seizasha, 1922.

Kobayashi Yukio. "Chianijihō seiritsu katei ni kansuru horon: Toku ni 'kokutai' gainen ni kanren shite I." *Kyōto Gakuen Hōgaku* 2–3, nos. 39–40 (2002): 53–108.

Kobayashi Yukio. "Chianijihō seiritsu katei ni kansuru horon: Toku ni 'kokutai' gainen ni kanren shite II." *Kyōto Gakuen Hōgaku* 1, no. 41 (2003): 153–194.

Kobayashi Yukio. "Nisso kihon jōyaku daigojō to chianijihō" (1959). In *Nisso seiji gaikōshi: Roshia kakumei to Chianijihō.* Tokyo: Yūhikaku, 1985.

Kodansha, ed. *Kodansha Encyclopedia of Japan.* Tokyo: Kodansha, 1983.

Koestler, Arthur. *The Ghost in the Machine.* London: Penguin, 1989.

Kojima Yuki. "Daihi no ote ni sugaru made." In Saotome, *Tenkōsha no shuki*, 43–73.

Kokumin Seiji Keizai Kenkyūsho, ed. *"Kokunai bōkyō" Sensen no sankyotō: Shiono, Suetsugu, Araki.* Tokyo: Kokumin Seiji Keizai Kenkyūsho, 1938.

Ko Miyagi Moto Shihō Daijin Kenpi Jikkōiin Jimusho, ed. *Miyagi Chōgorō shōden.* Tokyo: Ko Miyagi Moto Shihō Daijin Kenpi Jikkōiin Jimusho, 1950.

Konno Nobuyuki. *Kindai nihon no kokutairon.* Tokyo: Perikansha, 2008.

Koschmann, Victor J. *Revolution and Subjectivity in Postwar Japan.* Chicago: University of Chicago Press, 1996.

Kōsei Hogo Gojūnen Shi Henshū Iinkai, ed. *Kōsei hogo gojūnen shi: Chiiki shakai to tomo ni ayumu kōsei hogo*, vols. 1 and 2. Tokyo: Zenkoku Hogoshi Renmei, 2000.

Kōtō Hōin Kenjikyoku, ed. *Chian ijihō teian tōgi: Teikoku gikai ni okeru shitsugi ōtō giji.* Tokyo: Kōtōhōin Kenjikyoku Shisōbu Hensan, 1928.

Kudnani, Arun. "Radicalisation: The Journey of a Concept." *Race and Class* 54, no. 2 (September 2012): 3–25.

Kuroda Hidetoshi. *Yokohama jiken.* Tokyo: Gakugei Shorin, 1975.

Kushner, Barak. *The Thought War: Japanese Imperial Propaganda.* Honolulu: University of Hawai'i Press, 2006.

Laclau, Ernesto. "Fascism and Ideology." In *Capitalism, Fascism, Populism: Politics and Ideology in Marxist Theory*, 81–142. London: Verso, 1977.

Laclau, Ernesto. *Capitalism, Fascism, Populism: Politics and Ideology in Marxist Theory.* London: Verso, 1977.

Lampert, Matthew. "Resisting Ideology: On Butler's Critique of Althusser" in *Diacritics* 43, no. 2 (2015): 124–147.

Large, Stephen. "Buddhism and Political Renovation in Prewar Japan: The Case of Akamatsu Katsumaro," *The Journal of Japanese Studies* 9, no. 1 (Winter, 1983): 33–66.

Large, Stephen. "Nationalist Extremism in Early Shōwa Japan: Inoue Nisshō and the 'Blood-Pledge Corps Incident,' 1932." *Modern Asian Studies* 35, no. 3 (2001): 533–564.

Lee, Chulwoo. "Modernity, Legality, and Power in Korea under Japanese Rule."

In *Colonial Modernity in Korea*, edited by Gi-Wook Shin and Michael Robinson, 21–51. Cambridge, MA: Harvard University Press, 1999.

Lemke, Thomas. *Foucault, Governmentality, and Critique*. Boulder, CO: Paradigm, 2012.

Lewis, Michael. *Rioters and Citizens: Mass Protest in Imperial Japan*. Berkeley: University of California Press, 1990.

Loughlin, Martin, and Neil Walker, eds. *The Paradox of Constitutionalism: Constituent Power and Constitutional Form*. Oxford: Oxford University Press, 2007.

Macherey, Pierre. "Judith Butler and the Althusserian Theory of Subjection," translated by Stephanie Bundy. *Décalages* 1, no. 2 (2013): 1–22.

Maki, John M. "Japan's Subversive Activities Prevention Law." *Western Political Quarterly* 6, no. 3 (September 1953): 489–511.

Martin, James, ed. *The Poulantzas Reader: Marxism, Law and the State*. London: Verso, 2008.

Maruyama Masao. "Theory and Psychology of Ultra-Nationalism" (1946). In *Thought and Behaviour in Modern Japanese Politics*, edited by Ivan Morris. London: Oxford University Press, 1963.

Maruyama Masao. *Nihon no shisō*. Tokyo: Iwanami shoten, 1961.

Matsuda Toshihiko. "Shokuminchi makki chōsen ni okeru tenkōsha no undō: Kang Yŏng-sŏk to nihon kokutai gaku • tōa renmei undō." *Jinbun Gakuhō* 79 (March 1997): 131–161.

Matsuda Toshihiko. *Tōa renmei undō to chōsen • chōsenjin: Nicchū sensōki ni okeru shokuminchi teikoku nihon no danmen*. Tokyo: Yūshisha, 2015.

Matsuda Toshihiko and Yamada Atsushi, eds. *Nihon no chōsen • Taiwan shihai to shokuminchi kanryō*. Kyoto: Shibunkaku Shuppan, 2009.

Matsui Kazuyoshi. *Kokka sōryokusen to shihō hogo jigyō*. Tokyo: Hoseikai, 1938.

Matsumura, Janice. *More Than a Momentary Nightmare: The Yokohama Incident and Wartime Japan*. Ithaca, NY: Cornell University East Asia Program, 1998.

Matsumura Takao. "Mantetsu chōsabu danatsu jiken (1942 • 43nen) sairon." *Mita Gakkai Zasshi* 105, no. 4 (January 2013): 719–754.

Matsuo Hiroshi. *Chianijihō: Danatsu to teikō no rekishi*. Tokyo: Shinnihon Shuppansha, 1971.

Matsuo Hiroshi. *Chianijihō to tokkō keisatsu*. Tokyo: Kyōikusha, 1979.

Matsuo Kōya. "Kyōto gakuren jiken: Hatsudō sareta chianijihō." In *Nihon seiji saiban shiroku 4: Shōwa • zen*, edited by Wagatsuma Sakae, 64–96. Tokyo: Daiichi Hōki Shuppan, 1968–1970.

Matsuo Takayoshi. "Kageki shakaishugi undō torishimari hōan ni tsuite: 1922nen dai45gikai ni okeru." *Jinbun Gakuhō* 20 (October 1964): 247–267.

McLennan, Gregor, Victor Molina, and Roy Peters. "Althusser's Theory of Ideology." In *On Ideology*, edited by Center for Contemporary Cultural Studies, 77–105. London: Hutchinson University Library, 1978.

Miller, Frank O. *Minobe Tatsukichi: Interpreter of Constitutionalism in Japan*. Berkeley: University of California Press, 1965.

Minear, Richard H. *Japanese Tradition and Western Law: Emperor, State, and Law in the Thought of Hozumi Yatsuka*. Cambridge, MA: Harvard University Press, 1970.

Mitchell, Richard H. *Censorship in Imperial Japan*. Princeton, NJ: Princeton University Press, 1983.

Mitchell, Richard H. *Janus-Faced Justice: Political Criminals in Imperial Japan*. Honolulu: University of Hawaii Press, 1992.

Mitchell, Richard H. "Japan's Peace Preservation Law of 1925: Its Origins and Significance." *Monumenta Nipponica* 28, no. 3 (autumn 1973): 317–345.

Mitchell, Richard H. *Thought Control in Prewar Japan*. Ithaca, NY: Cornell University Press, 1976.

Mitchell, Timothy. "The Limits of the State: Beyond Statist Approaches and Their Critics." *American Political Science Review* 85, no. 1 (March 1991): 77–96.

Mitchell, Timothy. "Society, Economy, and the State Effect." In *State/Culture: State-Formation after the Cultural Turn*, edited by George Steinmetz, 76–97. Ithaca, NY: Cornell University Press, 1999.

Miyachi Masato. "Dai ni ji Ōmotokyō jiken: Senjika shūkyō danatsu no kiten." In *Nihon seiji saiban shiroku 5: Shōwa • go*, edited by Wagatsuma Sakae, 95–140. Tokyo: Daiichi Hōki Shuppan, 1969.

Miyachi Masato. "Morito Tatsuo jiken: Gakumon no jiyū no hatsu no shiren." In *Nihon seiji saiban shiroku 3: Taishō*, edited by Wagatsuma Sakae, 228–272. Tokyo: Daiichi Hōki Shuppan, 1969.

Miyagi Chōgorō. *Hōritsuzen to hōritsuaku*. Tokyo: Dokusho Shinpōsha Shupanbu, 1941.

Miyake Masatarō. *An Outline of the Japanese Judiciary*, rev. 2nd ed. Tokyo: Japan Times and Mail.

Miyazawa Toshiyoshi. *Tennō kikansetsu jiken: Shiryō ha kataru*, 2 vols. Tokyo: Yūhikaku, 1997.

Mizuno Naoki. "Chianijihō no seitei to shokuminchi Chōsen." *Jinbun Gakuhō* 83 (March 2000): 97–123.

Mizuno Naoki. "Chianijihō to Chōsen: Oboegaki." *Chōsen Kenkyū* 188, no. 4 (1979).

Mizuno Naoki. "Nihon no chōsen shihai to chianijihō." In *Chōsen no kindaishi to nihon*, edited by Hatada Takeshi, 127–140. Tokyo: Yamato Shobō, 1987.

Mizuno Naoki. "Senjiki chōsen ni okeru chian seisaku: 'Shisō jōka kōsaku' to yamato-juku o chūshin ni." *Rekishigaku Kenkyū*, no. 777 (July 2003): 1–12.

Mizuno Naoki. "Senjiki chōsen no chianiji taisei." In *Iwanami kōza: Ajia • Taiheiyō sensō 6: Shihai to bōryoku*, edited by Kurosawa Aiko et al., 95–122. Tokyo: Iwanami Shoten, 2006.

Mizuno Naoki. "Shisō kenji-tachi no 'senchū' to 'sengo': Shokuminchi shihai to shisō kenji." In *Nihon no Chōsen • Taiwan shihai to shokuminchi kanryō*, edited by Matsuda Toshihiko and Yamada Atsushi, 472–493. Kyoto: Shibunkaku Shuppan, 2009.

Mizuno Naoki. "Shokuminchi dokuritsu undō ni taisuru chianijihō no tekiyō." In *Shokuminchi teikoku nihon no hōteki kōzō*, edited by Asano Toyomi and Matsuda Toshihiko, 417–459. Tokyo: Shinzansha Shuppan, 2004.

Monbushō, ed. *Kokutai no Hongi*. Tokyo: Monbushō, 1937.

Monbushō, ed. *Kokutai no Hongi: The Cardinal Principles of the National Entity of Japan*. Translated by John Owen Gauntlett. Cambridge, MA: Harvard University Press, 1949.

Montag, Warren. *Althusser and His Contemporaries: Philosophy's Perpetual War*. Durham, NC: Duke University Press, 2013.

Montag, Warren. "'The Soul Is the Prison of the Body': Althusser and Foucault, 1970–1975." *Yale French Studies*, no. 88 (1995): 53–77.

Morita Akira. "Taishō shōnenhō no shikō to 'shihō hogo' no gainen." *Hanzai Shakai Kenkyū* 20 (1997), 64–86.

Moriya Katsuhiko. *Shōnen no hikō to kyōiku: Shōnen hōsei no rekishi to genjō.* Tokyo: Keisōshobō, 1977.

Moriyama Takeichirō. *Shisōhan hogo kansatsu hō kaisetsu.* Tokyo: Shōkadō Shoten, 1937.

Moriyama Takeichirō. "Hogo kansatsu no yōhi kettei no hyōjun." In *Shisōhan hogo kansatsu hō*, edited by Aomori Hogo Kansatsusho (1937). In Ogino, *Chianijihō kankei shiryōshū*, vol. 3, 69–71.

Mun Gyong Su. "Nihon kyōsantō to zainichi chōsenjin." In *Zainichi chōsenjin mondai no kigen*, 131–150. Musashino: Kurein, 2007.

Murai Hisashirō. "Fubo ha saijō no kami nari." In Saotome, *Tenkōsha no shuki*, 74–94.

Murthy, Viren, Fabian Schafer, and Max Ward, eds. *Confronting Capital and Empire: Rethinking Kyoto School Philosophy.* Leiden: Brill, 2017.

Myers, Ramon H., and Mark R. Peattie, eds. *The Japanese Colonial Empire, 1895–1945.* Princeton, NJ: Princeton University Press, 1984.

Nabeyama Sadachika. "Mizuno shigeoron ni shokuhatsu sareta." *Ronsō* 4:10, no. 19 (November 1962): 215–221.

Nabeyama Sadachika. "Tenkō o megutte." In *Kataritsugu shōwashi*, vol. 1, edited by Itō Takashi, 209–261. Tokyo: Asahi Bunko, 1990.

Nagashima, Atsushi. "The Accused and Society: The Administration of Criminal Justice in Japan" (excerpt). In

The Japanese Legal System: Introductory Cases and Materials, edited by Hideo Tanaka, 541–547. Tokyo: University of Tokyo Press, 1976.

Naikaku Jōhōbu, ed. *Shisosen kōshūkai kōgi sokki*, vols. 1–4. Tokyo: Naikaku Jōhōbu, 1938.

Naikaku Jōhōbu, ed. *Shisōsenten: Dainimen.* Tokyo: Naikaku Jōhōbu, 1940.

Naikaku Jōhōbu, ed. *Shisōsen tenrankai kiroku zukan.* Tokyo: Naikaku Jōhōbu, 1938.

Naimushō. "Chianijihōchū ni 'seitai henkaku' ni kansuru kitei o mōbeku shi to suru an ni taisuru hantai riyū" (1934). In Ogino, *Chianijihō kankei shiryōshū*, vol. 2, 41.

Naimushō Keihokyoku, ed. "Chianijihō kaisei hōritsuan." In Ogino, *Chianijihō kankei shiryōshū*, vol. 2, 46–76.

Nakamura, Takafusa. "Depression, Recovery and War, 1920–1945." In *Cambridge History of Japan*, vol. 6: *The Twentieth Century*, edited by Peter Duus, 451–493. Cambridge: Cambridge University Press, 1988.

Nakamura Yoshirō. "Genka ni okeru shisōtaisaku." *Kyōiku Panfuretto*, no. 323 (November 1938).

Nakamura Yoshirō. "Tenkō o yōsei sarete iru mono ha shisō jiken kankeisha nomi de nai." *Kakushin*, December 1938, 171–180.

Nakano Sumio. "Sano, Nabeyama tenkō no shinsō." *Kaizo*, July 1933, 200–204.

Nakazawa Shunsuke. *Chianijihō: Naze seitō seiji ha 'akuhō' o unda ka.* Tokyo: Chūōkō Shinsho, 2012.

Nihon Keisatsusha, ed. *Shisō keisatsu tsūron*, rev. ed. Tokyo: Nihon Keisatsusha, 1940.

Nihon Kyōsantō Chūōiinkai. "Shakai fashisuto kaitōha o funsai seyo!" *Mushin Panfuretto*, no. 10 (September 1931).

Nimura Kazuo. "Kantō daishinsai to kameido jiken." *Rekishi Hyōron* 281 (October 1973): 39–69.

Nishikawa Hiroshi. "Zainichi chōsenjin kyōsantōin • dōchō no jittai: Kei-hokyoku shiryō ni yoru 1930nendai zenhanki no tōkeiteki bunseki." *Jinbun Gakuhō* 50 (March 1981): 31–53.

Nolte, Sharon. "National Morality and Universal Ethics: Onishi Hajime and the Imperial Rescript on Education." *Monumenta Nipponica* 38, no. 3 (autumn 1983): 283–294.

Odanaka Toshiki. "Dai ichi kyōsantō jiken: Nihon kyōsantō sōritsu to chianijihō jidai zenya no saiban." In *Nihon seiji saiban shiroku 3: Taishō*, edited by Wagatsuma Sakae, 339–378. Tokyo: Daiichi Hōki Shuppan, 1968–1970.

Odanaka Toshiki. "Jinmin sensen jiken: Hansen • hanfashizumu seiryoku e no danatsu." In *Nihon seiji saiban shiroku 5: Shōwa • go*, edited by Wagatsuma Sakae, 273–328. Tokyo: Daiichi Hōki Shuppan, 1968–1970.

Ogino Fujio, ed. *Chianijihō kankei shiryōshū*, 4 vols. Tokyo: Shinnihon Shuppansha, 1996.

Ogino Fujio. "Kaisetsu: Chianijihō sei-ritsu • 'kaisei' shi." In Ogino, *Chianijihō kankei shiryōshū*, vol. 4, 505–771.

Ogino Fujio. *Sengo kōan taisei no kaku-ritsu*. Tokyo: Iwanami Shoten, 1999.

Ogino Fujio. *Shisō kenji*. Tokyo: Iwanami Shoten, 2000.

Ogino Fujio. *Shōwa tennō to chian taisei*. Tokyo: Shinnihon Shuppansha, 1993.

Ogino Fujio. *Tokkō keisatsu*. Tokyo: Iwanami Shoten, 2012.

Ogino Fujio. *Yokohama jiken to chianijihō*. Tokyo: Kinohanasha, 2006.

Ōhara Shakai Mondai Kenkyūsho, ed. *Taiheiyō sensōka no rōdō undō*. Tokyo: Rōdō Junpōsha, 1965.

Oka, Yoshitake. *Konoe Fumimaro: A Political Biography*. Tokyo: University of Tokyo Press, 1983.

Okudaira Yasuhiro. "Chianijihō ni okeru yobō kōkin." In *Fashizumuki no kokka to shakai 4: Senji nihon no hōtaisei*, edited by Tokyo Daigaku Shakai Kagaku Kenkyūsho, 165–229. Tokyo: Tokyo Daigaku Shuppansha, 1979.

Okudaira Yasuhiro. *Chianijihō shōshi*, new ed. Tokyo: Iwanami Shoten, 2006.

Okudaira Yasuhiro, ed. *Gendaishi shiryō 45: Chianijihō*. Tokyo: Misuzu Shobō, 1973.

Okudaira Yasuhiro. "Shiryō kaisetsu." In *Gendaishi shiryō 45: Chianijihō*, edited by Okudaira Yasuhiro. Tokyo: Misuzu Shobō, 1973.

Okudaira Yasuhiro. "Some Preparatory Notes for the Study of the Peace Preservation Law in Pre-war Japan." *Annals of the Institute of Social Science* 14 (1973): 49–69.

Ōya Shōichi. "Mizuno shigeo-ron." *Bungei shunju*, 33, no. 22 (December 1955): 124–135.

Park Kyong-sik. "Chianijihō ni yoru chōsenjin danatsu" (1976). In *Tennōsei kokka to zainichi chōsenjin*, 87–130. Tokyo: Shakai Hyōronsha, 1986.

Park Kyong-sik. *Tennōsei kokka to zainichi chōsenjin*. Tokyo: Shakai Hyōronsha, 1986.

Person, John. "Between Patriotism and Terrorism: The Policing of Nationalist Movements in 1930s Japan." *Journal of Japanese Studies* 43, no. 2 (summer 2017): 289–318.

Poulantzas, Nicos. *Fascism and Dictatorship: The Third International and the Problem of Fascism*. Translated by Judith White. London: Verso, 1979.

Poulantzas, Nicos. "Internationaliza-
tion of Capitalist Relations and the
Nation-State." In *The Poulantzas
Reader: Marxism, Law and the State*,
edited by James Martin, 220–257.
London: Verso, 2008.

Poulantzas, Nicos. *State, Power, Socialism*. Translated by Patrick Camiller.
London: Verso, 2014.

Read, Jason. *The Micro-politics of Capital:
Marx and the Prehistory of the Present*.
Albany: State University of New York
Press, 2003.

Rehmann, Jan. *Theories of Ideology: The
Powers of Alienation and Subjection*.
Chicago: Haymarket, 2013.

Rimer, J. Thomas, ed. *Culture and Identity:
Japanese Intellectuals during the Interwar
Years*. Princeton, NJ: Princeton Univer-
sity Press, 1990.

Robinson, Michael. "Forced Assimilation,
Mobilization, and War." In *Korea Old
and New: A History*, edited by Carter J.
Eckert, Ki-baik Lee, Young Ick Lew,
Michael Robinson, and Edward W.
Wagner, 305–326. Cambridge, MA:
Harvard University Press, 1990.

Robinson, Michael. "Ideological Schism
in the Korean Nationalist Movement,
1920–1930: Cultural Nationalism and
the Radical Critique." *Journal of Korean
Studies* 4 (1982–1983): 241–268.

Rosdolsky, Roman. "The Workers and the
Fatherland: A Note on a Passage in the
'Communist Manifesto.'" *Science and
Society* 29, no. 3 (1965): 330–337.

Ryang, Sonia. "The Great Kantō Earthquake and the Massacre of Koreans
in 1923: Notes on Japan's Modern
National Sovereignty." *Anthropological Quarterly* 76, no. 4 (autumn 2003):
731–748.

Ryle, Gilbert. *The Concept of Mind*. London: Penguin, 2000.

Sakai, Naoki. "Ethnicity and Species: On
the Philosophy of the Multiethnic State
and Japanese Imperialism." In *Confronting Capital and Empire: Rethinking
Kyoto School Philosophy*, edited by
Viren Murthy, Fabian Schafer, and Max
Ward, 143–175. Leiden: Brill, 2017.

Sano Manabu. *Sano Manabu chosakushū*. 5
vols. Tokyo, Sano Manabu chosakushū
kankōkai 1959.

Sano Manabu and Nabeyama Sadachika.
"Kinpaku seru naigai jōsei to nihon
minzoku oyobi sono rōdōsha kaikyū
sensō oyobi naibu kaikaku no sekkin
o mae ni shite komintaan oyobi nihon
kyōsantō o jiko hihan suru." *Shisō
shiryō*, May 1933.

Sano Manabu and Nabeyama Sadachika.
"Kyōdō hikoku dōshi ni tsuguru sho"
(1933). In Sano Manabu, *Sano Manabu
chosakushū*, vol. 1, 3–20. Tokyo, Sano
Manabu chosakushū kankōkai 1959.

Sano Manabu and Nabeyama Sadachika,
"A Letter to Our Fellow Defendants,"
trans. Andrew Barshay and Carl Freire,
in *Sources of Japanese Tradition*, 2nd ed.,
vol. 2, ed. Wm. Theodore de Bary,
Carol Gluck, and Arthur E. Tiedman,
940–947. New York: Columbia University Press, 2005.

Sano Manabu and Nabeyama Sadachika,
eds. *Nihonkyōsantō oyobi komintaan
hihan: Ikkoku shakaishugi ni tsuite*.
Tokyo: Musansha, 1934.

Saotome Yūgorō, ed. *Tenkōsha no shuki*.
Tokyo: Daidōsha, 1933.

Sartre, Jean-Paul. *Being and Nothingness:
A Phenomenological Essay on Ontology*.
Translated by Hazel E. Barnes. New
York: Washington Square, 1953.

Satō Takumi. "The System of Total
War and the Discursive Space of
the Thought War." In *Total War and
"Modernization,"* edited by Yamanou-

chi Yasushi, J. Victor Koschmann, and Ryuichi Narita, 289–313. Ithaca, NY: Cornell University East Asia Program, 1998.

Schencking, J. Charles. *The Great Kanto Earthquake and the Chimera of National Reconstruction in Japan.* New York: Columbia University Press, 2013.

Scheuerman, William. *Between the Norm and the Exception: The Frankfurt School and the Rule of Law.* Cambridge, MA: MIT Press, 1994.

Schmid, Andre. "Colonialism and the 'Korea Problem' in the Historiography of Modern Japan: A Review." *Journal of Asian Studies* 59, no. 4 (November 2000): 951–976.

Schmitt, Carl. *Political Theology: Four Chapters on the Concept of Sovereignty.* Translated by George Schwab. Chicago: University of Chicago Press, 1985.

Seifu. "Chianijihō [Kaisei hōritsuan]" (1934). In Ogino, *Chianijihō kankei shiryōshū*, vol. 2, 33–36.

Seifu. "Chian ijihō kaisei hōritsu shikō kijitsu no ken" (May 14, 1941). In Ogino, *Chianijihō kankei shiryōshū*, vol. 4, 105.

Seifu. "Fuhō danketsu nado shobatsu ni kansuru hōritsuan." In Ogino, *Chianijihō kankei shiryōshū*, vol. 2, 226–227.

Seifu. "Kantōshū shisōhan hogo kansatsu rei," "Kantōshū hogo kansatsusho kansei," and "Kantōshū hogo kansatsu shinsakai kansei" (December 18, 1936). In Ogino, *Chianijihō kankei shiryōshū*, vol. 3, 53–55.

Seifu. "Shin chianijihō" (March 10, 1941). In Ogino, *Chianijihō kankei shiryōshū*, vol. 4, 69–75.

Seifu. "Shisōhan hogo kansatsu hō shikō kijitsu no ken" (Ordinance 400), "Shisōhan hogo kansatsu hō shikō rei" (Ordinance 401), "hogo kansatsu sho

kansei" (Ordinance 403), and "Hogo kansatsu shinsakai kansei" (Ordinance 405), (November 14, 1936). In Ogino, *Chianijihō kankei shiryōshū*, vol. 3, 47–51.

Seimeikai, ed. *Shisō tenkōsha ha ika ni katsudō shite iru ka.* Osaka: Seimeikai, 1937.

Serizawa Kazuya. *"Hō" kara kaihō sareru kenryoku: Hanzai, kyōki, hinkon soshite taishō demokurashi.* Tokyo: Shinyōsha, 2001.

Shakai Mondai Shiryō Kenkyūkai, ed. *Chianijihōan giji sokkiroku narabi ni iin kaigi roku: Dai 50 kai teikoku gikai.* Tokyo: Tōyō Bunkasha, 1972.

Shakai Mondai Shiryō Kenkyūkai, ed. *Chianijihō ni kansuru giji sokkiroku narabi ni innkai giroku: Dai65kai teikoku gikai.* Tokyo: Tōyō Bunkasha, 1975.

Shakai Mondai Shiryō Kenkyūkai, ed. *Shisōhan hogo kansatsu hō ni kansuru sokkiroku: Dai69kai teikoku gikai.* Tokyo: Tōyō Bunkasha, 1973.

Sharp, Jasper. *Historical Dictionary of Japanese Cinema.* Lanham, MD: Scarecrow, 2011.

Shigeto, Yukiko. "The Politics of Writing: Tenkō and the Crisis of Representation." PhD diss., University of Washington, 2009.

Shihō Hogo Jigyō Renmei, ed. *Shihō hogo sōsho dai 19 shū: Kōa no soseki.* Tokyo: Zen Nihon Shihō Hogo Jigyō Renmei, 1939.

Shihōshō. "Chianijihōan sankō shiryō" (February 1934). In Ogino, *Chianijihō kankei shiryōshū*, vol. 2, 77–95.

Shihōshō. "Chianijihō kaisei an: Gikai teishutsu ni kettei, 'Yobō kōkin' ha sakujo" (January 1935). In Ogino, *Chianijihō kankei shiryōshū*, vol. 2, 222–223.

Shihōshō. "Dai ikkai hogo kansatsu shochō kaidō gijiroku" (November

25–26, 1936). In Ogino, *Chianijihō kankei shiryōshū*, vol. 3, 89–169.

Shihōshō. "Hogo kansatsu sho no kakujū." In Ogino, *Chianijihō kankei shiryōshū*, vol. 3, 353–355.

Shihōshō. "Kaisei chii hōan kara yobō kōkinsei o sakujo" (September 1934). In Ogino, *Chianijihō kankei shiryōshū*, vol. 2, 222.

Shihōshō. "Shisō gyōkei sankō shiryō" (February 1934). In Ogino, *Chianijihō kankei shiryōshū*, vol. 2, 95–99.

Shihōshō. "Shisōhan hogo kansatsu hō shikō rei dai san jō ni okeru tsūchi yōshiki ni kansuru ken" (February 4, 1937). In Ogino, *Chianijihō kankei shiryōshū*, vol. 3, 60–61.

Shihōshō Daijin Kanbō Hogoka, ed. *Shihō hogo shiryō 5: Hogo kansatsu seido sankō shiryō jō.* Tokyo: Shihōshō Daijin Kanbō Hogoka, 1936.

Shihōshō Daijin Kanbō Hogoka, ed. *Shihō hogo shiryō 6: Hogo kansatsu seido sankō shiryō chū.* Tokyo: Shihōshō Daijin Kanbō Hogoka, 1936.

Shihōshō Keijikyoku. "Chianijihō kaiseian sankō shiryō" (March 8, 1935). In Ogino, *Chianijihō kankei shiryōshū*, vol. 2, 228–237.

Shihōshō Keijikyoku. "Chianijihō kaisei hōritsuan" (December 13, 1933). In Ogino, *Chianijihō kankei shiryōshū*, vol. 2, 30–33.

Shihōshō Keijikyoku. "Shisō jimuka kaidō gijiroku" (May 1940). In Ogino, *Chianijihō kankei shiryōshū*, vol. 4, 19–63.

Shihōshō Keijikyoku, ed. *Shisō shiryō panfuretto tokushū 12: Tokuda Kyūichi, Shiga Yoshio, Fukumoto Kazuo ni kansuru yobōkōkin seikyū jiken kiroku.* Tokyo: Shihōshō Keijikyoku, December 1942.

Shihōshō Keijikyoku Shisōbu. "Nihon kyōsantō chūōbu kankei hikokunin ni taisuru tōkyō chihō saibansho hanketsu." In *Shisō kenkyū shiryō*, Tokushū No. 2, edited by Shihōshō Keijikyoku. Tokyo: Shihōshō Keijikyoku, 1932.

Shihōshō Keijikyoku Shisōbu, ed. "Shisō jimu ni kansuru kunrei tsūchoshū." *Shisō kenkyū shiryō*, Tokushū 1 gō, September 1932, 15–19.

Shihōshō Keijikyoku Shisōbu, ed. *Dai45kai teikoku gikai: Kageki shakai undō torishimari hōan giji sokkiroku narabini iinkai giji sokkiroku.* Shisō kenkyū shiryō, Tokushū 10 gō (Tokyo: Shihōshō keijikyoku, 1934). Republished by Shakai Mondai Shiryō Kenkyūkai, vol. 1, no. 8. Tokyo: Tōyō Bunkasha, 1972.

Shimane Kiyoshi. "Nihon kyōsantō rōdōsha-ha: Mizuno Shigeo." In *Kyōdō kenkyū: Tenkō*, vol. 1, edited by Shisō No Kagaku Kenkyūkai, 150–163. Tokyo: Heibonsha, 1959.

Shimane Kiyoshi. *Tenkō: Meiji ishin to bakushin.* Tokyo: Sanichi Shobō, 1969.

Shin, Gi-Wook, and Michael Robinson, eds. *Colonial Modernity in Korea.* Cambridge, MA: Harvard University Press, 1999.

Shiono Suehiko. "Jo." In Saotome, *Tenkōsha no shuki*, 1–2.

Shisō Jimukai, ed. "Tenkō ni kansuru jikō" (May 1934). In *Shisō jimukai dō gijiroku*, edited by Shakai mondai shiryō kenkyūkai, 1–143. Tokyo: Tōyō Bunkasha, 1976.

Shisō No Kagaku Kenkyūkai, ed. *Kyōdō kenkyū: Tenkō*, 3 vols. Tokyo: Heibonsha, 1959–1962.

Shōtokukai. "Zaidan hōjin shōtokukai gaiyō" (August 1936). In Ogino, *Chianijihō kankei shiryōshū*, vol. 3, 30–34.

Shūgiin. "Chianijihō kaisei hōritsuan" (1934). In Ogino, *Chianijihō kankei shiryōshū*, vol. 2, 41–45.

Sibertin-Blanc, Guillaume. *State and Politics: Deleuze and Guattari on Marx*. Translated by Ames Hodges. Los Angeles: Semiotext(e), 2016.

Sim Kil-bok. "Chōsen ni okeru shisōhan hogo jigyō no kensetsu no tame ni." In Kobayashi, *Tenkōsha no shisō to seikatsu*, 396–406.

Sipos, George. "The Literature of Political Conversion (Tenkō) of Japan." PhD diss., University of Chicago, 2013.

Skya, Walter A. *Japan's Holy War: The Ideology of Radical Shintō Ultranationalism*. Durham, NC: Duke University Press, 2009.

Smith, Carole. "The Sovereign State v Foucault: Law and Disciplinary Power." *Sociological Review* 48 (2000): 283–306.

Smith, Henry. *Japan's First Student Radicals*. Cambridge, MA: Harvard University Press, 1972.

Steinhoff, Patricia G. "Tenkō." In *Kodansha Encyclopedia of Japan*, vol. 8, 6–7. Tokyo: Kodansha, 1983.

Steinhoff, Patricia G. *Tenkō: Ideology and Societal Integration in Prewar Japan*. New York: Garland, 1991.

Steinhoff, Patricia G. "Tenkō and Thought Control." In *Japan and the World: Essays on Japanese History and Politics in Honour of Ishida Takeshi*, edited by Gail Lee Bernstein and Haruhiro Fukui, 78–94. New York: St. Martin's, 1988.

Steinmetz, George, ed. *State/Culture: State-Formation after the Cultural Turn*. Ithaca, NY: Cornell University Press, 1999.

Suzuki Kazuhisa. "Waga kuni no kōsei hogo jigyō no hatten to kokusaiteki hanzaisha shogū no dōkō." In *Kōsei hogo no kadai to tenbō: Kōsei hogo seido shikō 50shūnen kinen ronbunshū*, 131–160. Tokyo: Nihon Kōsei Hogo Kyōkai, 1999.

Suzuki Keifu. *Chōsen shokuminchi tōchihō no kenkyū: Chianhō ka no kōminka kyōiku*. Sapporo: Hokkaidō Daigaku Tosho Kankōkai, 1989.

Suzuki Takeshi. *Sano manabu ichimi o hōtei ni okuru made*. Tokyo: Keiyūsha, 1931.

Takeda Kiyoko. *The Dual-Image of the Japanese Emperor*. Translated by Ian Nash. New York: New York University Press, 1988.

Takeda Kiyoko. *Tennōkan no sōkoku: 1945nen zengo*. Tokyo: Iwanami Shoten, 1978.

Takeuchi Yoshimi. *What Is Modernity? Writings of Takeuchi Yoshimi*. Translated by Richard F. Calichman. New York: Columbia University Press, 2005.

Takeuchi Yoshitomo, ed. *Gendai nihon shisō taikei 21: Marukushizumu II*. Tokyo: Chikuma Shobō, 1965.

Takizawa Ichirō. *Nihon sekishoku kyūenkai shi*. Tokyo: Nihon Hyōronsha, 1993.

Takumushō Kanrikyoku. "Chōsen ni okeru shisō hanzai chōsa shiryō" (two parts, issued March 1935). In Ogino, *Chianijihō kankei shiryōshū*, vol. 2, 257–285, 286–317.

Takumushō Kanrikyoku. "Taiwan ni okeru shisō undō chōsa shiryō" (March 1935). In Ogino, *Chianijihō kankei shiryōshū*, vol. 2, 317–323.

Tanaka Hideo, ed. *The Japanese Legal System: Introductory Cases and Materials*. Tokyo: University of Tokyo Press, 1976.

Tanaka Tokihiko. "Toranomon jiken: Kōtaishi o sogeki shita Nanba Daisuke." In Wagatsuma, *Nihon seiji saiban shiroku*, vol. 3: *Taishō*, 439–483.

Tansman, Alan. *The Aesthetics of Japanese Fascism*. Berkeley: University of California Press, 2008.

Terada Seiichi. "Chōsen ni okeru hanzai genshō no tokuchō." *Hōseikai kaihō* 4, no. 3 (May 1920): 1–36.

Tipton, Elise. *The Japanese Police State: The Tokkō in Interwar Japan*. Sydney: Allen and Unwin, 1990.

Tokuoka Kazuo. *Chianijihō ihan jiken no saihan ni kansuru kenkyū*. Tokyo: Shihōshō Kejikyoku, 1938.

Tokyo Hogo Kansatsu Sho. *Jimu seiseki hōkoku sho* (1937). In Ogino, *Chianijihō kankei shiryōshū*, vol. 3, 175–224.

Tomita Kenji. "Shisōsen to keisatsu." In *Shisōsen kōshūkai kōgi sokki*, vol. 3, edited by Naikaku Jōhōbu, 113–136. Tokyo: Naikaku Jōhōbu, 1938.

Tozawa Shigeo. "Shisō hanzai no kensatsu jitsumu ni tsuite" (1933). In *Gendaishi Shiryō*, vol. 16: *Shakaishugi undō 3*, edited by Yamabe Kintarō, 15–36. Tokyo: Misuzu Shobō, 1963.

Tsuchiya Shukurō. *Yobō kōkin sho*. Tokyo: Banseisha, 1988.

Tsunazawa Mitsuaki. *Nō no shisō to nihon kindai*. Nagoya: Fubaisha, 2004.

Tsurumi, Kazuko. "Six Types of Change in Personality: Case Studies of Ideological Conversion in the 1930's." In *Social Change and the Individual: Japan before and after Defeat in World War II*, 29–79. Princeton, NJ: Princeton University Press, 1970.

Tsurumi Shunsuke. *An Intellectual History of Wartime Japan, 1931–1945*. London: KPI, 1986.

Tsurumi Shunsuke. "Kokumin to iu katamari ni umekomarete." In *Tenkō sairon*, edited by Tsurumi Shunsuke, Suzuki Tadashi, and Iida Momo, 7–30. Tokyo: Heibonsha, 2001.

Tsurumi Shunsuke. "Tenkō no kyōdō kenkyū ni tsuite." In *Kyōdō kenkyū: Tenkō*, vol. 1, edited by Shisō no Kagaku Kenkyūkai, 1–27. Tokyo: Heibonsha, 1959.

Uchida Hirofumi. *Chianijihō no kyōkun: kenri undō to kenpō kaisei*. Tokyo: Misuzu Shobō, 2016.

Uchida Hirofumi. *Chianijihō to kyōbōzai*. Tokyo: Iwanami Shoten, 2017.

Uchida Hirofumi. *Keihō to sensō: Senji chian hōsei no tsukurikata*. Tokyo: Misuzu Shobō, 2015.

Uchida Hirofumi. *Kōsei hogo no tenkai to kadai*. Kyoto: Hōritsu Bunkasha, 2015.

Uchikawa Yoshimi. "Naikaku jōhōkyoku no setsuritsu katei: Nihon fashizumu keiseiki no masu media soshikika seisaku." In *Masu mediahō seisakushi kenkyū*, 193–237. Tokyo: Yuhikaku, 1989.

Ueda, Atsuko, Michael Bourdaghs, Richi Sakakibara, and Hirokazu Toeda, eds. *The Politics and Literature Debate in Postwar Japanese Criticism, 1945–1952*. Lanham, MD: Lexington, 2017.

Ueda Seikichi. *Shōwa saibanshi ron: Chianijihō to hōritsukatachi*. Tokyo: Ōtsuki Shoten, 1983.

Umemori Naoyuki. "Modernization through Colonial Mediations: The Establishment of the Police and Prison System in Meiji Japan." PhD diss., University of Chicago, 2002.

Uno, Kathleen. "The Death of 'Good Wife, Wise Mother'?" In *Postwar Japan as History*, edited by Andrew Gordon, 293–322. Berkeley: University of California Press, 1993.

Ushiomi Toshitaka. *Chianijihō*. Tokyo: Iwanami Shoten, 1977.

Uyehara, Cecil H. *The Subversive Activities Prevention Law: Its Creation, 1951–1952*. Leiden: Brill, 2010.

Wagatsuma Sakae, ed. *Nihon seiji saiban shiroku.* Tokyo: Daiichi Hōki Shuppan, 1968–1970.

Wakabayashi, Bob Tadashi. *Anti-foreignism and Western Learning in Early Modern Japan: The New Theses of 1825.* Harvard East Asian Monographs 126. Cambridge, MA: Harvard University Press, 1992.

Walker, Gavin. "Primitive Accumulation and the Formation of Difference: On Marx and Schmitt." *Rethinking Marxism* 23, no. 3 (2011): 384–404.

Walker, Gavin. *The Sublime Perversion of Capital: Marxist Theory and the Politics of History in Modern Japan.* Durham, NC: Duke University Press, 2016.

Ward, Max. "Crisis Ideology and the Articulation of Fascism in Interwar Japan: The 1938 Thought-War Symposium." *Japan Forum* 26, no. 4 (2014): 462–485.

Ward, Max. "Displaying the Worldview of Japanese Fascism: The Tokyo Thought War Exhibition of 1938." *Critical Asian Studies* 47, no. 3 (2015): 414–439.

Ward, Max. "Historical Difference and the Question of East Asian Marxism(s)." In *East Asian Marxisms and Their Trajectories*, edited by Joyce Liu and Viren Murthy, 87–102. Interventions Series. London: Routledge, 2017.

Ward, Max. "Ideology and Subjection in Ōshima Nagisa's *Kōshikei* (1968)." In *Perspectives on Oshima Nagisa.* UTCP-Uehiro Pamphlet No. 7 (2015), 33–59.

Ward, Max. "The Problem of 'Thought': Crisis, National Essence and the Interwar Japanese State." PhD diss., New York University, 2011.

Washburn, Dennis, and A. Kevin Reinhart, eds. *Converting Cultures: Religion, Ideology and Transformations of Modernity.* Leiden: Brill, 2007.

Yagami, Kazuo. *Konoe Fumimaro and the Failure of Peace in Japan, 1937–1941.* Jefferson, NC: McFarland, 2006.

Yamabe Kintarō, ed. *Gendaishi Shiryō 16: Shakaishugi undō 3.* Tokyo: Misuzu Shobō, 1963.

Yamada Kenji. "Miyagi Chōgorō." *Tsumi to batsu* 34, no. 1 (1996): 47–53.

Yamagata Jirō. "Nanzan no shisōhan hogo kansatsu hōan." *Hogo Jihō* 20, no. 2 (February 1936): 9–18.

Yamagata Jirō. "Shisōhan hogo kansatsu hō no unyō ni kansuru yōbō." *Hogo Jihō* 21, no. 1 (January 1937): 34–36.

Yamaguchi Hayato. "Kyōsanshugi yori shūkyō e." In Saotome, *Tenkōsha no shuki*, 1–42.

Yamamoto Katsunosuke. *Nihon kyōsanshugi undōshi.* Tokyo: Seki Shobō, 1950.

Yamaryō Kenji. *Tenkō no jidai to chishiki-jin.* Tokyo: Sanichi Shobō, 1978.

Yokomizo Mitsuteru. "Shisōsen ni tsuite." In *Shisōsen tenrankai kiroku zukan*, edited by Naikaku jōhōbu, 1–3. Tokyo: Naikaku Jōhōbu, 1938.

Yoshida Hajime. "Chōsen ni okeru shisōhan no kakei narabini ruihan jōkyō" (1939). Shisō jōsei shisatsu hōkokushū (Sono 6) in *Shisō kenkyū shiryō: Tokushū dai 69 gō*, edited by Shihōshō Keijikyoku. Reprinted in *Shakai mondai shiryō sōsho: Dai 1 shū.* Tokyo: Tōyō Bunkasha, 1971.

Yoshimi Yoshiaki. *Grassroots Fascism: The War Experience of the Japanese People.* Translated by Ethan Mark. New York: Columbia University Press, 2015.

Yoshimoto Takaaki. "Tenkōron" (1958). In *Yoshimoto Takaaki Zenhūsen*, vol. 3: *Seiji shisō*, 9–34. Tokyo: Daiwa Shobō, 1986.

Yoshimoto Takaaki. "On Tenkō, or Ideological Conversion" (1958), translated by Hisaaki Wake. In *Translation in Modern Japan*, edited by Indra Levy, 102–121. London: Routledge, 2011.

Young, Louise. *Japan's Total Empire: Manchuria and the Culture of Wartime*

Imperialism. Berkeley: University of California Press, 1998.

Yuasa Katsuei. *Kannani and Document in Flames: Two Japanese Colonial Novels*. Translated by Mark Driscoll. Durham, NC: Duke University Press, 2005.

Yūgami Kōichi. "Jidai haikei ni tsuite." In *"Tenkōki" no hitobito: Chianijihōka no katsudōka gunzō*, by Kobayashi Morito, 268–277. Tokyo: Shinjidaisha, 1987.

Žižek, Slavoj. "The Spectre of Ideology." In *Mapping Ideology*, edited by Slavoj Žižek, 1–33. New York: Verso, 1994.

Žižek, Slavoj. *The Sublime Object of Ideology*. London: Verso, 2008.

Foucault, Michel, 11, 14, 54–55, 74–75, 116, 120, 143,
195n54, 208n18, 209n24, 209n29, 209n30, 234n9;
Discipline and Punish (1975), 53, 194n50; on dispositif,
87, 223n38; governmentality and, 17, 53, 56, 115; on
governmentalization of state, 139, 142; *History of
Sexuality*, Volume 1 (1976), 53; on ideology, 11–12;
power and, 13, 16, 51, 52, 55, 89, 192n35, 193n41, 194n48,
208n17, 208n20, 209n25, 225n55, 230n120, 235n112
4.16 Incident (1929), 61–62, 105
framing, frames, 26, 54, 56
France, 168
freedom of speech, 33. *See also* public speech
Friendship Society (Dōyūkai), 129, 137
Friere, Carl, 219n6
Fujii Eshō, 81, 104, 141; as chaplain, 129, 219n9,
226n65, 247n142; Imperial Renovation Society
and, 92, 130, 236n28, 245n122; Kobayashi and,
68–69, 91–92, 95, 122, 227n73, 232n150; "Reform
Methods for Paroled Thought Criminals," 118–20;
True Pure Land Buddhism and, 115–16; *Yomiuri
Shimbun* articles by, 82–83
Fujitani, Takashi, 6, 27–28, 36, 156, 194n48, 194n50,
248n9, 251n43
Fujita Shōzō, 6, 190n21
Fukunaga Misao, 219n7
Fukuoka, 166
Furuta Masatake, writes police training pamphlet,
46–47, 206n128

gaichi (outer territories), 33–34, 63, 213n76. *See also*
naichi (inner territory)
Gakuren (Gakusei shakaikagaku kenkyūkai; Student
Federation of Social Science), 57, 210n33
Gakuren Incident (1925), 58
Garon, Sheldon, 5, 6, 188n7, 189n16
genealogical method, 209n29
General Election Law (Futsū senkyo hō), 1925, 36
German Institute on Radicalization and Deradical-
ization Studies (GIRDS), xi
Germany, 132, 153, 166
ghost in the machine, 192n30; as metaphor, 3, 95, 145;
tennōsei as, 7–11
ghosts: of imperial state, 50, 125; of imperial subject
and subjectivity, 110, 111, 120, 125, 147; of Peace
Preservation Law apparatus, 114, 182; of reform
apparatuses, 183
Gluck, Carol, 6
Goldstein, Jan, 54, 56, 209n25
Gotō Fumio, 135
governmentality and governmentalization, 116, 139;
Foucault and, 13, 17, 53, 55, 56, 115–16, 194n50,
230n120, 235n112; governmental techniques and,
143, 147, 177, 179; of imperial state, 139, 142–43
Great Depression, 96
Greater East Asian Coprosperity Sphere (Daitōa
kyōeiken), 160

Guantánamo Bay, xiii
guarantor system and legal guarantors (mimoto
hikiuke), 72, 92, 150, 217n130
guardians (hogosha), 70
Guattari, Félix, 198n20, 199n33
guidance counselors and officers (hogoshi), 91–93,
104, 150, 245n128
guidance officials (hodōkan), 248n10, 254n80

Hall, Stuart, 193n41
Hara Yoshimichi, 61, 213n66
Harootunian, Harry, 12, 218n2
Hayashi Raizaburō, 30, 31, 139–40, 201n53
Hegelian philosophy, 233n153
High Court, 210n39
Hiranuma Kiichirō, 60
Hirata Isao, 10, 51, 66, 166, 169, 216n108, 247–48n2,
253n66, 253n67, 253n76; career of, 1, 50, 59, 64, 65,
77, 90, 241n91; defectors and, 67–68, 81, 188n1,
237n50; Itō on, 207n9, 216n105; lectures and writings of, 2, 103, 152, 165; on mission of Protection
and Supervision Centers network, 145–46, 152;
tenkō and tenkōsha and, 82, 84, 161–63, 171
Hirohito, 37, 183
historiography of tenkō, 79
hitenkō, hi-tenkōsha (unconverted), 134, 150, 180
Hitler, Adolf, 166
Hobbes, Thomas, *Leviathan*, 8, 191n26
hogo (protection), 229n110
Hogo Jihō (Aid and Guidance) (journal), 118, 137,
151–52, 229n109, 247n142; Kobayashi's writings
in, 100, 232n151; as successor to *Hoseikai Kaihō*,
100, 229n110; on thought crime and criminals,
103, 229n111
hogoshugi (protectionism or rehabilitationism), 70,
131, 226n68
Hokkaidō Collectivist Party Incident (Hokkaidō
shūsantō jiken), 1927, 210n37
Home Minister, 40, 60, 61, 200n45, 203n68. *See also*
Home Ministry
Home Ministry, 37, 59, 69, 131, 135, 200n39, 211n49,
230n125, 242n98, 254n96, 258n6; Antiradical Bill
and, 29–30, 35, 201n59, 202n67; documents of,
33, 34; Justice Ministry and, 4, 52, 134, 244n114;
Peace Preservation Bill and Law and, 23, 39, 40,
201n55; Police Affairs Bureau (Keiho-kyoku), 38,
180, 208n16; publications and reports of, 29, 46;
Thought War Symposium and, 161–62
Honda Shūgo, 220n19, 259n15
Hong Jong-wook, 6, 19, 189n9, 246n138; on tenkō
cases in colonial Korea, 73, 141, 155, 252n56
Honor and Harmony Society (Keiwakai) in Nagano,
129
Hōritsu Shimbun (Legal Times), 103
Hoseikai Kaihō (Bulletin of the Hoseikai), 100, 229n110
Hosei University, 225n56

interpellation, 88; Althusser and, 78, 195n56, 223n36, 224n46, 234n6; of individuals as subjects, 12, 86, 218n2

Inukai Tsuyoshi, 132

investigation, 65, 234n2

ISAS (Ideological State Apparatuses), 110, 119, 217n139, 218n2, 222n35, 241n92; Althusser and, 14–15, 17, 86–89, 102, 179, 192–93n95, 195n54, 195n56, 208n18, 223n36, 223n39, 223n40; family as, 122, 165; ideologization of rehabilitation and, 114–15; Imperial Renovation Society as, 78, 89, 90, 93, 102–3, 115, 120; mass tenkō and, 110–11; Peace Preservation Law as, 11–15; rituals of, 100–103

ISIL, ix, xi

Italy, 132, 166

Itō Akira, 142, 191n24, 215n96, 219n4, 226n71, 233n155, 233n156; on defection, 67–68, 232n146; on Hirata, 207n9, 216n105

Itō Hirobumi, 63; Meiji Constitution and, 7–8, 27, 62, 191n27

Itō Noe, 36

Iwata Chūzō, 133, 241n94

Jameson, Fredric, on aporia, 6, 190n20; on vanishing mediator, 94, 227n78

Japan, 52, 91, 99, 114, 121, 124, 126, 134, 148, 161–62, 172, 210n37, 213n76; Allied Occupation of, 3, 21, 179, 182–83, 258n10; China invaded by, 2, 18, 64, 109, 142–43, 148, 152, 160–61, 175, 229n110, 235n13; communism in, 1, 33, 35, 105, 166, 211n44; family system of, 93, 97, 103; foreign relations of, 30, 35–36, 40, 61, 151; holy war of, 177–78; Koreans in, 36, 109, 126; Meiji, 7–8, 27, 62, 191n27, 194n50; mission of, 126–29, 163, 237–38n56; modernization of, 5, 190n21, 191n23, 218n3, 222n32; postwar, 179–84, 219n6; social dislocations in, 96, 106; Soviet Union and, 35–36, 40, 61. See also Japanese Empire; metropole; and names of Japanese cities

Japanese, ethnic (minzoku), 11, 159

Japanese Communist Party. See JCP

Japanese Communist Party Labor Faction (Nihon kyōsantō rōdōsha-ha), 66–68, 83, 215n98, 237n43, 237n50

Japanese Empire, 4, 5, 11, 28, 63, 66, 72, 94, 126–29, 142, 156, 168–69, 190n18, 211n44, 213n76, 233n153, 253n63; communism in, 36, 105; ideology of, 6, 128, 153; Korea and, 58, 63, 84, 127–28; law and, 29, 33–34, 179; renovation of, 146, 165, 177; sovereign power and, 10, 73–74, 159

Japanese spirit (nihon seishin), 9–11, 88, 105–6, 117–19, 124–28, 148, 153–54, 159, 162, 166–68, 193n36, 253n66; converts and, 152, 170; as integrating force, 126, 237n51; Justice Ministry and, 2, 162; Koreans and, 127–28, 141, 156, 158; mastery of, 147, 160, 164; Protection and Supervision Centers and, 145, 146

Japanism, 104

Japan Labor Union Council (Nihon rōdō kumiai hyōgikai), 211n49

Japan Red Support Group (Nihon Sekishoku Kyūenkai), 230n122

JCP (Japanese Communist Party; Nihon kyōsantō), 2, 104, 157, 173, 182, 212n53, 222n33, 228n87, 231n144, 236n28; 4.16 Incident and, 61–62; affiliates of, 50, 63; arrest and imprisonment of members of, 49, 51, 81, 92, 226n64, 233n155; calls for abolishing monarchy, 59, 61, 66–67, 86, 88, 125, 162, 212n53; Comintern and, 59, 61, 79; conversion of members of, 16, 85–86, 103; defections from, 4, 17, 65–69, 77–82, 108, 117, 121, 219n10; dissatisfaction with, 66, 84; dissolution of, 35, 65–66, 113, 131, 220n12; as illegal, xi, 35; Kobayashi and, 91, 93, 94; leaders of, 1, 64–65, 180, 226n64; members of, 49, 51, 81, 84, 92, 103, 106–7; Mizuno and, 188n1, 219n7; Sano and Nabeyama and, 82, 219n9, 220n20, 259n14. See also communism; communists

Jessop, Bob, 11, 193n35

jihadists, 187n24

judges, 207n7, 208n12, 208n16

Judicial Protection Law (Hogo shihō, No. 204), 1950, 183, 184

Judicial Protection Services Law (Shihō hogo jigyō hō), 1939, 146, 184

Judicial Protection system, postwar, 259n20

juntenkō (semiconverted), 150, 177

juridical power, 53, 73. See also sovereign-juridical power

justice, 16, 52

Justice Minister, 105, 135, 200n45; Hara as, 61, 213n66; Hayashi as, 139–40; Koyama as, 132, 133–34; Ogawa as, 40, 43–44; Suzuki as, 37–38

Justice Ministry, xii, 2, 37, 72, 99, 103, 117, 127, 131, 145–46, 181, 226n68, 230n125, 241n88, 244n115; Antiradical Bill and, 29–30, 35; Corrections Division in, 105, 231n130; Criminal Affairs Bureau, 30, 38, 157, 212n63; Home Ministry and, 4, 52, 134, 244n114; officers of, 34, 104; Peace Preservation Law and, 23, 39, 40, 208n12; procurators and, xi, 57, 207n6, 208n16; Protection Bureau of, 138, 169, 178; reformers in, 69, 70; rehabilitation and, 92, 111, 117, 138–39, 146–47, 182–83; reports and publications of, ix, 33, 46, 93, 239n72; Supreme Court and, 59–60; tenkō and, 110, 168; thought crime and, 1, 72, 82, 131, 137–38, 242n100; Thought Criminal Protection and Supervision Law and, 17, 139–40, 155; Thought War Symposium and, 161–62

juvenile delinquents (hikō shōnen), 69, 71, 130, 184; laws concerning, 69–70, 72, 182; rehabilitation of, 16, 226n68, 245n128

Kaitō-ha defections, 67–68. See also Japanese Communist Party Labor Faction

kyōka, 229n118. See also moral suasion
Kyoto, 57, 129, 166
Kyoto Imperial University, 57

labor activism and activists, 36, 59, 181, 204n90, 211n49
Labor Faction. See Japanese Communist Party Labor Faction
Labor-Farmer Faction (Rōnō-ha), 137
Labor-Farmer Party (Rōdōnōmintō), 91, 211n49
labor procurators (Rōdō gakari kenji), 181
Lacan, Jacques, 223n36
Laclau, Ernesto, 88, 224n50
law, laws, 53, 197n10, 201n53, 209n25, 209n32; in colonies, 28–29; imperial state and, 5, 25, 29, 31, 51–52, 199n33; kokutai and, 24; legal positivism and, 198n22; legal rationality and, 24, 25, 198n22; legal system and, 189n13; rule of, 208n14, 208n16; sovereignty and, 135
League of Blood Incident (Ketsumeidan jiken), 1932, 132
League of Nations, 151
Lemke, Thomas, 193n35
Lenin, Vladimir Ilyich, 37, 107
liberal education, 104
liberalism, 40, 44, 126, 139, 194n42; expunging of, 161, 164, 237n54; Western, 147, 162
Los Angeles, xiii
Loughlin, Martin, 27
Lower House of Imperial Diet, 61, 132, 135, 139, 243n106; Antiradical Bill in, 32–33; members of, 37, 135; Peace Preservation Bill in, 40, 43
Lowry, Kevin, xi
loyal and productive imperial subjects, 55, 56, 75, 89, 168; tenkōsha reformed as, 114, 116, 143, 145. See also imperial subjectivity and subjects; subject, subjects
loyalty, 23, 55, 94–95
Loyalty Research Center (Taikōjuku kenkyūsho), 117

Makino Shizuo, 135, 243n106, 243n107
Manchukuo, 64, 152, 168, 175, 214n84, 238n59, 256n123
Manchu (Qing) monarch, 175
Manchuria, 63–64, 99, 175; Manchurian Incident (1931) and, 151
manuals and textbooks, 146–47, 150
March First Movement (Korea), 29, 30
martial law, 36
Maruyama Masao, 6, 181–82, 228n102
Marx, Karl, 98, 107, 194n44
Marxism, 67, 83, 96, 101–2, 119, 121, 125–26, 156, 162–63, 198n20, 216n105, 222n32, 253n66; expunging of, 95, 237n54; Kobayashi on, 91, 95–97, 101–2, 228n93; -Leninism, 57, 97, 104; Marxists and, 106, 137; Marxist theory and, 67, 107, 109, 151; religion and, 99, 232n150; renunciation of, 84, 170, 178; structur-

alist, 11, 193n41; thought criminals and, 147, 156. See also Comintern; communism; communists; JCP
maryoku (spell), 25, 197n13
Masunaga Shōichi, 141
materialism, 97, 106, 122, 227n86
Matsuda Genji, 32, 135, 136
Matsuda Toshihiko, 160
Matsumoro Itasu, 61
May 15 Incident (1932), 132
mediation, mediators, 88, 95, 122; Imperial Renovation Society and, 78, 84, 90
Meiji Constitution (1889), 15, 24, 33, 34, 61, 198n22, 201n55, 213n76; Article 1, 10, 23, 28, 42, 44, 47, 136; Article 4, 23, 47; Emperor Organ Theory and, 134–35; Itō and, 7–8, 191n27; kokutai and, 23, 25, 47, 62; preamble to, 27; Skya on, 190–91n21
Meiji ideology, 6, 107
Meiji period, 147, 162, 208n16
Meiji state and oligarchs, 6, 8
Metalworks Vocational Center (Kinzoku jusanjō), 178
metropole, 6, 29, 50, 113, 136, 140, 155–56, 180; altering the kokutai arrests in, 59, 60; colonies vs., 16, 18, 45; Korean tenkōsha in, 126–27. See also Tokyo
Mie, Mutual Love Society in, 137
militarism, 79, 180, 184
military conscription, 34
Military Police (kempeitai), 36
Minagawa Haruhiro, 104, 117
mind and body duality, 8, 86, 95, 191nn25–26, 192n30, 194n44, 227nn84–86
Ministry of Education, 129; Fundamental Principles of the Kokutai (Kokutai no hongi), 1937, 135
Minneapolis, Somali American terrorism case in, ix–xiii
Minneapolis Terrorism Disengagement and Deradicalization Program, xiii
Minobe Incident, 236n41. See also, Minobe Tatsukichi
Minobe Tatsukichi, 134–36, 205n96, 236n41, 242n103, 243n106, 243n107
Mitamura Shirō, 65
Mitchell, Richard H., 24, 189n15, 207n5, 207–8n9, 208n16, 208n17; Bix on, 189n17, 195n63; Peace Preservation Law and, 4–5, 69, 189n9, 218n3, 234n2; on tenkō, 52, 222n31
Mitchell, Timothy, 9, 192n35; on state-effect, 193n35
Miyagi Chōgorō, 34, 70, 81, 82, 90, 226n68, 239n72; as chief procurator, 219n9, 226n65; as director of Imperial Renovation Society, 92, 93, 138; Kobayashi and, 91–92
Miyagi Minoru, 65
Miyake Masatarō, 70, 174
Mizuno Naoki, 6, 19, 34, 203n76, 204n90, 210n39, 210n41, 251n44; on colonial independence, 39, 63; on Korea, 47, 57, 74, 207n5; on Peace Preservation Law, 47, 189n9

Mizuno Shigeo, 65, 68–67, 214n93, 215n96, 215n98, 216n105, 219n7; imprisonment of, 66, 188n1

mobilization, 146, 177, 189n11, 235n13, 251n43; colonial, 154, 160; conversion and, 152–54, 178; rehabilitation and reform and, ix, 1–2, 152, 250n24; spiritual, 18, 143; tenkō and, 2, 142, 160–72; for total war, 3, 11, 116, 229n110. *See also* National Spirit Mobilization Movement

Mochizuki Keisuke, 61

modernity and modernization, 5, 198n21, 218n3, 221n22

monarchy, 243n107; JCP calls for abolition of, 59, 61, 66, 67, 86, 88, 125, 162, 212n53

Mongolian People's Republic, 168

Montag, Warren, 12, 195n58, 223–24n44

moral guidance, 104, 119, 139

moral suasion (kyōka), 5, 102, 116, 189n16, 214n92

Morito Tatsuo, 29, 200n39

Moriyama Buichirō, 50

Moriyama Takeichirō, 139, 140, 150, 241n91, 245n128; at Justice Ministry, 138–39, 146–47; on stages of conversion, 147, 254n84

Murai Hisashirō, 231n140, 233n153

Mussolini, Benito, 166

Mutual Love Society (Kyōaikai), 137

Nabeyama Sadachika, 89, 219n8, 220n15, 244n114, 259n14; arrest and imprisonment of, 64–65, 82, 219n9; defection of, 100, 103–4, 124, 131, 237n43; renounces Comintern, 79–81, 158; socialism of, 103, 105–6, 123–24, 139, 230n124; on tenkō, 85–86, 222n32

Nagai Tetsuzō, in *Tenkōsha Memoirs*, 106

Nagano, 65, 91, 94, 129

Nagoya, 129, 138, 258n10

naichi (inner territory), 33–34, 63, 213n76. *See also* gaichi (outer territories)

Nakamura Yoshirō, 146, 169, 253n76, 254n80, 256n124; on tenkō, 163–66, 171, 254n84

Nakatani Sadayori, 135, 136, 243n109, 249n14

Nakazawa Shunsuke, 63, 132, 175, 203n76, 242n98

Namba Daisuke, 37

Naoki Sakai, 156

narrative, narratives: by converts, 104–5; of religious tenkō, 99–100; of self-negation, 96

National Committee in Response to the Current Crisis (Jikyoku taiō zenkoku iinkai), 152–54

nationalism, nationalists, 79, 99, 101, 104, 124. *See also* anticolonial nationalism

national laws (kokka no kokken), 31–32

national socialism, 105–6, 124, 133

National Spirit Mobilization Movement (Kokumin seishin sōdōin undō), 3, 18, 153, 173, 178. *See also* mobilization

National Thought (*Kokumin shisō*) (journal), 117

national thought defense (shisō kokubō), 146, 161–63, 164, 169, 173, 250n24

national thought policy (shisō taisaku), 230n125

nation-state, 18, 96, 97, 126, 156, 198n21, 237n56

nativism, 98

Nazism, 132

neo-Nazis, Trump and, 187n26

New East Asian Order (Tōa shinchitsujo), 160

New Peace Preservation Law (Shin-chianijihō), 1941, 174

Newspaper Law (Shimbunshihō), 1909, 29, 199n35, 200n39

Newspaper Ordinance (Shimbunshi hakkōjōme), 1873, 196n2

newspapers, 47, 204n90, 231n140, 236n31; *Asahi Shimbun*, 219n9; *Chōsen Nippō*, 141; Sano-Nabeyama letter in, 79–81, 219n8; *Star Tribune* (Minneapolis), xi, xii; *Tokyo Asahi Shimbun*, 47, 127, 229n113; *Yomiuri Shimbun*, 90, 167, 219n9, 220n15

1927 Theses (Comintern), 1, 59, 66, 188n2

1932 Theses (Comintern), 188n2

nonconverts (hi-tenkōsha), 113, 134, 180

Obama, Barack, xiii

Offenders Prevention and Rehabilitation Act (Hanzaisha yobō kōsei hō, No. 142), 1949, 183, 259n20

Ogawa Heikichi, 40, 43–44

Ogino Fujio, 63, 137, 191n24, 202n60, 204n86, 214n92, 226n66, 239n79, 242n100, 259n18; on Korea, 141, 154, 175, 257n143; on maryoku of kokutai, 25, 197n13; on Peace Preservation Law, 38, 244n116

Ōhara Institute for Social Research, 189n9

Ohara Naoshi, 135

Okada Ryōhei, 32

Ōki Enkichi, 200n45

Okinawa, 33

Okubo Genji, 220n12

Okudaira Yasuhiro, 72, 85, 86, 137, 174, 203n76, 207n5, 208n12, 208n17, 217n130, 220n10; on arrests under Peace Preservation Law, 62, 207n2; on kokutai, 24, 196n2, 196–97n8; on Peace Preservation Law, 4–5, 221–22n31

Ōmotokyō, 25, 137, 173

Ono Yōichi, as pen name of Kobayashi, 93, 94, 95, 97, 98, 108

onshi (imperial donation), 239n71

On the Control of Mass Movements (Taishū undō no torishimari ni kansuru ken), 1945, 180

ontology, political, 188n5, 198n22

Ordinances: No. 7 (Korea) (On the Punishment of Political Crime), 30, 210n39, 210n40; No. 86 (Chian keisatsu hō), 1932, 64; No. 129, 60, 61

Organized Crime Law (Soshikiteki hanzai shobatsu hō), 2017, 185n4

Osaka, 65, 69, 70, 153; Friendship Society in, 129, 137; procurators in, 72, 245n120

Ōuchi Hyōe, 29, 200n39

pacification, 2, 64, 163
pamphlets, 46–47, 206n128; by Nakamura, 163–64; published by tenkōsha groups, 153–54
paradox of constituent/constituted, 26–27, 42–47
parergon (Kant), 26
parole (karishakuhō), 2–3, 4, 78, 188n1. *See also* parolees
parolees, 69, 118, 142, 155, 170, 180, 183, 231n139, 247n143; assistance for, 75, 109, 151, 234n159; Imperial Renovation Society and, 109, 234n159, 245n122; under Peace Preservation Law, 149, 245n128; reform and rehabilitation of, 130, 146, 226n67; statistics on, 170, 246n138; thought criminals as, 140, 227n73
Pascal, Blaise, 87, 223–24n44
Peace Preservation Bill (Chianijihōan), 1925, 35, 37, 46, 173, 241n89; articles of, 39, 44, 200n47, 201n51; committee consideration of, 42–43; debates on, 15, 22, 26, 37–46, 59; drafts of, 38–39, 200n45; Hoshijima on, 40–41; in House of Peers, 43–45; private property system and kokutai in, 32, 201n55, 202n60. *See also* Peace Preservation Law (Chianijihō), 1925
Peace Preservation Law (Chianijihō), 1925, 3, 47, 56, 60, 65, 66, 131, 134, 137, 149, 179, 181, 185n4, 189n11, 189n13, 203n76, 208n12, 208n17, 210n39, 235n13, 244n119, 245n128, 251n46; arrests under, 1, 3, 60–63, 113, 118, 136, 140, 149, 162, 189n9, 207n2, 218n140, 233n154; articles of, 45–47, 63; crime defined in, xi–xii, 197n10; death penalty and, 51, 207n5; kokutai and, 45, 60, 68, 98; in Korea, 15–16, 44–46, 137, 148, 157, 200n44, 210n41, 251n41; Mitchell on, 189n17, 234n2; passage of, 21–48; policies and, 21, 142; private property system and, 60, 98, 201n55, 210n37, 237n50; prosecutions under, 218n140, 234n2; repeal of, 21, 180; repressiveness of, 155, 173; revision of, 22, 24, 28, 49, 58–62, 114, 129, 130–38, 149, 245n120; revision of 1928 of, 212n53, 212n63; revision of 1941 of, 18, 172–77; scholarship on, 3–7, 221n31; statistics on, 3, 62, 63, 118, 136, 189n9, 244n115; to suppress leftists, 173, 241n96; tenkō and, 120, 220n10; transformation of, ix, 50, 239n76. *See also* Peace Preservation Bill (Chianijihōan), 1925; Peace Preservation Law apparatus
Peace Preservation Law apparatus, 6, 17, 25, 50, 75, 179, 181, 195n56, 208n17, 234n6; Althusser's ISAs theory and, 11–15; birth of, 47–48; continued operation of, 177–78; conversion and, 117, 149; dynamism of, 111, 137; emperor system ideology and, 1–19; imperial subjectivity and, 102, 145; as instrument of repression, 11–15; modes of power in, 13, 55, 114–115, 147
Peace Preservation Law Revision Bill (1934), 130–34, 136, 138, 173, 175
Peace Preservation Law Revision Bill (1935), 134–36, 138

penal power (Foucault), 52, 54
Person, John, 133, 241–42n96
Philippines, 168
police, 36, 50, 59, 62, 151, 201n59, 202n64, 208n12, 214n88; Home Ministry and, 52, 208n16; tenkōsha and, 130, 247n142, 247n143; training of, 46–47, 206n128. *See also* Special Higher Police
Police Bureau, 38–39, 201n59
Police Law (1954), 180–81
political activism, political activists, 10, 36, 95, 99
political crimes, 3, 10, 22, 30, 181, 222n31. *See also* political criminals; thought crimes
political criminals, 71, 90, 104, 131, 134, 137, 147, 253n76; reform of, 5, 47–48, 55, 99; rehabilitation of, ix, 9, 17, 110, 179, 195n56, 232n150. *See also* political crimes; thought criminals
political groups, 30, 181, 200n39
political legacy of Peace Preservation Law, 179–81
political parties, 36, 47, 59, 66, 135, 240n82. *See also* names of specific political parties
political prisoners, 16, 230n122. *See also* thought criminals
political theory, 8, 197–98n20
popular front, 164, 168; groups of, 137, 173; strategy of, 228n98, 255n111
postcolonial studies, 237n49
poststructuralism, 193n41
Poulantzas, Nicos, 11, 13, 88, 149, 192n35, 193n36, 193n41, 224n50; on Althusser, 195n54, 217n139; on Foucault, 14, 53, 209n24; on paper, 72, 217n130; on state, 192n31, 199n33
power, 13, 14, 191n23, 225n55, 231n144; Foucault and, 12, 52, 192n35, 193n35, 208n20, 209n25, 235n12; modes and modalities of, 53, 147, 179; state, 3, 209n32
praxis, 84, 96–97, 99, 124, 182, 190n20, 232n150
preventative detention (yobō kōkin), 18, 131, 132, 134, 149; Peace Preservation Law revision (1941) and, 172–77; Preventative Detention Centers and, 174–75, 180
Prime Minister, x, 59–61, 132, 153, 161, 181, 249n24
Prince and Princess Takamatsu, 183
Prison Bureau, 249n14
prison chaplains, 71, 91, 95, 104, 151
prison wardens, 151, 230n125
private property, 201n59, 233n151
private property system (shiyūzaisan seido), xii, 32, 39, 40, 133, 201n55, 205n106, 255n114; in Peace Preservation Law, 98, 202n60, 210n37, 212n58, 237n50; in proposed revisions to Peace Preservation Law, 60, 132. *See also* rejecting the private property system
Privy Council (Sūmitsu-in), 41, 60–61
probation, 70, 259n20
procurator, procurators (kenji), 48, 50, 57, 65, 73, 118, 130, 138, 151, 163, 181, 208n12, 208n16, 210n40,